Peter's Vision
Of Christ's Purpose
in First Peter

by

Phillip A. Ross

Pilgrim Platform
Marietta, Ohio

Copyright ©2011 Phillip A. Ross
Edition: 10.1.2011

ISBN: 978-0-9820385-9-8

Published by

Pilgrim Platform
149 E. Spring St., Marietta
Ohio, 45750
www.pilgrim-platform.org

Biblical quotations are from the *English Standard Version*, Standard Bible Society, unless otherwise cited.

Printed in the United States of America

Dedicated to

Pastor Rodney Lord
Valley Harvest Church
Marietta, Ohio

toward Christian unity

BOOKS BY PHILLIP A. ROSS

The Work At Zion—A Reckoning, Two-volume set, 772 pages, 1996.

Practically Christian—Applying James Today, 135 pages, 2006.

The Wisdom of Jesus Christ in the Book of Proverbs, 414 pages, 2006.

Marking God's Word—Understanding Jesus, 324 pages, 2006.

Acts of Faith—Kingdom Advancement, 326 pages, 2007.

Informal Christianity—Refining Christ's Church, 136 pages, 2007.

Engagement—Establishing Relationship in Christ, 104 pages, 1996, 2008.

The Big Ten—A Study of the Ten Commandments, 105 pages, 2001, 2008.

It's About Time! — The Time Is Now, 40 pages. 2008.

Arsy Varsy—Reclaiming The Gospel in First Corinthians, 399 pages, 2008.

Varsy Arsy—Proclaiming The Gospel in Second Corinthians, 356 pages, 2009.

Colossians—Christos Singularis, 278 pages, 2010.

Rock Mountain Creed—The Sermon on the Mount, 350 pages, 2011

The True Mystery of The Mystical Presence, John Williamson Nevin and Phillip A. Ross, 355 pages, 2011

Peter's Vision of Christ's Purpose in First Peter, 317 pages, 2011

Peter's Vision of The End in Second Peter, 300 pages, 2012.

TABLE OF CONTENTS

Introduction..i

1. Sprinkled - 1 Peter 1:1-2...1

2. Inheritance -1 Peter 1:3-4...9

3. God's Power Revealed - 1 Peter 1:5-7.......................................18

4. Things Announced - 1 Peter 1:8-12...29

5. The Engine of Hope - 1 Peter 1:13...38

6. Holy Smoke! - 1 Peter 1:14-17..48

7. Believers In God - 1 Peter 1:17-21...59

8. Abide In The Light - 1 Peter 1:22-25..70

9. The Milky Way - 1 Peter 2:1-5..82

10. Destiny's Children - 1 Peter 2:6-8..94

11. Oxymoron - 1 Peter 2:9-10..104

12. Subordinate - 1 Peter 2:11-15 114

13. Three-In-One-in-Three - 1 Peter 2:16-20.............................124

14. Called To Suffer - 1 Peter 2:21..135

15. Following Jesus - 1 Peter 2:22-25...145

16. Modeling Submission - 1 Peter 3:1-4....................................152

17. Holy Women - 1 Peter 3:5-7 159

18. Unity - 1 Peter 3:8-9...168

19. God Favors Righteousness - 1 Peter 3:10-12........................179

20. Christian Readiness - 1 Peter 3:13-16..................................188

21. The Grace of Suffering - 1 Peter 3:17-20..............................198

22. Saved By Baptism - 22. Saved By Baptism............................205

23. Suffering Judgment - 1 Peter 4:1-5.......................................214

24. Gospel Hype - 1 Peter 4:6-10..222

25. God's Charisma - 1 Peter 4:10-11...229

26. The Lord of Hosts - 1 Peter 4:12-13.....................................236

27. Human Deconstruction - 1 Peter 4:14-17..243

28. Lord of the Aggregate - 1 Peter 4:17-19..251

29. Who, Me? - 1 Peter 5:1-3...262

31. The Plan - 1 Peter 5:8-11..279

32. The End - 1 Peter 5:12-14...288

Scripture Index..299

Alphabetical Index..302

INTRODUCTION

The text that lies before you provides an excursion into Peter's heart and his understanding of God in Christ seen through his first letter to the "elect exiles of the dispersion" (1 Peter 1:1). Of course it also comes from me and my perspective in the Twenty-First Century, long after Peter lived.

The methodology of this book, like all my books, is interactive. It is neither scholarship nor exegesis, neither historical fiction or eisegesis. The methodology is to engage the text faithfully and interactively. It is an effort to catch Peter's vision and read it back into the text in a way that interacts with Peter's context in order to shed light on our contemporary context in the hope that we can hear the message afresh. It is not so much an effort to explain the text as it is to see it in the light of Christ.

Can people read the Bible and understand the intent? Of course. How can I claim to know what was in Peter's heart as he wrote this letter? Because to some extent I share his heart in Christ. Because I know what Christ has done to my heart through regeneration, I know to some extent the central concerns in Peter's heart. Nonetheless, I am not infallible—not even close. So, I ask you to put on your own ears to hear and eyes to see so that you can identify and avoid my errors of both omission and commission in this work. Will there be errors? Of course, look for them and please let me know when you find something that concerns you.

I intend to raise more questions than I will answer as I shake loose some of our most fundamental but inadequate assumptions. My hope and intention is to provide a perspective from which to see Peter's letter in the light of Christ, to see Peter's letter from a Twenty-First Century perspective and in a way that honors God's intent. Sure, Peter was writing in his context, but God intended His words for Christians in every context. My mission is not mere discovery, but mining—digging deep into this mineral rich mountain. My mission is to take the ore that Peter has provided and refine it for use today. And I need you to pray for this effort and for this mission. It cannot be completed without you. If *you* don't understand what I'm trying to get at after you have read this book, then I will have failed. My intention is not to convince you of the rightness of what I'm saying, but to reveal the present applicability of what God was saying to us through Peter. Curiosity is a great help toward understanding. So, my job is to ignite your curiosity about what Peter was saying, not to satisfy you, but to stir you up (2 Peter 1:13).

I have found that reading Peter's letters through the eyes of faithfulness to God's trinitarian character (by assuming the reality of the Trinity) opens the text up in some fresh ways. The simple discipline of remembering that God's character is trinitarian opens up our minds to consider other perspectives and shades of meaning in the text that might otherwise be overlooked.

The Christian Trinity is absolutely unique in the history of the world, and that uniqueness provides a kind of Rosetta Stone for biblical interpretation and understanding. It is likely that my readers will not yet understand what I mean by this reference to the Trinity, and that is regrettable. I wish reality were more simple and that essential truths could be boiled down to bite-size nuggets for rapid consumption. But that is not the way that God created the world, nor the way that He reveals Himself. To see God we need to look at the whole, not simply at the bits and pieces.

While it is my intention to provide enough understanding of the hermeneutic of presuppositional trinitarianism[1] in the text to suggest the richness and depth of meaning that it unlocks, those who want to dig deeper into my methodology should consult my other books.

Reading Peter's letters is quite different than reading Paul's. Paul was a scholar who was trained in biblical academics, which involves focusing on specific meanings—definitions and implications. It usually means looking at something with a microscope in order to clarify what sometimes appears to be minutia. In contrast, Peter, who came to Christ as an uneducated fisherman (though he most certainly did not remain so), turns the microscope around (so to speak) to make it function as a telescope, and points it to God's future.

So, while Paul was often focused on the inner, personal realities of faithfulness, Peter was focused on the grand scheme of Christ's mission in the world. Where Paul was focused on particulars, Peter was focused on universals. While understanding Paul involves the personal experience of the Holy Spirit through regeneration, understanding Peter builds on regeneration and takes in the whole sweep of human history

---

1   This is what I call my methodology. It is simply the assumption of the reality of the
     doctrine of the Trinity as an essential characteristic of God and His world.

and casts a vision of the future in the light of Christ. For Peter the Old Testament was all the history he knew. He had, nor did he need, any other history book. As such, reading Peter without more than a passing familiarity with the Old Testament will surely lead you astray.

Paul came to Christ as a biblical scholar with a deep theological understanding of the Old Testament, and used his understanding as a backdrop for his explorations into the meaning of Christian faithfulness. Paul was plugging Christ into his understanding of the Old Testament.

But Peter came to Christ as a fisherman. Peter did not bring a full-blown understanding of Old Testament theology to Christ, as did Paul. Rather, Peter brought his ordinary understanding and experience of God's Messiah from the Old Testament and built upon it. In Paul's writing we find history brought to faithfulness, while in Peter's writings we find faithfulness brought to history, yet Peter was not looking backward. He was looking forward. His was a vision of hope toward the accomplishment of the purpose of God. Paul was focused microscopically, while Peter was focused macroscopically. So, while reading Paul clarifies the details of faithfulness, reading Peter magnifies the vastness of Christ's mission to the world.

These few introductory remarks are here to provide a alert: fasten your seatbelt and get ready to have your vistas expanded, at least that's what Peter has done for me. Reading Peter with trinitarian eyes brings the light of Christ to shine as a beacon for the world. Peter set the light of Christ as a lighthouse on a rocky shore to guide travelers, to point the way forward. And while Peter lit the lamp eons ago, it not only still shines today, but it shines more brightly today than it did when Peter lit it, and it promises to shine even brighter in the future.

This book is not a typical commentary on First Peter because it is more than mere exegesis. Peter's letters are like icebergs from God, in the sense that the actual text is above the waterline but the bulk, weight and significance of Peter's meaning lies below the waterline, submerged in the assumptions of context and subtext. What we exegetically find is completely true and can be trusted, of course. The part of the iceberg that we can see is real, solid and it can be measured in a variety of ways. But the greater weight and significance of the iceberg cannot be seen by the exegetical eye alone. Various instruments are required to see what is below the waterline. What is below is more impalpable, more imprecise, yet more real and more consequential as well.

My efforts here are to examine what can be seen of Peter's iceberg that is above the waterline, and to suggest the greater meaning that is below. It is not that the part of the iceberg that is below the waterline is determined by what is above, but that what is above is determined by what is below. The greater part cannot be seen exegetically. Critical analysis must give way to faithful incorporation and internalization. Understanding the Bible requires, not simply scientific objectivity but submissive and passionate subjectivity.

We must not be content to take truth from Scripture, we must also read troth into it. *Troth* is an old word that is part truth and part trust, and means fidelity. To get the most out of Scripture we must come to it covenantally, with agreement. To do otherwise is to read it with only one eye—myopically. My hope is not to simply read Scripture open-eyed, but to come to it with both eyes open. May the Lord God in Christ be our guide.

Phillip A. Ross
October 2011
Marietta, Ohio

1. SPRINKLED

Peter, an apostle of Jesus Christ, To those who are elect exiles of the dispersion in Pontus, Galatia, Cappadocia, Asia, and Bithynia, according to the foreknowledge of God the Father, in the sanctification of the Spirit, for obedience to Jesus Christ and for sprinkling with his blood: May grace and peace be multiplied to you.   —1 Peter 1:1-2 (ESV)

Peter begins by identifying himself. It was customary at that time to first indicate who the letter was coming from and who it was going to. This letter is thought to have been written around A.D. 60-68, during the decade preceding the Fall of Jerusalem in A.D. 70. This is an important detail because it provides the context, which involved the persecution of the church and the military build up of Roman troops prior to one of the most horrific sieges ever fought in terms of destructiveness and loss of life. Josephus claimed that 1,100,000 people were killed during the siege, most of whom were Jewish, and that 97,000 were captured and enslaved.[2]

This is important because, while mostly Jews died, Christian persecution increased by both the Romans and the Jewish establishment as the final destruction neared. The church had been growing, and it was thought to have threatened both the Romans and the Jews. And it did, though not militarily or politically. The church threatened the stability of the establishment inasmuch as the establishment was founded on and promoted sin—which it did. Sin and corruption were rampant. The Jerusalem establishment at that time was spiritually Jewish but politically Roman. Consequently, Christians were at odds in one way or another with just about everyone in Jerusalem. The Roman state was Pagan and the Jewish church was apostate. The apostasy of the Jews was nothing new. The Old Testament prophets had railed against it again and again.

---

2   Josephus, Flavius. *The Wars of the Jews*, VI.9.3, public domain.

So, the fact that the Temple establishment had fallen into apostasy again is no great revelation. Nonetheless, as the social tensions mounted in and around Jerusalem, so did the persecution of Christians.

This persecution was not like the later Roman persecutions when Christians were fed to the lions and killed for sport. Rather, this persecution began as all persecution does: with feelings of ill-will and distrust toward some group. The leading edge of persecution is always social and economic. It always begins with social discrimination against the suspect group and leads to housing and employment problems because people don't want to work with or live near the suspect group. That was Peter's situation, and the situation of Christians at the time.

ELECT

Peter identified himself as an apostle (*apostolos*). That means that he was a delegate, an ambassador or commissioner for Christ. The apostles were the leaders of the church. There has always been a lot of discussion and disagreement in the Christian community about whether Christian leaders are appointed or elected. Both arguments have some merit. So, why not choose both. Appointed leaders should also be recognized by those they lead, which means that they should also be elected. And elected leaders should be recognized by other leaders, which means that they should also be appointed. *Appointed* here means chosen by the other leaders because only they have the authority to appoint. And *elected* means approval by those they lead because only they have the authority to elect.

Peter went on to identify the people to whom he was writing: "To those who are elect exiles of the dispersion" (v. 1). The *Authorized Version* translated the phrase: "to the strangers scattered throughout." Note that he was not writing to people in Jerusalem. Jerusalem prior to its destruction was the context in which he wrote. However, at that time Peter did not know that Jerusalem would be destroyed in A.D. 70.

He knew that the church was under persecution, and in all likelihood people were leaving Jerusalem in anticipation of political upheaval and war. Not only had Jesus mentioned such a potential scenario (Matthew 24, etc.), but Paul had been a wanted man for decades. And Paul had also warned people that the proverbial writing was on the wall. It didn't take a political genius to see that Roman troops and siege provisions were amassing.

So Peter was also writing to Christians in other areas, to those who had left Jerusalem during the decade preceding Jerusalem's fall, and to all who would eventually be a part of the Christian dispersion. Don't undervalue the importance of this exile, because it plays a key role in the growth and evangelism of the church during this time. But neither do we want to brand it with the glowing overtones of historic import- ance by turning it into a museum skit of platitudinous pomp and face paint.

When we overvalue historic events we are tempted to turn them into theater, into shallow, artificial, dramatic events and miss or mis- construe how things actually happened. The situation would have been much like 1938 in Germany. Many Jews left, if they could. They knew that they were being persecuted as Hitler's machine began closing its grip on them. The pressure began with social devaluation and discrim- ination regarding jobs and housing. And while many Jews left, for a variety of reasons many couldn't leave.

DISPERSION

Again, who was Peter writing to? To those who had already left, for sure. But to call them "elect exiles of the dispersion" (v. 1) requires a point of view that would have been from the future, after people became aware that enough people had left Jerusalem to call it an exile and suggest that it was a diaspora, in the likeness of the exiles and dis- persions of former times. People in Jerusalem knew that it had been destroyed and Jews enslaved twice before. The destructions of Jerus- alem and the Temple were staples of Jewish history. We need to acknowledge that the phrase may have been a later interpretation and emendation of Peter's actual words by a copyist. This however does not mean that Peter did not communicate the idea in some form, only that someone else may have tried to clarify it after Peter's death in A.D. 67. We can't say for sure about that. But we can say that the *English Standard Version* translation is most certainly a modern embellish- ment.

The *Authorized Version* is probably closer to Peter's sense of the situation, "to the strangers scattered throughout...." Peter was writing to people who had left their longstanding homes in and around Jerus- alem. And they would have been strangers in their new nations and neighborhoods, but Peter was not writing to people who were strangers to him. Again the word choice is unfortunate.

PILGRIMS

The Greek word *parepidēmos* is only used three times in the New Testament, and is not the usual word for *elect* (*eklektos*). Some ver- sions translate it as *sojourners*, suggesting people residing in a foreign land, people who have a unity or an identity that is not shared with those with whom they live. Peter used the word to refer to the people of God, and to the fact that his Christian friends were at the same time both united and divided, that they had a common unity, common bonds, but were living in dispersion, not in a central location or even a common neighborhood.

Peter was writing to God's people, who had previously been geographically united but who were now, and for the foreseeable future, geographically dispersed. To call them the church in exile is inaccurate because it suggests that God's plan was to bring them all back to Israel someday, which was an Old Testament pattern of thinking. Israel had been destroyed before, and rebuilt. But that was not what God was doing with the church. God's plan was not to bring all Christians back to Israel, but to Christianize the nations, to send Christians out and plant them where they went. God was simultaneously bringing the people of God into the kingdom of God, and was bringing the kingdom of God to the earth, to the Gentiles.

Peter, an elected leader of the church, was writing to those who had elected him—the church, but who were now residing in foreign lands. The phrasing suggests Peter's leadership and authority, and that through this letter he was continuing to exert that leadership and authority.

He then named the countries or regions where these people had gone: Pontus, Galatia, Cappadocia, Asia, and Bithynia. All were in modern Turkey. Peter was writing to those who had migrated westward from Jerusalem. The direction of the migration would prove to be an important detail because of the foundational relationship between Christianity and Western Civilization.

Verse 2 provides an explanation of how this scattering of the people of God fit into God's larger plan, and provided assurance that things were unfolding exactly as God had planned, so that God's people could rest assured that God was still in control. Those who had left Jerusalem were running for their lives, escaping persecution and impending war. They had experienced the beginnings of the persecutions against them by the Jews and by the Romans. They knew the determination of the Jews who had been hounding Paul, who had a bounty on his head (Acts 25:3). And they knew the power and ruthlessness of Rome, who's empire controlled and defined most of the civilized world at the time.

WESTWARD

It is significant that God's people did not run eastward, away from the Roman Empire, but ran westward, toward it and into it. They seem to have chosen to live in civilization rather than apart from it. This was an important choice in that God's intent was to bring His kingdom to human civilization, rather than to have His people escape from it.

This happened "according to the foreknowledge of God the Father" (v. 2). This dispersion of God's people was not a surprise to God. *Rather,* said Peter, *it was all unfolding as part of God's plan.* Peter suggested that God knew what would happen. There has been much discussion in the church about God's foreknowledge, and it has led to much speculation. We can better contain the speculation by considering the root meaning of the Greek word (*prognōsis*). The word has simply been transliterated into English and is used primarily in medical settings. A medical prognosis is the determination or diagnosis of an illness. God, as the chief physician, had chosen to save humanity and on the basis of His prognosis issued a purification order to be carried out by the Spirit through a blood sprinkling of the saints upon the nations.

And we also know from Paul's writings that the destruction of Jerusalem was a necessary part of God's plan to bring the gospel to the Gentiles, and eventually to the whole world. Peter was implying that the dispersion of God's people westward was no accident, but was central to God's plan. Therefore, those who had been displaced from their homes in Palestine could take solace that they were on the leading edge of God's plan, that they were still in the will of God, that their dispersion served God's greater purpose.

TRINITY

We should also notice that Peter's reference to God the Father indicated that he was to some degree aware of what we call the Trinity. It was not common practice for Jews to refer to God as Father. But Peter was undoubtedly following the teaching of Jesus, who had taught His people to pray, *Our Father*, who art in heaven. Jesus often spoke of God as Father.

Is it really legitimate to suggest so much from such an apparently insignificant reference? Aren't I reading the doctrine of the Trinity into Peter's words? Yes, it is legitimate. And yes, to some degree I am reading the doctrine of the Trinity into Peter's words. And the reason that I'm reading the Trinity into Peter's words is because I share Peter's trinitarian perspective, and because I see His use of the doctrine of the Trinity. I share Peter's trinitarian perspective by grace through faith. I understand Peter's faith because I share it. And I understand the extent to which our common Christian faith, which is itself trinitarian, effects everything. So, I am confident about my understanding of Peter and of his trinitarian perspective.

Peter continued to explain what God was accomplishing through the dispersion of His people westward. It was part of the expansion of God's kingdom "in the sanctification of the Spirit" (v. 2). The *Author-*

ized Version reads "through sanctification of the Spirit." The Greek word *en* here literally means *by the instrumentality of*, and in this case he was talking about the instrumentality of the Spirit. The Spirit was the means or vehicle by which the dispersion of Christians out of Jerusalem was happening. The Spirit of God was causing and animating the dispersion.

SANCTIFICATION

So, it was not that those who had been dispersed had been separated from the Spirit, though they had been separated from some of their family and friends. Rather, said Peter, they had been carried away by the Spirit or in the Spirit. Actually it was the Spirit who had carried them away! This meant that, rather than being separated from the Spirit, they were actually in the will of the Spirit. And they could find much hope and comfort in this fact. Peter wanted them to celebrate this hope and comfort.

But it wasn't that this dispersion simply happened in or because of the Spirit, but that it was itself a kind of sanctification of God's people by the Spirit. Remember that the word *sanctify* means separated for a particular use or purpose. The Greek does not contain the words "of the" but has only one word—*spirit*. So, the two words—*sanctify* (*hagiasmos*) and *spirit* (*pneuma*)—translated "through the sanctification of the Spirit" could also be translated as "through spiritual sanctification."

Why do I make this point? Only because God doesn't grow or change. God doesn't undergo sanctification or growth, we do. The sanctification belongs to the people, not to the Spirit. The Spirit was sanctifying (separating) the people through the dispersion.

Because we understand that the Spirit is also God by the reality of the Trinity, we determine that the sanctification that Peter referred to was the sanctification of God's people. The dispersion of God's people was happening because it was the very means of their own sanctification.

We must also understand this trinitarianally and note that the sanctification served both the sanctification of the particular individuals involved and also the sanctification of the corporate body of believers as a whole—the church. Not only can individuals be sanctified, or grow in grace, but God's church as a whole is also sanctified as it grows in grace as a corporate body. In fact, these two aspects of sanctification are intimately related because of the trinitarian character of God's people.

Peter continued by mentioning that this was also happening "for obedience to Jesus Christ" (v. 2). Or as the *Authorized Version* rendered it "unto (*eis*) obedience." We note that obedience is central to God's purpose and to our sanctification, both individually and corporately. God's purpose unfolds through compliance or submission to His Spirit, who provides both direction and power for the accomplishment of His will.

SPRINKLING

Finally, Peter concluded that this was all happening, not only "for obedience to Jesus Christ" but "for sprinkling with his blood" (v. 2). The sprinkling of the blood of the sacrifice was an Old Testament liturgical practice that was used as a method, an instrument and a reminder of God's blessings (Leviticus 8:30, Hebrews 11:28, etc.). Being sprinkled by the blood of Christ was an allusion to the cleansing of sin and for the dispensation of God's blessings.

Paul wrote of this: "Therefore, brothers, since we have confidence to enter the holy places by the blood of Jesus, by the new and living way that he opened for us through the curtain, that is, through his flesh, and since we have a great priest over the house of God, let us draw near with a true heart in full assurance of faith, with our hearts sprinkled clean from an evil conscience and our bodies washed with pure water" (Hebrews 10:19-22).

However, Peter's mention of the sprinkled blood of Jesus Christ was not merely a reference to the cleansing of sin, but it carried the suggestion that the dispersed people of God were themselves the sprinkling of Christ's blood upon the nations. They were themselves like droplets of sprinkled blood that were in the process of being sprinkled upon the Roman Empire, or upon human civilization.

The implication was that just as the sprinkling of blood liturgically was a symbol of purification from sin, a symbol of sanctification in grace, so the dispersion itself was, not merely a symbol, but the very means of purification from sin and sanctification of the Gentiles, of the Roman Empire and of the world at large—not immediately, of course, but over time. God's people, who had themselves been sprinkled with the blood of Christ for the purification of sin, were themselves the sprinkling on the nations, on the world. They were in the process of carrying the purifying blood of Christ to the nations, which was God's great mission to the world.

INCREASE

Peter then closed the salutation section of his letter with a benediction: "May grace and peace be multiplied to you" (v. 2). The Greek word (*plēthunō*) doesn't literally mean multiplication, but suggests an abundant increase. The root of the word is like the English word *pleth-*

ora, which means an extreme excess. Peter was praying that God would grant an abundant increase of grace and peace for those who had been scattered westward.

The order of the words is important because it suggests that peace comes from grace, as if peace is a fruit of God's grace. But it doesn't work the other way around. God's grace is not the fruit of peace. While these two things go together peace is established on God's grace, but God's grace is not established on peace. The house must rest upon the foundation, not the foundation upon the house. Working for peace apart from God's grace cannot bring peace because peace issues out of God's grace. Thus, if people want peace they should "seek first the kingdom of God" (Matthew 6:33), and peace will be added as one of the many things that issues from God's grace.

Peter was also praying that God's grace would establish both peace in the hearts of those who had been dispersed, but also that the persecution that had been experienced in Jerusalem would stop. Remember that neither Peter nor those who had fled knew that Jerusalem would be destroyed in A.D. 70. Neither did they know the history of the early church, or of the Roman persecutions that were ahead of them. None of those things had happened yet.

But the fact of the difficulties that lay ahead of the church, or the ongoing history of the accomplishment of God's purpose and plan to bring the kingdom of heaven to earth, did not and has not dulled the effectiveness or power of Peter's benedictory prayer. Though the multiplication of grace and peace has not yet manifest completely in the four corners of the earth does not mean that significant progress toward this end has not been accomplished. Indeed, much progress has been made.

There is more reason to anticipate the completion of God's plan today than ever before, not only because of the extent of the expansion of Christianity in the world, but because to this day we can continue to proclaim with truth and integrity that God has kept His promise over all the intervening years.

God continues to keep His promises, and the dispersion of Christians into Western Civilization and from there to the whole world that had begun in Peter's day was the leading edge of God's movement to save the world.

2. INHERITANCE

Blessed be the God and Father of our Lord Jesus Christ!
According to his great mercy, he has caused us to be born
again to a living hope through the resurrection of Jesus Christ
from the dead, to an inheritance that is imperishable,
undefiled, and unfading, kept in heaven for you ...
— 1 Peter 1:3-4 (ESV)

Verse 3 is saturated in the doctrine of the Trinity to the point that apart from sharing Peter's assumption of the reality of the Trinity the verse cannot be fully understood. Peter was doing one of three things here, and likely all of them at once.

First, he was offering thanks and praise for God by extolling the blessings of the relationship between the Father and the Son, by suggesting that God Himself is blessed to have such a Son as Jesus Christ, and that Jesus Christ is blessed to have such a Father as Yahweh, the omnipotent, eternal and only existing yet trinitarian God of the universe. Each is blessed in His own right, and both are doubly blessed because of their familial relationship. In this case the verse is understood as an exclamation of praise and thanksgiving, and the verse is about Peter's state of appreciation. Here Peter is the central concern of the verse.

Second, Peter was simply describing the condition of God and Jesus as that of being blessed. Here Peter was not so much offering thanks and praise, as simply making an observation that both the Father and Son were blessed by their mutual relationship with the Other. In this case the verse is about the condition of God and Jesus. Here God and Jesus are the central concerns of the verse.

And third, Peter was commanding those to whom he was writing to make a practice of blessing or speaking well of God and Jesus and of their familial relationship. They are after all Father and Son. In this case the verse is about those to whom Peter was writing. And here the Christian community is the central concern of the verse.

Spirit

Having mentioned the Father and the Son, Peter then acknowledged the Spirit, but not in the way that we might expect because he acknowledged the Spirit by acknowledging the principle effect that the Spirit has in the world, which is regeneration. Just as we cannot see the wind itself, but only its effects—moving clouds, the rustling of leaves or the blowing of rain and snow—we cannot see the Spirit directly either. Air or wind is invisible. Similarly, we note that the word *Spirit* does not appear in this verse. And yet the latter section of the verse is all about the function and effects of the Spirit in the world.

Note also the means of the Spirit—"according to His great mercy" (v. 3). The Spirit functions by the grace and mercy of God. We (people) do not evoke, control or effect the activities of the Spirit. Rather, the Spirit moves by the grace and mercy of God alone. This is one of the central and most important but least understood elements of Christianity. Because people think that they seek God through various kinds of thoughts and actions, they think that they are able to request and secure the principle blessings of the Spirit though various spiritual disciplines like prayer, fasting, worship, etc. This is the natural spiritual urge that motivates people to engage religious behavior.

But Peter was saying here that the Spirit does not work like that. The Spirit is not directed by our passions, prayers or pleas. Rather, the engine and the steering wheel of the Spirit are God's grace and mercy alone. God functions according to His own will, not ours. God is not out to satisfy our hopes or dreams or our highest aspirations. Rather, God is out to satisfy and accomplish His own plans. So, He moves according to His own will, His own grace and mercy. And what does He do?

Peter said that He "has caused us to be born again" (v. 3). Some versions read "begat us again" (*American Standard Version*), "hath begotten us again" (*Authorized Version*), "has regenerated us" (*Modern King James Bible*), etc. The thing to note is that whatever God has done, He has already done it. The verbs are in the past tense. Our regeneration is not something to be hoped for in the future, but something already accomplished. Those who have not been regenerated have no understanding, reference or expectation of it. So, for those who are are genuinely aware of it, it has already happened and is the source of their awareness in Christ. This is not an insignificant point, but is again one of the most central and yet misunderstood elements of Christianity.

SEEKING

Christians are not people who are seeking to be born again at some point in the future. We are looking forward to a future resurrection, but only because we already enjoy a past regeneration. Christians are people who have already been born again at some time in the past. This is of critical importance because, first, if a person has not been born again, he is not a Christian. Being a Christian means that the Spirit of God has broken into your life, and changed your identity as a person. This began when Jesus Christ broke into human history and changed the identity of humanity by fulfilling and supplanting the archetype of Adam with the archetype of Christ.

And second, the whole mindset of seeking God is not what Christianity is about. The reason that Christians do not seek God or seek to be born again is that God is already present and active in their lives. So, it is nonsense to seek something that is already in your possession. (This, of course, does not mean that we somehow possess God, but rather that God possesses us. But either way, the point is the same.) God should not be sought out by Christians.

There are two reasons for not seeking God (Romans 3:11). First, because God is already at the very center and heart of their being. And second, because seeking God turns Christianity into a works-righteousness endeavor. Christians, do, however, seek to know more fully and engage more actively the will of God. But again, the will of God can only be sought by those who already know God personally and covenantally. People cannot seek God in order to become regenerate. Rather, God regenerates people in order that they are able to know Him.

Peter cut off both of these false approaches to Christian spirituality by acknowledging that the central purpose of the Holy Spirit—the regeneration of God's people—has already been accomplished. How was it accomplished? By the resurrection of Jesus Christ. Who has it already been accomplished for? For those to whom Peter was writing. And who was that? Christians who were on the move for or because of Christ. Ostensibly, it was Christians who were under persecution and fleeing from Jerusalem prior to its destruction. But by application, Peter was writing to all Christians who have been regenerated by the power and presence of the Holy Spirit in all ages, to all who are motivated and animated by the Spirit of Jesus Christ.

Note also that the Spirit caused (*anagennaō*) this to happen. The Greek word means to *bear, beget, be born, bring forth, conceive, be delivered of, engender* and *make*. The Spirit, and therefore the Trinity, is the progenitor of human regeneration. It has happened, is happening and will continue to happen because of the will and desire of God,

according to His grace and mercy, because of the propitiation of Christ
and by the power of the Holy Spirit.

TIME

And it happens in time. So, because time is a process, it involves
the past, the present and the future. And here's the critically important
but vastly unrecognized characteristic of time: time does not push the
present forward from the past.[3] Rather, time pulls the present forward
from the future. Why is this? Because God is the Lord of time. Because
God is the Lord of the universe, and the universe unfolds according to
His instruction and His timetable, and he knows the future because He
determines it.

This means that the power or the engine of time is not in the past,
not in history. It is not a power that pushes the present forward.
Rather, the power or the engine of time is in the future. It pulls the
present forward, like a kind of magnetic attraction. History, then, is not
the determining factor of the present or the future, but is more like a
wake left in the past, like a wave that spreads behind a boat as it moves
forward. The wake does not propel the boat forward, but is simply
evidence that the boat is moving. God, who is not in time, spoke His
decree from before time (*before* suggests that His decree precedes
time), which set the goal or endpoint of history in the future, and now
time is being pulled into the present toward that goal or endpoint.
God's decree is guaranteed by pulling time from the future because it
doesn't matter where the present is it will end up where God wants it.

Of course we can learn much from history because history is a kind
of time mirror. As we look into history we see a reflection of the track
of time. But we never see it as those who lived through it saw it. We
always see it from our own vantage point, which is in the future of the
past moment that we are looking at. We see the past from a future perspective because as we look into the past we are always ahead of it in
time.

HOPE

Christians are not merely born again, but are born again *into*
something, *through* something and *from* something. What are Christians born again *into* (*eis*)? Hope. It is more accurate to say that we are
born again into hope rather than simply born into hope because we are
born into the hopeless of sin. Most of the time, when people think of

---

3   Shortly after completing this manuscript I discovered a magazine article discussing
    "time-symmetric quantum mechanics" (*Back From The Future, Does the universe
    have a destiny—and could the laws of physics be pulling us inexorably toward our
    prewritten fate?*" by Zeeya Merall, *Discover*, April 2010).

hope they think of something in the future that they hope for. And Peter will get to this in the next verse. But for now he was focusing on a present hope, a condition or state of mind that is positively and presently expectant, a state of present expectation that looks forward to good things, even great things. Christians are born again into active hopefulness, into an optimism whose source is the infallible and omnipotent God of the universe, a hopefulness that cannot be disappointed because it both originates and concludes in God, who is gracious and merciful beyond our wildest expectations.

This regenerated hope is more than a generic optimism that things will turn out well. Rather, it is the particular confidence that God cannot fail to accomplish what He wills. It is a hope that is more knowledge than guesswork, more active anticipation than a giddy longing for distant happiness. The *Authorized Version* calls it *a lively hope*, which I like better than a *living hope*.

RESURRECTION

The means of this regeneration into hopefulness is the resurrection of Jesus Christ. Paul spoke of this: "For if we have been united with him in a death like his, we shall certainly be united with him in a resurrection like his" (Romans 6:5). To understand this we need to view it through trinitarian eyes. By this I mean that we need to look at it historically in the sense that our personal regeneration has already happened in Christ because Christ has already been resurrected. God decreed it, and Christ accomplished it, is accomplishing it and will finish accomplishing it in our resurrection.

The beginning and end points have been established. And history is simply running from the one to the other. The regeneration that culminates in resurrection is in the process of happening to God's people in a way that individuals can recognize in themselves in the present though it will not be completed until some future time.

People sometimes doubt the reality of regeneration because it is much more difficult to recognize in other people, and impossible to recognize if it hasn't happened to you personally. But once you recognize it, it is undeniable from that point forward. Furthermore, this resurrection, of which our personal regeneration is but a platform from which to launch the resurrection of God's people, His church, will happen in an increasingly robust way as time unfolds. And it will happen in the same way that it happened to Jesus Christ on Easter morning.

There are three phases or stages to our regeneration that lead to resurrection and they correspond to time—past, present and future. This process has happened in the past. It is happening in the present. And it will happen in the future. There are also three elements to our resurrection that correspond to 1) Jesus Christ (who is God Himself by the power of the Trinity), 2) to us as individuals and 3) to the community of God or the church of Jesus Christ as a corporate entity. This is because we have been created in God's trinitarian image. We are like God in the respect that Christians have a trinitarian-like identity. The third (the Holy Spirit) element of our trinitarian-like identity comes "online" through regeneration, when we find the beginning of the fullness of our identity in Christ.

Being in Christ is a key element because Christians are born again into Christ. In Christ, the three elements of our trinitarian identity become clarified. We retain our individual identities, but we also come to more fully realize our corporate identity as or in the church. And we see that Jesus Christ is at the center of both our individual identities and our corporate identity, holding them together, unifying them. So, there are three distinguishable and unique but inseparable parts to our identities as Christians: 1) being an individual, 2) being in the corporate church and 3) being in Jesus Christ, the Son of God and second Person of the Trinity.

Finally then, Christians have been born again *from* "the dead" (v. 3). Actually, in the Greek there is no definite article. So, a more accurate reading is that Christians have been born again *from death*. This more accurate reading then helps us better understand that the process of regeneration unto resurrection is a process that unfolds in time.

It happens in the relatively small time scale of individual lives, so that people can themselves know that they have experienced the change that we call regeneration. But it also happens in relatively larger corporate history or in the history of the church of Jesus Christ, which is more than two thousand years old to date, and counting. The resurrection of the church (the body of Jesus Christ) involves a kind of cascade that results from a critical mass of individual regenerations. That is to say that history will reach a point where God's truth will simply be historically undeniable.

In order to differentiate between regeneration and resurrection, which are both similar and distinct, we refer to the regeneration of individuals, but in the fullness of time when Christ comes again, all Christians will be resurrected with Christ into the church (the body of Christ), or the new city of God, which then comes down from heaven to earth in the sense that it issues from God's decree. However, we cannot completely differentiate between regeneration and resurrection, as if they are completely separate and unrelated things or processes. They are different, and yet they are also very similar. The primary difference is that one emphasizes the individual, and the other emphasizes the corporate. Yet, because they are a function of the Spirit, and because of the character of the Trinity, they are one and the same, yet different—distinguishable but inseparable.

Two things differentiate them. They are different in terms of time. Regeneration comes first in the lives of individuals, where resurrection comes later and brings individuals into the fullness of the corporate church, the body of Christ in glory. And they are different in terms of scope. Resurrection includes the corporate aspects of the body of Christ, the church, such that with the completion of the final resurrection, all of God's people are involved. Regeneration, on the other hand, includes only individuals. So, regeneration happens one individual at a time, but the final resurrection will happen all at once, in the fullness of time, in the twinkling of an eye (1 Corinthians 15:52).

Eternal Inheritance

Peter continued in verse 4 to say that God has caused us to be born again "to an inheritance that is imperishable." Inheritance is always a function of family rights—not individual rights, whether one is natural born or adopted. Inheritance applies only to the natural born or adopted children of the deceased. It is always a family matter. Christ is the only natural born or begotten Son of the Father because His Father is the Holy Spirit who impregnated or overshadowed Mary (Luke 1:35). And just as God is the Father of Jesus Christ by the Holy Spirit, so God is Father to all who are born again by the Holy Spirit. However, for the inheritance to take effect legally God must still go through the process of adoption on His end, which He has already done (Romans 8:15-17).

Peter went on to say that this inheritance "is imperishable, undefiled, and unfading" (v. 4). To say that the Christian inheritance is imperishable or incorruptible means that it exists outside of or apart from worldly sources of corruption. I say *worldly* not because some other kind of unworldly corruption might apply, but because corruption can also refer to biological things or even to metals. Rot and rust are kinds of corruption. But incorruptible also refers to legalities, where the lack of integrity or honesty can lead to bribery or other kinds of legal and political corruption, like dishonesty.

In addition, the Greek word (*aphthartos*) indicates shriveling, withering and spoiling—rot. This inheritance, then, is not something that is natural to this world, but is impervious to the natural rot and corrosion of this world. The word *undefiled* (*amiantos*) is similar, but refers to that which is not contaminated, that which is untainted. Contaminated with what? Rot, corrosion and corruption. The third word, *unfading* (*amarantos*) refers to perpetuity, or ceaselessness.

Finally, said Peter, this inheritance is "kept in heaven for you" (v. 4). The word *kept* (*tēreō*) does not mean that it cannot escape. That would be a different Greek word. Rather, *kept* here means that it is guarded from loss or injury by keeping an eye on it—watching it, monitoring it, caring for it, guarding it. And it is not so much that this inheritance is kept in heaven like a coin is kept in a purse. But rather, that it is kept by the instrumentality of heaven. Heaven keeps an eye on it to protect it from the three things that Peter mentioned—perishing, defiling and fading.

HEAVEN

In the same way that this inheritance is not like a coin that is kept in a purse, heaven is not like a purse in which a coin is kept. The analogy works both ways. In other words, the reference to heaven is not a reference to a place. It is a reference to the abode of God. The Greek word translated as *heaven* (*ouranos*) literally indicates a hill or a rise or something that has been built up. In addition, the abode of God can also refer to God's household as well as His house, as if God has an actual house or a specific place where He lives. But in fact, He does not because God is omnipotent, omnipresent, etc. There is nothing that can contain God. Thus, *household* is a better interpretation because it points to God's people.

All of this is to suggest that our usual idea of heaven being somewhere above the sky is more Greek than biblical, more Pagan than Christian. The biblical idea of heaven is more like saying that heaven is wherever God reigns, and particularly wherever His reign is celebrated. It is a reference, not merely to God's authority or jurisdiction, but to the celebration and worship of His authority and jurisdiction. Heaven is wherever God's sovereignty and reign are honored, celebrated and worshiped. Heaven is not merely a place, but is the active and present reign of God. Thus, heaven is as much a time as a place.

Putting this all together, we see that Christians are born again into an inheritance that is perfect and eternal. And this inheritance is not kept *in* heaven, but is kept *by* heaven, by the authority, jurisdiction and reign of God Himself because of the propitiation of Christ on the cross and through the instrumentality of the Holy Spirit. God watches over it like a hen watches over her eggs.

Y'ALL

And what is more, it is kept for *you* (*hēmas*). This is not the singular *you*, but the plural *you all*. It is not that heaven isn't kept for individuals. Of course, it is kept for individuals. But it is not kept merely for individuals, but for the *you all* of the corporate church of Jesus

Christ. Heaven is the godly authority and jurisdiction of all who are included in the corporate church, all who celebrate God's reign with honor, integrity and worship. And it is kept imperishable, undefiled, and unfading by the various authorities and jurisdictions of God's representatives on earth—His people.

Peter hasn't concluded this sentence yet, there is still more to come.

3. God's Power Revealed

...who by God's power are being guarded through faith for a
salvation ready to be revealed in the last time. In this you
rejoice, though now for a little while, if necessary, you have
been grieved by various trials, so that the tested genuineness
of your faith—more precious than gold that perishes though it
is tested by fire—may be found to result in praise and glory
and honor at the revelation of Jesus Christ.
—*1 Peter 1:5-7 (ESV)*

We are still in the middle of a long sentence. So, we need to remember what has come before. This sentence began in verse 3, where Peter was praising the trinitarian God for causing His people to be born again *to* hope through Christ's resurrection and *from* death. Peter's joy overflowed into a compound sentence when he added thanksgiving to God for causing His people to be born again into an eternal, pure and unchanging inheritance that heaven itself eternally protects.

So, the referent of the word *who* in verse 5 belongs to those who have been born again into all of this. These people, whom God caused to be born again, are also guarded by God's power. It is not merely that heaven keeps the inheritance of the twice born like a marble in a bag, but that the very power of God Himself protects them. Calvin recommended that verse 5 be translated as, "Who are kept by faith in the power of God unto salvation."[4]

And how does the power of God protect His people? *Through faith.* This phrase is used more than a dozen times in the New Testament to describe the agency of salvation, or in this case, the agency of rebirth since that is the primary subject of this section. The eleventh chapter of Hebrews contains a series of biblical examples of how faith served as the

---

4   Calvin, John. *Calvin's Commentaries*, Baker Books, Ada, Michigan, 1974, 1 Peter 1:5.

means of God's protection and care throughout the long history of His people. "Through faith we understand that the worlds were framed by the word of God" (Hebrews 11:3). "Through faith also Sarah herself received strength to conceive" (Hebrews 11:11). "Through faith he (Moses) kept the passover" (Hebrews 11:28). "Through faith (David) subdued kingdoms, wrought righteousness, obtained promises, stopped the mouths of lions" (Hebrews 11:33). "And these all, having obtained a good report through faith, received not the promise" (Hebrews 11:39).

Wait a minute! Wasn't Peter saying that the inheritance of God is received through faith? So, what does it mean that all of these Old Testament characters, who acted in faith, did *not* personally receive the promised inheritance? Doesn't Scripture teach that regeneration comes by grace through faith? Yes, it does. However, the Old Testament people needed to wait for the coming of Messiah for the propitiation of God and the outpouring of the Spirit on all flesh.

Isaiah had prophesied it: "A voice cries: 'In the wilderness prepare the way of the Lord; make straight in the desert a highway for our God. Every valley shall be lifted up, and every mountain and hill be made low; the uneven ground shall become level, and the rough places a plain. And the glory of the Lord shall be revealed, and all flesh shall see it together, for the mouth of the Lord has spoken'"(Isaiah 40:3-5). And John the Baptist proclaimed it "in the wilderness of Judea, "Repent, for the kingdom of heaven is at hand. For this is he who was spoken of by the prophet Isaiah when he said, 'The voice of one crying in the wilderness: Prepare the way of the Lord; make his paths straight'" (Matthew 3:1-3).

The Key

Jesus Christ, the Lord of human history who was both prophesied and proclaimed, is the key to the Scriptures and the key to human history because He is the object of faith that unleashed the promises of God upon the world. Before His advent people were saved by grace through faith in the certain hope of His coming in the flesh—which then happened! And after His resurrection people are saved by grace through faith in the resurrection of Jesus Christ and the certain hope of the full dispensation of His inheritance through the surety of our own regeneration and the ultimate resurrection of Christ's church, the people of God. Just as Jesus Christ was thrust into human history by the decree of God, so is the Holy Spirit thrust into the personal lives of Christians by the power of God.

Peter said in this verse that the salvation provided by Jesus Christ and guarded by God was "ready to be revealed in the last time" (v. 5). It had been hidden, covered over or veiled prior to the advent of Christ. But now following Christ's resurrection, it was ready to be revealed. Paul had said that the truth of the Old Testament law had been veiled from the Jews, but unveiled as people turn to the Lord (2 Corinthians 3:15-16). It is important to notice that it is both unveiled or revealed by the fact of the advent of Jesus Christ, and by the turning of people to the Lord. The unveiling and the seeing (turning to) of what has been unveiled are the same thing, process or fact.

There are two opposing views of how this happens. Some Christians believe that the turning to the Lord is the event that reveals or unveils God's salvation through faith in Christ, that God enables people to believe through their seeing, through their own free will to chose to accept and see.

And other Christians believe that it is God's salvation through faith in Christ that enables believers to turn to or see the Lord with belief. This is essentially a debate between grace and works. It's about the relationship between God's grace and human faith, and whether God's grace is unlocked by our faith, or our faith is unlocked by God's grace. It's about the keeping of God's law. There is no question about whether God's blessings come as a result of keeping His law (Deuteronomy 28) —they do. Of course, no one is able to keep it apart from Christ. So in Christ, the question becomes whether our believing is the result of our effort to honor Christ, or our effort to honor Christ is the result of our belief.[5]

Another way to phrase the debate is: who decides whether or not someone is a Christian? Do we make that decision ourselves by accepting Christ as our Lord and Savior? Or does Christ decide by enabling people to surrender to Him? Those who think that it is the former need to consult Matthew 7:21-ff. There, people who thought that they were themselves believers and disciples of Christ were rejected by Christ, which suggests that people can fool themselves.

Either way, all Christians actually do freely choose to accept Christ. The issue is not whether free will actually exists, or whether God manipulates people like puppets. We must neither be absurd ourselves nor think that the other side is so absurd. Rather, the issue is the relationship between God's grace and human free will. One side says that all people have been created with free will and can choose or reject Christ on the basis of their own free will. And the other side says that all people are born in slavery to sin and are without the will, the ability or the vision to see either their own bondage or the reality of God until

---

5   Christian obedience is not a matter of keeping the Old Testament law, but of keeping the law of Christ. The relationship between them is complex. See *Rock Mountain Creed—Jesus' Sermon on the Mount*, by Phillip A. Ross, Pilgrim Platform, 2011.

God gives them eyes to see and ears to hear by grace through faith in Jesus Christ.

Sprinkling

The debate is about the condition of infants at birth, whether new born infants are free from sin and unworthy of God's condemnation, or whether they are born into sin and worthy of God's condemnation. If people are born free of sin, then at some point they are free to choose to be saved by Christ. But if people are born in sin, they have no initial freedom to freely choose anything until and unless God grants them an alternative to their sin, and gives them the interest and ability to make such a choice. Note that this is a subtle and complex debate, and it cannot be settled by simplistic measures.

Too many people deny the complexity of the reality of the Trinity, which simultaneously insists upon both the diversity and the unity of the Godhead, and the diversity and unity of Christ's body—the church. Are there "good" people on both sides of this argument? Or are we all nothing but sinners apart from Christ?[6]

Peter weighed into this argument by saying that God causes people to be born again, that it is the dispensation of the Holy Spirit that results in personal regeneration. Peter said that Christians are selected according to God's prognosis through the instrumentality of faith, which leads to genuine spiritual sanctification, which results in obedience to the will of God and was producing the sprinkling of Christ's blood among the Gentiles through the dispersion of Christ's people.

Sprinkling was a liturgical act that was introduced by God through Moses for the consecration of Aaron and his sons for service to the Lord (Exodus 29). Thus, it was part of the ordination service in the Old Testament, and was a symbolic act. The sacrifice of the animal was done as a sign and seal of the covenant, and the sprinkling of the blood of the sacrifice symbolized the reception—or the sign (symbol) and seal (reception)—of God's covenant by the people. Blood makes a permanent stain, and served as a perpetual reminder of one's obligations and service to God's covenant.

Peter was showing how the sacrifice of Christ was being used by God historically in the same way that Temple sacrifices had been used liturgically. Liturgically, the sprinkling of the blood instituted and authorized those upon whom it was sprinkled as agents in the service of God. And that was Peter's point.

---

6   See: Romans 3:12; Genesis 1:31, 6:6-7; Exodus 32:8; Psalm 14:3, 53:1; Ecclesiastes 7:20, 7:29; Isaiah 53:6, 59:8, 64:6; Jeremiah 2:13; Matthew 25:30; Philemon 1:11; Ephesians 2:3, 2:8-10; Philippians 2:12-13; 1 Peter 2:25; Titus 2:13-14; James 1:16-17.

Those who had been scattered because of persecution as a result of their covenant faith in Christ were themselves agents in the service of God in Christ who had been sent out into the world to further sprinkle the blood of Christ as a sign and seal to be applied to more servants of God in Christ. These persecuted Christians on the run were in the process of revealing or unveiling the salvation of God in order to demonstrate the truth of God historically—not just in books but in actual history. They were the leading wave of evangelists sent out to unveil the gospel in the light of Christ in the midst of the final or end time that had begun.

A.D.

The introduction of the term "last time" is problematic because of the popularity of Dispensational end times speculation by contemporary Christians, who are convinced that the Bible predicts the destruction of the world and the transportation of a small number of Christians into heaven to escape the carnage and enjoy life on a new earth somewhere in a new heaven. Suffice it to say that this is not at all what Peter was talking about here.

Quite the opposite, he was talking about the change from the Old Testament Temple administration of God's covenant to the new administration (new at that time) of God's covenant through Jesus Christ. Peter lived on the leading edge of Christ's covenantal administration, looking forward to the unfolding of the new age that Christ inaugurated. This is the literal meaning of Peter's words. The Greek, *eschatos kairos*, points to the immediacy and contiguity of a special historical period of time.

And Christ's new age has indeed been significant in the history of the world. It was such a significant event in history that the world's authorities decided to recalibrate time on the basis of Christ's birth. Eventually the Roman Empire adopted the system that had been in use by Christians who celebrated Christ's eternal nature by dating their letters and works on the basis of His birth, and as a means to set a common, annual date for Easter. It was common to date things according to the reign of the current king. And because Christians understood Christ to be on the throne, they began dating things by His birth.

The *Anno Domini* (Latin for *The Year of Our Lord*) dating system was formally adopted in 525 by Dionysius Exiguus (or Dennis the Short, meaning humble), a Romanian monk who used it to compute the date of the Christian Easter festival, and to project future Easter dates. His system replaced the Diocletian era that had been in use because he did not want to continue the memory of a tyrant who had persecuted Christians. The last year of the old calendar, Diocletian 247, was immediately followed by the first year of his new dating table, A.D. 532.

Prior to this the years of the Julian calendar were identified by naming the consuls who held Roman office that year. He himself stated that the year his system was inaugurated was the consulship of Probus Junior, which was 525 years since the incarnation of our Lord Jesus Christ. This is the age or the "last time" that Peter referred to, which began at Christ's birth and continues today in the Twenty-First Century of the Year of Our Lord, sometimes referred to as the Common Era (C.E.), or as others call it: the Christian Era.

The point is that Peter was not talking about the end of the world, but the beginning of an new age of the covenant administration of Jesus Christ. In fact, the era of Christ's covenantal administration is eternal. It is without end because it represents the completion of God's work of creation and the inauguration of God's eternal Sabbath. Because Christ is the purpose (*telos*) of the world that God created, the practice of Sabbath worship also changed when Christ fulfilled God's purpose and brought the Old Covenant Sabbath practices to a conclusion.

We cannot read Peter's letters without understanding that Peter had a foot in both eras because he was a transitional figure between them, as were all of the Apostles. The change in covenantal administration that Christ brought dominated Peter's life and thought. It was a very big deal for him, and his writing is saturated with the idea of this covenantal change. Peter was very aware that he himself lived at the beginning of the last or end time, or the final and eternal age of the world.

Peter knew that his fellow Christians needed to understand what was happening to them in the midst of this historic and cataclysmic time between the ages, between the end of the Jewish age and the beginning of the Christian age. He knew that his fellow Christians needed to see the big picture so that they could make better sense of their own lives in the mosaic of world history. Thus, the end times does not refer to the destruction of the world, but to the purpose of the world in Christ.

TRIALS' END

This theme continues in verse 6, "In this you rejoice, though now for a little while, if necessary, you have been grieved by various trials." Those who had suffered persecution, and those who fled the destruction of Jerusalem by the Roman army according to the prophecies of Jesus Christ were in the midst of suffering many trials that accompanied their faithfulness. Life was not easy. The loss of jobs, homes, property and family brought much pain and difficulty. Moving is never easy, but under the circumstances of those days, it was both dangerous and painful.

Peter assured them that their difficulties were only "for a little while" (v. 6), not forever, but just for a season. The difficulties could not be avoided. History had hit a bump in the road and people were thrown off track—but it would only be for a season. Things would get better. There was a purpose in their suffering. That purpose was the sanctification and purification of their faith, which was more precious than gold. They were grieved by trials "so that the tested genuineness of (their) faith—more precious than gold that perishes though it is tested by fire—may be found to result in praise and glory and honor at the revelation of Jesus Christ" (v. 7).

The trials were God's means of testing or proving the saints. The word is *tried* (*dokimazō*) in the *Authorized Version*, and by implication it means *approved*. But it wasn't that God was testing a prototype to see if it would hold up under stress. Rather, God was firing the clay of faithfulness in the kiln of affliction in order to strengthen it. God knew what the end result would be, but those under Peter's care did not. So, he was writing to assure them that the end or purpose in it was that the process would "result in praise and glory and honor at the revelation of Jesus Christ" (v. 7).

Faith*less*ness complains and curses God in the face of difficulties. But faithfulness finds glory in the face of frustration. Faithfulness honors God in the presence of persecution. Faithfulness proposes praise when tempted and tried. Peter knew that this would be true for other believers because it had been true for him. He knew it from the inside. Peter knew that faith in Christ would trump anything that the world could throw at him because he knew that God was using faith to protect His people from temptations, and using trials to strengthen the faith of His people.

THE ELECT

It is important that we understand who Peter was writing to because it also shows us who God was guarding and protecting—and strengthening. According to verse 1 he was writing to the "elect exiles of the dispersion." These were the people whom God was working with, and there are at least four things to note about them: 1) They had been chosen, as opposed to having chosen themselves. 2) They were not residing in their homeland. 3) They had been scattered far and wide. And 4) in spite of their dispersion they were a unified group, not disparate individuals, but a cohesive group, a plural *y'all*, not a bunch of singular *yous*.

Why are these things important? Because God had chosen them as a group, a unit. Of course, they retained their individuality. But the point is that God's selection was group oriented first and individual oriented second. They had not been chosen because of anything in or of themselves. God is not a respecter of persons, of individuals.[7] Rather, they were selected for God's reasons and His purpose, and according to a group that He defined—for His own glory and for His church.

Of course, groups cannot exist without particular individuals. However, God was not choosing individuals in order to determine the character of the group, He was creating a group without regard for the character of the individuals because He was in the process of changing individual character to comply with His predefined group definition.

And what is more, because we know that salvation is by grace alone through faith alone, we know that this common purpose is a function of grace alone through faith alone. However, they were not chosen because God foreknew that they would have faith. No. Rather, they had faith because God had given it to them, as God has given people everything they have. We have nothing that God has not given us. Everything we have is the result of God's grace. So, if people have faith, it is because God has given it.

Peter's reference to their being exiles had a double meaning. They were exiles from Jerusalem, but they were also exiles from the kingdom of God, which is the true home of all Christians. It is not that our home is in heaven, as if heaven is some Gnostic, other worldly, spiritual zone somewhere in space or other dimension. Remember, heaven is the abode or reign of God, and is as much a time as a place. Heaven is where God's power, authority and jurisdiction are lovingly appreciated and honored. And that is where Christians are currently exiled from because the powers and principalities of our contemporary world do not appreciate or honor God's reality and authority. Again, God is gathering exiled Christians into His kingdom of heaven on earth, but that process won't be finished until He returns to complete it.

The fact that Peter mentioned that this group was dispersed indicates that his intention was to address them, not as individuals but as a group. It is at this point that the trinitarian character of Christians makes a huge difference that is often—usually—overlooked, even by otherwise faithful Christians. It is at this point that Christians tend to choose for themselves one or the other sides of various false dichotomies that lead to arguments and dissension among the brethren. It is in the failure to discern unity in diversity that Christian factions of every

---

7   Leviticus 19:15; Deuteronomy 1:17; 10:17; 16:19; 2 Chronicles 19:7; Proverbs 24:23; 28:21; Lamentations 4:16; Acts 10:34; Ephesians 6:9; Colossians 3:25; James 2:9; 1 Peter 1:17.

kind fail to honor Jesus Christ as the Second Person of the Trinity, and deny the power of the Holy Spirit to accomplish God's will.

It is much easier to flatten out the complexities and nuances involved in trinitarian relationships than to make the effort to sort it out. And people generally do what is easy. But doing what is easy creates an inaccurate understanding of reality. It ignores and negates important details and provides a shallow and deficient understanding of the reality in which people actually live.

THE TRINITY

Most Christians over most of Christian history have not sufficiently understood the doctrine of the Trinity, and have simply set it aside. It has long been the neglected doctrine. Unfortunately, the Charismatic/Pentecostal churches have captured this doctrine and misconstrued it, and grown that misunderstanding worldwide. But this kind of growth of errant ideas is nothing new to Christianity. Christianity has always struggled against heresy and apostasy.[8] Restoring sanity and biblical accuracy to the doctrine of the Trinity will not be easy. Apparently God doesn't want it to be easy.

Because the Trinity is somewhat difficult to understand, people have generally ignored it. But it is the central doctrine that differentiates Christianity from all other religions and cannot be ignored or denied without ignoring or denying the one thing that makes Christianity unique. To fail to understand and correctly apply the doctrine of the Trinity means failing to understand and apply Christianity itself.

The doctrine of the Trinity is a tricky issue because people actually engage the truth of the Trinity all the time. It is impossible not to engage it because God Himself holds reality together, and He is trinitarian. Thus, He holds His trinitarian reality together in trinitarian ways. Unfortunately, people are in the habit of not seeing the trinitarian aspects of reality, or of God. Apart from Christ they are veiled (2 Corinthians 3:13-18, Roman 1:18-20). People unacquainted with Christ simply look past them. Even most Christians look past the Trinity because they have been confused by history and circumstance. People simply take the reality of the Trinity for granted and fail to think about it. For the most part it is subconscious.

The things we take for granted are always the most difficult to see or perceive. Nonetheless, God calls people to the task of seeing and celebrating His trinitarian character. That's what the Bible is about—seeing God, acknowledging God so we can get our worship right, which will put our lives right, which will put our world right. Community wor-

---

8   For further discussion see: *Arsy Varsy—Reclaiming the Gospel in First Corinthians*, by Phillip A. Ross, Pilgrim Platform, 2008, p. 220-ff.

ship provides the proper context for the purpose of our individual lives. Worship provides purpose, meaning and hope in an otherwise purposeless, meaningless and hopeless world.

Furthermore, one of the central consequences of the failure to see and correctly apply the doctrine of the Trinity impacts the unity of the church. The unity of the church is a function of the Trinity. This is true because Christian unity is necessarily trinitarian unity because God is trinitarian, and that is the one thing that makes Christianity unique and different from all other religions and philosophies. And apart from recognizing and engaging the uniqueness of Christianity—it's trinitarian character—people fail to recognize and engage God in Jesus Christ through the Holy Spirit.

Consequently, the general ignorance and disregard of the Trinity, and of the implications of the Trinity upon the structure of reality and upon human character, are at the root of the failure of Christians to understand and practice genuine Christianity, and the failure to engage genuine Christian unity (trinitarian unity). The problem begins with wrong theological assumptions, with academics, with wrong thoughts and ideas, etc. It begins with how we see God and His world, but it doesn't end there. That error then cascades into every area of human life, both individual and social. Whenever and wherever we get our thinking wrong about something as fundamental as God and the character of reality, all other areas of human endeavor get infected with that wrongness.

Vision

Problems develop because we don't see things as they actually are. And those who have been created in God's image, but fail to see God or engage life accordingly, create difficulties for all of us. God calls it sin. But regardless of what people call it, the problems it creates are very real. And because unfaithful people cause these problems, the more unfaithful people there are in the world, the more problems there are. The problem, however, is not the people, but the sin—the unfaithfulness. It is not that we have too many people in the world, but that we have too much sin in the world.

The resolution of these problems requires correcting the root cause, the central thing that produces the problems. And in this case, that one thing is our understanding and application of the doctrine of the Trinity to God, to the Bible, to the church and to the world. We misunderstand who we are, who God is, who Jesus Christ is, who the Holy Spirit is.

And because there is complexity and subtlety in the doctrine of the Trinity, we focus on part of reality and ignore the rest. We overem-

phasize one thing and underemphasize another. People tend to sim-
plify the complexities of reality to fit their own expectations and preferences. People tend to cut off from their own consideration various
things that they themselves cannot account for. People tend to opt for
easier solutions, such as creating or relying on various habits and
superstitions to account for what they don't understand. Superstition
has always provided a stumbling block to the gospel. Christ came to
bring purpose and meaning to the world, and to put an end to all bad
habits and superstitions—ancient and modern.

"God's power" (v. 5) is uniquely found and expressed by the power
of the Trinity. Christ's "inheritance that is imperishable, undefiled, and
unfading, (and) kept (by) heaven" (v. 4) is kept by the power and reality of the Trinity. Christ's resurrection and our regeneration are functions of the Trinity.

The point of all of this is that the Trinity is completely unique to
Christianity and can only be understood in the light of Christ by the
power and presence of the Holy Spirit through regeneration, which
means that Jesus Christ is central to human identity and all human
activity. We must rethink our understandings of Christianity. Before
we can reach the world with the gospel, we must get it right ourselves.

REPENT!

The Lord's first sermon was a call to repentance—not mere
remorse for sin, but an actual change in our thinking and behavior.
Who was He preaching to? Jews—people who thought they were faithful believers. God doesn't want us to simply feel bad about our sin. He
commands us to abandon it. So, Christ's essential and eternal message
is always this same demand, which is also at the same time a gift of forgiveness. It is the forgiveness that provides the opportunity and the
power for the repentance—change.

We must as a people, as a society, rethink what we are doing. We
must as a people reconfigure how we are doing what we are doing. We
must as a people reevaluate why we do what we do.

It is not that we need to assert or insert Christ into our thinking
and doing, as if faith is a last ditch effort to force Christ on the world.
Not at all! Rather, we must see that Christ is actually already here,
holding everything together, providing context and syntax for everything that we do. So, people must stop ignoring Him and see that
Christ's activity of holding the world together is the foundation of
human sanity, human hope, human aspiration and inspiration, and
Christian unity. This is God's trinitarian will for the world.

4. THINGS ANNOUNCED

Though you have not seen him, you love him. Though you do not now see him, you believe in him and rejoice with joy that is inexpressible and filled with glory, obtaining the outcome of your faith, the salvation of your souls. Concerning this salvation, the prophets who prophesied about the grace that was to be yours searched and inquired carefully, inquiring what person or time the Spirit of Christ in them was indicating when he predicted the sufferings of Christ and the subsequent glories. It was revealed to them that they were serving not themselves but you, in the things that have now been announced to you through those who preached the good news to you by the Holy Spirit sent from heaven, things into which angels long to look.
—1 Peter 1:8-12 (ESV)

As we read Peter's letter we see that he was speaking about big ideas. He was applying the gospel to various elements of biblical history and showing how the gospel of Jesus Christ illuminates the Old Testament to provide additional understanding and perspective that was not available to the Old Testament saints. Peter provided here the beginnings for what we might call progressive revelation.[9] God's revelation through Scripture has grown increasingly richer and more robust over time. The church has also grown, and with it the body of

---

9   This is not to be confused or associated with the Progressive Movement in the current era. In the United States, the term *progressivism* emerged in the late 19th century in reference to a more general response to the vast changes brought by Modern industrialization. It was an alternative to both the traditional conservative response to social and economic issues and to the various more radical streams of socialism and anarchism which opposed them. Political parties, such as the Progressive Party, organized at the beginning of the 20th century, and progressivism made great strides under American presidents Theodore Roosevelt, Woodrow Wilson, Franklin Roosevelt, and Lyndon Johnson.

Christian literature has grown in both breadth and depth as well. Only those unfamiliar with it will dispute this fact.

Scripture continues to bring God's people to increasing maturity over time by providing a growing body of faithful Christian commentary, literature and increasingly mature saints.[10] The accumulation of this literature contributes to the maturity of God's people as they interact with it and add to it. This literature is not equivalent to the Bible. It will always be secondary to Scripture. It is not a replacement for Scripture, nor a correction of Scripture. Nonetheless, some of it is quite helpful. The wisdom of godly saints in the past and the present can be helpful because they have dealt with the same kinds of issues and concerns that we deal with today. Indeed, sin is always the same, and the gospel is always the same.

Not Seen

Peter knew that those saints who were on the run from the destruction of Jerusalem in his day loved Jesus even though they had not seen Him in the flesh. He knew that the joy of belief in Christ was not tied to the Lord's physical presence. Would this unaided faithfulness have been easier in Peter's day, when there weren't any Christian resources? Or in ours, when there is a glut of resources? In Peter's day there were no established Christian churches. There were no Christian colleges, little to no Christian literature.

Perhaps it's an unfair question because we know the benefits of these things, having lived with them all of our lives. In Peter's day they didn't have the hindsight that we have. Without a doubt, these resources can be immensely helpful. But Christians in Peter's day had no such idea.

Then again, on the negative side of all this, they would not have had the level of confusion that our churches, colleges and literature have brought us. We must not deny that many of the resources that Christians depend on do not further the cause of Christ, but retard it. For instance, while we must learn from the Early Church or the Reformation or the Puritans, we must not be bound to their errors. We must not work to return Christ's church to some historical bygone era. Rather, we must work to build upon biblical truth toward the continuing reformation and development of the church. *Semper reformanda!*

We have a wealth of Christian resources that those in Peter's day didn't have. That gives us an advantage that they didn't have—and greater responsibility. We can stand on the shoulders of other faithful saints who have gone before us. We can learn what they learned in

---

10 Obviously, all who call themselves Christian are not mature. And unfortunately, many are not even Christian. See Matthew 7:21-27. Lord have mercy!

much less time than it took them because we have the advantage of their faithful reflection and insights. But there is a down side to this, too. Apart from wisdom and discretion on our part, apart from guidance by the Holy Spirit, people can also learn and easily accept the errors of those who have gone before. History exposes us to both truth and error.

SEEN

Peter said that these saints he was writing to loved the Lord, though they hadn't seen Him. What did Peter mean by *seeing* the Lord? The Greek word (*eidō*) simply means *see*, and by implication it means *to know*. Peter didn't have our resources, nor could he have anticipated them or their diversity. So, it is unlikely that Peter had this perspective or the benefit of historical perspective in mind. It is quite likely that Peter did not intend to suggest the kind of knowing of the Lord that can be acquired through such resources. Our resources can give people a kind of secondhand knowledge of Christ, a knowing *about* Christ rather than a personal knowing *of* Him, and that is not what Peter was talking about.

Today people often think of seeing or knowing the Lord in academic or intellectual terms, and there is nothing wrong with such knowledge. The wealth of Christian resources available today can be of great help to faithfulness, but it can also provide a serious hindrance. Anyone can acquire intellectual knowledge, even the godless—and they do. But this was not the kind of seeing and knowing that Peter was talking about. Peter was talking about knowledge by faith, about direct perception. Peter was talking about how faith in Christ can inform, reform and transform people into the likeness of Christ. Of course, Christians don't ever become Christ, but we do become increasingly like Him.

People in Peter's day did not have the secondary sources that we have—creeds, confessions, commentaries, etc. They had to rely on the more immediate things like Scripture (the Old Testament and some letters from some apostles), things like prayer, fellowship and church authorities. The point is that in our day it is much easier to get distracted by secondary resources because there are so many of them. People can easily get distracted by secondary resources and secondary issues to the point that they lose track of the primary sources and issues. Again, this is more our concern than Peter's.

HOPE

Peter was talking about walking by faith, not by sight. Peter was talking about the reliability of faith to illuminate the truth. The writer of Hebrews said that "faith is the assurance of things hoped for, the conviction of things not seen" (Hebrews 11:1). Peter agreed.

But we must take care not to think of hope as the world thinks of hope. The world thinks that hope is a function of emotion and imagination, and not of knowing God. But apart from knowing God in Christ, there is no basis for hope, other than human imagination. Apart from Christ all we have are our own hopes and dreams, our own thoughts and desires. But Peter was not talking about our human hopes, but about God's eternal hope.

Only in Christ can Christian hope be grounded and fruitful. Christ is the fulfillment of God's hope, and God's hope is not imaginary. Christian hope is not based upon human imagination. Rather, Christian hope is based on God's decreed desire to save the world in Christ, and His relentless progress toward that end. He promised a Messianic salvation, and then sent the Messiah—Jesus Christ. The Bible is the story of God's faithfulness to His promises. We are encouraged to trust God's promises because He always keeps His promises.

Today, God is still in the middle of keeping His final promise of salvation in Christ. And yet faithfulness is not a matter of hedging our bets about whether God will eventually fulfill that promise or not. It has already been fulfilled because Christ has already come. It has already been fulfilled, but it's not over. This promise of salvation in Jesus Christ is an eternal promise. It is a promise that never ends its fulfillment because it is a promise of eternal salvation—not just eternal for you and me individually, but eternally active in the world, eternally working for the salvation of humanity. This hope is always new because new people are always coming to it. This hope has no end because this hope is the end, the purpose of God.

God is indeed bringing the world to an end, but not in the way that most people think. It's not that the world is going to end in catastrophe and be no more. Catastrophe is not the end that God has in mind. It may be a stumbling stone along the way—nations rise and nations fall —but God is not aiming at catastrophe. Salvation, not destruction, is God's end, His purpose. If there is to be a catastrophe it will be the product of those who hate and despise God, not of those who love and honor Him.

God's people are working toward salvation, not destruction. The end and means of the gospel is life not death, construction not destruction. Peter said that those who know God in Christ are filled with un-containable joy because they trust God's promise of salvation. The "end of your faith" (v. 9) as it is translated in the *Authorized Version*, is the purpose and outcome (*telos*) of faith. The fulfillment of God's salvation promise is the end or the purpose of the world toward which God is working.

Soul Salvation

Peter said that God intends to save our souls (*psuchē*). *Webster's Dictionary* (1828) defined *soul* as "the spiritual, rational and immortal substance in man, which distinguishes him from brutes; that part of man which enables him to think and reason, and which renders him a subject of moral government. The immortality of the soul is a fundamental article of Christianity. Such is the nature of the human soul that it must have a God, an object of supreme affection." Webster was a little carried away with the rationalism of the soul, but that was a product of his own time.

The Greek word (*psuchē*) simply means *breath* and alludes to human sentience or consciousness. But it doesn't simply mean self-aware. In the biblical context it means aware of God. From a trinitarian perspective our identity is caught up in Christ, who is the Second Person of the Trinity. We cannot know who we are as human beings apart from knowing who God is. God is to the soul as the center is to the circumference of a circle, in that it defines it at every point.

Again, it must be noted that from a trinitarian perspective the soul is not something that is a part of a person. The human soul is not like a man in a machine. It is our wholeness in Christ. The soul cannot be dissected or abstracted from the body. It is integrated into the whole of the body. People are wholes, not parts. To divide a person into his or her constitutive parts leads to the death of the person, not his salvation. According to Webster, our identity in Christ in humanity is what God intends to save.

Therefore, God's salvation of the human soul means the salvation of human beings, of course. But not merely the salvation of a collection of disparate human individuals. Rather, it means the salvation of human culture, human society in Christ. Because our individual identities are caught up in our corporate or cultural identity, both are involved in God's salvation. This is an important point because it means that we are saved as individuals but also as a biblical *kind* (Genesis 1:12) or species. We are saved as humanity in the corporate sense, as well as persons in the individual sense. These two aspects of our identity cannot be separated, nor should they be blurred. Rather, they are to be considered as elements of our trinitarian character.

Corporate Sustainability

Because God's salvation plan involves the integration of heaven and earth—it is to be on earth as it is in heaven (Matthew 6:10)—the corporate or cultural aspect of salvation must be what we might call *sustainable*. God knows that the number one enemy of sustainable culture in the world is sin, not pollution, not corruption, not overpopulation or climate change.

God's salvation plan involves the eventual elimination of sin, which will be accomplished gradually as God Himself becomes revealed more fully over time. God's revelation is progressive, and as the light of Christ shines brighter and more fully into the dark corners of the world, that light dispels sin as it saves people—eventually, ultimately. And it will do so completely.

Verse 10 tells us that the Old Testament prophets prophesied about the hope of Jesus Christ through God's grace, that Christ was alive and functioning in the Old Testament. The *Contemporary English Version* says it well: "Some prophets told how kind God would be to you, and they searched hard to find out more about the way you would be saved" (v. 10). The thing to notice is how Peter related the Old Testament to the saints of his own day, and to all Christians by implication.

Peter was agreeing with Paul that "these things took place as examples for us" (1 Corinthians 10:6). Things in the Old Testament happened for the benefit of those in Peter's day, and those in ours as well—which is only to say that we can and must learn from history. Things in the Early Church and in the Reformation and in the founding of America happened for our benefit. History benefits the future.

The *Contemporary English Version* continues, "The Spirit of Christ was in them and was telling them how Christ would suffer and would then be given great honor. So they searched to find out exactly who Christ would be and when this would happen" (v. 11). Peter testified that the Spirit of Christ was in the Old Testament prophets.

We understand this today, but in Peter's time this would have been an astonishing statement because the fullness of the doctrine of the Trinity did not manifest until Christ's advent and the dispensation of the Holy Spirit. Peter was indeed writing about something very new and very significant. The doctrine of the Trinity was not officially established until hundreds of years later. But this does not mean that the Trinity was invented by later theologians, only that it is a difficult doctrine to understand.

Later theologians could not deny that the church had been using the doctrine from its beginning, that the doctrine of the Trinity is everywhere in Scripture. Peter was saying that the Trinity was actually part of the Old Testament, that Christianity (the Trinity) did not begin with the birth of Jesus but began with God's purpose for creation.[11] Of

---

11   Natan, Yoel. *The Jewish Trinity*, Aventine Press, San Diego, California, 2003.

course, the Trinity was not fully manifest until the birth, life, death and resurrection of Christ, which is why the New Testament is part of the Bible.

Old Testament Truth Reloaded

Peter was making a trinitarian statement about the Old Testament. It is no wonder that the Jewish establishment didn't like the idea of the Trinity—they still don't. The Jews had uniquely defined monotheism in the midst of a polytheistic world. That was their claim to fame. Then, suddenly in Christ it seemed that trinitarianism stepped on the stage of history to usher in, not a religious movement to reestablish a Jewish monarchy or Jewish monotheism, but a completely new era of human history that would begin with the conclusion or end of Judaism.

The New Testament doctrine of the Trinity, however well or poorly defined at the time, was being read back into the Old Testament by Peter. Peter was looking for and seeing Christ in the Old Testament. And Christ was revealing more truth than had ever been seen before. The light of Christ illuminated the Old Testament in a new way, but not just the Old Testament—Christ illuminated life itself. It revealed God's end or purpose for creation. Peter said that, as this process developed, the glory of Christ would also increase—and it has!

It may be difficult for faithful Christians today to get excited about seeing Christ in the Old Testament because in our day there is nothing new about it. Then again, because so many Christians today are so ignorant of the history and theology of Christianity, such a thought just might actually provide for renewal. Certainly, in the light of the Trinity Christ's activity always brings a renewal to those who "get it," to those with eyes to see and ears to hear.

But the point is that Peter was saying that the revelation of God increases in the light of Christ over time. The "end" of the world is not a simple return to the Garden of Eden, forgiven and sanctified. But the "end" of the world is the city of God, the New Jerusalem come down from heaven into the garden. The "end" of the world is the purpose for which God created it. The end or purpose of God's Word is not to return the world to its beginning point, but to provide an improved beginning point in Christ—world without end. What began with God, was renewed in Christ and revealed here by Peter (and others) has continued for two millennia. And it shows no signs of abating!

Service

Finally, verse 12 tells us that this revelation was given, not to those who served themselves but to those who served *you*—the exiles of the dispersion (v. 1). By application, then, it was also given to all who serve other Christians, who help other Christians grow in faithfulness. This is important because it shows that God was more interested in those who acted in the service of others than those who acted out of self-interest. This means that God matures Christians through service to others, and not those who are overly focused on their own spiritual growth. Christianity is always other-directed and not self-directed.

An application of this idea is the growth that comes from reading and studying good Christian commentaries and literature. But that growth will quickly reach a plateau and rot unless people begin to apply what they learn. For instance, the failure to teach others what we are learning ourselves will turn our studies into a glorified form of navel gazing. To fail to move into Christian service is to fail to grow as a Christian.

This does not mean that everyone has to do church work, not at all. It means that everyone has to do kingdom work. God's love is about sharing and serving, not self-satisfaction or self-improvement. It is about being who God has made us in Christ in the midst of our ordinary circumstances.

Peter noted that those preachers who had taught the saints had preached to them by the power and presence of the Holy Spirit, who had come down to them from heaven. Those preachers were evangelists (*euaggelizō*), bearers of God's good news in Christ. The good news was, of course, the news of the gospel of grace, that through Christ's work on the cross God had been propitiated, and all who were or who would one day be in Christ were forgiven. Their relationship with God through Jesus Christ had been restored. They could begin anew, without the baggage of sin and guilt that people had carried around since Adam and Eve left the Garden.

This good news of the gospel of Jesus Christ was a new thing in Peter's day because Peter belonged to the generation who had seen the Lord in the flesh. It's not new anymore, and it is hard for people today to see it as being new. And yet, it is renewed every time some one "gets it." It's all about renewal, but it is not new to those who don't "get it."

Angels

Peter also spoke of angels. Sometimes when the biblical writers used the word *angel* (*aggelos*), they were referring to pastors, preachers, prophets and evangelists—those who brought the message of the good news of the gospel. This does not mean that there are not angels in heaven. Of course, there are angels in heaven! It just means that sometimes biblical authors wrote of such earthly gospel proclaimers as angels because proclaiming God's Word is the primary job of angels, even in the Old Testament.

If we understand the word this way, Peter was saying that he had a message that had stirred the hearts and aspirations of pastors and evangelists in the fledgling Christian community. He was saying that this doctrine had taken the Christian community by storm. It was very popular among Christians and was creating interest far and wide, especially among gospel proclaimers.

Was it popular because it predicted the end of the world in destruction? No. Of course it did anticipate the destruction of Jerusalem in A.D. 70 and the end of the Old Testament administration of the covenant, the end of Judaism. And these things were huge! But none of these things would amount to the complete destruction of the entire earth or the solar system. That was not what Peter was talking about.

Peter was talking about the end of one era and the beginning of a new era, the beginning of new possibilities and realities that would utterly change the world, the entire world. And they have! The changes in the world that have come since Christ walked on the earth and because of Christ—during the current Christian Era—are unparalleled in history.

In Peter's time, people—especially proclaimers of the gospel—were flocking to learn about Jesus Christ and how He enlightens the Old Testament, how the Trinity inhabits the Old Testament, what He means to the future. Indeed, Peter was less concerned about the end of the old and more concerned about the beginning of the new. Christ had come! The New Age had already begun. Halleluiah!

5. The Engine of Hope

Therefore, preparing your minds for action, and being sober-minded, set your hope fully on the grace that will be brought to you at the revelation of Jesus Christ.   —1 Peter 1:13 (ESV)

On the basis of all that Peter had said so far he made some recommendations for action. God was doing a new thing in Christ. That new thing was already in motion. The fullness of time had already arrived, the Messiah had already come to collect and dispense His inheritance to His people by the very power of God Himself. And He was doing this through those saints who had been scattered in the name of Jesus Christ. "Therefore" (v. 13), said Peter, *because of all this you need to be alert, to think straight and prepare your minds for action.*

There are three things to notice about this phrase. First, preparation is involved. Second, the sort of action involved requires right thinking. It is about getting our thoughts in the correct order. And third, the thinking involved must produce action. We must not confuse thinking about a thing with doing something about it. Thinking is not sufficient. Peter intended to show us what it means to be a faithful saint, how to live faithfully.

The *Authorized Version* translates this phrase as, "gird up the loins of your mind" (v. 13). This is a strong statement about preparation. We are to prepare ourselves to think deeply and clearly about Christ and the gospel, as if such thought would be strenuous and demanding. We are to understand these things correctly, which means biblically, from the perspective of the whole Bible, and especially from the perspective of the Old Testament.

For the saints Peter was addressing, the Bible was the Old Testament. Sure, they valued the histories and letters of the apostles and considered them to be equal to the Bible because of the light that they gave to the Bible, to the Old Testament. Reading the Old Testament from the point of view of the fulfillment of Jesus Christ shed new light on the ancient texts. Nonetheless, for them at that moment the Bible was the Old Testament. So, in order to read and understand Peter fruitfully we must read his letters through the eyes of the Old Testament and in the light of Christ. We must understand his allusions and references to the Old Testament lest we turn his letters into a product of our own imaginations.

DISCRETION

Peter also said to be "sober-minded" (v. 13). The Greek word (nē-phō) means to be discreet, to be sober, and to watch. Discretion isn't on our minds much anymore. It is an unpopular idea today because one form of the word—*discrimination*—has been hijacked by the Political Correctness Movement.[12] To be discreet means to be prudent, modest, wise and self-restraining. It means not doing whatever you want, not saying whatever you feel like saying, not being unrestrained in your expression. People often think that being free means that you can do or say whatever you want.

But actually, that isn't freedom at all. Consider a drunk, someone who is not sober-minded. Drunks often feel completely free to do and say whatever they want. So, they do. But in the morning they are often disgusted with themselves because they were under the influence. Under what influence? The influence of demon rum, without self-control, or whatever. Getting drunk does not make people free—quite the opposite. It simply removes inhibitions and allows unrestrained sin to dominate one's speech and actions. And sinners are not free, but are bound by their sin. Peter's point here was to recommend that people maintain their inhibitions, strengthen them, improve them.

Peter said that free people are self-inhibited, self-controlled, not uninhibited. Personal inhibitions are the bulwarks of social and political freedom. Free people are in control of themselves and their destinies. Free people do not relinquish that control to others, nor abandon it altogether. To be free is to be autonomous, to be self-governed, not ungoverned.

And here's the rub: sinners are not free. Sinners are bound to the desires and proclivities of their sin. Sinners do not have the freedom to abandon sin. Sin is their master. And the only way to get out from under the mastery of sin is through Jesus Christ. Sinners can only be free from their sin in Christ.

---

12 Political correctness is a term that denotes language, ideas, policies, and behavior that are seen as seeking to minimize social and institutional offense in occupational, gender, racial, cultural, sexual orientation, disability, and age-related contexts. In current usage, the term is primarily pejorative. More: http://en.wikipedia.org/wiki/Political_correctness.

So, Christians trade bondage to sin for bondage to Christ—which is the only actual, available option. Only Jesus Christ has the power and ability to actually be free. Apart from this trade, freedom is not real. And apart from this choice—to abandon sin in Christ—people cannot actually be free because apart from Christ sinners are under the mastery of their sin.

TRINITARIAN IDENTITY

Christians live and move and have their being in Christ. So, Christian freedom is freedom in Christ, freedom within the bounds of Christ. No one is free to break the law, which means that human freedom can only exist apart from the law in such a way that it breaks no law. This means that the only real freedom available is the freedom to live above the law—not in mere obedience to the law, but with genuine love, honor and regard for perfect righteousness. Everyone must obey the law, but those who are free are not free to ignore the law. Rather, they are free to fulfill the law in righteousness, if they are able—and only Christ is able to do that. Nonetheless, Christians freely strive toward that end.

It is at the point of defining freedom that we come up against the doctrine of the Trinity because it affects who we actually are as human beings. Here's how it works: We are individuals, but we are also social beings. Our social identities are determined by our belonging to various groups, and our human identity is based upon our belongings and associations. Such characteristics define us by refining the kind of persons we are. Our identities are caught up in various social groupings. Our lives are interwoven into various social fabrics, and it cannot be otherwise. Most of these identity groupings and associations are not entered into voluntarily. For instance, I am tall, male, Caucasian and American—none of which I chose, but which nonetheless contribute significantly to my personal identity.

It is in our social character that our freedom requires limits. For our freedom to be maximized our individual freedoms must not infringe on the freedoms of others, nor theirs on us. Freedom requires certain socially agreed upon limitations or rules that equally bind all people in order to provide the maximum freedom for everyone. Thus, individual self-imposed discretion—self-control, morality, refinement, aesthetics, etc.—produces maximum social freedom. And when people refuse to exercise self-control or discretion, the law must impose a generic, lowest common denominator kind of control upon them by civil government or legal sanctions.

Jesus dealt with this in His Sermon on the Mount. Christians are indeed out from under the legal imposition of the law because of

Christ's propitiation on the cross—and also because Christians exercise moral discretion or self-control. Christ made forgiveness real and sent His Holy Spirit to give His people the desire and the drive to please the Lord.

The Holy Spirit was dispatched to change human identity through regeneration. In Christ people are not who they used to be. And not being who they used to be, they no longer do the things they used to do, nor do they do things like they used to do them. Our being is like the headwaters of our doing. Human identity drives human behavior. People do what they do because of who they understand themselves to be.

So, when the Lord changes human being (identity), human doing (behavior) also subsequently changes—not right away, but over time. In the same way that a river cannot flow upstream, our doing (our behavior, our works) cannot change our being (our identity). That's why Christianity is not a works-righteous religion. Grace flows from being to doing, from identity to behavior, but not from doing to being. It's a one-way flow.

CHRISTIAN HOPE

"Therefore," said Peter, "...set your hope fully on the grace that will be brought to you at the revelation of Jesus Christ" (v. 13). We are to set our hope on God's grace, and when we do that we find that the hope that has been set on God's grace is the hope that God gives us. It is God's hope—not ours—and it is an eternal hope. It doesn't waver or waffle, and it doesn't end. God provides it, steadies it and maintains it. God inspires it and encourages it, and then fulfills it. This hope is God's hope, start to finish. He gives it to us, and by doing so He makes it ours —though it is always His.

But it is not ours in the sense that it is a common human hope. It is not a universal hope, not yet. Rather, it is a common *Christian* hope— the world knows nothing of it. The world berates and belittles it. The world cannot understand it. It belongs to all who have it—and they own it. Yet, all who have it received it from God.

The word *your* in verse 13 is plural, which means that it is ours to share and not mine or yours alone to keep. Christian hope is shared hope, and it is the hope that everyone will one day share. But we cannot keep it or give it to others as if it were a nut that could be saved up for a winter day. Only God can give it, and He gives it as He wills through Christ alone by the Holy Spirit. You and I cannot give it to another, but we can share it among others.

The thing that drives God is His own desire, grace and mercy to do as He pleases. That's why He's God. God only does what He wants to

do. Fortunate for us, He always wants to do us good. Even His admon-
ishments are for our good, not merely for our individual good but for
our corporate or social good.

The thing that draws Christians into faithfulness is this shared
hope. Hope is the vision that draws us into God's future. Hope is the
engine that pulls us forward. Hope is always optimistic, and never
pessimistic. We don't hope that bad things will happen. We might fear
that something bad will happen, but we don't hope for it. And because
God's hope is always a shared hope that does not belong exclusively to
anyone, it is always an optimistic expectation for good things for all
who share it. It is a community hope.

This hope cannot be poisoned, nor can it be thwarted. The worst
thing than anyone can do to it or about it is to ignore it. But ignoring it
doesn't make it go away. It remains a shared hope among Father, Son
and Holy Spirit regardless of what anyone else does with it or about it.
Ignoring it is simply a confession of one's own blindness. What the
blind cannot see does not disappear simply because they cannot see it.
It remains. But not seeing it, the blind stumble over it. It's amazing
that people stumble on God's hope for the well-being of humanity.
They stumble over it because they don't see it!

Nonetheless, God's hope is the engine of human development, of
human growth and improvement. And because this hope belongs to no
one in particular it belongs to all who share it in common with Christ.
This hope is not what makes us unique individually because it is the
same for everyone. It belongs to our common corporality in Christ.
That's where it is found. And that's where it is shared. Hopefulness is a
necessary characteristic of the body of Christ, of those who are in the
body of Christ, the church.

Unfolding Fulfillment

There is also the sense of a future fulfillment of this hope in the
sense that more grace will be given "at (or *by* or *through*) the revelation of Jesus Christ" (v. 13). Grace will abound (2 Corinthians 2:9)
because of the revelation of Jesus Christ and it will abound by (or
through) His revelation. Christ's revelation is progressive as it unfolds.
And its unfolding is slow "as some count slowness" (2 Peter 3:9). But
there is both a necessity and a purpose in God's slow but steady progress toward the full revelation of Jesus Christ.

The necessity of it comes from our own hardheadedness. People
are slow to learn. Christians don't get an instant information download
the moment they are born again. It doesn't work like that. We get an
immediate perspective change, but the information and the application

of the change take time—a lot of time, apparently—more than we expect or want it to take.

The purpose of God's slowness is His "long-suffering toward us, not purposing that any should perish, but that all should come to repentance" (2 Peter 3:9). Yes, God wants all people to come to repentance, and all extant humanity will eventually come to it, even if it is too late for them personally (Romans 14:11)! Eventually.

The historic formulation of this biblical issue, known as Limited Atonement or Particular Redemption, sets up a problem where there isn't one in Scripture. The idea of limited atonement frames the issue as a false dichotomy by making an argument between limited or unlimited atonement. Is God's atonement limited or unlimited? It's both!

So, choosing one or the other side of this atonement argument is always wrong because Scripture does not frame the issue like this. Arguing in this traditional way has proven to be futile, divisive and fruitless. We must see this traditional argument in the fullness of its biblical context.

James Jordan, for example, speaks of God growing all humanity into a corporate bride for His Son.[13] Of course, some individuals will reject God and His Son. Not everyone will repent, and those who refuse to repent will be pruned from the Branch and thrown into the fire. So, this side of glory there are people who refuse to repent and are destined for hell. But on the other side of glory all extant humanity will be caught up with the Lord and His salvation will be complete. Will there still be individuals who reject God? Probably, but humanity as a whole, with near unanimity, will be caught up in His salvific embrace (1 Thessalonians 4:17).

When will that glorious Day come? Andre Crouch, an American song writer, said, "Soon and very soon, We are going to see the Lord." Peter said that "the day of the Lord will come as a thief in the night" (v. 10), which means that it will come unexpectedly. Jesus said that we "must be ready, for the Son of Man is coming at an hour you do *not* expect" (Luke 12:40).

This has serious implications because almost every Christian today believes that the Day of the Lord is near—imminent. Crouch said it will be sooner than people think. Peter said it will come unexpectedly. And Jesus said that it will not come as we expect it will, neither when we expect it nor how we expect it. T.S. Elliot said that the world will end, "Not with a bang but a whimper."[14]

---

13 Jordan, James B. *Crisis, Opportunity and the Christian Future*, Athanasius Press, Monore, Louisianna, 1994, 1998, 2004.
14 T. S. Eliot, *The Hollow Men* (1925), a poem in public domain.

I'm to the point that I don't believe that humanity will ever end (2 Samuel 23:5; Psalm 119:142, 139:24, 145:13; Isaiah 40:8, 45:17, 51:6, 51:8; Ephesians 3:9-11; 2 Thessalonians 2:16; Titus 1:1-3; Hebrews 13:20; Revelation 11:15). Sure, nations rise and nations fall, civilizations come and go, but God doesn't. God is saving His people for eternity. God intends to renew and restore the earth, not to its original glory, but to the revealed and progressive glory of His Son, Jesus Christ. God's plan is redemption (Hebrews 9:12), renewal (Titus 3:5), revival, reformation, reconfiguration, reconstruction, renovation, restitution, reclamation, revitalization—whatever you want to call it! The end will be a new heaven and a new earth come down from heaven. Sure, the first one will be gone, but God's people won't. The slowness of the coming kingdom is for our benefit and God's glory. God's glory needs the largest possible group of people to give Him praise and honor. And we need God's greatest grace and mercy because we are all such dunderheads.

RENEWAL

In the same way that these saints to whom Peter was writing were not to focus on the impending destruction of Jerusalem, nor to get caught up in it physically or emotionally, so we are not to focus on the impending destruction of whatever godless society we inhabit, we are not to get caught up in that which perishes. We are, rather, to focus on what does not perish. The revelation of Jesus Christ is about that which does not perish—Christ the Lord.

This gradual but relentless revelation is the always-new-thing that God is doing. It's always new because it is always unfolding in new ways. The Greek word translated as *revelation* (*apokaluptō*) literally means to take the cover off or unveil. Jesus Christ was being revealed—unveiled. He was being unveiled then and He is being unveiled further today, right now! The unveiling is itself an eternal process because it is the unveiling of the infinitude of God. And that unveiling is gracious, merciful and slow, as some count slowness because many people are dull and hardheaded as God counts dullness and hardheadedness.

The current focus of Christians on the various end times scenarios of the various millennial positions is a function of the poverty and paucity of our contemporary vision of God's gospel. The process of gospel revelation has gotten sidetracked. Too many Christians are too small-minded to consider the immensity of Christ unveiled. Paul said that the Jews had a difficult time with it (1 Corinthians 3:11-16). So do we today.

People today are still too fearful and self-concerned to consider the greatness of the glory of God in Christ—even Christians! And we must repent of it! We must say *no* to the small-minded end times scenarios that so plague and cripple our churches and distract our people from seriously engaging this life in this world for the long run. The churches are suffering an epidemic of narrowmindedness that has turned Christians against one another, like dogs fighting over a dead rabbit, desperately trying to get our share of the end times goods, hoping to get raptured out of life's difficulties and brought back for life's eternal goodies. This is not what Peter was talking about or what the Lord has in mind.

Yes, I understand that "the gate is narrow and the way is hard that leads to life" (Matthew 7:14), but a narrow gate is not the same thing as a narrow mind, nor is a hard way the same as a hard head. Rather than serious consideration and submission to the wideness of God's grace, which provides the gate and the way of salvation, people reject God and retreat into their own narrowmindedness and hardheadedness, into a kind of me-and-Jesus mentality that is essentially self-centered.

Too many Christians want to reserve salvation for themselves or for their own particular group, denomination or church and cut themselves off from other views of Christianity. And it seems that the closer two views or denominations are, the more they have to differentiate themselves from each other. But that is not what God has in mind. Most of the world thinks that Christians are narrowminded and hardheaded—and for the most part they are right!

Grace & Election

The grace that comes by the revelation of Jesus Christ is an increasing grace. It grows over time because the revelation of Jesus Christ increases over time. As the revelation increases, so does the grace—and our understanding follows suit. All of this is to say that Christians grow in grace and in faithfulness over time. And where such increases are not in evidence to one's self and to others there is a need to revisit Peter's instructions to prepare our minds for action, to be sober-minded, to set our hope fully on the grace that will be brought in the fullness of the revelation of Jesus Christ (v. 13).

For some people this progressive revelation might appear to be works-righteousness. And that might be the case if the person considering this possibility is not someone Peter was addressing. If the letter was not written to you, then it does not apply to you. Who was Peter writing to? "To those who are elect exiles of the dispersion" (v. 1), to God's people scattered for the cause of Christ, to the elect. For the elect this process of growth is a function of grace and salvation. But for those who are not elect, engaging it is a matter of works-righteousness and damnation because it doesn't work.

Jesus spoke of the same thing. "So the last shall be first, and the first last: for many be called, but few chosen" (Matthew 20:16, *Authorized Version*). The doctrine of election has been the source of much difficulty in the church. And that difficulty runs very deep, so deep that the last phrase of this verse was either added to the source of the *Textus Receptus* or deleted from the source of the *Codex Sinaiticus*.[15] The doctrine of election is at the heart of this issue, and in this verse we find evidence for one of the deepest, most divisive and most complex arguments in biblical history.

There is no doubt that Jesus spoke the words, "for many are called, but few are chosen" (Matthew 22:14). The issue is: how important were these words? And how do they apply to Christianity? Because Peter said that he was writing to the elect, they certainly apply here.

There are two possible ways to interpret this phrase. First, that it applies to all Christians because all real Christians are elect Christians. The other interpretation is that, while all Christians are called by God to faithfulness, the distinction of election pertains to church leaders who are elected to office. This second understanding suggests that Peter was writing to church leaders.

Calvin wrote of Matthew 22:14, "I enter no farther, at present, into the question about the eternal election of God; for the words of Christ mean nothing more than this, that the external profession of faith is not a sufficient proof that God will acknowledge as his people all who appear to have accepted of his invitation."[16] Calvin argued that all genuine Christians are elect or chosen by God.

Albert Barnes clarified the same verse by saying, "It does not mean, therefore, that the great mass in the church are simply called and not chosen, or are hypocrites; but the great mass in 'the human family,' in the time of Christ, who had been 'called,' had rejected the mercy of God."[17] Barnes argued that the verse did not pertain to the church, but to the world.

In his second letter Peter clarified the relationship between calling and election. "Therefore, brothers, rather be diligent to make your calling and election sure, for if you do these things, you shall never fall" (2 Peter 1:10). Thus, we see that Peter intended to suggest that he was providing instructions for all who are called to Christ, and that having

---

15 The words, "for many be called, but few chosen" are deleted from Matthew 20:16 in most modern translations of the Bible but they are in the King James Bible. This is because there are differing Greek manuscripts. For a discussion of this see Theodore Letis, The Institute for Renaissance and Reformation Biblical Studies, 6417 N. Fairhill, Philadelphia, PA, 19126, http://kuyper.org/thetext/.

16 Calvin, John. *Calvin's Commentaries*, Baker Books, Ada, Michigan, 1974, Matthew 22:14.

17 Barnes, Albert. Barnes *Notes on the Old and New Testaments* , Baker Books, 1983, Matthew 22:14.

been called, all Christians should aspire to adopt the character qualities and life habits of Christian leaders, if not to actually become church leaders. As Paul said, "Be imitators of me, even as I also am of Christ" (1 Corinthians 11:1). Peter will have more to say about this in the next few verses.

6. Holy Smoke!

*As obedient children, do not be conformed to the passions of
your former ignorance, but as he who called you is holy, you
also be holy in all your conduct, since it is written, "You shall
be holy, for I am holy." And if you call on him as Father who
judges impartially according to each one's deeds, conduct
yourselves with fear throughout the time of your exile...*
—*1 Peter 1:14-17 (ESV)*

There could hardly be a clearer call to Christian obedience than
verse 14, where Peter gave instructions on how to be obedient by
not conforming to the passions of our former ignorance. Notice
that Peter tells us how to do it by giving us a negative command. He
said, *In order to be obedient, don't do this one thing!* By providing a
negative instruction he provided the maximum freedom possible.
Obedience can be done any way at all, except this one way: "do not be
conformed to the passions of your former ignorance" (v. 14).

We must not lose track of the fact that Peter was writing to elect
Christians, whether election refers only to leaders or to all who are
genuinely saved. In fact, he was further defining what it means to be an
elect Christian. Elect Christians are those who are not conformed to the
passions of their former ignorance. Peter believed that Christians were
or should be people who have passed through a major change, from a
state of ignorance to the state of a conscious, intentional abandonment
of that ignorance in Christ. Yet, there is more to this than simple abandonment because at the same time we are called to take up a perspective
or worldview that will replace our former ignorance.

The Greek word translated here as *ignorance (agnoia)* literally
means not knowing, and is from the same root as the English word
agnostic. This verse means that Christians must abandon any and all
commitment to not knowing ultimate truth, to agnosticism and its vari-

ants. Agnostics deny that they have any ultimate knowledge regarding the existence of God. Agnostics are philosophical relativists and moral fence-sitters. Agnostics don't believe in any claims of ultimate knowledge, which means that agnostics are Postmodern in their basic philosophical orientation.

PHILOSOPHICAL RELATIVITY

But this verse says more than this! It also says that Christians cannot be Postmodern or philosophical relativists because Peter here calls Christians to *not* be conformed to any view that does not know God. He calls this perspective *ignorance* and insists that one of the first acts of Christian obedience is to abandon it. Why is it among the first things to be abandoned by obedient Christians? Because Peter said that the instruction he is providing here is for children, for the immature. As Paul said, "When I became a man, I gave up childish ways" (1 Corinthians 13:11). And Peter said that ignorance of God in Christ is childish—immature.

Interestingly Peter did not say that people should give up their intellectual commitment to philosophical relativity—though they most certainly should. Rather, he said that they should give up their passion (*epithumia*) or lust for it. Peter did not here make any attempt to address or counter agnosticism as a philosophy or false teaching. He simply told people to abandon their passions that are based on philosophical relativity.

But why would people be passionately attached to philosophical relativism? I can understand being passionately attached to some ultimate position, but it seems that relativism should be undergirded by passivity and nonchalance, not passion. After all, it's just relativity. There's nothing permanent or of ultimate value or importance involved. No relativist can know anything for sure. So, why care? Why bother being passionate about it? Nonetheless, Peter identified passionate relativity and forbade it.

Interestingly, as Postmodernism becomes more popular we find that people are in fact passionately committed to it. Of course, we also know that the attraction to relativity issues from an aversion to God according to Romans 1. People who hate God will passionately embrace anything except God.

HOLINESS

Peter was not content to simply provide negative advice, so in verse 15 he said something positive: "as he who called you is holy, you also be holy in all your conduct." He calls Christians, whether leaders or ordinary Christians, to be holy (*hagios*), to be morally blameless and

ceremonially consecrated. It was not enough to simply demand that
Christians be holy and let us define holiness ourselves. He said that we
are to be holy as Christ is holy. Christ is to be the model of the holiness
toward which we aspire. That is a high calling, a moral imperative, a
demand for moral behavior that is faithful to biblical law.

There is a lot of resistance to the idea that Christianity demands
conformity to a particular set of moral principles—guides, even laws.
People are very afraid that when Christians focus on the moral
demands of Christianity it becomes legalistic, narrowminded, burden-
some and restrictive. As we know, an overemphasis on rules, which is
the definition of legalism, is a very real problem in our contemporary
church, and in contemporary society as well.

Do you realize that there is a form of conservative legalism and a
form of liberal legalism, each having different sets of hard and fast
rules? Yes, liberals can be as blindly committed to their rules as conser-
vatives can be to theirs. It is not that rules are bad, but when we expect
too much of rules they can dampen the spirit. Nonetheless, Peter made
it quite clear that there can be no faithfulness apart from genuine
Christian morality—the morality of Jesus Christ, informed by careful
study of Scripture and empowered by the Holy Spirit. Peter knew that
the gospel was aiming at relationship not rules, love not ideology or
theology. But neither are we to abandon rules or theology.

Resistance against Christian morality issues out of a wrong understanding or false teaching—a wrong teaching. While Christians are to
be moral, we are not to base our morality on a set of rules or principles
that can mechanically determine behavior in any situation. Christian
morality issues out of a personal relationship with Jesus Christ, not
from an orthodox understanding of biblical principles.

While biblical principles are important, relationship with the Lord
is essential. Where morality is defined as motivation based on ideas of
right and wrong, Christian morality is motivated by God in Christ
through the Holy Spirit. The Trinity is at the heart of it. It is a living
morality, not a mechanical morality. And yet, it is also a principled
morality, where various principles are established through the study of
Scripture.

However, even principles can become mechanical and stifle the
spirit of creativity and freedom apart from regeneration. Christian
morality or behavior cannot simply be programmed like a computer,
regardless of the sophistication of the algorithm. Christianity does not
provide a mere program for humanity. It provides a relationship with a
Person—God in Christ through the Holy Spirit.

PIETY

The Pietists in the 1700s and 1800s had a sense of this and reacted against the intellectual efforts to systematize Christianity by the Reformers. Luther, Calvin and others developed systems of biblical understanding and explanation, some better than others, but all were turned into mechanical systems by various followers. We can't blame those followers. They were simply trying to understand the Reformers and be faithful to the Early Church Fathers. Many people found solace with Augustine and others who had also attempted to do this same kind of systematization. What the Reformers failed to realize was that the underlying philosophy that guided these kinds of efforts had been infected with Greek rationalism.

Of course, systematizing Scripture is immensely useful for helping us better understand God's character, purpose and activity in the world. But it is also dangerous because it can lead people to think that God is a system or a principle—even a force—rather than a Person. Systematizing can make us think that part of God's character is all of God's character. We know that God usually operates according to principles. For instance, some of those principles are commonly called the Laws of Nature.

But it is equally important that we understand that God is not bound by any set of principles. We see evidence for God's boundlessness in the various biblical miracles. The miracles seem to violate the ordinary rules of operation in the world. However, they are not miracles or violations to God. They are miracles to those who understand God too narrowly, too rigidly. God does not violate His own principles.

Over time Reformation churches refined and improved the intellectual systems by which they understood God and Scripture. Various systems of Protestant theology developed. And the better they got at systematization, the more mechanical Christianity became. The Pietists reacted against that mechanical approach to Christianity by emphasizing the response of the heart and under emphasized the intellect. The Pietists had their problems too, but they were on to something important, something that Peter was talking about here. Then, as Pietism itself fell prey to systematization, it introduced and strengthened individualism,[18] which helped to prepare the way for the Age of Enlighten-

---

18 Individualism makes the individual its focus and so it starts with the fundamental premise that the human individual is of primary importance in the struggle for liberation. Classical liberalism (including libertarianism), existentialism and anarchism (especially individualist anarchism) are examples of movements that take the human individual as a central unit of analysis. http://en.wikipedia.org/wiki/Individualism.

ment.[19] And the Enlightenment then took Christianity into the apostasies of Modernism and Liberalism (or Secularism).[20]

The intention of the Pietists was to return religion (Christianity) to its focus on the heart, on personal faithfulness and morality, and to abandon the focus on the intellect that had been all the rage following the Reformation. They observed, and rightly so, that an over-emphasis on the intellect tended toward Liberalism and the kinds of social and sexual permissiveness that dominated ancient Greek society.

THE REFORMATION

The Reformation had been seeded, nurtured and birthed by scholarly intellectuals: Wycliffe, Hus, Luther, Calvin, etc. All were university trained scholars who had gone back to the original languages of the Bible and discovered that the Roman Catholic Church had made a mess of Scripture and buried the heart of Christian faith in their various traditions. Tradition had simply swallowed truth.

The original Reformers rebooted Christianity by translating the Bible, not from the Latin texts that had been in use by the Roman Catholic Church, and not into Latin, the language of scholarship. Rather, they provided a fresh translation into several common languages—German, English and French. They worked to recover the original meaning of Scripture, made it clear, and were able to give it to the people more economically and widely because of the invention of the printing press.

We must also remember that the moveable type printing press had just been invented. Prior to this time, books were very rare and expensive. The printing press along with less expensive paper and binding began making literature cost effective and available to the common people, to the less educated. So, the combination of the university educated Christian intellectuals and the uneducated or home educated Christian people proved to be problematic.

The intellectuals believed that understanding and practicing Christianity required intelligence and scholarship to study and understand the Bible. The uneducated thought that the intellectuals were teaching that Christianity was an intellectual endeavor, that faithfulness was a matter of understanding the Bible correctly. And, of course, that is part

---

19 The Age of Enlightenment (or simply the Enlightenment) is the era in Western philosophy and intellectual, scientific, and cultural life, centered upon the 18th century, in which reason was advocated as the primary source for legitimacy and authority. http://en.wikipedia.org/wiki/Age_of_Enlightenment.

20 Liberalism encompasses several intellectual trends and traditions, but the dominant variants are classical liberalism, which became popular in the Eighteenth Century, and social liberalism, which became popular in the Twentieth Century. http://en .wikipedia.org/wiki/Liberalism.

of what they taught the people. Understanding the Bible correctly is very important.

But the focus on intellectuality was not the focus of the earliest Christians, many of whom couldn't read and didn't have Bibles. So, the Pietists set out to correct this misunderstanding or overemphasis on the intellect. And to make their point they set their Pietistic system in stark contrast to the intellectual systematizations of the Reformation.

Note the irony of the Pietists developing a system to counter the over-systematization of the intellectuals. Nonetheless, the starker the contrast that could be made, the clearer the Pietists thought that they could make their point. So, they overemphasized the heart and under-emphasized the mind. They overemphasized the individual response and under-emphasized the corporate commitments.

Pietism, initially a Lutheran movement, became quite popular. The children of Pietism include Wesleyanism, Methodism, Brethren churches, the Holiness movement and Pentecostalism. In England and America the Wesleys led the way, having been deeply influenced by the Pietism of the Moravians. They developed a simplified method for teaching Pietism. Laypeople—people without theological training—were taught how to gather a Bible study group, and the Wesleys fed them Pietistic curriculum and new music.

The response was fantastic and thousands of these groups became churches in a fairly short time. Methodism was born on the fringes of society among the lesser educated or ordinary people. Methodism was largely a lay movement, at least more so than other denominations.

In a way Pietism tried to address Peter's injunction to be holy as Christ was holy. The root of the Greek word translated *holy* (*hagios*) is the same as the root of the word translated as *sanctified* (*hagiazō*). Sanctification includes growth and maturity, of course—but also separation. It is a particular kind of growth and maturity. It is moral growth, maturity and increasing conformity to Christian morality and separation from sin. Such growth is a good thing, a biblical thing, and it needs to be encouraged, not discouraged.

Revival As Revolution

Pietism and its new methods went too far in the rejection of the intellectual side of Christianity, and too far in its emphasis on the individual. Because the movement was so popular among non-intellectuals, and because it was so easy to bash the intellectual side of the faith in order to make the emotional aspects stand out so much more clearly, the Christian Pietists set their hearts against the Christian intellectuals. And that opposition within the church, then set the minds of the intellectuals against the Pietists in response. This breach in the Christian community continues to this day, and has proven to be one of the more difficult divisions to overcome. But overcome it we must.

The breach came about because of the intellectual separation of head and heart over the issue of holiness. And that is where it must be repaired. Peter had called the church to holiness, to sanctification, to growth and maturity. That call is not just a call to the heart, it is also a call to the head. It is not just a call to the individual, it is a call to the community. It is a call to the whole person, and to the wholeness and unity of all those who are in Christ. Not only must our hearts be warmed by the gospel message, our minds must be sharpened by it as well. Not only are individuals to respond to the gospel of grace, but the church as a whole—a union—must also respond with unity.

The result of this breach in the Christian community has created both Liberalism on the one side and Fundamentalism on the other. Liberalism was a reaction against the errors of the Pietistic movement which had devalued the role of the intellect in Christianity. That devaluation drove the intellectuals further into their heads in order to defend themselves against attack.

At the same time, this breach that overemphasized the intellect led to the rise of Fundamentalism, which was a reaction against the errors of these increasingly liberal Christian intellectuals. The more the intellectuals stressed intellectualism, the more the Fundamentalists rejected it—which then caused the intellectuals to emphasize it all the more. Both reactions drove the two groups farther apart.

The church must repent of both errors, both extremes. We must reclaim, not the middle—as if the goal is a halfway commitment to the errors of both extremes. No, we must reclaim the wholeness and holiness of the Christian faith. Christianity is not half head and half heart. It is all head and all heart. It is not a compromise, but a proclamation of comprehensive truth.

TRINITY

Thus, the wholeness of Christianity will be most fully manifest through the perspective and expression of God as the Trinity. The comprehensiveness of God is found only through the doctrine of the Trinity. And the doctrine of the Trinity requires the progressive revelation of Jesus Christ that was being unfolded at the last or end time. This was the end time of which Peter was speaking. It was/is the time, not of the destruction of the world, but of the completion and fulfillment of the revelation of Jesus Christ for the world. Growth in both wholeness and holiness, in both unity and sanctification, understanding of both ultimacy and particularity, can only be rightly gained from the trinitarian perspective. This is why only God in Christ through regeneration

by the power and presence of the Holy Spirit can heal the breach from
both sides.

Peter justified his call to holiness by citing the Old Testament. Why
bother with holiness? Because, said Peter, "it is written, 'You shall be
holy, for I am holy'" (v. 16). Peter cited Leviticus 11:14, 19:2 and 20:7.
Again, we see that the basis for Peter's comments are found in the doctrine of the Trinity by equating the God of the Old Testament with
Jesus Christ. He could acknowledge that "the revelation of Jesus
Christ" (v. 13) was tied to God's demand for holiness in Leviticus
because he knew that Jesus Christ was the God of the Old Testament.
Holiness is one of God's most important characteristics, and is at the
heart of God's mission to the world.

The *Contemporary English Version* translates verse 17 as, "You
say that God is your Father, but God doesn't have favorites! He judges
all people by what they do. So you must honor God while you live as
strangers here on earth." This is not a repudiation of the doctrine of
salvation by grace alone, though when considered apart from counter-
vailing verses it can seem like it is. We must understand that God
judges people on the basis of their behavior. God's judgment is a moral
judgment. But He doesn't play favorites. He calls for faithfulness and
holiness, and then measures our response, and provides rewards and
punishments on the basis of His measurements. God employs both the
carrot and the stick.

JUDGMENT AS DISCERNMENT

At first blush, this, however, does not sound like Protestant Christianity! How can we understand this verse in the light of the doctrines
of grace? First, we must accept Peter's letters as Scripture, as the very
Word of God and not attempt to avoid or blunt the plain meaning of
the words. What Peter said is completely true and can be trusted
because it is God's Word. We must not deny Peter's statement. We
must also hold fast to the doctrines of grace. Scripture holds these two
perspectives (the doctrines of grace and judgment according to works)
together and so must we. Of course, this is much easier said than done.

Does the fact that God judges people on the basis of works (*ergon*)
contradict the doctrine of salvation by grace alone? No. The problem is
that the answer to this conundrum—the doctrine of the Trinity—is not
stated as clearly as we would prefer it to be, but is scattered throughout
Scripture as various presuppositions, allusions, beliefs and assumptions.

God has given us various biblical problems to solve because solv-
ing them requires a particular perspective, the perspective of what I
call presuppositional trinitarianism. That's a fancy (or technical) way

of saying that we must see that Scripture reveals the reality of God as Trinity with or through eyes of faith. The solution of the problem requires the application of personal faith in Christ to Scripture, which means that it is available only to the regenerate or through regeneration in Christ.

Peter's focus here is the revelation of Jesus Christ (v. 7) at the last time (v. 5), which means that Peter understood that Jesus Christ is the second Person of the Trinity, and that the revelation of the unity of God as Father, Son and Holy Spirit is progressive over time, and that the advent of Jesus Christ began the final phase of the revelation of God as the Trinity. Peter emphasized in verse 16 that God's holiness or uniqueness is intimately related to human holiness and the uniqueness of our own human identity in Christ. Created in God's image our human character is like God's trinitarian character—not perfectly like it, but as a dim reflection of it. God is holy, therefore we are called to realize our holiness in Christ, and not just *my* holiness or *your* holiness (individual holiness), but *our* holiness (corporate holiness) as Christ's church.

John also spoke of this: "I do not ask for these only, but also for those who will believe in me through their word, that they may all be one, just as you, Father, are in me, and I in you, that they also may be in us, so that the world may believe that you have sent me. The glory that you have given me I have given to them, that they may be one even as we are one, I in them and you in me, that they may become perfectly one, so that the world may know that you sent me and loved them even as you loved me" (John 17:20-23). John was talking about the holiness of God in Christ in us, in the church.

Office

What exactly is holiness? The Hebrew word (*qôdesh*) indicates something sanctified, consecrated, dedicated or set apart for a particular purpose. Sanctification suggests increasing freedom from sin. To consecrate means to endow something with a particular function or purpose. Dedication, like consecration, categorizes a person or thing by assigning a special purpose for it, or giving it a special function.

A holy person is set apart from other people for a particular purpose, function or task. Of course, the sanctified person must still function in the world, in the midst of sin and corruption. But by definition, in order to be holy such a person must not be contaminated by sin and corruption. So, the holiness is the setting apart of the person from sin and corruption by Christ and in Christ—*through* Christ.

The holiness is the distinction or the difference, the separation or segregation of the person from the sin and corruption by God. It is as if

God provides the sanctified person with an inoculation against the effects of sin and corruption—not perfectly, but increasingly over time as the person grows and matures in Christ. This can be done through a kind of spiritual inoculation that keeps sin from sticking, growing or developing in an individual. And/or it can be done by separating the individual from the contagion of sinful influences.

Traditionally, religious leaders are consecrated or dedicated to the office they are to occupy. That means that office holders are to be faithful, and that other people are supposed to allow them special privileges in order to fulfill their office and hold them accountable for their decisions and actions, to see them in a different light (the light of Christ), to have higher expectations regarding them and to relate to them with honor and respect. Of course, office holders are to be worthy of such honor to the best of their ability.

That honor and respect are always to be given for the office that is held, and only for the individuals who hold office inasmuch as they fulfill the high calling of the office. That usually means that such people—office holders—have greater authority and responsibility among those they serve in order to fulfill the requirements of their office.

One of the problems in our day, and in every age, is the fact of sin and corruption of Christian leaders. Leaders cannot be completely separated and physically sealed off from the rest of society in order to keep them from the contamination of sin and corruption. In fact, such an effort is wrong-headed because it fails to see that the insulating agent is not mere distance from sin, but Christ Himself. It is also wrong-headed because it runs from culture rather than working to transform it. Perhaps it is the working to transform culture in the light of Christ that constitutes the work (*ergon*) in verse 17 that God judges.

Thus, social isolation is not a sufficient response to sin and corruption. And yet, isolation from temptation does in fact provide some help for the immature who don't yet have the strength or discernment to resist sin. Temptation is conquered progressively through the practice and mastering of Christian discipline, which the Lord summed up in His Sermon on the Mount.[21] But maturity takes time to grow.[22]

In order to properly manage additional responsibility and authority, office holders must also evidence mature sanctification. They must be more holy than the average person, which means that they must be more spiritually mature in both heart maturity and head maturity, both emotionally and intellectually. They must demonstrate personal mastery of whatever areas of responsibility and authority they are to

---

21 See footnote 5, page 20.
22 See *The Wisdom of Jesus Christ in the Book of Proverbs*, by Phillip A. Ross, Pilgrim Platform, Marietta, Ohio, 2006.

provide leadership for. Sanctification means spiritual growth and maturity, and in the case of biblical Christianity that means understanding that the purpose and function of Scripture—Old Testament and New—is the revelation of Jesus Christ as the second Person of the Trinity. That revelation is God's ultimate purpose, according to Peter.

TRINITARIAN WORLD

The revelation of the Trinity began in the Old Testament. For instance, Isaiah reported that a serif or angel "called to another and said: 'Holy, holy, holy is the Lord of hosts; the whole earth is full of his glory!'" (Isaiah 6:3). God is thrice holy—holy as the Father, holy as the Son, and holy as the Spirit. In confirmation of God's trinitarian character John reported that "the four living creatures, each of them with six wings, are full of eyes all around and within, and day and night they never cease to say, 'Holy, holy, holy, is the Lord God Almighty, who was and is and is to come!'" (Revelation 4:8). The repetition of the word *holy* is an allusion to the Trinity, found in both testaments.

John reaffirmed the trinitarian character of God and folded time into the definition of the Trinity by telling us that God spans past, present and future. In order to see and understand God as Trinity we cannot bind God with the ordinary distinctions or categories of time. God is in time, as evidenced by the Father/Son relationship, but is not time bound. And in order for human beings to make sense out of God's timeless being we must view time with trinitarian eyes or in trinitarian categories. Thus, God as Trinity in the Old Testament is the same as God as Trinity in the New Testament, because God does not change.

As an act of faith we must impose trinitarian categories upon all of reality because the trinitarian God has created a trinitarian reality for Himself and His trinitarian creations. We must see the world through trinitarian eyes. Apart from the Trinity our vision and understanding are occluded by a kind of myopia—a blindness or shortsightedness. Apart from the Trinity we fail to see all of the colors of the rainbow of reality. Unless we bring regenerated, trinitarian eyes to Scripture we fail to see God (John 3:3).

Faithfulness to the Trinity in this way opens us to the only God who actually exists. It opens us to (and opens to us) the progressive revelation of the trinitarian God of Scripture made increasingly clear through the advent and reign of Jesus Christ. The revelation of Jesus Christ in the last time that Peter was speaking about is the unveiling of the Trinity in history (His story, God's continuing story).

7. Believers In God

And if you call on him as Father who judges impartially according to each one's deeds, conduct yourselves with fear throughout the time of your exile, knowing that you were ransomed from the futile ways inherited from your forefathers, not with perishable things such as silver or gold, but with the precious blood of Christ, like that of a lamb without blemish or spot. He was foreknown before the foundation of the world but was made manifest in the last times for the sake of you who through him are believers in God, who raised him from the dead and gave him glory, so that your faith and hope are in God.
                                              —*1 Peter 1:17-21 (ESV)*

Peter said in verse 17 that if we call on God we must honor God. And God doesn't care about who we think we are. That might sound contradictory to what we have been taught to believe, but Scripture says several times that God does not honor persons (Deuteronomy 10:17, 16:19; 2 Chronicles 19:7; Job 34:19; Proverbs 24:23-24; Luke 20:21; Acts 10:34; Galatians 2:6, 6:7-8; Ephesians 6:9; Colossians 3:25).

It means that God doesn't make judgments that are based on individual identity. It means that whatever social position we occupy or whatever role we play is inconsequential to God. The things that are most important to us as human beings are often the least important to God. So, when we call on God, when we ask Him for His attention, He doesn't care who we are—rich, poor, sick, healthy, Jew, Gentile, American, Iranian, President, janitor, etc. None of that matters. According to verse 17 He cares about what we do, how we act, how we live. And because action follows thought, He cares about what we think and believe about *Him*, but not about our race, roll, position, status or wealth. What is important is not what we think of ourselves, but what God thinks of us, and what we think about God.

It is true that every individual human being is unique. But God doesn't love us for our uniqueness. God does not play favorites based on the ways that we differ from other people. Of course, He doesn't despise us for our uniqueness, either. Our individual uniqueness as persons is fine with God. He made us that way. God is pleased with His creation and His creatures (Genesis 1:31). But our uniqueness is not what makes us Christian—or faithful.

Alone

Nonetheless, God found it to be not good for the man He made to be alone (Genesis 2:18). Being alone or unique (singular) is not sufficient. The perfection we are called to is not found in our uniqueness (Genesis 1:27). We commonly understand Genesis 1:27 to be about the necessity for marriage. And that is certainly part of what it means.

Humanity would die out if not for marriage and child rearing. But when we realize that marriage is the most fundamental covenant relationship that human beings can be involved in apart from Christ, we see that God also meant that it is not good for people to be without covenantal relationships. Human wholeness apart from covenantal relationship is impossible. But this verse is not just about marriage.

Biblical marriage is a threesome—husband, wife and God. God has always been at the center of the marriage covenant because marriage is God's idea. He initiated it and He holds it together. Marriage—family— is the means by which God now creates people. And His covenant with humanity is the way that He creates human society or culture.

Thus, the aloneness of Adam before Eve had been created is at the heart of the person that God does not honor. God does not honor any person who is outside of His covenant because God always relates to humanity covenantally. People outside of God's covenant are nothing to God. God does not respect individuals. He doesn't relate to us on the basis of our individuality, but on the basis of our covenantality. That's what this idea of God not honoring persons means. People apart from God's covenant are without honor. This is what it means to have a personal relationship with Jesus Christ.

Adam had originally been created as a solitary human being—an individual, and that was not a good thing. It is not good for one person to exist alone, isolated from others. It doesn't merely mean that people should be married. It means that people must be in covenant with God and with one another. It means that people must not deny or ignore the corporate or trinitarian aspects of human identity. Adam's premarital state was not the ideal human condition. Individuality alone is not good. God didn't merely create individuals, He created biblical kinds (Genesis 1:11, 12, 21, 25). God did not merely create a solitary man, He created the human race to be an earthly kind or species.

Nor was it sufficient for Adam alone (or any individual) to be in covenant with God. God and Adam were in relationship, in covenant in the Garden when God said that it was not good for Adam to be alone. Prior to Eve's creation, Adam had a job cataloging the world (Genesis 2:19). This means that he was a scientist because that's what scientists do. They name and classify things.

ORIGINAL SIN

God had given Adam the prohibition against the tree of the knowledge of good and evil. And what exactly was that prohibition? The idea that it was an apple tree is completely unsupported by the text. It is a ruse to hide the real meaning of this most important story. It is another instance of extra-biblical misdirection, an instance of Satan's cunning subtlety—his craft or specialty, as he misdirects our attention to apples or sex, rather than the actual original sin.

Scripture uses the word *tree* here as an allusion or metaphor. Being a metaphor, the idea of a tree represents something else. The Hebrew word ('êts) stems from a root word ('âtsâh) that implies the idea of closure, as in closed eyes. From this sense of the word it can be understood that God forbade the closing of one's eyes to, or the failure to see, good and evil. And that is exactly what Adam and Eve did regarding the Serpent and his temptation. They closed their eyes to God's command, and failed in and of themselves to discern whether the Serpent or the tree was good or evil. They wouldn't take God's word for it and couldn't determine it on their own. They believed Satan and doubted God. They doubted God's analysis and believed their own.

We might translate Genesis 2:17 as, *But closing your eyes to good and evil is not nourishing or sustaining, and the day that you find such a thing nourishing you shall surely find that it will not sustain your kind.* The allusion to a tree suggests a complex system that links earth and heaven, dirt and sky, root and branch. The tree of knowledge represents an intellectual system or way of understanding the world that has virtual roots and branches. The thing that God forbade was the development of an intellectual system or way of understanding the world that is devoid of God's determination of good and evil, or is value neutral. He forbade it because it is a lie. And because good and evil are value judgments, it suggests the development of an intellectual system (a philosophy or science) that is completely objective, where objectivity means devoid of personal value judgments, the belief that one can be value neutral.

THE TREE OF LIFE

The tree of life, in contrast, was a tree or a way to systematically understand the world based upon God's Word, a way that God had predetermined to be good because it is of Him. And since God provided the better tree of life, the fundamental idea was that philosophy (systematic knowledge symbolized by the idea of a tree) and science (the cataloging of the world, the fruit of the tree) must be developed in the light of God, with reference to God and His Word. God and His Word, His advice, His law, His wisdom and His prohibitions apply to everything because they apply to the tree of life, or the systematic understanding of life—root and branch, so to speak.

Value judgments are at the heart of human activity and identity. Human consciousness, human freedom requires people to evaluate and judge everything. Such judgment and analysis provides the definition of what it means to think. That's what thinking is. Adam was a taxonomist,[23] which means that the central thing that human beings do is taxonomy—classification, categorization, organization. We evaluate, classify and group things and ideas.

That's the way that we understand our world. The way we organize the world determines the way we live in it. Our organization of the world determines how we live in the world. Taxonomy, the first science, provides the basic resource for science, where science is the application of taxonomy, and technology is the application of science. Taxonomy classifies and categorizes the things of the world so that science can analyze them. Technology then builds upon science by manipulating the things of the world according to their scientific taxonomy.

GOOD AND EVIL

What about good and evil? Ideally, the idea of good represents the force of attraction, and the idea of evil represents the force of repulsion. Think of magnetic forces. Good attracts, evil repels. People are supposed to be attracted by what is good and repelled by what is evil. The desire for good is supposed to hold society together, but the desire for evil tears society apart (Psalm 34:14, 37:27). So, when people get good and evil confused, destruction results (Isaiah 5:20, Amos 5:14-15, Matthew 7:17-19). The confusion or reversal of good and evil is the human trajectory or momentum in the world known as original sin.

Christ's mission is to fix the problem of sin through the revelation of Himself (through regeneration by the Holy Spirit) as the Second Person of the Trinity. That's His mission as evidenced by the first Christian creed that Christ is Lord (Luke 2:11; John 11:27; Acts 10:36).

---

23 A biologist who specializes in the classification of organisms into groups on the basis of their structure and origin and behavior.

By means of this revelation God is demonstrating to the world that He is intimately involved with everything, that He actually and literally holds the world together and that everything is a product of His grace and glory.

There are no objective facts in the world apart from God because God provides the only objectivity that human beings can actually know. Consequently, philosophy and science that are devoid of the values and judgments of God (Scripture) are branches on the tree of the knowledge of good and evil. The tree of the knowledge of good and evil is the way of understanding the world based upon our own (human) evaluation, and we are forbidden to engage it. Human beings are unable in- and of-themselves to correctly determine what is good and what is evil. Original sin has skewed our moral compass such that it is unreliable.

In verse 17 Peter noted that God judges impartially, that is to say objectively, without partiality. Human beings do not and cannot in- and of-themselves judge or evaluate anything objectively or impartially. Human beings always have a particular subjective perspective that shapes and skews our understanding, where God alone has a universal and objective perspective because of His trinitarian character.

So, God doesn't value human judgments—human preferences, human perspectives, human worldviews. To God these things are unreliable, untrustworthy and evil because they are not perfectly objective (Leviticus 19:15). Relying on these things leads to death, leads to a culture or way of life that is not sustainable.

We cannot escape our subjectivity, except as we are born again into Christ where we then have conscious though imperfect access to the Trinity by faith in Christ. Christians die to themselves, to their subjectivity, to their old ways of life, their old beliefs and superstitions, and rise to new life in Christ. Christians rise into the wholeness of corporate union with the Trinity through regeneration—not perfectly, but sufficiently.

Correct Belief and Behavior

Peter's recommendation to "conduct yourselves with fear throughout the time of your exile" (v. 17) also means that we should conduct ourselves with wisdom because the fear of the Lord is the beginning of wisdom (Psalm 111:10). To fear God is to live in His wisdom, to live on the basis of God's judgments (evaluations). We must understand and apply God's wisdom—God's evaluation of good and evil—to everything. Why should we do this?

Because we know Christ, said Peter in verses 18-19. Because we know that we have been ransomed from the futile beliefs and practices that we inherited from our forefathers. Christians are free from the futility of everything in the past, free from all previous history, free from the shame of our own historic guilt. The presence of Jesus Christ in the world means that from the time of His birth forward, from the life of Jesus Christ forward, people can no longer rely on their forefathers—their history, whether Jew or Gentile. From that day forward, we must not look to the past for guidance because Christ has come. God stepped into the present moment to reveal Himself in and through Jesus Christ. Jesus Christ lived, died for our redemption, was resurrected and is now pulling history forward from the future, from heaven.

The guiding light of history is now the light of Christ's fulfillment of the ancient promises of God. That fulfillment is both a past and a future reality. It is past in that Christ has already come and died for the propitiation of God and the redemption of His people. And it is future in that Jesus Christ will one day return to collect and complete His people. It is also present because that is exactly what He is doing right now.

Christ's resurrection was the first fruit of the corporate resurrection of Adam's race. Adam's race or humanity is being resurrected (or regenerated) in Christ. History is currently in the midst of the birth pangs of this worldwide resurrection. It began with Jesus Christ and will be completed in the future. It is from the future completion of this process, decreed by God from outside of time, the place or realm wherein Christ has been resurrected into, the place He ascended to, that He is pulling history forward. He's already there making preparations (John 14:2-3), and His people are already in the process of following Him. This is what being a Christian is all about.

Drawn To The Light

Again, history is not being pushed forward from the past, but is being pulled forward from the future. Why? Because in the light of Christ we can see God's trinitarian truth, and that vision draws people into God's goodness. Prior to seeing the trinitarian light of Christ, people could not see God's ultimate truth, and were repulsed in fear of His wrath. Apart from Christ, God's truth was veiled. But in Christ the veil is removed (2 Corinthians 3:16) and God's goodness draws people to Him. Whereas apart from Christ people are repulsed by the fear of God. Apart from the light of Christ people cannot see God. So, they speculate on the basis of their own imaginations and the darkness of their fear apart from Christ.

Peter also said that what draws people into the future are imperishable things, not perishable things like gold and silver. Apart from Christ people are driven by concerns about money—food, shelter, clothing, etc. In Christ, in the light of Christ, everything becomes different. In Christ people are drawn not driven. And they are drawn by imperishable, intangible, immeasurable things like love, truth and beauty. In Christ money is still money. It still does what it does. But people relate to it differently. Money is no longer the driving force of individuals or of society. In Christ money takes a back seat to God, to God's goodness, to God's love, truth and beauty as the motivating force of behavior.

Christ has ransomed His people, not with money or other worldly valuables, but with His own precious blood (v. 19), with His own death. The *blood of Christ* refers to His death on the cross. From time immemorial if someone somehow saved your life, you then owed that person your life. You became a bond servant to him in order to pay your debt of life to him, and you were in debt until he released you. Following this pattern, the Bible teaches that all who find themselves alive following Christ's death on the cross owe their lives to Christ because He has saved humanity. His death on the cross has saved human kind from ultimate destruction, the death of humanity. Apart from Christ, God would have already destroyed humanity.

Christ did not just save individuals, but by saving individuals He has also saved the human genus or kind—the whole or wholeness of humanity. This involves the ongoing and future salvation of humanity into eternity. When God warned Adam about the forbidden tree He said, "but of the tree of the knowledge of good and evil you shall not eat, for in the day that you eat of it you shall surely die" (Genesis 2:17). The last phrase suggests, not the mere death of Adam as an individual, but the death or genocide[24] of Adam's race, the death of the culture of Adam.

CHRIST'S MISSION

This announcement of Adam's death was also the context of Christ's mission to ransom and redeem Adam's race. God is not interested in the death of humanity—not at all! God has spared the death of humanity. God is interested in life not death, redemption not punishment, freedom not subjugation, glory not gore. The culture of Adam—of unrepentant humanity—will one day become the culture of Christ. Jesus initiated this operation and the Holy Spirit is in the process of completing it. The Old Testament set up the coming of Christ. The New Testament is the story of the impact of His arrival. And the ongoing

---

24 It is most definitely **not** that Christians are waging genocide on non-Christians. That is not what this means. Rather, God intends to regenerate humanity in Christ in order to keep us from bringing extinction upon ourselves. So, it is a war, but not a war with worldly weapons (Ephesians 6:12-18).

history of the world chronicles the advancement of the Kingdom of God on earth.

It is important to understand that the Early Church did not get Christianity wrong, they simply got the infancy of the church. How could it have been otherwise? The church is a body and must grow into maturity. The goal of Christianity is not to return to its infancy, but to grow and mature in Christ. Our destination is in the future, not in the past. I am not the same person I was as an infant, but I'm not a different person either. An oak tree is not an acorn, but neither is it other than an acorn. And so it is with the church, with God's people, who are the body of Christ.

When the population of the world was small it was easy to deny the sovereignty of God in Christ. But as the population continues to grow it will become increasingly difficult to deny and will ultimately be realized by everyone extant. This is the revelation of Jesus Christ that Peter was talking about in verse 7. Jesus Christ was the "lamb without blemish or spot" (v. 19) who provided the required sacrifice. Following that sacrifice, God's revelation of Jesus Christ began to unfold in human history throughout the world, among the Gentiles. And it continues to this day. We have made much progress. And yet in terms of how far we have to go, we've barely begun.

Peter then summed up this argument: "He was foreknown before the foundation of the world but was made manifest in the last times for the sake of you who through him are believers in God, who raised him from the dead and gave him glory, so that your faith and hope are in God" (vs. 20-21). There is a lot packed into these verses.

GOD'S GRAVITAS

Christ was not foreknown by us, by humanity. Human beings have no access to any foreknowledge of Christ or of anything else because we are time bound creatures. Only God is not bound by time. It is God's trinitarian character that frees Him from time because it identifies God as both particular and universal, both individual and corporate, both here and hereafter, both past and future—and, of course, always present. It is only through God's trinitarian character that we have knowledge of God's timelessness. But we don't know it like God knows it—experientially. We only know about it abstractly. To us it is an idea, but to God it is reality.

Why would God bother with all this? Why give the Law to Moses and set up the kingdom of Israel though David, only to lose it through Solomon? Why send His only begotten Son only to die the most horrible death known to man, and then destroy the Temple that He had so meticulously built? Why would God, who is perfectly glorious and self-sufficient, go to all this bother?

Peter said that He did it for us so that our faith and hope will be securely tethered to God, because faith and hope are the engines of God's glory. God's glory is the gravity by which He holds the universe together. The unifying force that binds the universe together is a function of God's truth, beauty and goodness—His glory. These things are the glory of God. They are at the heart of God's gravitas, God's weight and power.

It is through worship that people give glory to what they have faith and hope in. Whatever people believe and hope for is the object of their worship, regardless of whether they engage that worship ceremonially or practically. Worship is the outworking of human beliefs and hopes—at church, at home, at school, at work. The location doesn't matter. Worship is what people do. Everything that we do is an expression of worship. And our idea of God, whatever it may be, is the foundation upon which our understanding rests, and to which our worship points.

So, why did God bother? God sent His Son in order to increase His glory. God's glory is the glue or gravity of human culture. So, the greater the culture, the greater the need for the glue, and the greater the glory. And the greater the glory, the greater is God's power to hold humanity together in a sustainable pattern of life with Him, ad infinitum.

The increase of human faithfulness increases God's glory and results in the ability of the world to support more people. How so? Because corruption—which is the absence of truth, beauty and goodness—leads to death. Righteousness, on the other hand, is the manifestation of God's truth, beauty and goodness, which leads to life. How?

Science and technology flourish in a social environment of righteousness—truth, beauty and goodness, but wither in a social environment of corruption—falsehood, ugliness and evil. Thus, science and technology allow the world to support more people through various advancements in agriculture and engineering. And as people understand this more fully, more people will give glory to God.

However, it is not just the quantity of people that matter. It is the character of the people that matters most. It is the righteousness of people that matters because science and technology depend upon righteousness, on truth, beauty and goodness. And the only righteousness available to human beings is the righteousness of Christ, who is the source of all truth, beauty and goodness.

REBORN INTO BELIEF

It is through Christ that people "are believers in God" (v. 21). No one can believe in God apart from being born again in Christ by the power of the Holy Spirit. All actual Christian belief is necessarily trinit-arian because the fullness of God is not exposed apart from the Trinity. God raised Christ from the dead. Believers are in Christ, who was Him-self raised from death. Therefore, believers are raised in Christ, born again into Christ, into the body of Christ. God raises individual believ-ers into the corporeality of the church, the body of Christ. Christian immortality includes the immortality of the temporal aspects of our unique individualities. Yet, the immortality of our individual unique-ness is swallowed by the immortality of Christ, the body of the church (1 Corinthians 15:54).

Paul said that being born again does not mean that Christians would then be unclothed, "but that we would be further clothed, so that what is mortal may be swallowed up by life" (2 Corinthians 5:4). Paul's allusion to clothing might also be literally understood as saying that *being in Christ does not mean that we are divested, but that we are invested.*[25] Being swallowed up like this doesn't mean that we lose any-thing. It is not like being merged into an amorphous ocean of being. Rather, we gain everything. Our uniqueness becomes more unique in Christ because we have been freed from bondage, from sin.

It is unrepentant sinners who are less unique as individuals because they continue to be controlled by sin, which is utterly predict-able. Sinners are predestined in all of its negative meanings, in the sense of fate, destiny, kismet or determinism. Whereas, Christians are free in Christ to be the unique individuals that God created them to be. In Christ people are more unique, more authentic, more loving, more kind, more considerate, more everything than people who are not in Christ.

This is the belief and hope of God in Christ, and in Christ this is our belief and hope. This belief, this hope fuels the church. It fuels genuine evangelism. Evangelism, then, depends upon all of us to make all of this true in our own lives and in the church. Sinners are to be res-cued from a sinking ship, but if the ship that they are rescued to is also in the process of sinking, they have not actually been rescued. So, we must shore up the ship of Christ, the church.

This is the model of humanity into which Christians are growing. Of this Peter said, "Therefore, brothers, be all the more diligent to make your calling and election sure, for if you practice these qualities you will never fall" (2 Peter 1:10).

One of the disturbing things of our present day is that the light of Christ reveals what is in the darkness. What we are seeing right now all over the world is the darkness of humanity apart from Christ as the

25 Clothes suggests vestments. Invest: Place ceremoniously or formally in an office or position.

light of Christ shines into this fallen world. And it is horrible, frighten-ing!

However, we must remember that it is the light of Christ that allows us to see the horrors of life without Christ. So, we must not get distracted or frightened by the darkness. We must focus on the light. For the light of Christ is our only salvation. Come, Lord Jesus! Come.

8. Abide In The Light

*Having purified your souls by your obedience to the truth for
a sincere brotherly love, love one another earnestly from a
pure heart, since you have been born again, not of perishable
seed but of imperishable, through the living and abiding word
of God; for "All flesh is like grass and all its glory like the
flower of grass. The grass withers, and the flower falls, but the
word of the Lord remains forever." And this word is the good
news that was preached to you.   —1 Peter 1:22-25 (ESV)*

Calvin complained that Erasmus had mistranslated the first word
of verse 22 by putting it in a past tense, as if Peter was congratu-
lating people on the accomplishment of having purified themselves. Rather, said Calvin, it is a call for action, not the observation of
an accomplishment. Calvin said, "The meaning is, that their souls would
not be capable of receiving grace until they were purified, and by this
our uncleanness is proved."[26] While we don't want to forget that this is
only one phrase in a complex sentence by Peter, we must not continue
until we understand this phrase—and there is much in it.

The Greek word in question (*hagnizō*) turns the idea of sanctification into a verb. And in fact it does mean to purify, where purification is
a process of separating what is good from what is evil and isolating them
from one another. Purifying is not simply a matter of washing, but
always includes the idea of separation. To wash a garment is to separate
the dirt from the garment in such a way as to remove the dirt and pre-
serve the garment. Applied as Peter uses it here, *purification* means the
reduction and eventual elimination of evil or moral impurity from one's
life, whether in thought or behavior. In this way the idea of purity
requires separation from worldliness.

---

26 Calvin, John. *Calvin's Commentaries*, Baker Books, Ada, Michigan, 1974, 1 Peter 1:22.

SOPHISTICATION

But what is this worldliness from which Christians are to be separate? In 1 Corinthians 1:26 Paul mentioned that few Christians had come from "worldly standards" of success. The *Authorized Version* understood the idea of worldly standards as being wise after the flesh, of being mighty, and noble—smart, powerful and influential. Another word for worldliness is *sophistication*.

So, being separated from worldly standards would require separation from those who had achieved worldly success, from the smart, the sophisticated, the powerful and the influential. The monastics of the Middle Ages understood this to mean retreating from the dominant culture of the time and its influences, and going into cultural isolation. So, they went to the desert or the mountains for solitude, away from the worldliness of the dominant culture, away from everything sophisticated.

But that is not what God has in mind. Of course, some solitude is good, avoiding worldliness and sophistication can be very helpful in many ways. But God intends to change human culture, not to simply retreat from it, nor to give up on it. And changing it requires being in dialog, in relationship with those who are smart, powerful, sophisticated and influential.

The emergent/emerging church understands this to a degree, as have the many expressions of Christian liberalism throughout history. Indeed, liberals are always on the cutting edge of sophistication and worldly influence. So it is only natural that they have sought to engage the cutting edges of worldly culture, to put the church on the cutting edge of cultural expression and development. Such interaction is necessary. However, there is a problem with being on the cutting edge. God intends this kind of interaction to result in cultural improvement that He can support, cultural improvement based upon His principles.

WASHING OUT

The problem is that people are adaptable. Adaptability is both a strength and a weakness at the same time. The problem is that cultural engagement and interaction cuts both ways. The problem is that a sponge cannot clean a thing without getting itself dirty. The church cannot affect worldly culture without suffering exposure to the infectiousness of sin. In the process, what is good comes in contact with what is less good. As Christians bring God's Word and the gospel of Jesus Christ to the world, the evil in the world becomes less impure—and that's a good thing!

But at the same time the resultant culture of the church becomes increasingly like lukewarm dishwater in God's eyes, neither hot not cold, not so bad but not so good either. Church contamination cannot be avoided. This is an important observation because washing dishes does produce lukewarm dishwater. The process gets the water cool and dirty. And if the water is not changed, over time the dishes get less clean. Over time Christian evangelism gets less effective because the difference between the church and the world becomes less meaningful. And that is not what God is after, though it may be an improvement over the previous filth of unadulterated worldliness for those being reached.

The instrument of cultural improvement—the church of the redeemed boldly, clearly and correctly proclaiming the gospel of Jesus Christ—cannot avoid contact with the culture it intends to improve. It cannot avoid becoming contaminated with worldliness in the process of reaching the world with the gospel. Bringing sinners into the church increases the level of sin in the church. This cannot be avoided.

DANGERS

There are two dangers that must be protected against. First, over time the boundaries between Christians and non-Christians become less clear. Immature Christians are less able to discern the marks of genuine Christianity and are more eager to share their new-found salvation in Christ with everyone. And this is a good thing! But it has a down side. When the focus on evangelism dominates, the focus on sanctification and maturity in Christ diminishes—not always, but too often. The temptation of immature Christian evangelists is to blur the boundaries of church membership (discipleship and discipline) because it is easier to get people to join the church if these biblical demands are not clearly articulated (John 6:66).

The other danger for the church in this situation involves giving control of the church to those who are less spiritually mature, less morally pure. The temptation is to get new recruits into church membership too soon and once in, to get them on committees, boards and in leadership, thinking that this will help mature them. It will, but it won't help the church to have such immature leadership.

As churches reach out to the lost, they must maintain their structures of authority and discipline because the spiritually immature will challenge the authority of godliness because it offends their as yet unsanctified worldly tendencies and habits. Therefore, they will undermine church authority and discipline if at all possible. They will not do so with evil intentions, but with good intentions that are simply less mature, less biblically informed and more shortsighted. Their good intentions are admirable on one hand, but not sufficient on the other.

Nonetheless, once this process of undermining begins in a church it is very difficult to correct. If the undermining happens at all, it happens because those already in the church are not sufficiently mature in their orthodoxy and/or their orthopraxy. Thus, the arguments of the immature will appeal to the immature, and when the immature dominate in practice or in office, they will teach and promote their own immaturity with the best of intentions. People cannot teach what they do not know and practice.

It is important to note that God did not destroy the church at Laodicea, whose love of the Lord had grown lukewarm (Revelation 3:16). Every church, every Christian who is hot for the Lord will cool as s/he interacts with the gospel coldness of the world and/or the coldness of church apathy. They will do so because the world withdraws from the purity of godliness in the same way that piping hot drinks are rejected until they cool. This same thing happens in churches.

The difficulty is that the world can only tolerate lukewarm Christianity, but effecting the world for the Lord requires hot Christianity. The world always rejects what it most needs. The medicine is bitter to the patient. But worldly tastes—preferences—are repugnant to God. What pleases the world offends God, and vice versa.

So, God spit the church at Laodicea out of His mouth, which only means that it was not pleasing to Him. It is important to see that He did not destroy it, or call for its destruction. Rather, He called the Laodiceans to buy His refined gold and to adorn white garments, to get from Him the things that He values. God insists on the purity of the church, that His churches be expressions of hot Christianity, of moral purity, if you will. What is lukewarm must be heated up to please the Lord, to cleanse sinners and to keep humanity from ultimate destruction.

Seeing And Wearing Righteousness

How are people warmed up? Before modern times, people had to wear more warm clothes, to put on a sweater or a coat or long underwear to get warm. Jesus counseled the church at Laodicea "to buy from me (Him) gold refined by fire, so that you may be rich, and white garments so that you may clothe yourself and the shame of your nakedness may not be seen, and salve to anoint your eyes, so that you may see" (Revelation 3:18).

The cure for the lukewarm is the purchase of godliness—righteousness—to cover their nakedness. Refined gold is heated to a molten state, where the impurities float to the top and are skimmed off. The resultant product is pure gold. The impurities are separated from the gold by fire—heat, or refinement by purgation.

The cure was to purchase white garments, another allusion to Christ's righteousness. But it was not just the purity and warmth of the gospel that the Laodiceans needed. They also needed eye salve (*kollourion*), eye medicine. Their problem was not merely their lukewarmness, but their vision, the way that they saw things. Their understanding of God's truth was faulty.

They were to separate themselves from impurity and cover their nakedness with godliness. But they also needed medicine that would improve their vision, so that they could see God's solution to their problems. The Laodiceans had three problems: 1) their love for the Lord had grown lukewarm, but 2) they could not see their own problem, so 3) they did not want what would cure them. That's exactly where people are today. We, too, need to purchase righteousness to cover our nakedness. We, too, need eye salve.

But can righteousness be purchased? Solomon thought so. "Buy truth, and do not sell it; buy wisdom, instruction, and understanding" (Proverbs 23:23) What does it mean for God to call the Laodiceans to get God's gold, God's garments to cover their nakedness and God's eye salve? It means that in their lukewarmness, which was the consequence of their own worldly success, they had lost the sense of embarrassment for their own moral laxity.

They had taken the first steps of faithfulness, grown successful and rested on their laurels, thinking that they were done. The combination of the ideas of evil and nakedness does not mean that sex is evil. It means that sex is easily coopted by evil. It means that people are not usually in control of their sexual urges or expressions, or that such control is weak. The best targets for our enemies to use against us are our own weaknesses. The weakest link in a chain is the easiest one to break.

SEX & MARRIAGE

Generations of Christians have misunderstood the biblical instructions about sex, to the delight of Satan. It is not that sex is evil or bad. It is wonderful and good. But it is an area of human weakness, so it must be handled carefully. It's not that God wants to end human sexuality, not at all. Rather, God uses it for His purposes. It's not simply about procreation. It's about human bonding, and God has drafted it as a work horse for the establishment of His covenant with humanity, and as an engine of culture. Consequently, He has dictated strict standards about how it is to be engaged.

We call it *marriage*. And it is an important lynchpin of human faithfulness and moral purity. It's not the only way to faithfulness and moral purity, but it is without a doubt the most important because it is the most common. Through marriage God binds Himself to people through love, satisfaction, commitment, honor, obedience, kindness, patience, perseverance, truth, intimacy, integrity, etc. Marriage—family —is the crucible in which these things, these character qualities, are learned and practiced. And where the family fails to inculcate biblical godliness, it becomes much, much more difficult to redeem or reform in society at some later point.

Is marriage necessary for spiritual purity or maturity? No. But it is the most common and widely accessible way for most people to protect their most natural weakness from the destructive forces of evil. Please understand that this recommendation for marriage has too little in common with the contemporary practice of marriage in the world today. To understand God's call to the marriage covenant we must not substitute our contemporary humanistic ideas of marriage with the biblical description of it.[27]

For instance, let me suggest that according to Scripture marriage is not between one man and one woman, but is between one man, one trinitarian God and one woman. Apart from God's involvement, marriage is not what it was created to be. From a human perspective, the biblical marriage covenant is most like God's covenant with humanity in that it is primary, intimate and life long. The call to faithfulness and purity is much more than mere biblical sexual morality or marital fidelity, but it is never anything less.

Soul Salvation

It is also important to note that Peter's injunction to purity is not simply about the flesh. In fact, Peter doesn't mention the flesh. He said to purify our *souls (psuchē)*, our psyche. The psyche is the center of our thoughts and feelings. Traditionally, it is the seat of the faculty of reason. We might also understand the soul as our humanity, where humanity is understood as our capacity for moral and intellectual life.

The soul is that aspect of our lives that makes us human, that makes us who we are, remembering that in Christ we are more than mere flesh. In Christ we share or participate in Christ's trinitarian character. He is in us (John 17:23). We are in Him (John 6:56). The human soul is that which is eternal, that which provides for the stability of human being, that is persistent over time. It is not that we are bodies who have souls, but that we are souls who have bodies.

---

27   Jonathan Leeman, in *The Church and the Surprising Offense of God's Love: Reintro-ducing the Doctrines of Church Membership and Discipline* . IX Marks, Crossway Books, 2010, notes that contemporary people have made an idol of love. Where the Bible teaches that God is love, people have reversed it and think that love is God. They then impose their own romantic and unbiblical ideas of love upon God and Scripture, thinking that they are being biblical.

And how are we to purify our souls? Through "obedience to the truth" (v. 22). And what is *truth (alētheia)*? The Greek word literally means *not hidden*, that which is not a lie, not a deception. The prefix "a" means *without*. Of course, Satan is the father of lies and deception (John 8:44). So, obedience to truth requires separation from Satan. It means without Satanic involvement or deceit, without original sin, without the deceit that fooled Adam and Eve in the Garden. This truth is not merely intellectual. Though it has intellectual components, we must not think that truth can be understood apart from actual behavioral compliance. Understanding and obedience, like grace and works, or love and marriage, ought not be separated. To separate them is to kill them, to drain the life from them.

Peter said that the result of our obedience must be "a sincere brotherly love" (v. 22). It must result in a compassion for humanity that actually serves the betterment of humanity, as God defines betterment. Brotherly love requires that we see others as family.

Peter's admonition is directed at Christians and church leaders, so it is directed at the church. In the church all are family. This is not an insignificant point, but acknowledges that God has redefined the human family as all who acknowledge God as Father. All who do the will of God are brothers and sisters in Christ (Matthew 12:48-50). But neither can we separate doing God's will from knowing God's will. The knowing increases the doing, and the doing increases the knowing.

ONE ANOTHER

As brothers and sisters we must "love one another" (v. 22), which means that our love must be genuine and reciprocal. It must flow both ways. James Jordan says that we must "one another one another," referring to the various one another passages in Scripture. Peter does not here call us to love the unlovable, but to return the love that we have been shown. We are to demonstrate love to others because God has demonstrated love to us, a love which is most clearly manifest in the life and death of Jesus Christ.

Reciprocal love is the foundation for Christian charity. Not that Christians cannot practice charity where reciprocal love does not exist, but that love apart from being reciprocal is not fully Christian. Christians are to provide charity first to other Christians as an expression of reciprocal love in order to increase the momentum of Christian love, and secondarily as a means of evangelism for the watching world.

This kind of love is not tit for tat. It is not that we are to love others because they have loved us, but that we are to love others because

Christ has loved us. We are to pass Christ's love for us forward to our brothers and sisters in Christ first, and then to the whole world, in the same way that family is to care for family first, but not to neglect neighbors.

The "city on a hill" (Matthew 5:14) that is to describe Christ's church is not a place of civil welfare, but a place of reciprocal love among Christians (John 13:34). It is the manifestation of the light of Christ among the residents of the "city." This reciprocal love must also be *sincere* (*anupokritos*)—without pretense, hypocrisy or dissimulation. It is to be unfeigned. It is to be agape love (*agapaō*)—selfless and without non-marital sexual involvement or implications. Agape love issues, not from our feelings, not from a sense of guilt or compassion, but from the primary commitment to serve Jesus Christ. It is not to be engaged in order to salve our guilt or enhance our social position. It is not to be done to impress our neighbors or those we serve.

It must be done with humility and in secrecy (Matthew 6:3), as much as possible in order to protect the recipients from shame and those who give it from pride. It must also issue from a pure heart. Our motives and intentions must be pure—godly. This means that it must be done with intention and fervency, with single-minded devotion to Jesus Christ, the only person worthy of such devotion.

Love that is exercised for the sake of anything else tends to contaminate the love with objectives that detract from and undermine the quality and purity of genuine love. Christians are not to exercise love in order to grow spiritually or to benefit themselves or the church, though genuine love will benefit both. Christians are not to exercise love or charity for the purpose of tax deductions, though tax deductions may be available.

MONEY

In fact, tax deductibility can turn charity into a self-serving action that undermines its purity and detracts from its service to God by focusing on its benefit to one's self. It muddies the waters of Christian charity and sticks the nose of the state into the tent of the church. This does not mean that we should not claim appropriate tax deductions. Given the condition of the civil government today we should do all we can to legally reduce our tax liabilities. Rather, it means that civil government should not be giving tax deductions for charitable giving because charity is primarily to be the work of the church, not the state. It is not the state's function to provide charity or to control the economy. But that's another issue.

Nor is the economy simply about the flow of money and credit, goods and services. Economy is a biblical term, *oikonomia*, which literally means *household management*. Yes, it pertains to money, but also to much more than money. The contemporary understanding and usage of the term focuses exclusively on financial management, to the detriment of the wholeness of the actual economy. The state uses the term *economics* to influence financial investment and flattens out the definition of the term by ignoring all other meanings. But by ignoring the other meanings or aspects of the economy, it fails to nurture them. It starves them and thereby reduces the vitality of genuine economic development by ignoring the foundation of economic development.

The current economic crisis is the result of state intrusion into the economy—generations ago. The definition and understanding of economy in strictly financial terms tends to strip the biblical household manager—the head of the household—of his most important responsibilities by inserting an artificial layer of civil administration between him and God. Economy is not simply about money, nor is money simply about numbers or spending.

Thinking about economy as the world currently does turns household management into an abstraction that is manipulated from Washington D.C., rather than something actual that is managed by the heads of the households under God. It usurps the biblical economic management responsibility of heads of households and gives it to Washington. It influences household and business management with inappropriate concerns. It guides the attention and money of the family with the concerns of the state through tax incentives. From a biblical perspective business management is to be a function of household management because the purpose of business is household stability and cultural longevity. The state has a role to play, but that role is not to direct or usurp the responsibilities of household or business management.

Born Again

Peter went on to note that Christians have been "born again" (v. 23) as a kind of foundation for all that precedes and follows. This concern is a repetition of what he said in verse 3: "he has caused us to be born again to a living hope through the resurrection of Jesus Christ from the dead." Peter said nothing about how to get born again, probably because he had already said that it is God who causes it.

What are you to do if you are not sure if you have been born again and want to be born again? Peter will bring this issue up many times and admonishes all Christians to make their calling and election sure (2 Peter 1:10) by practicing the various character qualities that he mentions in both of his letters. The manifestation of Christian character qualities provides a kind of proof of regeneration. Being born again is not about speaking in tongues as commonly understood. It is about using our tongues in the service of Jesus Christ.

Peter also wanted to make sure that no one misunderstood the kind of regeneration he was talking about. It was "not of perishable seed but of imperishable" (v. 23). The idea that it is a kind of seed suggests husbandry or the raising—farming—of born again Christians. It also suggests that there is a seasonal aspect to regeneration because to everything there is a season (Ecclesiastes 3:1), especially farming.

Who is the farmer of regeneration? Jesus Christ, the Groom of the Bride, the one who husbands the Bride (the church), God's family. The word *husband* is a verb that means to economize or manage. Farmers husband their animals. To have a husband is to have a manager. To be a husband is to be a steward. It is not a term that communicates oppression, but love, care and responsibility. The shepherd is not trying to oppress his sheep, nor the rancher his cattle, nor the farmer his chickens. He is trying to keep them healthy, happy and growing. Their health, happiness and growth serve his own interests.

Nonetheless, the central concern of this phrase is the perishable versus imperishable distinction. We might understand it today as sustainable versus unsustainable development, in the sense that being reborn of imperishable seed suggests a new lease on life that produces sustainable human development, a sustainable life, a sustainable family, a sustainable culture.

SUSTAINABLE DEVELOPMENT

Is it legitimate to connect Peter's concern about being reborn of imperishable seed with the contemporary concerns about sustainable development? Absolutely, because apart from having an eternal (long range) perspective that is genuinely concerned about the longevity and well-being of humanity, sustainable development will not be possible.

Of course there are differences between sustainable economic development and biblical spirituality, but there are also many useful similarities and overlaps. There are spiritual and heavenly aspects, but there are also bodily and worldly aspects. And these various aspects regarding human sustainability are not to be in conflict with one another, but are to be in ultimate harmony.

How does the idea of the regeneration of the imperishable seed work? Peter said that it works "through the living and abiding word of God" (v. 23). That means that it works through the Bible, but because it is about regeneration it also means through the Holy Spirit. And because Peter is talking about Jesus Christ, it means through Jesus Christ.

Thus, it all happens through the reality of the Trinity because Jesus Christ is the second Person of the Trinity. It works through all of these various means. And that means that it works through God alone in Christ alone through Scripture alone by the Holy Spirit alone for the glory of God alone. This aloneness points to the singularity of God's purpose in history.[28] And that singularity brings Father, Son and Holy Spirit in contact with past, present and future.

God's Word is indeed living and abiding. It is alive and it lives forever. This means that God's word is eternally available and always relevant. Our job is not to make God's word relevant to the passing world, but to make ourselves and our society relevant to the eternality of God. It is not that God needs to know where we are coming from— trust me, He knows. He doesn't need to be told what we think or how we think.

We don't need to translate God's Word to suit the language, preferences and ideas of our society. Rather, we need to adapt the language, preferences and ideas of our society to be in harmony with God's Word. We need to know what God thinks and how God thinks. We need to learn to speak His language. We must not attempt to adapt God's Word to the world. Such adaptation is too often syncretistic and sinful. Rather, we must adapt ourselves to God. We must allow God to remake us in the image of Jesus Christ.

SEASONS

Peter then quoted Isaiah 40:6-8: "All flesh is grass, and all its beauty is like the flower of the field. The grass withers, the flower fades when the breath of the LORD blows on it; surely the people are grass. The grass withers, the flower fades, but the word of our God will stand forever." This is poetry and metaphor. He is saying that humanity has seasons of growth just like everything else. There are seasons when humanity swarms and seasons when it recedes. Humanity ebbs and flows. That is the natural pattern of the natural world and the natural man Adam and his race.

It is against this pattern of growth and decline that Jesus stands as an eternal beacon of God's light and eternal life. He stands with God's Word, in God's Word. He is God's Word. Against the temporal cycle of boom and bust stands the eternal continuity of God's Word, the only anchor in the sea of change in which we live. The imperishable seed represents the idea of continual growth and maturity. It is a metaphor for human life in Christ, and suggests life eternal, where growth and

---

28 For a discussion of singularities see *Colossians—Christos Singularis*, by Phillip A. Ross, Pilgrim Platform. Marietta, Ohio, 2010.

maturity do not cease. It has a heavenly application, but it also has a worldly application—and that has been my focus here.

Peter then defined the gospel: "this *word* is the good news that was preached to you" (v. 25). Here Peter used the Greek word *rhēma* (*word*), where in verse 23 he used *logos* (*word*). We are born again by the *logos* of God, whereas we to preach the *rhēma* of God. What is the difference? Let me suggest that *logos* refers to the logic of God and *rhēma* refers to the rhetoric of God. One represents the skeleton or structure of God's thinking (*logos*), and the other represents the clothes or robes in which or by which God is presented (*rhēma*). The *logos* is the engine, the power or juice. The *rhēma* is the appeal, the raiment or adornment.

Gospel preaching requires that the *rhēma* reflects the *logos*, that the rhetoric serves the logic, that the description matches the reality, that the appeal is filled with effectiveness. The gospel that is preached is never other than the gospel that is personally lived. So, our preaching always reflects our own understanding and our understanding always reflects our own practice. Thus, the problem with too much contemporary preaching is that it comes out of lukewarm churches, which are always the most worldly and successful churches. When churches measure success as the world measures success, the gospel that most impacts the world through them is the lukewarm gospel of the Laodiceans because the world can better tolerate that.

Consequently, the biblical cure for lukewarm preaching is not fire and brimstone, not intensity of appeal, but simple, personal faithfulness on the part of the preacher. However, genuine faithfulness in the churches always requires faithfulness of the leadership and faithfulness of the followership. Both must work in tandem for genuine biblical faithfulness to manifest. Our practice—leaders and laity—must be in line with the gospel.

We must own and wear God's refined gold and His white garments. Christ's righteousness must cover our nakedness, His eye salve must cure our blindness. We must put our money on these things—godliness, Christ's righteousness and God's vision for the world. We must invest in these things, support them, promote them.

But before we can promote them, we must have them ourselves. They must actually operate correctly in our own lives and churches. And that is our problem.

9. The Milky Way

*So put away all malice and all deceit and hypocrisy and envy
and all slander. Like newborn infants, long for the pure spiritual milk, that by it you may grow up into salvation—if
indeed you have tasted that the Lord is good. As you come to
him, a living stone rejected by men but in the sight of God
chosen and precious, you yourselves like living stones are
being built up as a spiritual house, to be a holy priesthood, to
offer spiritual sacrifices acceptable to God through Jesus
Christ.*   —1 Peter 2:1-5 (ESV)

Of verse 1 Calvin wrote, "After having taught the faithful that they
had been regenerated by the word of God, he now exhorts them
to lead a life corresponding with their birth."[29] Calvin answered
the question about how we know that we have been born again. Contrary to the popular notion that people must have a vivid experience that
results in regeneration, Calvin said that Peter had taught that the
faithful could know that they had been born by the Word of God by the
character of their new life in Christ. Peter taught this truth to them so
that they would know it, so that they wouldn't miss it.

This issue is about who exactly are the faithful, and how they know
how to be faithful. How do they know that they actually are faithful?
First of all, Peter wrote promiscuously to the scattered and elect exiles of
the dispersion. Were all who had been dispersed members of the elect?
If they took their families and children with them, were all of the children elect? This question about who is a Christian and who isn't is both
difficult and persistent. Because people continue to be born and born
again, the issue is never finally resolved. Everyone in every generation
must ask it of themselves, and every church must ask it of their membership. Are you a Christian? How do you know? Are you sure?

---

29 Calvin, John. *Calvin's Commentaries*, Baker Books, Ada, Michigan, 1974, 1 Peter 2:1.

This is not an invitation for people to insist on some kind of experience or to become morosely introspective. Peter was not encouraging doubt. He was encouraging faithfulness. The simple answer is that being a Christian means being faithful to Christ by living a faithful life. The difficulties arise out of our own sin and faithlessness. The positive answer is clear. The negative answer is dark and cloudy. Being a Christian is simple but not easy. Pretending to be a Christian is complex and confusing precisely because it tries to avoid the serious difficulties. Nonetheless, because so many people do pretend, the complexities of faithlessness must be revealed for what they are.

Put Away

Peter provides the simple answer: Christians "put away all malice and all deceit and hypocrisy and envy and all slander" (v. 1). Though he makes no reference to Jesus Christ in this verse, Christ is everywhere assumed because Christ is revealed through the removal of the things Peter named. These evil things are part of the darkness that the light of Christ dispels. Peter called attention to these things in order to renounce them.

Malice (*kakia*) is the desire to see others suffer. It usually arises out of a kind of jealousy that feels guilty about itself in the face of joy and happiness because, having renounced the forgiveness of Christ, it knows that it does not deserve joy or happiness, and cannot tolerate such things in others. Malice is to be renounced.

Deceit (*dolos*), *guile* in the *Authorized Version*, refers to a decoy or a replica that is used as bait in order to put someone at a disadvantage. It is a matter of taking advantage of people through deception, particularly of those who are simple, honest and amenable. Those who are unacquainted with worldly deceitfulness. Deceit is to be renounced.

Hypocrisy (*hupokrisis*) is a matter of pretending to be something that you are not. It is pretending to be anything other than the person who God actually created you to be, which necessarily means the person you are to become in Christ. All failure to live as God has instructed in the Bible through the light of Christ involves hypocrisy. Thus, faithlessness and hypocrisy are cut from the same cloth. Hypocrisy is to be renounced.

Envy (*phthonos*) is ill-will toward others. It is difficult to separate envy from jealousy. But it is not necessary to do so because they are twins from the loins of the father of lies and deceit, Satan. Envy and jealousy work frantically to fill the emptiness of the human soul apart from God. Emptiness apart from Christ is not only a bottomless pit, but the more attention the emptiness is given, the deeper the pit appears to be. And the deeper the pit, the more that people have to do to try to fill it or hide it. Envy cannot be overcome with personal will power or might. It must be starved to death—ignored. Envy is to be renounced.

Slander (*katalalia*) or *evil speakings* in the *Authorized Version* is the last term on Peter's list. Slander speaks evil of others by defaming them. Slander involves character assassination, or attacking the character of others as a way of making one's self look better by comparison. Slander is to be renounced.

Peter simply demands that Christians put these things away. Of course, this is easier said than done. Sin is tenacious and stubborn. It is a matter of habit, and habits are hard to break. And what is more, it is impossible to break the habits of sin apart from regeneration in Christ. However, regeneration does not make people instantly mature Christian adults. It makes them babes in Christ, immature Christian infants. Christians are to grow up in Christ.

SIN'S DECEPTION

Going from what seems like mature sinnerhood to immature sainthood is an embarrassment in the eyes of the world. From a worldly perspective, it looks like regression rather than progression. Sinners always think that saints are unacquainted with the ways of the world, and that their lack of worldly experience—their lack of experience in sin—needs to be matured by exposure and acclamation to the wickedness of worldliness. For instance, sinners think that it is good for people who are sexually inexperienced to experience the loss of sexual innocence by exposure to sexual immorality, and that such a loss of innocence by sinful experience results in maturity and wisdom.

The world understands maturity to be a product of what the Bible calls foolishness and sin, in the sense that growth in worldly maturity requires active and intentional sinfulness. "Big boys" dare little boys to break moral taboos as a show of bravery and/or freedom. And oddly enough we find that little girls are trying to be brave "big boys" who are unafraid to sin, too. They erroneously think that the engagement of sin produces maturity, whereas Christians believe that maturity avoids sin. At least, that is what Christians are supposed to believe. The more mature the Christian, the more the avoidance of sin. But this does not mean a lack of interaction with sinners, it means engaging in sin less and less over time.

The reality, though, is that our churches are so corrupted by worldliness that Christians too often follow the world with regard to its definition of maturity. For instance, the typical "coming of age" story for too many Christians is not about the retention of moral purity in the face of sin and the growth of faithfulness to Jesus Christ, but is a story about temptation, fall and redemption.

However, temptation, fall and redemption is not a story arc of growing in the sincere milk of the Word. Temptation, fall and sin is an Old Testament story, not a New Testament story, a worldly story, not a mature Christian story. The Old Testament morality stories are about covenant establishment and covenant disloyalty, leading to reestablishment. Over and over again Israel lost her way only to have a prophet arise and reestablish God's covenant. But with Christ we have the fulfillment of the law, which results in the final covenant. Following Christ no new prophets arise because in the light of Christ mere prophets are retrograde. Christ has come to break the cycle of covenant renewal and unfaithfulness followed by more renewal. Christ unleashed the means of covenant fidelity—God's Holy Spirit through regeneration—once and for all.

Old/New

Indeed, the story of temptation, fall and redemption is so common in our contemporary culture as to be universalized in literature and movies. Yes, it is the story of humanity that has been captured in the Bible through the stories of the great patriarchs. All were sinners who fell in one way or another, and who were then redeemed by the grace of God. The story is common, even universal because of Adam's role as the federal head of humanity, because of his archetypical model for humanity, and his failure of obedience.

The Bible is the story of the redemption of sinful humanity. The Old Testament provides documentation of God's treatment of Israel and of Israel's fall apart from Christ. And the New Testament is the story of God's redemption of the whole world, using Israel as a fulcrum for the advent of Jesus Christ and His propitiation of God on the cross for the sins of all extant humanity.

But here's the stickler: Christ died once for all (Hebrews 10:10). His death and resurrection put an end to the Old Man by giving birth to the New Man in Christ. The New Man in Christ is to grow beyond the Old Man because the power of Christ has conquered sin and death once and for all time, from Christ forward. Christ has redeemed humanity. Of course, that redemption comes one sinner at a time, but it must not be denied or neglected that Christ applies His work of redemption on the cross for all extant humanity to individual sinners. Christ's redemption brings the corporate character of humanity, now forgiven in Christ in God's eyes, to bear upon individuals so that God no longer sees the person as an individual, but as a corporate member of a forgiven humanity in Christ.

So, from Christ forward, the story of human redemption is no longer the story of temptation, fall and redemption because Christ has brought human redemption to a foregone conclusion in human history. Jesus Christ has brought (is bringing) redemption to all extant humanity. This is not Universalism, it's Postmillennialism. It does not mean that every person ever born will be saved, but that one day all extant humanity will be saved. So, from Christ forward the story of human redemption began anew with Christ's redemption and grows into sanctification as it moves toward the fullness of the revelation of Jesus Christ to the glory of God.

In other words, all those stories of human redemption that move from temptation to fall and redemption are Old Testament stories, Old Testament patterns that deny the reality and power of Jesus Christ in history by ignoring the reality of Christ's redemption as the new starting point. And they fail by not starting with the foundation of Christ's redemption. To begin with temptation and fall is to deny the ability of Christ's redemption to actually effect human development *once for all*.

Christian stories don't flow from temptation to fall and redemption. Christian stories *begin* with redemption, they build upon Christ's redemption. They don't culminate with it. Christ is the redemption of the old world, the Old Man. In Christ the old story, the old pattern is dead and buried. In Christ the Old Man is dead. To begin anywhere other than with Christ is to fail to begin with the New Adam. The advantage of living on this side of Christ's advent is that we begin with Christ. We don't begin with Adam. We begin with sin redeemed, not sin expressed. The old way was to begin with Adam. In Christ humanity has been recreated. "The old has passed away; behold, the new has come" (2 Corinthians 5:17). To neglect this foundational fact is to commit the error of a false start.

Have Tasted

Peter dealt with this in verse 2. "Like newborn infants, long for the pure spiritual milk, that by it you may grow up into salvation—if indeed you have tasted that the Lord is good" (vs. 2-3). Most modern translations treat verse 3 as a conditional statement, but the *Geneva Bible* translates it as "*because* ye have tasted that the Lord is bountiful." We are not to grow up into salvation *if* something happens. We are to grow up into salvation *because* something has already happened. Christ has come! Peter tells the saints to begin their story with the new birth. Of course, many saints have taken a long and winding road prior to their new birth in Christ. But now, since Christ that story is old-hat. That's not the new story, that's the old story. That's the old beginning, not the new beginning.

It is well past time to let the old story go, to leave it in the past, rather than to continually rehash it in the present, in the light of Christ. And this is true both individually and culturally. Being a Christian is not a matter of being tempted and falling only to be redeemed once again, over and over. Every generation does not need to re-experience Adam's sin. Christ's advent provides a kind of reboot for human history, human culture. Jesus Christ has taken care of Adam's sin. Christ came to fix that particular problem! In Christ humanity is done with that.

Being a Christian is a matter of being born again and growing in faithfulness and maturity in Christ. Being a Christian does not mean starting with the Fall, with temptation and sin, and finding resolution in the infancy of redemption. Sure, that's a real story. But it is the story of the change from Old Covenant to the New Covenant. It's the story of the First Century church, of the infancy of the church. That's what Peter means by "grow up into salvation" (v. 2). The *Authorized Version* translates the phrase as "that ye may grow thereby." Jesus Christ provides a new starting point, a new beginning for humanity, both individually and corporately. Yes, God's people were once infants in Christ. But they—we—must grow up in Christ, and not wallow in spiritual immaturity. To grow in Christ is to let go of what is not in Christ.

We are to grow by the spiritual and sincere milk of the word. What milk? The milk of the *word* (v. 2). But this *word* is not *logos* or *rhēma*, but *logikos*. The sincere milk of *logikos* is more substance than style, more logic than rhetoric, more reality than panache. Certainly we are to grow through study of the Bible, but *logikos* does not simply refer to Scripture. It refers to the kind of thinking that comes from Bible study. It is not simply rehashing the biblical stories, nor finding application of them for our current experience, but is rather the active and ongoing development of God's story (history) in the light of Christ.

The advent of Jesus Christ inaugurated a new humanity with a new human history, a new humanity for which the old pattern of temptation, fall and redemption no longer applies. That old story is the cesspool from which Christianity was freed, and is not the story of the new life in Christ. The new stories begin with the light of Christ in redemption and grow in sanctification into glory. The new stories begin with Christ, not Adam. They grow in righteousness, they don't succumb to temptation only to need redemption again and again. They grow into glory, they don't backslide and regurgitate only to backslide and regurgitate again.

GET OUT OF THE RUT

One of the problems with contemporary Christians is their tendency to wallow in the past, in their stories of temptation, fall and redemption. Consider most Christian testimonies over the past hundred years and you will find this old pattern. In our Evangelical churches we find that people "come forward" again and again, that people find Christ at some crusade-like event or other only to later backslide because of some failure to resist temptation and fall, only to require re-redemption again and again. Too many Christians are stuck in the Old World rut of temptation, fall and a redemption that doesn't get them to the next level of maturity in Christ. A little of this kind of thing is understandable. Even Paul struggled with it (Romans 7). But it's way too common today.

Seldom do we hear a testimony like, "I was born into a Christian family and a faithful church, and have grown into sincere godliness to the delight of my family and friends." Indeed, it sounds boring because we are inundated with the more exciting stories of temptation, fall and redemption. It's not the the old stories are untrue, but that they are inadequate to the more subtle textures of life in Christ. Nor does it mean that there is no struggle in sanctification. Rather, the struggles of sanctification are different than the struggles of redemption.

Yet, that is the story that Peter calls Christians to live and embrace. We are to drink the milk of Christian thinking (*logikos*) as new babes in Christ and grow up into salvation. In Christ we don't begin with temptation and fall. That was the old story, not the new story. That was the way of the prodigal son, not the way of the Christian saint. The prodigal was a Jewish son, a son of the old way, not a Christian son of the new way. The prodigal son was a transitional story. We must not get stuck in the transition.

The story of the prodigal is not to be humanity's eternal story. We are to learn from that story and grow beyond it because we have tasted that the Lord is good. The repetition of the prodigal story as a common human spiritual experience is not the Christian way. The point of that biblical story was to illustrate the necessity of the regeneration of both Jew (the older brother) and the Gentile (the prodigal son). That was the situation of God's people when Jesus told that story. The prodigal son got out of the rut. The end of the prodigal story is the beginning of Christianity.

Our stories this side of Christ's redemption are to issue from the goodness of the Lord, not from the sinfulness of lost people, not even lost people who are forever finding Christ again and again. Finding Christ is a good thing, don't get me wrong. But we must grow beyond simply finding Him, and actually engage Him, grow in Him. People who live on this side of Christ's advent don't need to go looking for Him. He has already come. He found us when He saved humanity from death on the cross.

Jesus isn't lost, and neither are those in Christ this side of Christ's redemption. May the church in our day end its self-indulgent romance with the prodigal son! Christians are not to be perpetual prodigal sons. Christians should not start their stories in prodigal lostness. We are to begin in Christ not in Adam, in salvation not prodigality. For Christ's sake it's time to grow up!

Building Blocks

Growing up into the fullness of salvation is a process. It doesn't happen all at once. It takes time and practice. Our stories should be about our time and practice in faithfulness. Peter said that we are being built up as a spiritual house as we come to Christ, through the process of growing into Christ. And to emphasize the corporate character of our salvation, our commonality, Peter noted that each Christian is but a single building block in a complex corporate structure. We are not only part of a larger whole, but our incorporation into the the larger whole is the purpose of our salvation.

This does not in any way denigrate the value of the individual Christian. The individual stones are important. A building is only as strong as its weakest stone. So each stone needs to be well-formed and well-fired (kilned), mature in Christ. But the purpose of the stone is to be incorporated into the building. Each stone has a place, a position and a purpose related, not to itself, but to the building, to the body of Christ.

Christians are living stones who are alive because of the regenerating power of the Trinity. Christians are alive, which means that we eat and grow and reproduce, which is the definition of living things. We feed at Christ's table, grow in Christ's church and reproduce in Christ's world. Our feeding is essential, our growth is mandatory and our reproduction is necessary. Yet, life in Christ is difficult.

Why is it difficult? Because, as Peter noted, Jesus Christ was "rejected by men" (v. 4). The cause of Christ is an offense to the world. The world is not only opposed to the spiritual house (or economy) that Christ is building with His people, but the world is opposed to His method of building it.

At this point in history, the world accepts the old story. The world is comfortable with stories of temptation, fall and redemption because they keep things in a familiar rut. The old stories keep us in the old rut. History is cyclical, the old story repeats itself again and again, but never gets out of the old rut. However, Christianity is the end of that story. And the beginning of a new story. The story of the prodigal son is a transitional story, not a foundational story.

In the sight of God, Christ and His people are chosen and precious. Christ is the foundation for the new story of redemption that doesn't begin with temptation and fall. This new story begins with redemption in Christ and grows into sanctification and glory. So when this new story repeats itself again and again, it does so dynamically as it goes from redemption to sanctification into glory. Each repetition begins with redemption and new growth, new understanding, and the new growth jumps out of the rut into uncharted territory as the incorporation of Christ expands into the world. The new story is the growth of the Christian household (or economy). The new story is redemption and maturity, not sin and redemption.

HOLINESS

Peter also called this "spiritual house" a "holy priesthood" (v. 5). A priesthood is at its root a group of people who live in common covenant with one another in order to serve God. The idea of holiness suggests otherness, sanctification, and separation from what is common, what is sinful. So, Christians who live in covenant together have in common that which is otherwise uncommon—God's forgiveness and redemption. That is to say that Christians live in a way that is distinct and different from the societies in which they dwell. In some way or another they live distinctly—differently—from the unforgiven and unredeemed society.

But Christians are not to be a subgroup of the larger society in the same way that Irish Americans, for instance, are a subgroup of Americans. No, Christians are a subgroup of something completely other than the society in which they live. The correct designation would be American Christians, not Christian Americans.[30] Christians belong to the realm of heaven, which is distinct from earth. Christians have dual citizenship. We are citizens of heaven and citizens of some particular earthly nation.

The Greek word *hierateuma* is translated as *priesthood* suggests a hierarchy of people who can read and write, and who are living in common covenant with God. The root of *hierateuma* is related to the word *hieroglyphics*. A hieroglyph is a picture that represents an object or idea. The point is that representation is at the heart of priestcraft. The priest mediates or represents God to his people and also represents his people to God. He takes God's concerns to the people through preach-

---

30 This distinction is very significant because it indicates which identity takes precedence, whether one's national identity and loyalty supersedes one's religious identity or visa versa. For Christians religious identity takes precedence because it is eternal.

ing, and the people's concerns to God through prayer. Priests also represent God by representing God's authority, and the representative
authority of priests is always derivative and hierarchical by definition.

Peter said that Christians compose a priesthood. Thus, this is what
Christians do. Christians are a priesthood united in Christ, active in but
independent from the society in which they live. Christians live in a
representative covenantal hierarchy. Christians are not dependent on
the world (the society in which they live) for their thoughts and ideas,
but translate the written thoughts and words of God (Scripture) for
their people. We are not to adapt God's Word to suit the culture, we are
to adapt the culture to suit God's Word.

Holy priests live apart from the influences that distract and interfere with their holiness and with the purity and truth of God's message.
Yet, they must also live in the midst of those influences in order to
bring God's love and God's Word to the unredeemed. They must live *in*
the world, but not be *of* the world. They must live in the midst of
worldly influences, but not be influenced by them, not be subject to
their influence. This requires steadfast discipline and maturity, and is
why evangelists should not be recent converts (1 Timothy 3:6).

In Christ Christians have direct access to the throne of God
(Hebrews 4:16). However, that access does not mean that each Christian has an individually unique access, as if God speaks differently to
each person. No. Christians have a common access to God because of
their common covenant. Consequently, Christians do not speak however they want on behalf of God, but speak out of their independent
and separate (from the world or society in which they live) but common union in Christ, their common covenant. Christians are united in
Christ with all other Christians who are united in Christ.

This common Christian union is not created by signing agreements. This union was created by God and has been signed with the
blood of Christ. This union is entered, not by signing a pledge card and
gathering with like minded individuals, but by growth and maturity in
Christ through regeneration by the power and presence of the Holy
Spirit. But this union is not about separation from the physical world
into some sort of ghetto.

Rather, it is separation or independence from the beliefs and values of the world while living in the midst of the world (society or culture). It is not a retreat from the world, but involves bringing Christ to
the world through their own lives, of manifesting the beliefs and values
of Christ in their own lives as the central act of evangelism. It is not
mere physical separation, but is spiritual and moral distinctness from
the world in the sense that Christians are not motivated or directed by

the spirituality or morality of the world, but by the spirituality and morality of God through Scripture in the light of Christ.

While living in the midst of the sin and corruption of the world Christians find guidance and direction from another quarter, from God's Word in the light of Christ. It is not simply that Christians find Scripture to be interesting and fellowship with other Christians to be beneficial, but that Christians value Scripture and fellowship more than their jobs and their families, more than their cars and their homes. Christians desire God like babies desire milk.

PRIESTCRAFT

As priests Christians are to offer up "spiritual sacrifices" (v. 5). The emphasis on *spiritual* here means that these sacrifices are not the blood of bulls or rams. They are not physical, but spiritual. Spiritual sacrifices are prayer, praise and thanksgiving—the things that please God. To be a Christian priest is to live a life of spiritual sacrifice, of prayer, praise and thanksgiving in the midst of a world of malice, deceit, hypocrisy, envy and slander (v. 1).

Christians find solace, meaning and purpose in Christ. Christian life begins with redemption in Christ, not with our old lives of temptation and fall. Meaning and purpose are not found in the world, they are found in Christ in spite of the world. And because meaning and purpose are not found in the world, Christians impose meaning and purpose on the world, not impose them on others but impose them upon *themselves*. That is the Christian mission: to impose the meaning and purpose of Jesus Christ upon one's self as the cure for human lostness, human brokenness, human sin; and then to impose or assert or understand Christ as the object of one's faith and understanding of the world, of the culture or society in which one lives.

Christian's are to impose biblical belief, hope and faith upon their own lives and upon their own understanding of God's world. We are to see things, to understand things, as God understands them. We are to begin in Christ not in Adam, and we are to think Christianly, in biblical categories with biblical logic toward biblical purposes. We are to impose the perspective of the Bible upon our own lives and our own families as we share the blessings of faithfulness. We are to see the world through the lens of Scripture by shining Christ's light on everything. We are to institute a philosophical imposition upon our own thinking—to live by faith, not by sight (Romans 1:17; Galatians 2:20, 3:11-12; Hebrews 10:38, Hebrews 11:9). Faith is first a presupposition, and then an assertion. Yes, faith is an assertion, not an argument.

How does this happen? How are we to do this? While it is true that it happens only as a consequence of being born again, it is not true that people just plug into the spirit as if God downloads His truth into them. Rather, said Peter, Christians must grow up into it. And how do children grow? They are taught and trained in the love and admonition of the Lord (Ephesians 6:4). Peter was teaching these new Christians about how to grow into salvation, into faithfulness. Peter was feeding the saints pure spiritual milk—milk, not meat! That fact that Peter understood his teaching as milk should give us pause and astonishment because it seems so meaty to us.

Am I?

How can Christians know if they are truly saved? How can we know if we are doing the will of God? How can we make our calling and election sure? By regularly drinking the milk. By practicing the presupposition. By imposing the faith upon our own thoughts. Christians will love it, even crave it! Christians will digest Peter's milk and not choke on it. Those who are growing in Christ won't be able to get enough of it. Those who are doing the will of God will want to do the will of God all the more. They desire to please God, and that desire draws them into Christian practice and maturity.

Of course, salvation comes by God's grace alone. And sanctification also comes by grace alone. It's all of grace alone. And of this grace James wrote:

"Therefore put away all filthiness and rampant wickedness and receive with meekness the implanted word, which is able to save your souls. But be doers of the word, and not hearers only, deceiving yourselves. For if anyone is a hearer of the word and not a doer, he is like a man who looks intently at his natural face in a mirror. For he looks at himself and goes away and at once forgets what he was like. But the one who looks into the perfect law, the law of liberty, and perseveres, being no hearer who forgets but a doer who acts, he will be blessed in his doing. If anyone thinks he is religious and does not bridle his tongue but deceives his heart, this person's religion is worthless. Religion that is pure and undefiled before God, the Father, is this: to visit orphans and widows in their affliction, and to keep oneself unstained from the world" (James 1:21-27).

How is this possible? By the grace that converts the desire to flee from God in fear and disgust into the desire to grow near to God in Christ in love and thankfulness. It begins with this milky way that Peter wrote about.

10. DESTINY'S CHILDREN

For it stands in Scripture: "Behold, I am laying in Zion a
stone, a cornerstone chosen and precious, and whoever
believes in him will not be put to shame." So the honor is for
you who believe, but for those who do not believe, "The stone
that the builders rejected has become the cornerstone," and "A
stone of stumbling, and a rock of offense." They stumble
because they disobey the word, as they were destined to do.
—1 Peter 2:6-8 (ESV)

To say that something "stands in Scripture" (v. 6) means that
Scripture attests to whatever it is as a central foundation, teaching or doctrine. It means that whatever it is that stands is very
important. The thing that Peter was describing in these few verses
required his acknowledgment that—whatever it is—it is a true and
essential teaching of the Bible. He had to state this fact because whatever it is, it is consistently denied, denigrated and ignored by everyone
who does not hold Jesus Christ to be the trinitarian Son of God
incarnate in human flesh.

So, what is this thing that stands in Scripture? It is the manifestation of Jesus Christ in the flesh, and it provides the cornerstone that
reveals the reality of God as Trinity. And the reality of the Trinity reveals
the central and most important characteristic regarding the reality in
which human beings exist.

The doctrine of the Trinity is the cornerstone that was laid in Zion,
and is the central testimony of Scripture. And what or where is Zion?
For Jews the term *Zion* was a figure of speech that referred to the city of
Jerusalem and the landed estate of Israel. It referred to the reality of
God's earthly mission, that God's intent was to save humanity by estab-
lishing a godly culture on earth as there is in heaven (Matthew 6:10).

God's mission is a rescue mission, of course. But that mission is not merely to free people from harm or evil. It is that, of course, but not merely that. It is also a mission to free people for health and well-being. It is not merely a mission to rescue people from a world of evil and transgression, but a mission to establish a just and sustainable culture through godly order, biblical order. Of course, God's mission is to rescue people *from* something bad, but also a mission to rescue people *for* something good, to rescue people from what will eventually kill us, and into something that will sustain us indefinitely.

Not Elsewhere

Indeed, eternal life means the preservation of life. God's mission is not to beam people up into some heavenly ethereal realm where all of our personal desires are satisfied and we lack nothing that we want. There is no such ethereal realm. There is no other dimension that is in some other location that is accessible to people from this dimension. All of reality's dimensions are bound up together in the trinitarian reality in which God has created, and we already live here. The new Jerusalem that will one day come down from heaven (Matthew 19:28, 24:3; Revelation 21:2) does not refer to a new world arriving from space, but to this world that will be renewed at a future time. It is not talking about new dirt, but about a new age (*aiōn*).

God's mission is not to remove people from this sinful earth, but to remove sin from this peopled earth. Yet, God's mission is not a mission of removal or destruction, it is a mission of regeneration and replenishment. And the realization of God as Trinity is the cornerstone of that mission. Sin cannot simply be extracted as if it is a bad gene sequence. Rather, the whole faulty and sinful genome sequence must be replaced by a perfect and sinless genome sequence, if I may use genetics as an analogy. And using this analogy does not indicate some physical change in the genome sequence. It simply means something as fundamental to human life as genetics.

This analogy does not mean that sin is actually genetic, though it has genetic manifestations and consequences. It means that sin functions *like* a bad gene in a genetic sequence in that it produces developmental problems. Another analogy suggests that sin works like the multiplication function in math, in the sense that one thing (a product) is generated from another (a factor). Sin has a kind of internally consistent logic.

Grace

The central lesson of the Bible is that the fullness of human identity is not a function of race, but is a function of grace. God's people are not blood related like the Old Testament Jews understood blood relationships. Rather, God's people are related by grace, through adoption and inheritance, which is the central teaching of Scripture. God "has made all nations of men of one blood to dwell on all the face of the earth, ordaining fore-appointed seasons and boundaries of their dwelling" (Acts 17:26, *Modern King James Bible*). Humanity is a biblical kind or species, and the variations within that species are not important to God. Color, race and nationality are insignificant to God.

Consequently, human identity based upon race or blood, family or nation, is a false identity—not because it is wrong but because it is inadequate to the reality of humanity in the light of Christ. It is insufficient. Of course we are like our biological families and like the nations in which our families reside in both nature and nurture. We tend to look like them and act like them. Nationalities are simply extensions of family or genetic relationships. And those relationships are both important and real, but they are inadequate to the fullness of human character because they do not allow for the complexity of the trinitarian reality in which we actually exist. A blood based human identity falls short of the reality.

This is the central teaching of Scripture to which Jesus Christ testifies through His advent as the Son of God manifest in human flesh, and whose primary mission is to bring salvation to the whole extant world. This is the mystery of the Trinity that remains veiled until it is revealed by God Himself.

Wholeness

It has been said that the whole is greater than the sum of its parts. In themselves, parts have no similarity to the whole because the whole is a feature of a completely different order than the part. The whole cannot be accessed or described by the language of parts. What is partial cannot encompass what is whole. Similarly, a human being is also greater than its constituent parts. A human being cannot be assembled by surgically connecting arms, legs, torso, head, etc. The wholeness of the parts, its life or soul, is something additional, something different, something of a completely different order. It is something God-breathed (Genesis 2:7).

Peter said that whatever it is that is "contained in Scripture" (v. 6) reveals the trinitarian wholeness of humanity as it reveals God in Christ. The wholeness of humanity is contained in Christ. What is it that is contained in Scripture? Let me suggest that it is the analogous whole of humanity that is greater than the sum of the parts. The reference to Scripture is not a reference to a particular book (Genesis,

Exodus, Matthew, Mark, etc.) but is a reference to the whole and the wholeness (and the holiness) of Scripture.

That which is greater than the sum of the parts is revealed by, through, in and as Jesus Christ through regeneration, which is related to Christ's resurrection. Or we could say that it is revealed as Scripture is read in the light of Christ. The wholeness and perfection of human identity is contained in Scripture when read in the light of Christ, when it is seen with regenerate eyes, when faith is imposed. Why? Because regeneration brings the regenerated individual into union and unity with Christ.[31]

How can I say that Jesus Christ is the wholeness of humanity, that He is that which is greater than the sum of the parts? Because Peter so identified this fact by telling us that Jesus Christ is the "cornerstone chosen and precious" (v. 6). The *Him* in which we are to believe is Jesus Christ, the divine Son of God manifest in human flesh. The *Him* in which we are to believe is the Trinity, the only God who actually exists.

TRINITY

A cornerstone is the stone that defines all other stones and identifies the building as a whole. All other stones are laid with reference to the cornerstone, and the cornerstone is inscribed with the identity of the building. The Trinity, manifest in Christ, is the cornerstone of biblical faith. The Trinity is the defining characteristic of God's actuality. All other beliefs about God are false if they lack reference to and identity in the Trinity.

Peter quoted and alluded to Psalm 118:22, "The stone that the builders rejected has become the cornerstone." The allusion to a stone compares Christ to a stone. Peter said in verse 5 that Christians are "living stones that are being built up as a spiritual house." Christ is the cornerstone and Christians are living stones. The building or structure, also known as the church or body of Christ in which people are to dwell, is a spiritual house or an economy.

An economy is a system of production, distribution and consumption—that's what people do in homes, particularly in agrarian homesteads or farms. People organize into societies in order to produce, distribute and consume. We forget that modern production processes are just that—modern. Being modern doesn't mean that they are bad or that the biblical message and way doesn't apply to them. It does. Modern production and distribution use different processes and procedures, but not different purposes. The purpose of an economy is the

---

31 For more on this see *The True Mystery of The Mystical Presence*, by John Williamson Nevin and Phillip A. Ross, Pilgrim Platform, Marietta, Ohio, 2011.

same as it has always been—to support and sustain human life. An economy is a kind of spiritual house.

The point is that Christ is not just any old stone. He is the cornerstone of the church, the basis upon which economies exist. And a cornerstone is the fundamental thing from which a building is begun, developed, planned or explained. So, sure Christ is the cornerstone of the church. But more importantly He is the cornerstone of reality itself. Jesus Christ is God incarnate, and God holds reality together. God is of central importance to humanity and to reality. Thus, the Trinity is the cornerstone of all reality in the church and out.

BELIEF

Therefore, said Peter, "whoever believes in him will not be put to shame" (v. 6). This is oddly phrased. The Greek literally means that believers will not be joined with shame. The idea is that they will not participate in what is shameful. This idea was also mentioned by Paul in Romans 5:1-5:

> "Therefore, since we have been justified by faith, we have peace with God through our Lord Jesus Christ. Through him we have also obtained access by faith into this grace in which we stand, and we rejoice in hope of the glory of God. More than that, we rejoice in our sufferings, knowing that suffering produces endurance, and endurance produces character, and character produces hope, and hope does not put us to shame, because God's love has been poured into our hearts through the Holy Spirit who has been given to us."

Note the emphasis on sanctification, on growth and maturity, and the central place of the Holy Spirit, which underscores the role of the Trinity in the process of sanctification, of maturity and development.

Paul also quoted the stone of stumbling phrase in Romans 9:33. Peter was undoubtedly quoting and referring to Romans 9 as well. The idea that everyone who believes in Christ, in the Trinity, will not be put to shame also destroys the false arguments about human identity being based in blood or family ties, and the false arguments about human identity being based on gender or work. Christian identity is not a function of gender (Galatians 3:28). Rather, taught Peter and Paul, human identity is incomplete and inadequate unless it is first and foremost based on God in Christ, on the Trinity. Therefore, human identity based in bodily attributes opposes Christianity and violates religious freedom.

The idea that God is no respecter of persons or individuals[32] means that God judges on the basis of wholeness not parts, on types not indi-

---

32 Scripture references listed in footnote 7, page 25.

viduals. So, special civil rights based on bodily attributes, personal preferences or cultural idiosyncrasies attempts to establish human identity apart from Christ. Salvation is a matter of being in Christ. In a sense, it doesn't matter who we are in Christ, it only matters that we are in Christ. Of course, being in Christ changes who we are as individuals, so it actually becomes important. Perhaps it would be better to say that God doesn't care who we were before we came into Christ because our being in Christ changes everything.

Peter went on to say that because Christian character and identity are caught up with Christ through regeneration, believers receive honor. It is an honor to be in Christ. But unbelievers, who reject the cornerstone are themselves rejected by the cornerstone. Unbelievers are without honor in God's eyes and are rejected by their own unbelief. They disqualify themselves from God's kingdom by their refusal to believe. Peter said, "They stumble because they disobey the word" (v. 8), and yet that very disobedience was appointed for them. They were destined or appointed (*tithēmi*) to it. What does that mean?

God has decreed everywhere in Scripture that unbelievers cannot be included in His kingdom. Unbelief is the rejection of forgiveness. It is the failure to acknowledge the reality of sin. It is the denial of one's own personal complicity in sin and, therefore, of one's own need for forgiveness. It is a self-identity that denies sin, and by that very denial it ignores the reality of sin. And by that ignorance of sin it subscribes to a self-identity that includes sin because it does not recognize it. And God cannot tolerate sin.

God's decree, then, becomes real as it is actualized in human history. If God had merely decreed it, but Christ never manifested in human form or no one ever actually got saved or damned, the decree would contain only an empty promise and an empty threat, and would be nothing. It would be less than real. A decree that has no actual effect has no basis in reality.

Consequently, both salvation and damnation are necessary for God's decree to be real, for His Word to be reliable. The failure to believe in heaven and hell as realities issues from the failure to believe in the truthfulness of God's Word. The denial of sin or of hell is really a denial of the veracity of God's Word. Thus, unbelievers identify themselves, not by what is true, not by God's Word, but by what is false, by their own thoughts and imaginations apart from God's Word.

OBEDIENCE

In addition, by tying unbelief to disobedience, Peter linked believing with biblical obedience. Believers are not set free from the demands of obedience to the Bible. Rather, believers are set free from sin so that

they are able to live in gospel obedience to the Bible in the light of
Christ. Belief without obedience is as deadly as obedience without
belief because it isn't actually obedience. Only when obedience and
belief occur together do they contribute positively to human identity
and longevity. Only when obedience flowers into belief can belief reinforce or feed obedience. Obedience is necessary in order to believe
fully, completely and with assurance.

And because they are linked, a deficit in one can be countered by
an emphasis on the other. So, when people find themselves in disobedience they can correct the situation by focusing on recovering or
strengthening their belief, on the study and understanding of biblical
doctrine. And when people find themselves with doubts or inadequate
belief and understanding they can correct the situation by focusing on
obedience, on being obedient to what they already know and/or
believe.

Why does this work? Because in Christ belief and obedience are
fused together into one thing, and we call this one thing faithfulness.
Being faithful requires both belief and obedience, and failure or privation in either one weakens or destroys faithfulness.

In verse 7 Peter said that Jesus is precious to believers but a stumbling stone to unbelievers. The contrast between precious and stumbling is awkward in English. The two ideas don't fit neatly together.
The Greek word translated as *precious* (*timē*) literally means value or
valuable. The idea of precious suggests something that is loved, honored and cherished. On the other hand, the idea of stumbling or being
offended suggests, not valuelessness, as if stumbling is related to
apathy. Rather, stumbling suggests something hated, something painful, loathsome and despised. The one thing is embraced (precious), and
the other is rejected (stumbling stone). One is an attraction, the other
is a repulsion.

It is almost like the two poles of a magnet or a battery, a positive
and negative pole. One type of person tends toward one pole and another type of person tends toward the other. Verse 8 alludes to this
issue. "They stumble because they disobey the word, as they were
destined to do" (v. 8). This is very much a Romans 9 issue about election and predestination.

The Greek word (*tithēmi*) is translated in various places as
destined, appointed, doomed, set, put, laid and *bowed down*. The
word is contrasted with an idea of putting something in an active and
upright position, and therefore suggests something in a passive and
horizontal position. It is almost like the difference between being
awake and upright and being asleep and horizontal. The person who is
awake is destined to respond to things, and the person who is asleep is

destined not to respond. The person who is awake is aware of the trinitarian character of reality, of God. And the person who is asleep is not.

BREAKERS AND KEEPERS

Consequently, the difference between these two reactions to God,
God being precious versus being offended by God, is a contrast
between being awake and being asleep. It is not about individual persons, nor about individual performance. It's about the ground of performance. You can't perform if you are asleep.

So, if it is true that God does not respect persons, and both the Old
and New Testaments agree about this, then God's predestination, while
it is understood by individuals to give them direction and purpose in
life, is not directed at individuals as individuals by God. God doesn't
simply judge or predestine individuals on the basis of their individual
behaviors or character. That's not the way it works.

Rather, God primarily judges on the basis of type or group membership according to God's own definitions and assessment, not ours.
And the two groups or types by which God primarily judges are covenant keepers and covenant breakers. We might also suggest that those
who keep God's covenant are awake to God and those who don't are
asleep to God. Covenant keepers are one type and covenant breakers
are another type.

Covenant keepers are judged and predestined on the basis of
Christ's righteousness and propitiation on the cross, freely given and
imputed to sinners, not because of anything unique in them as persons
but because of God's grace. Such sinners then acknowledge God as
God, which is demonstrated by their belief and behavior. Christ is the
prototype of being awake to God that believers emulate, and they are
judged on the basis of the reality of the faithfulness of the prototype,
not on the basis of their conformity to it.

This quickly gets more complicated than we are used to thinking.
People are not judged or predestined on the basis of their individual
belief or behavior, nor on how well they emulate Christ, the prototype.
Rather, people are initially judged on the basis of God's justifying grace
alone. It is not that if our belief or behavior measures up to God's
expectations, He then justifies us. That's works-righteousness! Rather,
God judges people justified, and on the basis of His judgment alone,
are they then able to properly ground faithful belief and establish faithful behavior. Justification precedes faithfulness, faithfulness does not
precede justification.

From our human perspective the result of God's grace can be seen
in individual faithfulness and obedience, but only for those who are
awake to it. Those who are asleep to God don't notice it. It is not that

our individual faithfulness and obedience need to be perfect, but that our desire to please God needs to be genuine in God's eyes. And remember, God can accurately read our hearts. Faithfulness then manifests in the gifts of the Spirit and those gifts are then appreciated by the Spirit and by those led by the Spirit.

FAITH

Faith is a particular kind of presupposition, that of believing, of actively trusting that the trinitarian God is real. Thus, the predestining factor is that people who are awake to God operate on the basis of faith in the reality of God, and people who are asleep to God don't. People who believe in God assume God to be real, whereas people who don't believe in God assume God to be not real. Both are assumptions. The reality of God is not at the foundation of faithless thinking. The assumption of God's trinitarian reality is the deposit of faith, if I may use traditional language.

Being faithful requires the presupposition that God is actually real, and the presupposition that God is not real results in faithlessness. So, faith in God is the determining factor regarding the longevity of humanity as a whole or as a type because faith links people with God, where the lack of faith breaks the link. But because faithfulness requires the imitation of a prototype, it is not the faithfulness of the individuals that is the primary concern. It will not due for people to accurately imitate a faulty prototype. Thus, the primary concern is the integrity of the prototype.

The central determining factor regarding human longevity is the faithfulness, perfection and righteousness of the prototype into which the individuals are growing—Jesus Christ. God first judges on the basis of the prototype, not on the basis of individual conformity to the prototype. In Christ, God has introduced a new human model. The old model (Adam) is being phased out, and will soon be out of production entirely. Faith, then, leads people to grow into God's blessings and longevity and the absence of faith leads people to fall into God's curses, into death and destruction.

So, race, blood, family, gender and job mean nothing to God, nor to Christian identity, because God doesn't care about these personal characteristics with regard to salvation. This is what it means to say that God is not a respecter of persons. Paul wrote to the Galatians that "there is neither Jew nor Greek, there is neither slave nor free, there is no male and female, for you are all one in Christ Jesus" (Galatians 3:28). And to the Colossians, Paul wrote that "there is not Greek and Jew, circumcised and uncircumcised, barbarian, Scythian, slave, free; but Christ is all, and in all" (Colossians 3:11). None of our personal characteristics or distinctives play any role in salvation. The only thing that determines our justification by God is the role that Christ plays in our lives. What matters is whether we are awake to God as Trinity in reality.

Is Christ your prototype? Are you awake or not? If you can answer affirmatively, you are destined to salvation, if not you are destined to damnation. No matter how we answer—and yes or no, awake or asleep, are the only choices available—we are all children of destiny. If you are awake, sit up, take nourishment, and prepare for the day of the Lord. If you are asleep, you won't be able to hear me. This argument will be meaningless nonsense to you.

11. OXYMORON

But you are a chosen race, a royal priesthood, a holy nation, a
people for his own possession, that you may proclaim the
excellencies of him who called you out of darkness into his
marvelous light. Once you were not a people, but now you are
God's people; once you had not received mercy, but now you
have received mercy.   —1 *Peter 2:9-10 (ESV)*

The idea that Christians are a chosen race is both interesting and dangerous, particularly because race has been such a contentious issue for so many centuries. And because Christianity is a matter of grace, not race. So this issue is problematic. Why, then, does Peter mention a special race? Is this really what he means?

Since Peter linked two words, let's consider the phrase "chosen race." We'll start with the idea of being chosen. In the Greek the word is *eklektos*. It is the same word used in 1 Peter 1:2: "Elect according to the foreknowledge of God" (*Authorized Version*), but in this verse the *Authorized Version* translates verse 9, "But ye are a chosen generation." The idea of being elect and being chosen are identical.

We might ask who does the electing or the choosing, but neither of these verses answer that question. That's why I mentioned in a previous chapter that it could mean having been chosen or elected by God, or having been chosen and elected as officers of the church, which would mean having been chosen or elected by God as well, but through a human agency. Nonetheless, the word puts these verses in the middle of the long-standing debate about election. It is enough to simply call our attention to this as a possible context.

Was Peter aware of the debate about election? Absolutely! The Jews have been criticized about their understanding of being God's elect or chosen people for long time. It didn't set any better with Old Testament people than it did with New Testament people.

Moving on, we look next at the word *race, genos* in the Greek. It literally means kin—family. So, sometimes it is translated as *kind, kindred, nation, stock* or *generation*. Because the *Authorized Version* renders the word as *generation*, it also may be a reference to regeneration, to being born again, since Peter has been emphasizing that idea quite a bit. We might think of regeneration as being born in Christ, as a reference to the family or kin of God. Peter was suggesting that those who are regenerate in Christ are a new race, a new kind or species, a new nation, a new people, a regeneration of humanity. God is creating a new people in Christ, which has been one of Peter's most fundamental and consistent messages. So, this idea is a good fit for the context.

Again, we must clarify exactly who this chosen generation is. Peter used the word *humeis*, which is translated as *you* or *ye*. It is the irregular plural of you, and doesn't refer to a particular person but to a particular group—the church. Nor does it refer to a particular generation in history, not those who were alive when Jesus walked the earth, nor to those who were alive when Jerusalem fell.

Rather, it is a reference to the ongoing regeneration of a new kind of people in Christ. It refers to the church. And it refers to the church in the plural, as a whole, which is important because of its trinitarian implications. God has chosen the wholeness of regenerate people on earth, a new Adam, a people who are born again in Christ. These are God's elect.

Kingly Priests

The next phrase, a *royal priesthood*, is of special importance. The Greek means exactly this, so there aren't any translation problems or special linguistic insights. However, as we compare what we know about the Bible and the various jurisdictions that are implied by the words *royal* and *priesthood*, we find an allusion to the people of Jesus Christ and to the special function that they are to play in the world. The allusion to royalty suggests the jurisdiction of civil government, and the allusion to priesthood suggests the jurisdiction of church government.

It was John Calvin who brought the idea of the threefold office of Christ into prominence.[33] It was then picked up by most of the subsequent Reformed churches, and adopted by most Lutherans as well. The threefold office presents Jesus Christ as prophet, priest, and king, who in his saving work fulfilled all these anointed offices of the Old Testament.[34]

33 Calvin, John, *Institutes of the Christian Religion*, Book 2, Ch. 15, public domain.
34 Muller, Richard A. *Dictionary of Latin and Greek Theological Terms* (Baker Book

So, Peter's allusion to the church as a royal priesthood suggests that the Christians, who compose the regenerate body of Christ, have a role to play in civil government as Christians. This is a very divisive and disputed idea.[35] I'm not going to do much with it here, other than call it to our attention and provide a quick overview of its history.

From the time of Constantine forward the Roman Catholic Church (the only church in existence for the first thousand years of Christianity) battled against the various European kings over the issue of the role of Jesus Christ and His church in the larger society. It is my understanding that this issue is also at the heart of the issue regarding the *filioque*, the basis of the primary dispute between the Roman and Orthodox churches which led to their separation in A.D.1054.

The *filioque* is an ongoing dispute about whether the Holy Spirit proceeds from the Father alone or from the Father and the Son. At its root, it is about the role of the church in society, whether that role is limited to the church or whether it touches upon civil government. If it proceeds from the Father alone, it is conceived of as heavenly or spiritual, and pertains only to the church. If it proceeds from the Father and the Son, it is conceived of as both heavenly and earthly, and pertains to church and civil realms.

I'm not going to expand this argument here, but simply note that Peter suggests here that the church does have a role to play among royals as well as among priests. This role does not eliminate the separation between the jurisdictions of church and state, but suggests the idea of cooperation at various points, and that Jesus taught a kind of sphere sovereignty under the God of the Bible.

PRIESTLY KINGS

And just in case we missed the importance of this idea that Christ and His church have a role to play in both church and state, Peter repeated the idea with different words in the very next phrase: "a holy nation" (v. 9). It's the same oxymoron, the same conflation of ideas that mix church and state. This idea has been hotly disputed because of the failure to adequately understand the doctrine and role of the Trinity as I have been discussing here and elsewhere.[36]

The way to understand the biblical argument that Christ has fulfilled and therefore occupies the threefold offices of human society—

House, 1985), p. 197.

35 For instance: North, Gary. *Political Polytheism: The Myth of Pluralism*, Institute for Christian Economics, 1989.

36 I have presented this trinitarian perspective in *Arsy Varsy—Reclaiming the Gospel in First Corinthians* (2008), *Varsy Arsy—Proclaiming the Gospel in Second Corinthians* (2009), *Colossians—Christos Singularis* (2010) and *Rock Mountain Creed—Jesus' Sermon on the Mount* (2011), Pilgrim Platform, Marietta, Ohio.

prophet, priest and king—while maintaining the important biblical separation between these offices requires the understanding that God's trinitarian character implies that God has created a trinitarian world inhabited by trinitarian people who have been created in God's image.

For those who have eyes to see, the whole of life and reality fit together under God and in Christ. And conversely, apart from God or apart from Jesus Christ, life and reality cannot be whole or complete (or perfect). The harmony and cooperation in the Godhead provides a model for harmony and cooperation on earth. Because there is harmony and cooperation in the Trinity there can be harmony and cooperation in the world among Christ's people because they have similar characters. The emphasis is on Christ's people because acknowledging and understanding the Trinity, understanding our role in Christ and Christ's role in the wholeness of reality, are essential to the process.[37]

PECULIAR PEOPLE

The next phrase that Peter used to describe this group is even more unusual. He called them "a people for his own possession" (v. 9), or as the *Authorized Version* translated it, "a peculiar people." There is no better verse in Scripture to illustrate the trinitarian character of God's people. The Greek sense of these two words suggests an oxymoron, a particular universal or something individually corporate. It is a amalgamation of the one and the many, which suggests a trinitarian character because the doctrine of the Trinity provides the only philosophical solution to explain the existence of both particulars and universals.[38]

In the Greek, the word *peculiar* (*peripoiēsis*) suggests ownership, and the English definition of *peculiar* suggests the characteristic of individuality. A peculiar thing is uniquely individual. It is a one-of-a-kind thing. The contrast created by putting these two words together, *peculiar* (*peripoiēsis*) and *people* (*laos*), suggests a unique group or a population that is made up of a new, different or unique kind of individual, a new typological model (Christ, not Adam). And that this group or these individuals are owned or somehow belong to Another, to God. Ownership by God implies that God is involved in their identity.

TRINITARIAN PEOPLE

The difficulty with understanding the reality of the church as something trinitarian is at least twofold: First, we are not used to talking in these terms so it may sound odd and engender unnecessary sus-

---

37 This is important, see footnote 31, p. 97.
38 See footnote 36.

picion. But secondly, we are very used to assuming the trinitarian character of reality in the sense that no one has difficulty understanding the relationship between an individual and a group. Actually, everyone is quite used to dealing with trinitarian realities, but not of thinking of them as being related to the biblical doctrine of the Trinity.

Because the traditional explanation of the Trinity is philosophical, complex and has been erroneously characterized in other worldly terms that have their origin in Greek philosophy rather than the Bible, we are used to simply dismissing the idea of the Trinity from our ordinary thinking and experience, ignoring it because it is mysterious and people have come to think that it is generally unknowable. I'm suggesting that the traditional understanding of the Trinity is not wrong, but inadequate to its reality. I'm arguing that the Trinity is neither completely mysterious nor unknowable, but is actually quite ordinary inasmuch as God is involved in ordinary life.

For instance, church membership is a very common idea, and it is not usually associated with the doctrine of the Trinity. However, the idea of membership is central to the idea of the trinitarian character of the Godhead, of the world in which we live, and of the mystery of human identity in Christ (1 Corinthians 12:12).[39]

Group membership is everywhere in the world. When Adam was naming the animals, he was grouping them. Members of a group can act individually by performing various activities on behalf of the group. Assuming that the acting individuals have official leadership or representational roles and requisite authority, they can act on behalf of the group without losing their individual identity, or their corporate role and identity. In addition, groups exist over time in the sense that various individuals can come and go without destroying the integrity or definition of a group. All of this is very trinitarian.

So, why is this important? Peter said that the reason for the existence of this chosen generation, this royal priesthood, this holy nation, this peculiar people is to reveal a truth (1 Peter 1:5, 7, 13) and proclaim a message (v. 9). The Greek word is *exaggellō*, which is made up of two words *ek* (out of) and *aggellō* (angel or messenger). The church, who are the people of Jesus Christ, is to be a representative messenger for God.

And there are two aspects to this message. One is spoken and one is embodied. There is a verbal component to the message and a life component. Christians are to speak a message, and to live a message. Both the lips and the lives of Christians are to announce something

---

39 This idea is treated extensively in Arsy Varsy—*Reclaiming the Gospel in First Corinthians*, by Phillip A. Ross, Pilgrim Platform, 2008.

about God—His trinitarian character and the involvement of that character in their own lives as individuals and as a group, as a whole.

EXCELLENCE

And what is the message? What are Christians to proclaim? Peter said that the purpose for the existence of this chosen generation, this royal priesthood, this holy nation, this peculiar people is to proclaim "the excellencies of him who called you out of darkness into his marvelous light" (v. 9). The purpose is to reveal God in Christ, to show the world the new life or regeneration of Jesus Christ in the individual lives of Christians and in the corporate character and unity of the church. The purpose is to proclaim by word and by life or demonstration how Christ has changed His people and how they are to relate to one another in Christ.

The Bible was "written so that you may believe that Jesus is the Christ, the Son of God, and that by believing you may have life in his name" (John 20:31). The fact that Jesus is the Son of God is a trinitarian fact. His Messiahship provides the universal prototype, model or example for the manifestation of Christ in our lives, individually and corporately. Father, Son and Holy Spirit are mediated to humanity through Jesus Christ. To believe in Jesus Christ is to practice the prototype, to imitate the Original, to presuppose the preeminence of God in every area of life.

The *English Standard Version* reads that we are to proclaim Christ's *excellencies* (*aretē*). The *Geneva Bible* translated the word as *virtues*. The *Authorized Version* translated it as *praises*. The Greek word literally means *manliness, valor* and *excellence*, all of which point to the perfection of the prototype—Christ.

And what exactly has this prototype done? He has called us individually and corporately out of darkness and into His marvelous light. This *calling* (*kaleō*) is not an invitation but a command, a declaration. When a light is turned on in a dark room, the darkness is not invited to receive the light. The darkness has no choice in the face of light but to disappear. The light simply reveals the contents of the room. Darkness is nothing (no thing), and light simply reveals this fact. In the darkness we are free to imagine, we are even bound to our imaginations. But in the light we are free from our imaginations about what is in the darkness. If someone is in the room and a light comes on, he or she can decide to remain in the light or leave. He or she might pretend that the light isn't on, but that doesn't change the fact that it is on. He or she might be blind, but their blindness does not effect the reality of the light.

The first thing that people see when light comes into their darkness is the mess they have made of their lives. The absence of light is a huge handicap. It is like being blind, and no one in their right mind wants to be blind. When light comes into our darkness, and we see who we are, who we have been and what we have been doing, when we see the mess we have been making in the dark, it is only normal that we feel embarrassed and guilty. That embarrassment and guilt can make people react with anger and lash out at the light that exposed the mess. It is also normal to want to fix the problem. We want to clean up the mess and get things straightened out. But because we have known nothing but darkness, we don't know how things are supposed to be in the light.

Therefore, we need help. We need a model, a prototype, to show us how we are supposed to live in the light. And apart from such a model or a prototype, we have no idea because we have only known darkness. The role and advantage that Jesus Christ provides is that He knows only light because in Him there is no darkness (1 John 1:5). Because He is the source of light, everywhere He goes He brings light. That's why we need to follow Him where He goes, and why we must take Him with us wherever we go.

FULL OF WONDER

But His light is not mere light. Peter described it as *wonderful* (*thaumastos*) light. The Greek word means that which produces wonder. The root of the word means to look closely at or examine. Thus, the light not only causes us to wonder, to be curious and look closely at things, but it is the very means by which we may do so. The light allows us to see, and apart from the light we cannot see.

We usually don't pay any attention to the source of light. We just look at the things that are illuminated by the light. No one goes into a room, turns on the light and stares at the light bulb. The purpose of the light is to illuminate other things, to show their existence and true character. At the same time, we must not fail to consider the source of the light because the kind of light makes a big difference. Things look differently in green or blue light than they do in white or yellow light. And black light is completely different.

So, the kind of light we have is important because it colors everything we see. Whatever we see, we see in the character of the available light. And the purpose of the light is revelatory. The purpose is to reveal what is in the room. And the contents of the room are seen in the character of the available light. For purposes of analogy and illustration, we say that Christ is the light (John 1:9).

God's purpose is to reveal His world to us. And when we see God's world in its truest reality, in the light of Christ, we see it as His world because He created it and He sustains it. Everything in the world can be best known, most fully known, in relationship to God, who created everything and whose light allows us to see things in their clearest, fullest and most revealing way.

Revelation

Similarly, the purpose of God in Christ is to reveal the trinitarian character of the Godhead and of His world in time, in history. Time is inherent in the fullness of the Godhead in the sense that time is essential for the relationship of father and son. A father/son relationship can only exist in time, and it necessarily implies time. Theologians sometimes talk about God as the eternal breaking into the temporal, or the infinite breaking into the finite, or the ultimate breaking into the proximate. We can also speak of God as the corporate breaking into the individual, or the universal breaking into the particular. All of these descriptions are from God's point of view.

To speak of the same thing from our human perspective we can talk about the temporal being flooded with the eternal, the boundaries of the finite being broken down by the infinite, the proximate being blurred by the ultimate, the individual being born again into the corporate, or the particular redefined by the universal. But however we talk about it, we see that by regeneration God expands our individual identities to include some aspect of His corporate identity—at least part of it. The light of Christ reveals that we are in Christ, and Christ is in us. We are mutually in one another, and not only Christ and me, but Christ and us—the church, the body of Christ. Membership is at the heart of who we are in Christ, and who we are in Christ has become our identity in the world, as well.

Becoming A People

Once we were not a people, said Peter quoting Hosea 1:9-10, but now we are God's people (v. 10). The difference between not being a people and being a people is a matter of corporate identity, of becoming an identifiable group. And at the center of that corporate identity is God because we belong to God and are the people of God. Ownership is always a function of identity. Because Jesus Christ fulfilled the role of Israel's Messiah by satisfying the law of God and fulfilling the offices of prophet, priest and king, Peter was saying that Christ's fulfillment of these things has also fulfilled or completed the identity of the God whose people we are.

When rightful ownership of something lost is restored neither the character of the owner nor the character of the thing that was lost changes. And yet the relationship between them changes in the sense that a wholeness of identity is shared between them. The lost thing and the owner belong together. Their proper relationship is then restored.

In the Old Testament the Jews understood themselves to be God's people. God introduced both trinitarianism and monotheism to the world through the Jews, who were the people of the God of the Bible. But God is not merely monotheistic. He is that! But not that alone. With the advent and fulfillment of Jesus Christ as God's Messiah we are able to see that Jesus Christ revealed a larger, more ultimate and universal truth about God—that God is trinitarian.

And furthermore, God's trinitarianism does not change His monotheism. He is both monotheistic and trinitarian at the same time, without mixing the natures of either. He is both individual and corporate, proximate and ultimate, finite and infinite, temporal and eternal—all at once, and without confusion.

This is at the very heart of the character of the Trinity, and because we are creatures of the trinitarian God who live in a world created by the trinitarian God everything in us and in our world has been created in the image of the trinitarian God. We are the trinitarian people of the trinitarian God, who is none other than Jesus Christ, the second Person of the Trinity. Thus, to be the people of God is to share and participate by way of membership in the trinitarian character of God in time, in history, in reality—in God's church, in the body of Christ. The restoration of God's people brings peace and wholeness to an otherwise restless and broken world.

We were without mercy, but now in Christ we become mercy-full. We were once without God's grace and compassion, but now in Christ we become grace-full and compassionate (passion-full). It is not simply a matter of God being gracious and merciful to us by inviting us into His house, into His wholeness. But it is a matter of God having actually changed our very character and identity as individuals, of course—but also as a people, as a group, as His church. It is as a group or in Christ's church that people find the sense of right or correct belonging and wholeness.

Changed

God's grace and mercy are not like a coin that He has given us to pay the entrance fee into His house. Rather, it is more like we have been dipped into a dye that has permanently changed the color of our skin to God's favorite color.[40] Or to change analogies, it is like being

---

40 For more on baptism and dyeing see *Trinitarian Baptism*, by Phillip A. Ross, Pilgrim

dipped into an acid bath that dissolves the barnacles of accumulated ungodliness that have attached themselves to us during our godless and lost stint on this sinful earth.

God cannot allow such barnacles (sin) in His house. So, He removes them. Actually, because we live in time, because we are a people and not simply individuals, a whole and not simply a collection of parts, and because God has brought us into our proper Father/Son relationship through regeneration by the power and presence of the Holy Spirit, the completion of the process of barnacle removal takes time. It takes time because we live in time. Nonetheless, the fact that it takes time does not in any way suggest or mean that God's acid dip will not in fact completely remove all of the barnacles. It only means that the completion of the process takes time. The final result is guaranteed from the beginning.

In Christ we have become something that apart from Christ we were not. Our identity has changed through incorporation into Christ (the body of the church). And while this identity change is not a character change, it causes a change in character as we increasingly live out our new identity in Christ in time. In Christ individuals become a people, a whole. In Christ those who had not received grace and mercy receive grace and mercy. People move from being in the class or group called *unredeemed* into the class or group called *redeemed*. In Christ people from every nation, race and tongue become one people as they are swept into the growing unity with the prototype of the New Adam, who is none other than Jesus Christ, our Lord and Savior.

Platform, Marietta, Ohio, forthcoming.

12. SUBORDINATE

Beloved, I urge you as sojourners and exiles to abstain from
the passions of the flesh, which wage war against your soul.
Keep your conduct among the Gentiles honorable, so that
when they speak against you as evildoers, they may see your
good deeds and glorify God on the day of visitation. Be subject
for the Lord's sake to every human institution, whether it be to
the emperor as supreme, or to governors as sent by him to
punish those who do evil and to praise those who do good. For
this is the will of God, that by doing good you should put to
silence the ignorance of foolish people.   —1 Peter 2:11-15 (ESV)

Peter reminded the saints that they were on the run, that they were not to think of themselves as being at home because they had left their homeland. They had no place in Jewish culture nor any place in the pagan cultures in which they now lived. They were to remember their pilgrim status at all times. They had fled Jerusalem because of the persecutions and impending destruction. Peter knew that these new Christians on the lamb would need to create a Christian culture that would be distinct from both the Jewish and pagan cultures of Rome or Greece, distinct from any culture that had ever existed on earth. Yet, it wasn't that they had to create this culture themselves, but that God was in the process of using them to create a new human culture, a new way of being human.

In this verse there was one foundational instruction that Peter focused on. They were "to abstain from the passions of the flesh" (v. 11). This is most commonly and correctly understood as abstinence from sexual immorality, not engaging sex outside of marriage. And yet, Peter insisted on more than the denial of the mere physicality of fornication or adultery because his guidance was not against the mere act of illicit sex, but was against the *desire* for it. They were not simply to avoid such behavior, but were to avoid the lust or passion (*epithumia*) for it. Peter begged them not to desire it, and to avoid any and all circumstances that would stimulate that desire. Christians are not to want it.

SEXUAL DESIRE

But why is God so concerned about sex and marriage? In the degradation of our world today we might be tempted to think that Peter was a bit over the top regarding his aversion to sexual expression or implication, that God Himself may be psychologically repressed.

But this would be wrong on two counts. First, neither God nor Peter is opposed to sex *per se*, but only to sex outside of biblical marriage, apart from God's covenant. Peter understood that God has drafted the passion of sexual desire to serve God's purpose. God intends that the desire for sex work toward the eradication of sin and evil and the establishment of purity, honesty and integrity among human beings.

Thus, the desire for sexual expression should lead people into the virtues of love, honor, purity, honesty and integrity, both personally and socially. And this is to be accomplished through the civilizing forces of biblical marriage, forces that produce maturity and responsibility in families. Out of that maturity and responsibility in and among families would then arise the biblical integrity and faithfulness that is responsible for social, scientific and economic development, which also depend upon honor, purity, honesty and integrity. Such progress, then, would raise communities out of poverty and subsistence level existence. The Lord was establishing a culture of maturity and responsibility upon the foundation of the ultimate trinitarian truth of God in Christ that would provide an eternal, stable and enduring point of reference for human definition and social morality.

Since the time of Adam's rejection of God in the Garden of Eden humanity has been adrift in a sea of sin and moral relativity. After the Fall, right and wrong, good and evil were no longer determined by God, but by human reason or self-justification under the influence of Satan. This is the basis of all paganism and false religions. How can I say that? Because of the definition of paganism. A pagan, according to the dictionary, is a person who does not acknowledge monotheism, who does not acknowledge the fact that there is only one God who actually exists. And the second definition points to people who are motivated by the desire for sensual pleasures. Note that the current definition of a pagan focuses on two things: 1) monotheism and 2) sexual desire. I didn't come up with this, it's in the dictionary. And it is in the dictionary today because it is in the Bible.

As Christians we find the dictionary definition lacking because of its focus on monotheism. As Christians we understand that the monotheistic God of the Bible is actually trinitarian, which then expands the definition of paganism to include both Judaism and Islam, the other monotheistic religions. These religions would not be pagan in the classical sense, but would be pagan from an orthodox Christian perspective because of their monotheism. As Christians we understand that pagans are people who do not acknowledge the Christian Trinity and/or who do not "abstain from the passions of the flesh" (v. 11). Consequently, the only people who are not pagan are faithful Christians. So, the word *pagan* functions for Christianity like the word *Gentile* in the Old Testament in the sense that it included everyone who is not Jewish.

SEXUAL MORALITY

This also begs the question: why is there a link between God and sex? What is that connection? And the answer is necessarily trinitarian in the sense that sex bridges the gap between (or establishes the connection between) father and son, an essential aspect of the Trinity. The most fundamental connection between fathers and sons is procreative. And the link between fathers and sons is a particular manifestation of the link between proximate and ultimate, particular and universal, individual and corporate and temporal and eternal—the one and the many. One father may have many sons.

Procreation issues out of the temporal unification of male and female that reproduces another person. Thus, each human individual is at the most fundamental level a union or amalgam of mother and father. An individual is at the genetic level a complex combination of the genetic uniqueness of the mother and the genetic uniqueness of the father. God at creation created a perfectly unique genetic sequence or human prototype (Adam). Later, God then intervened by removing part of Adam's genetic sequence (a rib) and grafted an antonymous (a kind of opposite) sequence onto it which became Eve, the human female prototype. Thus, Eve became a biologically antonymous being to Adam. Eve became inwardness to Adam's outwardness. She became the feminine to his masculine.

And the link or connection between them, between Adam and Eve, between masculinity and femininity, is God, the trinitarian Creator of everything. Even language itself reflects these differences. God as Trinity defines and enables both human individuality and human unity. The human kind (genus or species) was created in the image of God as the trinitarian prototype (Adam). God established the link or relationships between the male and the female of the human species, and God called that link, not sex but covenantal marriage. It is also important to note that the link is not merely biological (pertaining to sexual relations), but is also cultural and social (pertaining to social order, intention and purpose). And the cultural aspect of the marriage bond or link is necessarily covenantal. Marriage is a covenant that was established by God as a bridge between human sexuality, and the spiritual link between individuality and sociality.

Such are the biological, spiritual, covenantal, cultural and social aspects of human sexuality and marriage. This is why God insists that marriage and sex be handled in accordance with His instructions. All sexual expression apart from God's instructions is forbidden because it undermines the character of the Trinity and destroys the human emotional connection between promise making and promise keeping (between social order, individual intentionality and God's purpose).

In addition, note that all science, technology and economic development necessarily issue from and depend upon honesty, integrity and purity. Economic development needs these things in order to provide the consistency and orderliness of the world that is required for such development. That is to say that science and technology depend upon handling the truth of the reality in which we live with honesty and integrity. This simply means that the data of science must be handled with integrity and honesty in order for science and technology to function.

SOUL

Why is any of this important? Because the "passions of the flesh ... wage war against your soul" (v. 11). To understand what Peter means by this it is necessary to understand what the soul is. There are many different definitions and ideas about the soul. Some people say that it is the psyche or the spirit, others say that it is the rational element of human thinking, and others say that it is something eternal that survives death.

For our purposes we are going to agree with Scripture generally, that the soul is that which survives death and lives eternally. It is something common to all people in the sense that everyone is involved in soul stuff. And furthermore, the soul is the prize for which God and Satan are fighting. To side with God in this war is to end up in God's eternal heaven, and to side with Satan is to end up in Satan's eternal hell. Thus, both God and Satan at some level are engaged in a struggle for what we might call the sustainability of human culture in the sense that they are vying for souls to exist indefinitely in one place or another. God has one vision for human sustainability (eternal heaven) and Satan has another (eternal hell). God thinks that heaven is good and hell is evil, and Satan thinks that God has them reversed.

However, the difference between heaven and hell is not simply that one is good and the other is evil. Rather, God and Satan employ competing definitions of good and evil. What God calls good Satan calls evil and vice versa. So, both God and Satan are fighting for what they themselves define as good. Satan does not understand himself to be trying to institute evil, but is instituting what he mistakenly believes to be good.

It is not that good and evil are locked in an eternal struggle, but that the actual struggle is about the definitions of good and evil. It is quite literally a war of words and ideas. And words—language—issue(s) out of beliefs, out of faith and presuppositions about reality. The theater of this war is both philosophical and theological. It is a war of worldviews, of beliefs, of assumptions and cultures.

In verse 11 Peter suggests that the earthly theater of this war tends to focus on human flesh, on sex and other fleshly pleasures, not exclusively but substantially. The lust or passion for temporal satisfaction wars against the establishment of eternal security. Thus, the opposites of temporal/eternal, particular/universal, proximate/ultimate and individual/corporate are at war with each other philosophically and theologically. Here I am speaking of, not a literal war but a clash of philosophical opposition based on the logic of mutual exclusion, which teaches that one or the other can be true, but not both.

Only one or the other of these conflicting worldviews can be established as being ultimately true regarding the reality of human life. This is the classic, Western philosophical problem of the one and the many that was introduced by Plato and has stumped Western philosophy ever since.

However, the actuality of the Trinity and of the trinitarian character of human life provides for the philosophical reconciliation of these warring opposites without the destruction or denial of either the one or the many, neither the proximate or the ultimate. Only the Trinity allows for diversity within unity. Pantheism destroys (undermines) unity, and monotheism destroys (undermines) diversity. Only through the doctrine of the Trinity can this philosophical dilemma be satisfactorily reconciled, which means that only the Bible, understood and interpreted from the Christian trinitarian perspective, can reconcile them. The central philosophical and theological conflicts of human civilization, in which the world is currently embroiled, can only be reconciled by the reality of the trinitarian God of Christianity.[41]

---

41   This is a major theme in much of my writing, so I will not repeat this argument here.

OUTSIDERS

Verse 12 then throws us a curve because, while Peter has been talking about proper relations between believers, he now speaks of our behavior among Gentiles, among unbelievers—pagans. He said that our dealings with nonbelievers must be both honorable and honest. The Greek word (*kalos*) has a foot in each term. So, not only are Christians to treat other Christians with honor and honesty, but we are to treat everyone with honor and honesty.

And it is not up to us as individuals to define the term or to determine how we are to understand and manifest it. Rather, we are to look to and depend upon Scripture alone to provide definition and direction for our lives, our beliefs and behaviors. And the reason that we are to treat unbelievers with honesty and respect by keeping all of our thoughts and actions toward them above board and on the table for all to see is because it will encourage them to treat us the same way. Right?

Well, this is true, but it's not exactly what Peter said. He said that we must treat those who speak against us and do evil to us with honor and honesty so that they can clearly see that we return good for evil, that we are not caught up in the self-perpetuating cycle of anger and revenge. We must break that cycle by risking our own harm. That's the only way it can be broken. We can't model the way to break it unless the onus for revenge is squarely upon us, and we then refuse to engage it. We must look evil in the proverbial eye and say *no*! And our commitment must be both verbal and behavioral.

Unbelievers need to remember our good treatment of them when they call upon God to save them from some difficulty. People are all hardwired to call upon God to save them when they come face to face with a serious threat that they can do nothing about. On that day and in that circumstance God will use their memory of our faithfulness to either draw them into faithfulness themselves, or to explain to them why they are on the receiving end of damnation.

And if it weren't hard enough that believers have to treat unbelievers with honor and honesty, believers must also be willingly subject to every human institution of government, even though said institutions have no respect for God or His justice. Note that Peter tells believers to be subject to government even when the emperor thinks that he is supreme, even when he thinks that he is above God.[42]

---

42 Of course, there are times and circumstances when people must oppose their leaders, both civil and religious. But such opposition must not be done as individuals lest the result be anarchy. Rather, opposition must unfold biblically and within the biblically based institutions of society. The American Revolution properly understood, though not perfect, serves as an example if we consider the impetus and process, but not the result. See *The Bible and the American Revolution*, by John Winter, http://www.spi-

Evil cannot be defeated by opposing it with more evil. Violence is not the solution to violence. Rather, evil can only be defeated by being overwhelmed by the genuine goodness of God's grace and mercy enfleshed and practiced by God's people. We must not be drawn into fighting evil with evil, fear with fear, etc. We must simply stand our ground and meet everything that is thrown at us with grace and steadfastness to love our enemies, and to do good to those who do us harm.

We are to obey God and not man (Acts 5:29), particularly in the heat of battle. The difference is that the decision to disobey civil authorities is not for individual believers to make, but is to be made higher up the chain of authority so that the authority addressed (the civil authorities) are met with a comparable authority (church authorities or other civil authorities). It is incumbent to respect authority at all times because the very structure of truth and civilization depends upon maintaining the structures of authority.

Peter was here speaking of individual behaviors, which is indicated by his reference to sexual morality, to personal morality. But in Acts, Luke recorded a decision made by the apostles as the governing body of the church. "But Peter and the apostles answered, 'We must obey God rather than men'" (Acts 5:29). Christian civil disobedience must have the sanction of the church. It is not something that individuals can or should do apart from the authority of the church.

For instance, the legitimizing factor of the Civil Rights Movement of the 1960s in America came only as the churches got involved. That Movement gained legitimacy because of the involvement and authority of the Christian churches. And as that happened, the leaders of the civil government began to come on-board.

The phrase "for the Lord's sake" (v. 13) is composed of three Greek words that literally mean *through the Lord*. Thus, the phrase literally means that we are to be subject through the Lord to every human institution. The Lord is the means by which we are to be subject to human institutions, and that is also why it is important to involve the church whenever civil disobedience is contemplated. Individuals are not free to simply do whatever they want, or to oppose whatever civil policy they don't like. Rather, as individuals we must always act in obedience to an authority greater than ourselves—always.

GOVERNMENT

Verse 14 describes the primary function of civil government: "to punish those who do evil and to praise those who do good." The Greek does in fact mean both *punishment* and *praise*, but the general idea is that civil government is to discourage what is evil and to encourage what is good. And this naturally leads to the question of who determines what is good and what is evil? How are these things defined and determined? The question throws us back to Genesis, to Adam and Eve in the Garden, and to God's prohibition of the tree of the knowledge of good and evil (Genesis 2:17).

Again, we must note that such decisions are not to be made by individuals, but only by higher church authorities in consultation. And in this case, because of the nature of the concern and the ultimate categories that must be engaged to consider the question regarding good and evil, we must appeal to an ultimate authority. Because good and evil are ultimate categories, they must be addressed with ultimate authority. Because good and evil are extreme opposites on a continuum and cannot be defined by anything that is relative in character, we must appeal and yield to whatever authority has ultimate jurisdiction. In this case, the only authority that has such jurisdiction is God Himself and Jesus Christ by the implications of the Trinity and the specific direction in Matthew 28:18-20, etc.

But neither are we to engage in individual interpretation of Scripture. Peter will engage this concern in his next letter. In these verses Peter raised the question of doing God's will. He will further clarify it in his second letter. But because of various issues raised here, we will look ahead at how we can know the will of God in specific matters. He tells us how eternal concerns can have temporal application.

"And we have something more sure, the prophetic word, to which you will do well to pay attention as to a lamp shining in a dark place, until the day dawns and the morning star rises in your hearts, knowing this first of all, that no prophecy of Scripture comes from someone's own interpretation ('private interpretation' in the *Authorized Version). For no prophecy was ever produced by the will of man, but men spoke from God as they were carried along by the Holy Spirit" (2 Peter 1:19-21).*

We will treat this more fully when we come to it in 2 Peter. But for now let it suffice to note that human beings can know good and evil only on the basis of Scripture and can understand Scripture correctly, not on the basis of our own individual, intellectual efforts but on the basis of consultation with regenerate church elders who respect the authority of the church in the light of Christ and by the power and presence of the Holy Spirit. Again, we see the involvement of trinitarian categories for the determination of good and evil in practical ways that effect people in ordinary ways. Because Christianity is trinitarian God's eternal Word has temporal application.

Understanding and interpreting Scripture is not something that should be done in private, as an individual, but rather should be done as an elder and in a community context. Why? Because the effort to do so as an individual neglects and/or denies the trinitarian aspects of the church and the representational reality in which we live. Such neglect or denial then undermines truth itself. The effort to understand and/or interpret Scripture privately, individually, is itself a denial of the trinitarian character of Christianity and of reality.

So, if you are gifted and driven to study, understand and interpret Scripture, seek the office of elder in a local church as a way to develop, mature and authenticate your work. Seek to understand and interpret Scripture in the light of Christ and by the power of the Holy Spirit in consultation with other faithful believers.

GOD'S WILL

Peter continued, "For this is the will of God, that by doing good you should put to silence the ignorance of foolish people" (v. 15). When he said that *this* is the will of God, he meant that the will of God is what he has been talking about: to abstain from the passions of the flesh, to behave honorably among pagans, and to be subject to all legitimate human institutions.

The purpose of doing the will of God is to silence ignorance and foolishness (Psalm 63:11, Isaiah 52:15). The Greek word translated *ignorance (agnōsia)* suggests agnosticism, the doubt and denial of God. Thus, the way to answer agnostics and atheists is to simply do the will of God. The *foolishness (aphrōn)* that Peter had in mind includes by implication what we call feelings or emotional responses that conflict with sound judgment.

In our world today we find an abundance of these two religious expressions: 1) ignorance or agnosticism and 2) foolishness or sympathetic emotionality. Agnosticism is religious belief that is guided by doubt. And sympathetic spirituality (foolishness) is religious belief that is guided by emotionalism, particularly the emotionalism of sentimental fiction and patriotic propaganda. Indeed, doubt and pathos, driven by guilt and pity, dominate contemporary American culture and religion.

However, it is not that people can become faithful by doing the will of God, but rather that those who are faithful engage the will of God. Consequently, the simple effort to abstain from the passions of the flesh, to behave honorably among pagans, and to be subject to all legitimate human institutions, cannot bring about the faithfulness that is so needed today. Peter was not talking to pagans, but to faithful Christians. Thus, Peter was not suggesting that doing the will of God is a cure for paganism, but rather, doing the will of God provides a faithful witness to pagans about the truth of the gospel. And that witness will either bring pagans into the faith by the power and presence of the Holy Spirit or it will justify their rejection of God and all that God stands for.

Either way, God's will to separate the wheat and the tares at His harvest will be accomplished.

13. THREE-IN-ONE-IN-THREE

Live as people who are free, not using your freedom as a coverup for evil, but living as servants of God. Honor everyone. Love the brotherhood. Fear God. Honor the emperor. Servants, be subject to your masters with all respect, not only to the good and gentle but also to the unjust. For this is a gracious thing, when, mindful of God, one endures sorrows while suffering unjustly. For what credit is it if, when you sin and are beaten for it, you endure? But if when you do good and suffer for it you endure, this is a gracious thing in the sight of God. —1 Peter 2:16-20 (ESV)

What is freedom? Most people think that being free means that you can do whatever you want, that free people are not encumbered with restraints. And I suppose that if the world consisted of only one person then this might be true. But human beings are necessarily social, no one human being can exist alone (Genesis 2:18). So that kind of freedom does not apply to human beings. And when people attempt this kind of completely unrestrained freedom, they find that the unrestrained freedoms of one person impose various restraints upon others who also have unrestrained freedom, which then destroys the idea of completely unrestrained freedom.

For instance, if my freedom includes having whatever I want, and I want something that you have and you want to keep, and I take it from you, then your freedom to have whatever you want has been restricted by my freedom to have whatever I want. There are always social limitations to human freedom, which means that human freedom is always necessarily limited and restrained. In addition, the individual who is completely free is always necessarily self-bound because he is always limited by his own wants and desires. And more often than not, the more free people are, the more they think that they deserve everything they want simply because they are free. The more free people think they are, the more selfish they tend to become.

Such an idea of pure, unrestricted freedom is nonsense. Such an idea is not freedom at all, but is the very heart of depravity, sin and tyranny. The very definition of sin is slavery to one's self, slavery to one's own desires. Being a slave to sin means doing exactly what you want without any restraints. And that is exactly how many people understand freedom.

GOD'S FREEDOM

Now it's true that God Himself does have this kind of unrestrained freedom. Not even death can constrain God. God is completely unencumbered. He is directed by nothing but His own will, and to a great extent that is what makes Him God. God is not bound by any law, even His own. God is not bound by law because God's will defines law. Neither is God bound by the laws of nature. He can circumvent such law anytime He wants. We human beings call such circumvention *miracles*, but God only experiences and knows such things as "doing what He wills." That's what it means to be God. God serves no one except Himself. Fortunately, God is good.

However, God is also trinitarian, and this is very important because it makes a huge difference for God's behavior. The fact that God is trinitarian plays a central role in God's freedom, and in ours. There is no area of His life that is not effected by God's trinitarianism, nor any area of human life or living, either. God's trinitarian character means that God is both individual and corporate, one and three simultaneously and in such a way that no element of either His individuality or His corporality[43] are diminished in the slightest. Rather, both are enhanced and expanded. The trinitarian character of God both enhances and increases God's greatness in depth, breadth, weight and character. Indeed, there is nothing greater than God.

God's trinitarian character effects God's freedom in same way that it effects ours. The fact that God is three Persons yet one Person, and that God's central commitment is self-service means that each Person of the Godhead is in primary service to the other Persons of the Godhead. So, God's focus on self-service is actually a focus on service to others.

Granted that God's service is directed only toward Himself, but fortunately for us there is nothing in this universe that is not directly related to God. And this means that God's self-directed concern is a concern for the well-being of the universe as a whole. And because God

---

43 This is a reference, not simply to God's body, but to the body of Christ as Paul discussed the term in his letters to the Corinthians. See footnote 8, page 26.

is eternal His self-concern, his self-service, is the engine of a kind of perpetual motion machine, except that God is a Person not a machine. Thus, God is a perpetual motion or eternal Person, a Person who does not die, a Person without limits.

SERVANTS

"Live as people who are free, not using your freedom as a coverup for evil, but living as servants of God" (v. 16). Human freedom is always a function of service to God. There is no other freedom that is possible. All other supposed freedom is actually slavery to self and sin. Sin is the failure to acknowledge our proper relationship to God with obedience, praise, thanksgiving and joy. People are not free to do whatever they want, but are free only to the extent that they actually acknowledge and serve God and the interests of God, the God of the Bible, because He is the only God who actually exists. Only by serving God can people be free from sin.

And just as God's freedom is always manifest in service to His own corporate interests, so human freedom, because we are creatures of God's image, is always manifest in service to God and His corporate interests, as well. However, humanity is a creature of God, which means that God's interests always take precedence over those of humanity. The creature serves the Creator.

This is all well and good, but how does it actually work? How can freedom be manifest through service? Am I suggesting that the highest form of human freedom is slavery to God? And if so, how can that possibly be? How can freedom be manifest through slavery? Well, that is exactly what I am saying because that is exactly what Peter was saying. And it works out this way because of who God is and who we are in the image of God. People who are in Christ advance the freedom of God. The Trinity is both the foundation and the capstone of all freedom. Or we can say the same thing more warmly: God's love is both the foundation and the capstone of all freedom.

TRINITY

When God is understood to be purely monotheistic, freedom is turned into tyranny because God's self-concern is not other-directed but self-directed. And because God is self-directed God's people are self-directed, which means that people who believe in monotheism tend to promote tyranny. Unfortunately, this is the way that most people today understand God, particularly in the West because of the Judeo part of our Judeo-Christian heritage. Even most Christians have failed to sufficiently understand the doctrine of the Trinity and its implications, and because of this, they have always understood God as monotheistic, in spite of the emphasis on the doctrine of the Trinity. The Trinity, while acknowledged, has yet to be widely understood, explained or appreciated.

Don't get me wrong, Christians have unconsciously made use of the doctrine of the Trinity, as has nearly everyone in the contemporary world. But people have not connected the realities of the doctrine of the Trinity with the presuppositions that sustain their own lives, and much less have people consciously acknowledged that these presuppositions originate and are upheld by the only real God of the Bible Himself. Nor have they begun to engage the implications of the doctrine of the Trinity. And failing to make these connections, people fail to be grateful and thankful to God.

Apart from actual, personal regeneration in Christ, the doctrine of monotheism cannot provide for the subtleties and distinctions of the true identity of the Godhead as Trinity, much less the implications for those who have been created in His image. To genuinely understand the Trinity, it must be more than an idea. It must become an actual, personal reality through the power and presence of the Holy Spirit.[44]

Monotheism apart from Christ is totalitarian. Monotheism as a theology is spiritually mono- or uni-dimensional. The God who created the world and humanity is trinitarian (Genesis 1:26) or tri-dimensional. Adam's Fall then produced polytheism or the relativity of ultimate truth evidenced by the fact that Adam and Eve became "like gods" (Genesis 3:22).

God then set in motion His plan to reveal and establish His trinitarianism by sending His Son to manifest in human flesh and atone for our sins in history (Genesis 3:15, the *protoevangelium*). However, because the world is a complex reality God needed to provide the necessary context in history (the Old Testament) for us to understand the doctrine of the Trinity. From the time of the Fall forward humanity has been engaged in a religious struggle (Genesis 3:15) between polytheism (or philosophical relativity) and monotheism (or unitarianism), until Christ came to establish the reality of the Trinity and adjudicate between these embattled worldviews.

THE LONG WAR

However, in the midst of this struggle God continued to provide for the progressive revelation of the Trinity in and through history. So, we find evidence of the Trinity throughout the Old Testament.[45] And though this evidence is spotty and difficult to discern, it is sufficient in

44 See footnote 31, page 97.
45 For instance: Richard Deem. www.godandscience.org/apologetics/triunity.html, Reasons To Believe, P.O. Box 5978, Pasadena, CA 91117. Or Natan, Yoel. *The Jewish Trinity*, Aventine Press, San Diego, California, 2003.

the most significant places where God (Yahweh) reveals Himself. Furthermore, because all of humanity is opposed to God because of Adam's sin, the Trinity (as an idea and even more as a reality) is opposed by both polytheists and monotheists. The Bible itself is the story of this opposition.

It is significant that the Jewish God, Yahweh, went on to assert His trinitarianism against the backdrop of ancient pagan mythology (the fruit of Adam's Fall). God's revelation as the monotheistic unity was so powerful that it sometimes obscured the reality of God's trinitarian character even among the Jews themselves. And repeatedly the Jews fell into the idolatry of monotheism so that God sent prophets to reconvict Israel of the ancient truth of God's Trinity and its consequent social morality. The articulation of this story required such clarification that God sent His Son to establish the reality of the second Person of the Trinity in the flesh.

God's decree and promise to reveal and establish Himself through His Son (Messiah) in human history shifted into second gear with the advent of Jesus Christ. Peter was fueling this effort.

Of course, it must be noted that Christianity is also monotheistic and cannot abide any other gods either (1 Timothy 2.5). But Christianity's monotheism is trinitarian. The God of Christianity is textured. He is interwoven and intertwined in reality like strands that make up a textile fabric (Ecclesiastes 4:12). He is complex rather than simple. The oneness of God is threesome in the same way that God's threesomeness is unified.

And yet, God is not polytheistic. God is not omnidimensional, but is tridimensional—Father, Son and Holy Spirit. Neither is God unidimensional. Each Person of the Godhead provides a dimension, a cluster of interrelated but independent attributes and properties—Persons actually—of the triune God that are reflected in God's creation and in His creatures, particularly in humanity. Why is humanity a special creation? Because humanity has been given the gift of the Word—language, a form of historical communication.

LANGUAGE & REALITY

Human language is not simply an immediate person to person communication but is also shared widely and is preserved from age to age in writing. This makes it more than simply person to person. It is that, but more than that. This gift allows humanity to communicate with itself over time and throughout history, much like God communicates with Himself in the Trinity. The gift of language that God has given humanity is necessarily historical because it creates a timeline, a story or perspective that grows over time because we learn from the past, from history. Other creatures communicate, but none have this gift of language and history as people have it. Language allows humanity to be developmentally progressive, to accumulate knowledge.

Father, Son and Holy Spirit are in consultative unity. They actually consult with One Another and have differing perspectives, different characters and attributes, but not differing opinions. Thus, they are in fundamental unity at all significant points and over time. Their differences do not meld into one thing or one perspective, but retain their uniqueness without losing their unity.

Humanity has a similar kind of consultative unity that is linguistic, reflexive and historical. And because humanity has been created in God's trinitarian image and participates in God through regeneration, humanity also has access to God's reflexivity through God's communication to humanity through the Bible. We have access to God through His Word in Scripture. It is real access to the only real God.

Thus, human communication is not simply person-to-person, but is also God-to-person, God-to-people, people-to-person, person-to-people and people-to-God. It is this complex, spiritual dimension of being human in all its fullness that comes alive in Christ through regeneration and provides access to God's thoughts and perspective found in the Bible. This spiritual communication with God is neither completely mysterious nor mystical. It is, rather, complex, multidimensional and historical.

It is through access to written history that we can see God's activity in the life of humanity, in His-story. And born again believers can see it in a way that provides growth and maturity for humanity, both individually and corporately. Humanity is a multifaceted single yet complex entity that exists in time. Our lives in time, in history, exist only on the foundation of God's existence in time. Humanity in Christ is able to exist in time because we participate in God who has created the world in time. We have been created in God's image and recreated in Christ's likeness.

FORBEARANCE

Consequently, human freedom is a reflection of God's freedom. But because humanity is a lesser who participates in the corporate being of a Greater (the trinitarian God) through God's covenant and in Christ, and who is like God only in mirror dimly (1 Corinthians 13:12), our freedom is not manifest in self-concern like God's freedom is. Rather, human freedom is manifest in concern for God because God's concern is for the greater good. Just as the Persons of the Trinity enjoy self-governed cooperative freedom, so human freedom can only be self-governed and cooperative as well. Our participation in God through spiritual regeneration also provides for God's participation in us. Regeneration brings people into a new identity that is corporately inclusive of God in Christ through the Holy Spirit. That identity in Christ, then, provides the presuppositional foundation for biblical faithfulness.

All I have said here is that real human freedom issues from the power to act or speak or think without externally imposed restraints. Real freedom is not freedom without restraint, but is responsible freedom, freedom to live in response to God in Christ through the Holy Spirit. It is not the freedom to do whatever we want to do, but is the freedom to do what God wants us to do.

There is no other freedom than this. And just as this freedom looks like slavery to those who don't personally know it, who don't personally know Jesus Christ as Lord and Savior, so what looks like freedom to do whatever you want is actually slavery to sin, slavery to the selfishness of the small-minded self-concern of individualism.

Only by the trinitarian God in Christ are the narrowminded limitations of monotheism broken open to reveal the deeper texture of the Godhead, of His creatures and His creation. Only in the Trinity can the reality that people live in but deny by their beliefs and behaviors be explained and understood at the deepest levels. Only through the Trinity can sustainable peace be made manifest in this world. How?

ACTIVE OBEDIENCE

"Honor everyone. Love the brotherhood. Fear God. Honor the emperor" (v. 17). It would be difficult to be more specific or practical, or more controversial. By *honor* (*timaō*) Peter means that we are to value people, to hold people in esteem. He didn't say to love everyone, probably because love that applies equally to everyone is both unreal and unsustainable. By definition love is a special relationship, so when it is equally applied to everyone it loses its specialness. The effort to love everyone dilutes love of its most important characteristic, its specialness, its uniqueness.

But in spite of love's uniqueness, other people can be valued and honored. Other people can be respected across the board, without distinction. If this single admonition could be obeyed, it would put an end to war because it is impossible to kill those we respect and value.

When Peter said to "Love the brotherhood " (v. 17), he meant other Christians, brothers and sisters in Christ. While the Greek word (*adelphotēs*) simply means *brotherhood*, it refers to the church, the body of Christ. By saying this Peter noted an important difference between Christians and other people.

We are to honor and tolerate unbelievers, but we are to love other believers. There is to be a special relationship between believers that is not shared among unbelievers. That special relationship is to be un-qualified *love* (*agapaō*), selfless love that serves others without expect-ing anything in return. This is important because it notes that Christians are to serve God above all else.

Christians are not to be in service to other people who do not honor or value God. Toward such people Christians are to be respect-ful, kind, courteous, etc., but we are not to entertain or promote their godless values or concerns. The admonition to love the *brotherhood* puts a focal point on our love and keeps it from dissipating in an ill-founded attempt to apply it promiscuously to everyone.

Next, Peter admonished believers to "Fear God" (v. 17). The Greek word is *phobeō* and is the root of the English word *phobia*. A phobia is an anxiety disorder characterized by extreme and irrational fear. Obvi-ously, there are two problems with this definition from a Christian per-spective.

First, Peter's recommendation to have a God phobia does not con-stitute a disorder. It is not a dis-order but if anything is a pre-order in the sense that "The fear of the LORD is the beginning of wisdom" (Psalm 111:10, etc.) and wisdom is the foundation of all order. A God phobia is the foundation of all real order, personal orderliness and social order.

Second, a God phobia is not an irrational fear, but is the most rational of all fears. "For who in the skies can be compared to the LORD? Who among the heavenly beings is like the LORD, a God greatly to be feared in the council of the holy ones, and awesome above all who are around him?" (Psalm 89:6-7).

Dictionaries today are not written by believers. Rather, dictionary writers today quite intentionally make every effort to write God out of all definitions because they do not believe in Him. This is not some grand conspiracy on their part, but is the simple result of decades of godless indoctrination in our schools, colleges and universities. Unbe-lievers simply believe God to be a false idea, and have no intention of writing what they believe to be falsehoods into the dictionary. Non-etheless, God says that the fear of Himself is the presupposition that is required for true wisdom.

THE EMPEROR

Peter's last instruction in this verse is more difficult. "Honor the emperor" (v. 17). It is simply an extension of Peter's first instruction to "Honor everyone." But here he means that we must not forget that the injunction to honor everyone includes those involved in civil govern-ment, and particularly the one person who is often the most difficult to honor—the king, the emperor, the president, the person at the highest level of civil authority.

It is particularly irritating that Peter did not qualify this to mean some particular king or emperor, or some particular kind of civil leader. People usually add their own qualifiers by thinking that Peter meant to say that we should honor only those kings who are themselves honorable, trustworthy, upright, etc.—or at least those who do not engage in intentional deceit, murder, hypocrisy or denial of God in Christ. But that is not what he said. Peter simply made no qualifications. "Honor the emperor" (v. 17). By implication this means to honor all who have authority.

Peter's instructions here can be boiled down to three things: 1) honor all people, 2) love all Christians, and 3) fear God. Honor is the basis for civility and manners, which are to be extended to all people. There is no excuse for incivility, discourtesy or being rude to anyone, ever—period. Neither is there any excuse for failing to abide in genuine Christian unity. The fact that Peter used the word *brotherhood* simply reflects the fact that he believed in household authority and biblical headship.

He most certainly did not mean that we should exclude women from our love, from our selfless service. Indeed, special biblical provisions are made for women who are outside of any household or headship relationships. So, rather than excluding women, Christianity has made a special effort to include them.

Finally, then, the admonition to fear God is by implication and application an admonition to be biblically wise. Upon the fear of God rests the love of God, and upon the love of God rests the understanding of God, the standing under God.

Just in case people might miss the intention of Peter's admonition, he provided this clarification: "Servants, be subject to your masters with all respect, not only to the good and gentle but also to the unjust" (v. 18). Back in verse 16 Peter said that Christians are to live as servants or slaves (*doulos*) of God and in verse 18 he addressed those servants again, but here they were Christians. He intentionally used the Greek form of the word for servants (*oiketēs*) that indicates the lowest level of household servants in order to include all servants, and to suggest the proper attitude of humility and meekness that all of God's people are to have. All of God's people are to regard themselves as the lowest of the lowly, to be on par with the most despised of the despised.

And again, to insure that we understand how far our service is to extend before we revolt in disgust against those who hate and despise God, he added that we are to "respect, not only ... the good and gentle but also ... the unjust" (v. 18).

REVOLUTION

Indeed, Christians are to avoid violent revolutions because violent revolutions destroy and distort history. Revolutions destroy homes, businesses, commerce and learning—the accumulations of history. Rather than fighting revolutions, Christians are to educate themselves in the ways of the world (but not in the values of the world), so that God can bring about change from within.

Christians are to work for peaceful change and social progress that provides sustainable economic development because God knows that sustainable economic development is a blessing that is reserved for the obedient and faithful (Deuteronomy 28:1-15), for those who love, appreciate, value, honor, respect and acknowledge God in Christ as the truest and finest revelation of the only actual and trinitarian God of Scripture.

Peter then tells us why he has recommended this strategy for both sanctification and evangelism. It is interesting that Peter's plan serves both of these efforts with one unified focus for belief and behavior. "For this is a gracious thing, when, mindful of God, one endures sorrows while suffering unjustly" (v. 19).

Here he means that grace is best communicated or revealed by graciousness under fire. But, of course, he doesn't mean merely composure under fire, but *godly* composure under fire. The being "under fire" part should be a cause to take refuge in God, to turn to prayer and praise for perseverance and preservation. And the faithful will have no hesitation in doing so. They will not only depend upon faith and prayer, which will serve their own sanctification, their growth in grace and maturity, but will also serve as primary instruments for evangelism as those who are near the saints witness them clinging to God in Christ through prayer and praise.

Emphasizing the fact that God's grace is particularly suited for this kind of service regarding both sanctification and evangelism, Peter notes, "For what credit is it if, when you sin and are beaten for it, you endure? But if when you do good and suffer for it you endure, this is a gracious thing in the sight of God" (v. 20). Enduring a just beating for actual sin that has been committed communicates justice, not grace.

Those who suffer the ravages of sin with poise and endurance simply receive what they justly deserve as sons of Adam. Justice, while a characteristic of the biblical God that does actually serve the maintenance of social order, has nothing to do with God's grace. And because of this, justice does not provide an attractive beacon of light for unbelievers. Indeed, the execution of justice is simply not attractive. There is nothing noteworthy in it. People get what they deserve. So what?

Unjust Suffering

Rather, God's grace is revealed by unjust suffering and the preservation of faithfulness in the face of fury. That's exactly what Jesus did on the cross. And that is why His story continues to attract masses of people. First and foremost, such suffering and faithfulness in circumstances unworthy of such a response runs so much against the grain of human behavior that it demands our attention. It forces a question, unlike the exercise of justice, which simply provides an answer. People usually have no questions about just punishment for sin. It is sometimes called comeuppance. But grace and poise in the face of personal harm, kindness in the face of abuse, love in response to hate, these things foist questions upon all who observe them.

Why doesn't he fight back? Why is he being treated that way? Whence comes his strength, his grace, his poise?

This is the question that God most wants to plant in the hearts of unbelievers because it is the question that only Christ can answer. This question cannot be driven into people, like a stake into the heart. It cannot be planted in anyone's mind, except by the power of God. This is the question whose answer is the grace of God alone. Causing this question to well up in the hearts of people is the goal of all evangelism.

Evangelism should not attempt to provide an answer to various spiritual questions that people have. Evangelism should not be an attempt to answer questions for unbelievers because unbelievers cannot understand the correct answers until they become believers. So, it is worse than a waste of time to try to answer the questions of unbelievers because it puts the answers in the wrong context. Evangelism is not an answer.

It is a question. The heart of the gospel is best communicated by the astonishment of seeing grace under fire. The best method of evangelism answers a question that cannot be asked, that cannot even be conceived by unbelievers until they are shocked out of their unbelief.

Real evangelism travels best across bridges of astonishment and amazement that the engrained and ingrown patterns of anger and revenge that so dominate all human experience are broken by nothing discernible to the naked eye. The astonishment of seeing good returned for evil plants a question that can only be answered by the love of Jesus Christ. The amazement of seeing unjust suffering borne and engaged with gentle kindness and forgiveness burns a searing question into those who see it. That is the question that the Lord is looking for. Ask that question and you will be saved.

14. CALLED TO SUFFER

For to this you have been called, because Christ also suffered
for you, leaving you an example, so that you might follow in
his steps.   —*1 Peter 2:21 (ESV)*

One of the most curious things about Scripture is found in its understanding and practice of freedom. The fact that Christ has set us free is indisputable (Galatians 5:1). But this freedom in Christ is not any kind of freedom that the world can recognize because it is freedom from the godless assumptions that guide the values of worldly commitment. While the world generally understands freedom to be permission to do whatever a person wants, that is most emphatically not what Peter or Paul or Christ Himself understood or taught. The biblical idea of freedom has always been understood to be freedom *from* sin, whereas the world's idea of freedom is freedom to do what the Bible calls sin.

Many people try to limit the worldly idea of human freedom by suggesting that one person's freedom must not impose upon or harm anyone else. And that is a good and noble idea that works to a point, but fails to address the sin issue. Sin imposes itself upon sinners and harms them in the process. Of course, people must not impose their own personal desires or preferences upon others, as if other people must conform to their likes and dislikes, or even to their understanding of right and wrong. Those who say that we must not be judgmental are, of course, right when one person's behavior restricts or opposes another person's behavior.

But the hard, cold fact of reality is that whatever common sense or commonly held values of the past have been superseded by the teaching of multiculturalism over the past fifty or so years, if such commonality ever actually existed. There are no universally held social values in America today. And I suspect that there never have been any, not really.

What America is or what it is supposed to be has always been hotly disputed. America has never actually agreed unanimously about anything. Thinking that these United States (or humanity) can be united by anything other than Jesus Christ is a delusion of biblical proportion.

LIKE-MINDED

Of late, the advances in communication technologies have facilitated the formation of affinity groups between like-minded people who share common interests. One of the results of this is that people today more often choose to communicate with those who are like themselves and to eschew communication with people who believe or behave differently than themselves. This has contributed to the development of cultural fragmentation that causes communities to be increasingly less geographically defined.

Various cultural groupings of society are enabled by the technological advances in personal communication. People increasingly choose to converse with their friends, with people who share their own views and values. And because time is limited with our busy, contemporary lifestyles, people also increasingly choose *not* to interact with people who are different from themselves.

The result of this development is that people have become used to communicating with their friends, with people who share their basic views, values and assumptions. But this accommodation simultaneously makes people less able to communicate with those who do not share such things. This inability arises partly because of the time and difficulty involved with addressing different assumptions and presuppositions about reality. Getting people to recognize their own assumptions is actually quite difficult. It is much easier to interact with people who share our basic assumptions, our likes and dislikes, than it is to interact with people who do not understand or share our views and values.

Conversation with this latter group is increasingly difficult because it requires a more rigorous presentation, explanation and defense of the unspoken assumptions and beliefs that people hold because those assumptions and beliefs are not shared. And, not being shared, they are called into question in a thousand ways by people who do not share them. Again, interacting meaningfully with people who do not share our most fundamental values and assumptions about the world is actually quite difficult. Misunderstanding is common and attempts at clarification and explanation require increased sensitivity and complexity. Often the more clear one person is about something he is trying to explain, the more the other person is able to disagree with the various particulars.

COMMUNICATION TECHNOLOGY

The bottom line is that the rise of communication technologies that facilitate affinity groups also tend to cause an erosion of social tolerance because of the lack of common presuppositions that support common views and values. Modern communication technologies provide a foundation of subtext[46] for social commerce that is increasingly unshared and uncommon. The more the communication technologies advance (or proliferate), the more raw information there is to communicate and comprehend from an increasing number of disparate perspectives. And because time is limited and individual interests differ, the less people share a common subtext, a social or cultural perspective or story. It is the common story or perspective that provides shared values and presuppositions that facilitate trusted communication precisely because of that sharing.

Think of television as social communication. In the early years a few stations broadcast common programming to everyone. But over time more stations came on line. Then cable broadcasting was developed, and now we have the Internet. Each new medium increases the amount of raw information being disseminated. And the more information that is pumped out, the less information is held in common. There is not enough time in a day to hear all of the various perspectives being broadcast. And with less common information being absorbed by individuals, communication between individuals becomes increasingly difficult.

Thus, the current situation is that the subtext of social communication that is supposed to establish the common context for meaning and understanding no longer issues from a common story, experience or perspective. The result is that it is increasingly difficult for people to express themselves because they need to clarify the differing subtexts and contexts to those who do not share them. Subtext and context are usually assumed, and it is difficult for people to articulate them adequately and intelligently to those who are habituated to a different historical era or a different subtext and/or context. Making our assumptions and presuppositions clear to people who do not share them is quite difficult.

All of this is to say that it appears that advances in communication technologies seem to be fragmenting common sense or common experience or commonly held assumptions. People who share a common culture share a common story and experience about who they are, who they have been in the past, and who they are coming to be in the future. Individuals find personal meaning and belonging in such stor-

---

46 Subtext: The unvoiced thoughts, feelings, meanings, and motives that underlie the words that are actually spoken.

ies, in shared cultural stories and perspectives. And the more people there are who share a common story or common culture, the greater the sense of personal meaning and belonging people tend to have, the more unity and cohesion a society enjoys. Conversely, the fewer people who share a common story or common culture, the less personal meaning and belonging people tend to have. That is, in a multicultural society people are more likely to run across others who do not share their views, values and assumptions, and communication with those people becomes increasingly difficult.

The opposite view is also compelling. That view suggests that modern communication and affinity groups provide for deeper social bonding precisely because the group members come with a boatload of already shared views, values and assumptions. Because they don't have to take time establishing these things, they can begin with them and take their relationships all the deeper because of it. And the result is that the groups are much more homogenous and harmonious when there are common subtexts and contexts—which is true, which also means that the smaller subgroups in a multicultural society are becoming more closely bonded. Such bonding is good, except that it also contributes to the calcification of subgroups and their potential entrenchment in isolation from others.

The rub comes when people in such groups need to communicate with those outside of their group. It is at this point that the difficulties come to the fore. We could say that affinity groups cause the subgroups of a society to become all the more firm. And that firmness poses a potential problem with regard to the larger elements of social unity and cohesion.

His Story

Peter acknowledged that Christ had come to call people into the greatest story the world has ever heard. The story of the incarnation of God in Christ is the entire human story (history). The whole story (the wholeness of human history) is required in order to reveal God's trinitarian character and the truth of the world that God created.

This relates to the argument about communication above because Peter said that Christ was calling all of humanity, that Jesus Christ is the prototype for a renewed humanity, that the biblical story of Jesus Christ is the universal story of humanity. Thus, the biblical Christian story is the most fundamental and foundational common story of humanity. The story of Jesus Christ can only be rightly understood when it is understood to apply to all people, to humanity as a whole, and to the whole of human history.

This is not an argument for Universalism because, while Christ applies to all of humanity, He doesn't apply in the same way to all of humanity. This is not an argument that all people will eventually be saved. Rather it is the argument that the only reason that some people go to hell is that Jesus Christ has jurisdiction of all humanity (Matthew 28:18). Thus, God's judgment through Jesus Christ has created a kind of human watershed in history. Christ's judgment causes some people to go one way and others to go the other way, but it affects all humanity.

When Peter said "for this" (v. 21) he was pointing to everything that he had said so far in his letter. And Jesus most certainly intended that God's calling into covenant renewal was a call to all of humanity. At Jesus' birth the angel assured the Shepherds, "Fear not, for behold, I bring you good news of great joy that will be for all the people" (Luke 2:10, see also John 3:35, 6:37, 6:39, 12:32, 13:3, 17:21, etc.).

There is great confusion about who Jesus actually called to covenant renewal because, on the one hand, everyone has been included in Christ's call, but on the other hand, everyone does not exhibit covenant faithfulness. Many people mistakenly think that because all are called but all do not respond positively, God's sovereignty is called into question. The error that gives rise to this question is an error about the character and extent of God's covenant.

While Christ's call is universal, not everyone is treated the same by God. Believers are received by God differently than unbelievers. The fact that God's covenant applies to all humanity is evidenced by the fact that those who will not be conformed to faithfulness in Christ will be damned. The fact that ultimate punishment will ensue is a consequence of covenant disobedience. The punishment ensues because the covenant is in effect for the disobedient.

So, we can clear up the confusion by asking, *Will everyone who has ever lived be ultimately saved?* And the biblical answer is emphatically *no!* But will all people who are at some future point in history alive at the same time ever know and experience the joy of covenant obedience and blessing? Here the biblical answer is *yes*, but only in the fullness of time in the kingdom of heaven. The salvation of humanity is God's ultimate intention. Jesus came to inaugurate the kingdom of God on earth, and in the fullness of time it will be complete.

All this means is that the culture of biblical Christianity has been planted in this world by Jesus Christ and will grow until it covers the whole earth, until at long last every *living* person believes. But that's a long range vision and goal. For now the wheat and the tares are growing together, which means that the world is growing both better and worse at the same time.

A Change of Master

Now that we know the extent of Christ's call, Peter reminds us of what we have been called to—the suffering of faithfulness. We have been called from slavery-to-sin to slavery-to-Christ. Our servant status has not been changed, but who we serve has been changed. Paul reminded the Romans: "But thanks be to God, that you who were once slaves of sin have become obedient from the heart to the standard of teaching to which you were committed, and, having been set free from sin, have become slaves of righteousness" (Romans 6:17-18). And that righteousness is not our own, but Christ's because there is no other.

We must understand that mere obedience to God's law does not result in righteousness because the revelation of God's law apart from Christ falls short of the revelation of God's trinitarian reality. By God's design, the law cannot be fulfilled apart from Christ. The rigidity of monotheistic obedience is not sufficient because love is more than mere obedience. The singular focus of monotheistic theology is not sufficient to reveal the depth and breadth of God's trinitarian reality. Salvation is the fruit of God's love for us, not the reward of our love for Him. When God loves His people He loves Himself because He loves the power and presence of His Holy Spirit that manifests in His people through the regeneration of His people.

The Gift

The Holy Spirit is the gift of grace that God gives, and anyone who does not personally yet know the Holy Spirit, anyone who has not yet been regenerated by the Holy Spirit, does not yet possess the gift of grace—or rather, is not yet possessed by the gift of grace. God's grace has already been freely given to all humanity through Jesus Christ, who alone bore that gift to the cross for the propitiation of sin. There is nothing anyone needs to do or can do to acquire this gift for themselves because it is not a gift that has been given *to* any individual in particular.

Rather, it is a gift that has been given *through* Christ's people in general. It was not simply given *to* us as individuals because God is not a respecter of persons or individuals, but is given *through* His church as the redeemed community of God in Christ. It is not a gift *for* us, but is a gift *through* us. It has been given to us so that we may give it to others. It is not ours to keep, but is ours to give away. Keeping the gift kills it, but passing it forward brings it to life. And while people cannot pass on what they do not actually possess, Christians can pass on to others the graceful mercy that was given to and through Jesus Christ.

The Holy Spirit is not mine or yours, but belongs to Christ's church, and potentially to everyone through regeneration—but only according to God's will. God Himself is the engine of salvation, not us and our decisions. The purpose of receiving God's grace is the sharing of God's grace. Those who try to keep the gift for themselves are spiritual misers, whereas those who pass the gift forward are spiritual stewards. Like the parable of the talents (Matthew 25:14-30) we are to invest God's grace and mercy in others. We are to give it away, to invest it in order to grow it. That's what Jesus did for His disciples, and He is our prototype, our model.

TRUST

Being faithful means trusting Christ. And trusting Christ means giving trust to others. It means not distrusting others. And this is the point at which Christian suffering comes into play because a lot of people are untrustworthy. A lot of people will abuse the trust you give them and take advantage of you. They will take what you have and abandon you when you need help.

Why are people untrustworthy? Because they themselves do not trust others. Because they do not pass the gift of trust forward. They doubt the trustworthiness of others because they themselves have abused the trust that has been given to them. They know themselves to be untrustworthy and extend that untrustworthiness to others. They lead with doubt rather than trust. They presuppose that other people are unworthy of trust, often because they themselves have had their trust broken by others. People lie to others because people have lied to them. Because people have been hurt by the lies of others, they protect themselves by not submitting to the vulnerability that is required when trust is extended to others.

People think that doubt provides a kind of protection against the pain of broken trust. *Once burned twice shy*, says the old aphorism. However, Jesus Christ teaches that the old aphorisms of the world are superstitious nonsense, particularly this one. Doubt does not provide any protection at all against the pain of broken trust. In fact, it amplifies it by creating more doubt and distrust in the world, which then brings more pain and heartache because the failure to trust results in the failure of trust.

Jesus' solution to the problem of broken trust is to refocus the source of the trust. It is most certainly true that people are untrustworthy and unrighteous. Paul reminded the Romans that "all have sinned and fall short of the glory of God" (Romans 3:23). Indeed, no one is righteous or trustworthy in- and of-themselves. So, our trust ought not to be placed in unrighteous, unworthy people. People are not to be trusted. And that's a fact! This is a lesson that is well-taught in the world. Much pain and suffering are caused by misplaced trust.

Jesus' solution to this problem was to trust God in all things by being the Person who modeled a life of complete, utter and unmitigated trustworthiness. He simply trusted God, trusted that God's Word was completely true and lived on that basis. But doing so required Him to extend trust to others, to trust that God was leading and guiding Him in all things. God insists that His people trust one another. Did this mean that Jesus was vulnerable? Yes. Many people, who turned out to be unbelievers, took advantage of Him, and they still do. Did Jesus suffer pain and difficulty because of the trust that He extended to others? Absolutely.

He trusted Himself to God in the midst of the society in which He lived, and that society abused and abandoned Him. He was abandoned by His own religious culture and was then also abandoned by the civil state—Rome. He was tried and convicted by a pack of lies and the distortion of truth. But He submitted to all of the world's abuse and authorities in order to demonstrate obedience to God's authority. He trusted and submitted His life to the Jews (church) who betrayed Him, and to the Romans (state) who crucified Him.

And by His submission He demonstrated a better way, a way that has forever changed the world for the better. Christianity is not the cause of the problems in the Western world—war, pollution, graft, greed and corruption. Rather, it is the failure of Christianity that is the cause of the problems in the Western world. Western civilization began in faithfulness to Jesus Christ, but over time the population of the faithless has exceeded the population of the faithful. As trust in the vision or revelation of Christ has diminished in the larger society, the structures of Western civilization have weakened. It's funny how the vision of God's ultimate trustworthiness seems to hold human culture together—but it does! You can believe it or not, but you cannot escape the consequences of your choice.

Christ has called all humanity to trust God, and to extend that trust to others as the replacement for doubting God and extending that doubt to others. Like begets like, so doubt begets more doubt, and trustworthiness begets more trustworthiness.

CREDIBILITY

Do you realize that the recent financial crisis has been a crisis of trust? Trust is required for debt and credit. Trust and its companions, truth and integrity, are essential to economic viability. They also provide the foundation of science and technology. Money, science and technology grow out of truth, trustworthiness and integrity.[47]

47 I will return again and again to this observation, which is supported by Rodney
Stark's book, *The Victory of Reason: How Christianity Led to Freedom, Capitalism,*

"For to this you have been called, because Christ also suffered for you, leaving you an example, so that you might follow in his steps" (v. 21). This translation is awful because it suggests that following Christ is a mere possibility. Peter was not hoping that Christians *might* follow Jesus. Rather, he was pointing to the road that Christians *must necessarily* follow. A better translation would be "leaving you an example to follow in his steps."

It was not sufficient for Peter to suggest the general direction that Christians must go, nor to specify the particular road to take. Peter found it necessary to instruct Christians to follow in Jesus' precise footsteps. It is more like crossing a mine field where our feet must go exactly where His feet went.

But at the same time, don't think that Peter was recommending that we all go out and get ourselves crucified. We are not to play the historical role that Jesus played. We have our own roles to play. Nonetheless, we are to engage life with the same kind of trust that Jesus had. To use Jesus as a model for our lives does not mean building an exact, machine manufactured replica. It means using the same principles, the same Spirit, expressing the same kind of love and devotion to the same God that Jesus knew and loved, but doing so in the context of our own individual lives, our own cultures and histories.

We are to follow Christ's love, patience and service to God. We are to learn from Christ's life, not blindly copy it. Paul taught the same thing in Romans 8:29: "For those whom he foreknew he also predestined to be conformed to the image of his Son, in order that he might be the firstborn among many brothers." Paul taught that all of God's children are foreordained to conform to the image of Christ because He was the first-born among many brethren. Christ, the body of Christ, is the prototype for a new humanity. As Christ suffered and died, so we will also suffer and die. And yet, suffering is not the point. It is not simply pain and death that makes people Christian. Rather, suffering is simply part of the process of turning a culture of doubt into a culture of trust. It is a stepping stone to something better.

Peter will remind his readers in the next chapter that "it is better to suffer for doing good, if that should be God's will, than for doing evil" (1 Peter 3:17). And Paul taught the Thessalonians: "See that no one repays anyone evil for evil, but always seek to do good to one another and to everyone. Rejoice always, pray without ceasing, give thanks in all circumstances; for this is the will of God in Christ Jesus for you. Do not

---

and Western Success, Random House, 2005, and others. Capitalism, science and technology are intimately related to the development of truth, integrity and social cooperation in a world that is stable, consistent and rational. Each and all of these things are both the basis of and the fruit of the Christian biblical worldview that has been in the process of coming to light since Christ's birth.

quench the Spirit. Do not despise prophecies, but test everything; hold fast to what is good. Abstain from every form of evil" (1 Thessalonians 5:15-22). That's our model. These are the precise footsteps we are to follow in.

May the Lord give you the common sense to receive by grace God's own trust in His Son to accomplish His will, and the desire and ability to pass that trust forward to others.

15. Following Jesus

He committed no sin, neither was deceit found in his mouth.
When he was reviled, he did not revile in return; when he
suffered, he did not threaten, but continued entrusting himself
to him who judges justly. He himself bore our sins in his body
on the tree, that we might die to sin and live to righteousness.
By his wounds you have been healed. For you were straying
like sheep, but have now returned to the Shepherd and Over-
seer of your souls.   —*1 Peter 2:22-25 (ESV)*

A t verse 22 Peter further describes the model that Jesus set for
His followers. Christians are to imitate Jesus in some very
specific ways. Because Jesus "committed no sin, neither was
deceit found in his mouth" (v. 22), Christians are to avoid sin and deceit,
as well. But this will not be as easy as we might first suspect. We are
sinners from birth, so how are we to avoid sin. That's like asking a fish
to avoid water, or a leopard to avoid having spots (Jeremiah 13:23). We
are all born into sin. And if this isn't bad enough, we are also to avoid
deceit, which means that we cannot fudge on the command to avoid sin.

The demand to avoid both sin and deceit forces us to depend on the
only actual remedy that there is for sin—the forgiveness of Jesus Christ.
To deny sin or to try to apply any other remedy is a matter of deceit,
either fooling ourselves or others about the extent and tenacity of sin.
So, here we see that Peter's first concern pertains to sin and its remedy.
And the failure of people to take this first step of the journey of following Jesus means that any other steps that people might try to take will
fail inasmuch as the sin issue has not been not dealt with.

Peter continued, "When he was reviled, he did not revile in return;
when he suffered, he did not threaten, but continued entrusting himself
to him who judges justly" (v. 23). Following suit, we are not to revile or
threaten others and to trust ourselves to the ultimate Judge. In short,

we are to be Christlike. We are to be willing to suffer for doing good. It's not that suffering itself is good, it's not. Rather, we are to do what is good and right according to God's wisdom not our own. And if that brings difficulties, suffering or persecution, then so be it. We are to persist in being who Christ has called us to be. And the more people who do this, the less suffering there will be in the world. And conversely, the fewer people who do it, the more suffering there will be.

SURROGATE

In case people did not understand the mechanics of salvation, Peter added that Christ was the surrogate for human sin in that He received the punishment for sin that was not His (v. 24). All sin necessarily incurs a consequence or punishment. So, Jesus Christ stepped into the seat of punishment on the cross, sheltering His people from the blow of just punishment for sin by taking it Himself. He threw Himself on the grenade of punishment, so to speak, in order to contain the damage inflicted by the punishment. He took the punishment for the sin of humanity upon Himself.

Because God is an infinitely perfect being with an infinitely perfect sense of justice, there is no sin so slight that does not require punishment. And because God is trinitarian in character, sin against God manifests in trinitarian ways. Because God is three dimensional, sin against God manifests in three dimensions. Sin manifests physically—length, width and height, and temporally—past, present and future. This is only to say that sin manifests in particular and individual ways, in universal and corporate ways, and in spiritual and abstract ways.

But Christ's surrogacy is not just about sin and punishment. Peter also said, "By his wounds you have been healed" (v. 24). People in the church are used to hearing this, but if the truth be told it is a very odd idea. How can wounds inflicted on someone else heal me? Why would they have anything at all to do with me? The doctrine of substitutionary atonement is itself a uniquely trinitarian idea. The only sense that can be made of it is trinitarian sense. How so?

Christ's suffering was very real, but it also represents the suffering of humanity for sin. The point is that His representation of our suffering is also very real, even though it is an abstract concept. Was Christ healed from His wounds and suffering? Scripture doesn't clearly say so, but we know that His resurrection returned Him to His preincarnate state, which was a condition of perfection in God. So, yes, He was ultimately healed. And His healing, his resurrection, represents the ultimate healing and resurrection of humanity, as well. And here His representation is also very real. This kind of representation works because of the trinitarian character of reality.

REPRESENTATION

To learn more about this, explore what is called *Representation Theory*, a branch of mathematics and philosophy that studies abstract structures by representing their various elements with other forms. The idea is that what happens in the representation also happens in reality. The representation actually corresponds to the reality. That's how math and science work. Squiggles on a page that represent abstract ideas actually have an applied effect in the world (off the page, if you prefer). Thinking and consciousness are dependent upon these kinds of representations and their integrity and veracity in the so-called physical world.

Thus, Christ's wounds heal me because the reality of substitutionary atonement heals the breach between humanity and God. Christ as the Second Adam, or the federal and representative Head of humanity mediates between God and humanity. There is an actual correspondence between Jesus Christ and His people that is uniquely trinitarian.

Of course, *my* wounds won't heal *you*. So, there must be another principle or element of representation involved. Christ represents me and you, everyone really. He is the Federal Head of humanity. That's the role He plays in history. He is the new prototype for human beings. Adam was the first Federal Head and prototype and Christ is the second or the new Federal Head and prototype. Christ represents humanity to God and at the same time Christ represents God to humanity. He has a uniquely mediating representative role and position.

So, those individuals whom He represents are those for whom He paid or satisfied the price of human sin. The price He paid, death on the cross, was sufficient for all humanity through all time. Jesus Christ actually represents humanity, but I don't. So, His wounds heal me, but my wounds don't heal anyone. Or do they?

If I am willing to suffer for Christ and be engaged in doing His will, then I am extending His will and His character on earth and providing a witness to Him that extends and embodies His reach in this world. And because His wounds, His propitiation on the cross, actually heals, then my active participation in Christ extends His healing ministry, as does yours. So, my suffering for Christ, when it arises because I hold fast in obedience to God's will, serves as a beacon or witness to the ultimate and real salvation provided by Jesus Christ. Thus, it actually does extend Christ's ministry in the world.

HEALING THE BREACH

You may wonder why people need healing. They seem okay and life is good. So, what's the problem? Peter answered this question. "For you were straying like sheep, but have now returned to the Shepherd and Overseer of your souls" (v. 25). Peter alluded to Isaiah 53:6. It has long been known that people are like sheep. Christ also referred to it and Peter simply acknowledged it here.

Sheep are dumb. They are narrowminded, shortsighted, hunger-guided and easily get blindsided. Their vision is poor, their legs are weak, they are top heavy and easily set topsy-turvy. They have no defenses and many enemies. Their only protection is to stay with the flock because it increases the chances that they will not be the one that gets eaten. Yet, they easily stray from the flock because they have poor eyesight and a short attention span. They have no discernment and will eat what makes them sick because of it. And their wool grows so much that it is a danger to them, so they have to be sheered regularly for their own well-being.

This is the way that God sees people. People are worse than sheep because of sin. People are narrowminded, short-sighted, hunger-guided, head-strong, stubborn sinners with poor insight, weak resolve, few defenses and little discernment. But our central problem, our major wound is sin. We can no more not be sinners than sheep can not be stupid. We are all born into it. Peter's comparison of people with sheep is not flattery. Apart from a shepherd, sheep would likely disap-pear as a species because they couldn't survive. They are born in seri-ous need of domestication.

But, said Peter, you have returned to the Shepherd, which is an allusion to Christ as the Great Shepherd (Hebrews 13:20). The Christi-ans to whom Peter was writing were flocking under the care of Christ the Shepherd. Straying is a matter of going one's own way, and it pro-vides an interesting contrast. Remember that Peter was writing to the "elect exiles of the dispersion in Pontus, Galatia, Cappadocia, Asia, and Bithynia" (1 Peter 1:1). So, these were Christians who had been scat-tered across the known world, fleeing persecution and impending destruction of Jerusalem. In one way they were scattered, wandering and straying, but in another way they were being gathered and protec-ted by their Great Shepherd into distant folds (John 10:16).

OVERSIGHT

How is Jesus like a shepherd? He is the Overseer (*episkopos*) of our souls. The Greek word is composed of two other words. One (*epi*) means to superimpose or to lay one image on top of another. And the other (*skopos*) can mean to peer about, or to conceal, or to watch (like a guard, sentry, or scout). Or it can mean a goal, depending on the con-text. Here it means *one who watches over or guards*. The *Authorized Version* translated the word as *Bishop*.

And what does the Overseer watch or guard? Our souls, that vital force which animates the body and shows itself in breathing. There is a connection between breath and brain function because the brain needs a constant supply of oxygen to function. Brain damage begins about three minutes after receiving no oxygen. Though this is a modern insight, it is a human truth and might provide a link between the idea of the soul and the mind or the rational mind. Surely the ancients had some experience with oxygen privation and brain damage. The Overseer watches and guards our souls, our minds, our lives and vitality.

Christ, the Great Overseer, protects the principle of our animation because He is the creator, preserver and redeemer of life and of human vitality. Contrary to popular opinion, the Overseer is not there to curtail creativity or to be a proverbial wet blanket to the enjoyment of human life. Not at all! Christ is the very source of creativity and even of life itself. Rather, it is actually the world that is dominated by a crippled spirit that stifles creativity by keeping people chained to sin.

What passes for creativity in this world is nothing more than sin in drag, sin dressed to conceal its true nature—pretending to be something that it is not. What God calls sin, sinners call normal human behavior. Just as God is opposed to sin, sin is opposed to God. God's intention is to maximize human enjoyment of life for all people, to maximize what we may call sustainable human freedom, both socially and individually.

To be free means to not be under either compulsion or restraint. So, freedom is always an expression of free will. However, biblical freedom takes into consideration the trinitarian character of human beings and of the world in which we actually live. Christians know that only God has absolute free will. The rest of us are encumbered with limitations of time, talent, treasure, accessibility, opportunity and interest. I suppose that interest should be listed first because it is always the first limitation that is engaged. If we aren't interested, the other things don't matter. Only after interest kicks in do we look to our available time, abilities, opportunities and resources regarding our decisions to do as we will.

The Overseer of our souls provides both positive and negative services. He encourages, inspires and interests us in various things in order to lead us toward some things or activities. And he discourages, frightens and bores us with others in order to lead us away from some things and activities. Ideally we are attracted to what is good, wholesome and healthy and not interested in or discouraged from what is bad and harmful for us.

The Overseer is the gatekeeper of human freedom because freedom is about the life and health of the soul. Where sin leads to the death of the soul, the Overseer preserves the life of the soul. And while this verse does not explicitly say so, it suggests that Christ is the shepherd and overseer. This means that Christ is both directly and indirectly involved through His representative authorities.

THICK DARKNESS

Peter had been a Jew all of his life and was familiar with the Jewish Bible. He knew that Ezekiel foretold that God Himself would be the shepherd of His people. "For thus says the Lord GOD: Behold, I, I myself will search for my sheep and will seek them out. As a shepherd seeks out his flock when he is among his sheep that have been scattered, so will I seek out my sheep, and I will rescue them from all places where they have been scattered on a day of clouds and thick darkness" (Ezekiel 34:11-12).

But Peter had been changed by God and was now a Christian. So, he was not merely quoting the Old Testament, but was alluding to the divinity of Christ and to the Trinity of the Godhead precisely because he was alluding Christ's role as the Great Shepherd of His people. He was alluding to the fulfillment of Ezekiel's prophecy regarding Jesus Christ. Note that Ezekiel said that God would be *among His sheep* on the day of cataclysm (Peter's reference to clouds and darkness), and that God Himself would not only rescue them but would be among them. This was an allusion to Christ's humanity. Peter was talking about the fulfillment of this promise.

Peter was writing during the decade prior to the destruction of Jerusalem in A.D. 70. He witnessed the Roman military buildup and anticipated that Rome would use the army that was at the door. Peter was acknowledging that the destruction of war was at hand.

Since the death of Jesus, Christians and their sovereign God had been increasingly blamed for various problems and difficulties experienced in the Roman Empire. That blame was undoubtedly a consequence of the Christian proclamation that God is sovereign. And since God is sovereign, He must be responsible for the collapse of the Jerusalem economy and its attendant problems. Christian persecution had been increasing as more Christians left Jerusalem to escape the coming difficulties. Their departure in turn contributed to the economic problems of Jerusalem as they took their money and businesses with them. An economic depression set in.

Peter was writing to Christians who had left Jerusalem and who were in the process of gathering together in foreign lands with other Christians who had left. And this explains his reference to their having returned to the Shepherd and Overseer. They were gathering together in foreign folds (John 10:16) in the name of Jesus Christ. Peter was

writing to Christians who were in various stages of leaving Jerusalem
and establishing homes and communities elsewhere.

Indeed, the establishment of Christianity among the Gentiles was a
kind of exodus in that people of all kinds and nationalities were leaving
Jerusalem under the spiritual leadership of Jesus Christ, the new
Moses. Though Christians were scattering from Jerusalem, they were
gathering in Christ. In spite of the geographical distances between
them, Peter called attention to their unity in Christ which bound them
together as the New Israel of God in Christ.

16. Modeling Submission

Likewise, wives, be subject to your own husbands, so that even if some do not obey the word, they may be won without a word by the conduct of their wives, when they see your respectful and pure conduct. Do not let your adorning be external—the braiding of hair and the putting on of gold jewelry, or the clothing you wear—but let your adorning be the hidden person of the heart with the imperishable beauty of a gentle and quiet spirit, which in God's sight is very precious.
—1 Peter 3:1-4 (ESV)

At chapter three Peter turned his attention to the primary jurisdiction of personal morality—the family. It is in the family where individuals first encounter other people, and where the concerns of freedom and responsibility are inculcated—or not. People learn manners and morals from their parents—or not. So, Peter turned his attention to the responsibilities that parents have for modeling faithfulness to their children because if manners and morals are not learned in the family at a young age they are most likely not learned at all.

He began this section with the word *likewise* (*homoiōs*) in order to provide a link between what he had been talking about generally with this specific example of how all these things play out in the family. And it is of particular interest that he began with wives rather than with husbands.

No doubt, his intent was to connect the behavior of wives with his instruction in 1 Peter 2:13-14: "Be subject for the Lord's sake to every human institution, whether it be to the emperor as supreme, or to governors as sent by him to punish those who do evil and to praise those who do good." Here Peter tied the idea of submission to the emperor, who represented civil government. Civil government, the glue of civilization, requires our submission. And here in chapter three he turned his attention to family government. Peter was taking the general principle of sub-mission[48] to Christ and showing how it applied in family life. Submission to Christ means submission to Christ's representative authorities. Peter identified the emperor as a representative authority of God. Paul referred to the civil magistrate as a deacon (Romans 13:4). But most people would never even meet the emperor, so Peter used an example of obedience to authority that was closer to home.

I understand that Peter's instructions regarding the sub-mission of wives to their husbands will for the most part fall on deaf ears in today's world. There are too few contemporary women who believe such a thing and even fewer who actually practice it. So, my comments here will undoubtedly offend our contemporary sensitivities. However, such offense is not my intention, and I will endeavor to not offend anyone unnecessarily. My intention is to explicate Peter's words as best as I can, knowing that our lives today are not unaffected by the historical context in which we currently live. So, a brief review of some of the history that has brought us to our contemporary situation will be in order.

DEFERENCE

When Peter said "likewise" (v. 1), he meant that just as husbands are to be subject to the emperor, wives are to be subject to their own husbands. Peter was articulating a kind of chain of command. There are two concerns here: the general character of submissiveness and the particular relationship in which such submissiveness is to manifest. Peter did not say that women were to be submissive to men as a general rule. Rather, he said that wives are to be in sub-mission to or with their own husbands. The relationship of mission and submission belong to the general structure of God's covenant and also to the marriage relationship. Biblical marriage is not a contract, wherein equals are involved, but is a covenantal relationship that is part of a chain of representative authorities.

This is not a statement about the equality of men and women, it is a statement that the role of husband and the role of wife do not have the same authority or responsibilities. The issue is not equality of being or of rights. God recognizes only two categories of human beings: covenant keepers and covenant breakers. All other categories are meaningless to God, who does not distinguish between male or female, slave or free, rich or poor, black or white, etc. People are not the same, not

---

48 By breaking this word into its constituent parts we can more easily understand the biblical definition of the word. Those who are in sub-mission understand that they are serving a greater mission, and that their immediate supervisor or authority also works in sub-mission to God's mission in Christ. All who are in sub-mission to Christ are in sub-mission together, not as equals but as coworkers.

equal, and it is foolish to think that they are. People have different interests, abilities, capacities, skills, opportunities, and resources.

Marriage and family are the first institutions in which biblical authority is exercised, which make them primary targets for God's enemies. The destruction of biblical marriage and family authority will eventually bring the destruction of all biblical authority because the family is the cradle of civilization. An attack on the cradle is an attempt to destroy the fount, spring or first exercise of biblical authority.

"Likewise," said Peter, "wives, be subject to your own husbands" (v. 1). Why does the issue of authority begin with wives rather than husbands? Because genuine biblical authority is not something that can be claimed, but rather it must always be given and received. Authority that is self-claimed tends to be authoritarian, but authority that is willingly and lovingly bestowed upon another suggests honor and authenticity.

Self-centered authority always leads to abuse and corruption because its root is pride, whereas other-directed authority leads to service because its root is sacrifice. The exercise of authority that is directed toward others and understood as service rendered to God in Christ, service that is trinitarian in character, serves the purposes of truth, honor, integrity, justice and love.

Authority is not first and foremost the power or right to give orders, as every contemporary dictionary suggests. Rather, authority is first and foremost the ability to receive and obey orders. Apart from the necessity of receiving and obeying orders personally one's self, the giving of orders can only be established on the basis or foundation of one's own authority.

CHAIN OF COMMAND

What is the option? God is the ultimate source of all authority and any authority that denies, undermines or contradicts God's authority stands against the God of the Bible, the only real God who actually exists, and is therefore opposed to genuine authority. Authority always exists as a chain of command because authority is always necessarily representative. No one but God has original authority. Everyone else is in service of God's authority, or opposing God by denying, undermining or contradicting God's authority.

Thus, Peter begins with wives because unless wives willingly and gladly grant honor and authority to their husbands, they deny, undermine and contradict the very definition of authority, and claim for themselves an authority that is greater than the biblical authority over them that God has given to their husbands. Authority is always a personal issue that has social consequences.

Wives always model sub-mission to the mission of their husbands, and their children see the wife's sub-mission to the authority of her husband—or not. They model it well or they model it poorly, but they do model it. When children see how their mother serves the greater mission of their father, who also serves the greater mission of God in Christ in their own families, they learn the proper roles and methods of authority and sub-mission, and are encouraged to join in sub-mission to Christ through obedience to their parents. Those children who do not see the sub-mission of their mothers are not likely to live in sub-mission themselves.

There is much to be gained by Christian families living in sub-mission to Jesus Christ and to His various representatives. But there is also much to be gained beyond the family, as well. Peter called attention to the evangelism that is wrought in the world by those who live in sub-mission to Christ. Why is obedience to authority important? Because "even if some do not obey the word, they may be won without a word by the conduct of their wives, when they see your respectful and pure conduct" (v. 1-2). This is one of the most important ways that people can be a witness to Christ for their friends and neighbors, and more importantly, for their own children.

Wives living in glad and willing sub-mission to their faithful husbands provide a very powerful witness to the gospel of Jesus Christ. People can be won to Christ without a word about Christ ever being spoken. Of course, wives are not prohibited from speaking about Jesus, and should do so every chance they get. Peter was simply acknowledging that actions speak louder than words.

Another reason that this is so important is that it provides authentication for the faithful sub-mission of husbands to Christ. A faithful wife will distinguish between her husband's own faithful, godly sub-mission to Christ and his faithless, godless refusal to submit to Christ. She must in turn submit to the one and resist the other. Of course, the only way that she can do so is to study and understand Scripture herself. She must understand the Bible correctly if she is to live in correct sub-mission to her husband.

In fact, a faithful wife provides the first corrective to a wayward husband. Much of a wife's role and responsibility as a wife is to serve as a kind of vice-president of the family corporation, of which her husband is the God-ordained president.[49] And the job of the vice-president is to provide counsel to the president. To be effective she must understand herself to serve the same mission as the family franchise. She must understand the mission of the franchise and be in full and com-

---

49 Husbands must understand that the family corporation is a franchise owned by God.
    Thus, husbands are bound by the terms of the franchise, God's covenant.

plete agreement and support of it. This again means that she must observe and support the mission of her husband and be in complete agreement and support of Christ's mission as well because all authority on earth and in heaven has been given to Jesus Christ. And again, this means that she must understand the Bible correctly.

A wife in faithful sub-mission to her own husband is a very attractive force because she reflects and models God's mission of love and care for His people. A wise wife exercising sub-mission to and with her husband implies that her husband lives in compliance with God's covenant, that he is God's ordained head of his family, and that he is worthy of her love and honor. Such a marriage is a walking billboard for God.

People want to be loved and the sight of genuine love, respect and honor in a marriage is a truly beautiful and attractive thing. Such a marriage beautifies the neighborhood and the culture in which it abides. Indeed, there is no higher art than the art of biblical marriage. Such a marriage provides everything that an artist wants and needs—love, respect, honor, attention, satisfaction, fulfillment, expression, creativity and companionship.

ADORNMENT

It is not surprising that Peter turned his attention to feminine adornment. Everyone knows that men are to be strong and women are to be beautiful. Children certainly know it. "Do not let your adorning be external—the braiding of hair and the putting on of gold jewelry, or the clothing you wear—but let your adorning be the hidden person of the heart with the imperishable beauty of a gentle and quiet spirit, which in God's sight is very precious" (vs. 3-4).

Here Peter shared the secret of true human beauty. True beauty is not what is seen on the outside, but is what is not seen on the inside. True beauty always rests on the right foundation. If it is true that beauty is in the eye of the beholder—and it is, then the art of beauty is to allow the eye of the beholder to imagine the best possible scenario that it can conceive. The art of beauty is to suggest, not to reveal. The things that are the most beautiful allow people to impose the highest values and virtues that they can imagine upon the object of art without being restricted by the personal limitations of the artist.

This only happens when the values and virtues of the art appreci-ator are in harmony with the values and virtues of the artist, when the values and virtues of the artist become transparent to the art appreci-ator. And when this happens both parties refer to the experience of the art as transcendent because the limitations of the individual artist's values and virtues do not obscure God's greater and transcendent values and virtues that are suggested by the art.

Peter was not banning external adornment. He was putting it in its proper context. There is nothing wrong with wearing gold or braiding your hair or wearing fine clothing. These things serve as a kind of human label because they suggest the refinement of human character. The function of a label is to identify the contents of the package. The label is not the content, but should accurately reflect the character of the content. Outer adornment is only a problem when it fails to accurately identify the inner character, or when it is overdone and serves as a crutch to prop up the lack of genuine refinement and maturity.

As an aside, it is curious that today we find that people do not want to be "labeled" and yet they spend inordinate amounts of time, energy and money styling their exterior lives to match very narrow and particular demographics. People work very hard at labeling themselves, but complain when other people label them, or acknowledge the label they have created for themselves. Labels simply serve as categories, and human beings are hardwired to make categorical distinctions, to put the various things of experience into categories in order to understand them. So, being upset that people label other people is like being upset that cows produce milk. This analogy is rich because human categorization or taxonomy provides the foundation for science and technology, which are, in fact, very good things when used in covenant faithfulness.

What is actually disturbing regarding the phenomenon of labeling is not the fact that it happens, but that our own self-assessment seldom matches the reality of our inner character. And labeling makes this clear. We don't like to think of ourselves as sinners, and the reality of such a consideration is truly disturbing. It's supposed to be! However, the solution to this problem is not the forbiddance of labeling, but growth and maturity of character in Christ.

At the center of Peter's description of a beautiful woman is "the imperishable beauty of a gentle and quiet spirit" (v. 4). The idea of perishing is the opposite of the idea of imperishable, and it suggests the body of flesh by implication. Peter used the same word (*aphthartos*) in chapter one, where he was talking about all the saints as obedient children, who should not be conformed to the passions of their former ignorance (1 Peter 1:14).

He went on to say, "Having purified your souls by your obedience to the truth for a sincere brotherly love, love one another earnestly from a pure heart, since you have been born again, not of perishable seed but of imperishable, through the living and abiding word of God; for 'All flesh is like grass and all its glory like the flower of grass. The grass withers, and the flower falls, but the word of the Lord remains forever.' And this word is the good news that was preached to you" (1 Peter 1:22-25). He was anchoring the beauty of a submissive wife to the model of Christian faithfulness broadly conceived.

Thus, there are four things that he attached to the idea of imperishability: 1) obedience to the truth, 2) brotherly love, 3) regeneration and 4) God's Word. The order is not significant, but the presence of all four elements in the lives of believers is. He was telling women that these are the foundational elements of godly beauty, and that godly beauty is the highest ideal or model for human beauty.

So, women who want to be beautiful need to master these things and not spend inordinate resources on things like gold, braids or clothes—outer accoutrements. Rather, said Peter, seek real beauty, eternal beauty, inner beauty, the beauty of faithfulness and Christian character that increases over time, not the outer beauty that shrivels and dies over time. Indeed, the beauty of faithfulness and Christian character are the only things that we can take with us into God's heaven.

17. HOLY WOMEN

For this is how the holy women who hoped in God used to adorn themselves, by submitting to their own husbands, as Sarah obeyed Abraham, calling him lord. And you are her children, if you do good and do not fear anything that is frightening. Likewise, husbands, live with your wives in an understanding way, showing honor to the woman as the weaker vessel, since they are heirs with you of the grace of life, so that your prayers may not be hindered.

—1 Peter 3:5-7 (ESV)

Verse 4 ends by telling us that the imperishable beauty of a gentle and quiet spirit is very *precious* (*poluteles*). The *Authorized Version* translates *poluteles* as "of great price." Of course, it doesn't actually cost God or us any money, so *price* is not really the right word, even though it's not a wrong translation. *Precious* is better than *great price*, but *precious* makes it sound delicate and tender rather than valuable.

The idea is that God values a gentle and quiet spirit among women. But He also values it among men. God would have everyone be gentle, kind, considerate, quiet and humble. Paul's list of the fruits of the spirit are not gender specific and include "love, joy, peace, patience, kindness, goodness, faithfulness, gentleness (and) self-control" (Galatians 5:22-23).

It is not a sexist thing where God wants to keep women in their proper place—not at all! Rather, God wants to keep everyone in their proper places because the failure for people to be in their proper places is a function of immorality. Righteousness is a matter of knowing and living in one's proper place, of exercising our spiritual gifts within the particular contexts of our calling. And there is nothing heavy-handed about the Christian calling to live according to God's righteousness.

Rather, it is immensely freeing and satisfying to live and work according to our own particular gifts and abilities in the service of genuine truth and righteousness under the guidance, protection and assistance of the Holy Spirit.

Scripture is about the establishment of representative government in all of the various governmental jurisdictions: individual (conscience), family, church and civil. If human society is going to function well, if people must exercise and enjoy the maximum freedom possible, we need to understand our various roles and positions, and we must engage them with honesty, honor and integrity. In order for authority to function properly in society, it must function properly at all levels. The biblical chain of command functions through the various representative authorities established by God through Scripture. Representative government requires social authority, and social authority begins with individual acknowledgment of the highest authority—Jesus Christ (Matthew 28:18).

Conscience As The Basis For Social Organization

The establishment of Christian conscience is what Christians usually mean by having a personal relationship with Jesus Christ. It is how such a relationship works. That relationship provides the foundation for conscience, and the study and understanding of the Bible provides the data that feeds and nurtures the conscience in Christ. Apart from responsiveness to the authority of Christian conscience, which comes about as the fruit of personal regeneration and Christian education, authority tends toward totalitarianism on the one hand or anarchy on the other. Authoritative power tends to coalesce into a unitary whole and lead to totalitarianism, or to dissipate into nothing and lead to anarchy.

Only Christianity provides for the reciprocity and balancing of these ultimate tendencies through the trinitarian character of reality itself, mediated by Jesus Christ. Only the doctrine of the Trinity provides for the reality and simultaneous existence of harmonious jurisdictions of multiple authorities. Only the Bible, Old Testament and New, correctly defines the jurisdictions. And only Jesus Christ properly mediates between them all.

In order for this to work properly, people must also be responsive to the authority of the church(es). Such churches must have properly defined, commissioned and functioning pastors, elders and deacons who are all personally regenerate and educated in the values and virtues of an historical, orthodox Christian worldview. In addition, church members must also actually honor and respect the authority of their church leaders. And, of course, people must also be responsive to civil government in its various local, regional and national jurisdictions, which means that people need to have some level of actual involvement in civil government by being responsible citizens, as well.

Clearly, a biblically structured society is a complex, multifaceted organism that involves each and every member of society to be actively involved in the service of the greater good that is defined by Scripture. To say that all of this is to be defined by Scripture does not mean that other books are not read or consulted. It simply means that the structure and definitions are drawn from and supported by the Bible. It means that the Bible is the primary source for definitions and structure.

When Jesus provided bread and fish for the five thousand, He said to his disciples, "Have them sit down in groups of about fifty each" (Luke 9:14). He was reproducing the social order that Moses instituted under the guidance of Jethro. Moses called for "able men from all the people, men who fear God, who are trustworthy and hate a bribe" to be placed "over the people as chiefs of thousands, of hundreds, of fifties, and of tens" (Exodus 18:21). Indeed, Moses used this simple pattern of government to establish social order.

The general principle that Moses used was representative government regarding the authority of society. The leaders then represented God to the people by teaching them about God, and they represented the people to God by bringing the prayers and concerns of the people to God in worship. Thus, the leaders mediated between God and His people. It was a very simple plan and to understand it correctly we must not get bogged down with the wooden literalism of exact details but see the general patterns.

Moses kept the size of the smallest groups manageable so that their leaders would not be overwhelmed and individuals would not get lost in the crowd. The maintenance of small groups simply allows for better communication and representation. It also provides more opportunities for more leaders to be involved. And the more leaders there are, the more representative the social fabric.

Returning to Peter's point, Christian leaders should also model a gentle and quiet spirit. It is not the purpose of social leadership to whip people up into various states of emotional frenzy. The mob mentality of emotionally frenzied people is a detriment to social order. Rather, the purpose of representative leadership is to teach and model Christian character, to teach Scripture and to exercise the functions of public worship in small group settings that provide for maximum intimacy with God and mutual social bonding by all involved.

Plain Old Beauty

In verse 5 Peter suggested that faithful women of old provided a model for social order through their imperishable beauty of a gentle and quiet spirit through sub-mission to/with their own husbands. That is the biblical model for social order that persisted throughout the Old Testament and which according to Peter has been inherited by the New Testament. And we must keep in mind that Peter's admonition of gentle humility supports Paul's various admonitions against the pride of position and authority. The worth of people as individuals is not based upon any characteristics of worthiness in God's eyes, for God is not a respecter of persons.

God insists that all of His people be humble, honest and honorable and that each and every person play the role that God has given with humility, honesty and honor to the best of their ability and in all circumstances. Individual roles are a function of the gifts that God has bestowed and the social context in which He has placed various people. While some people have more or less authority and responsibility, such differences are neither based upon, nor do they indicate, any measure of God's love or respect for particular individuals. God simply wants everyone to be faithful to their various stations. Life in Christ is not a competition between people. If anything Christianity is a team sport.

Peter cited Sarah's obedience to Abraham and her deference to him as *lord* (*kurios*). *Kurios* is the same Greek word that is used elsewhere to refer to Christ, and means *supreme authority*. Sarah could give her complete allegiance to her husband because she knew him to be honestly faithful to God to the best of his ability. He represented God to Sarah. However, while Peter here addressed wives, the burden was not simply placed upon the wives to submit, but is also upon the husbands to be worthy of such sub-mission. Sarah could only love and honor Abraham to the extent that Abraham loved and honored God.

So, men: if you want your wives to be more submissive to you, you must be more submissive to God. Take your concern about the submission of your wife and add it to the exercise of your own sub-mission to God in Christ and His various representative authorities. This is your calling. Do this and your wife's love, honor, respect and sub-mission will fall into its proper place. Husbands cannot force their wives to honor them, they can only be worthy of such honor. And no one is or can be worthy in their own right (Romans 3:23). Rather, all human worthiness is founded upon and issues from Jesus Christ. Only Christ is worthy (Revelation 5).

Peter's advice to wives, and by implication to all who live in some sort of sub-mission—which includes everyone, was for them to do good, to be virtuous, and to not be afraid. The key for wives to trust and honor their husbands is to first trust and honor God in Christ and then by helping their husbands to be who God has called them to be, to help their husbands find their identity and role in Christ's church.

This means that they must not only know and understand Scripture, but that they must know and understand their husband's identity and role, his views and understandings of Scripture. Furthermore, they must agree and support him in his role and his sub-misison to God in Christ. Husbands and wives need to work together to accomplish God's mission in their respective spheres of influence, to be in sub-mission to God individually, and then by helping each other be the kind of people that God has called them to be. Only in this way can they be the kind of family that God has called them to lead.

CONTINUITY

By citing Sarah and Abraham, Peter called attention to the fact that the biblical tradition of marriage taught in the Old Testament has continued into the New Testament. The development and revelation of biblical marriage continues from the Old Testament into the New Testament. There is no break in this tradition, but there is growth, refinement and correction provided through the light of Christ. Marriage has changed in the light of Christ, as everything else changes in the light of Christ. And yet the light of Christ does not provide any sort of fundamental break in the biblical tradition of marriage relationships. Rather, it refines and strengthens them.

The other thing that Peter advances through this recommendation is the continuing mission of God's grace. By citing Abraham as the model husband, he both indicates that God's mission of grace was active in the old administration and that it, too, continues into the new administration of God in Christ. Just as Abraham was saved by grace and nurtured by Sarah, so are husbands in the new administration saved by grace and nurtured by their wives. Sarah's sub-mission to Abraham was of great value in God's sight—and in Abraham's. Husband and wife are not merely joined to one another in the marriage covenant, they are joined together in covenant *with God*. God is the covenant issuer and holder regarding biblical marriage.

GROWTH

At verse 7 Peter turned to address husbands more directly because he knew that much of what he had said regarding wives has many implications for husbands, as well. First, husbands and wives are to live together intelligently, with knowledge and wisdom. This means that knowledge, wisdom, intelligence, understanding and mutual education are to be at the very foundation of their covenantal relationship.

This is more important than having sex together. Each must be committed to helping the other grow in knowledge, wisdom, intelligence and understanding by spending time together in the pursuit of biblical education.

Peter brought together two ideas in this verse: dwelling and understanding. Husbands are to integrate knowledge, understanding and teaching as a key element in their households. And because Peter was here addressing husbands, his point was that husbands should spend time teaching their wives. He was providing instructions for husbands about how to minister to their households. Husbands are to *husband* their families by providing Christian education and worship in their homes.[50]

Of course, such teaching is not to be a one way street that flows from the husband to the wife. This is not a license to ignore, denigrate or otherwise speak down to one's wife and children. Rather, it is a personal call to the husband to exceed his wife in knowledge, wisdom, intelligence and understanding. Not that husband and wife are in some kind of competition, they most assuredly are not. Nonetheless, Peter was simply calling the husband to the highest degree of perfection that he is capable of (Matthew 5:48).

He was to have greater authority and responsibility in the family because he is the head of the household. Being the head of the household is not a justification for dominance, but is a demand for servant leadership in morality, Christian education and worship. And an honest wife will not begrudge her husband's intelligence or ability but will herself be submitted to helping him grow and mature for the sake of the growth and maturity of her family and children.

Subsidiary

Peter then speaks of "showing honor to the woman as the "weaker vessel" (v. 7), which provides a bevy of problems for modern women who are looking for an excuse to be offended. Peter was not speaking generally here, but was speaking of the relationship between husbands and wives, not of men and women generally. Nonetheless, overly sensitive women have generalized the phrase as if it pertains to all men and women. It has been turned into the foundation of the Women's Movement, as if it teaches or suggests that men as a class have abused women as a class by forcing them into subservient social positions. Unfortunately, there is too much truth to this accusation, but it is a truth that is to have no part in the lives of regenerate Christians. This

---

50 For a resource see "Directory for Family Worship," *Westminster Confession of Faith*, 1646, public domain.

presupposition is then read into Scripture, as if Scripture teaches it (which it does not!) and is seen as a validation of that perspective.

Have men abused women? Have husbands abused wives? Yes, of course. But has every man abused every woman? Has every husband abused his wife? No, of course not, thanks be to God in Christ.

Nonetheless, abuse tends to accompany faithlessness. Those who abuse their authority are not faithful to Christ because Christ forbids such abuse. Thus, abuse tends to decrease as men grow in faithfulness. We must understand that the abuse of authority is a sure sign of faithlessness. It cannot be denied that abusive men are faithless, irresponsible and immature. In order to reduce and eventually eliminate abuse, abusers—men—must be branded with a kind of Scarlet Letter.[51] The remedy for abuse is for men to become increasingly faithful, responsible and mature. The question is: How can this be accomplished? How can men be inspired to greater faithfulness, responsibility and maturity.

Peter appealed to the reality that women are as a rule physically smaller and weaker than men, and coupled it with the fact that their physical weakness should, if anything, increase the obligation to honor them. It should go without saying that a husband should honor and respect his own wife as an expression of his love for her.

But because sin has so coarsened the natural sensitivities of men Peter needed to remind men of their own obligations to honor the women they love. The phrase in question should be less an affront to women because of their natural weakness than it is an offense to men for their natural faithlessness. The gist of the verse is that men should honor their wives. The phrase says no more nor any less than that.

Peter continued to point to the equality of men and women, husbands and wives, regarding salvation as he told them why they should honor their wives. Because "they are heirs with you of the grace of life" (v. 7). Women are no less heirs of God's grace than men. Paul mentioned this several times (Galatians 3:28, etc.). And more particularly, wives are heirs of God's grace with their faithful husbands. It is a corporate family inheritance, not an individualistic, blood-based inheritance. Human sonship in God's kingdom has always been a matter of adoption—grace not race, bread not blood.

Does this mean that women are saved by the faith of their husbands? Of course not, no more than baptized infants are saved by the faith of their parents! However, in both cases faithful husbands and faithful parents will insure that their wives and children are exposed to the means of grace—God's Word. Therefore, such wives and children actually do have an advantage over others who have no such faithful

---

51 Nathaniel Hawthorne, *The Scarlet Letter* , 1850, public domain.

head of household because they will be exposed to God's Word regularly and faithfully. "So faith comes from hearing, and hearing through the word of Christ" (Romans 10:17).

PrayerWorks

The final phrase of verse 7 provides the ultimate reason for husbands to teach the Bible to their wives and children, and to encourage faithfulness in their families by modeling faithfulness themselves: "so that your prayers may not be hindered" (v. 7). Peter understood the value of prayer, and wanted to insure its effectiveness among church families.

By teaching the Bible and leading their families in regular, prayerful worship husbands can increase the effectiveness of their own prayers. Peter's teaching provides a win/win situation in which everyone involved benefits. The engine of these various benefits is the faithfulness of husbands to love, honor, teach, protect, nurture and care for their families in tangible, spiritual, helpful, kind, faithful, loving and effective ways. Any man who honestly and seriously engages this engine will not be met with wifely resistance.

To understand what Peter meant requires understanding what prayer is and how it works. Prayer is not a means of asking God for what we want. This common misunderstanding is based on Jesus' conclusion to the parable of the fig tree: "Truly, I say to you, if you have faith and do not doubt, you will not only do what has been done to the fig tree, but even if you say to this mountain, 'Be taken up and thrown into the sea,' it will happen. And whatever you ask in prayer, you will receive, if you have faith" (Matthew 21:21-22).

We know that no particular biblical teaching can be understood apart from the larger context of Scripture. And here, when we take Jesus' words alone and apart from all context it does seem as if He turned prayer into a cosmic vending machine, as if Jesus means that we can have whatever we want if we will only believe hard enough.

This understanding is almost correct, but not quite. John 14:13 provides a corrective: "Whatever you ask in my name, this I will do, that the Father may be glorified in the Son." The corrective is asking in Jesus' name. However, the word *Jesus* is not to be used as a talisman or magic word that will unlock the stores of heaven. Rather, to ask in Jesus' name means to ask in His character, to imitate His character and then ask God.

This changes what is asked for. Luke recorded the character of Jesus saying, "Father, if you are willing, remove this cup from me. Nevertheless, not my will, but yours, be done" (Luke 22:42). Jesus always served His Father's will, so when we imitate Jesus' character, we also endeavor to serve our Father's will and not our own. And God will grant what is in harmony with His own will.

This perspective is also present in Matthew 21:22, but it is not as clear. According to Matthew, Jesus said, "whatever you ask in prayer, you will receive, if you have faith." Here the qualifier is having faith. But it doesn't mean having the right quantity or intensity of faith, as if people can have whatever they want if they will only believe hard enough. Rather, Jesus meant that people had to have right faith or to have faith rightly, correctly. And in this case correct faith is the desire to do the will of God, not to have whatever we want for ourselves.

When people ask God for what He wants them to have, He will provide it because it is His will for them to have it. Having faith or asking in Jesus' name always means asking for what God wants us to have, and when we do that our prayers will be much more effective. This is what Peter was alluding to, and what he was calling husbands to engage in order to increase the effectiveness of their prayers. And these things, while directed toward women, are actually a great benefit for all Christians.

18. UNITY

Finally, all of you, have unity of mind, sympathy, brotherly
love, a tender heart, and a humble mind. Do not repay evil for
evil or reviling for reviling, but on the contrary, bless, for to
this you were called, that you may obtain a blessing.
                                                    —1 Peter 3:8-9

Peter addressed wives and husbands and then turned his attention
to both husbands and wives as he called for unity in verse 8. The
goal or purpose (*telos*) of what Peter had been writing about was
for all to be like-minded. Christ's people have sympathy, brotherly love,
tender hearts, and humble minds. Peter's words are not only a call for
these things, but provide a description of what Christians are to be like.
Not only are these things to be true of Christians, but where these things
are not true, Christianity is missing. Thus, Peter's words both call the
church to faithfulness and judge the churches for faithlessness at the
same time.

This matter of being like-minded is not as simple as it first appears.
If Christian history means anything, and it does, then like-mindedness
does not mean cookie-cutter similitude. Nor does it mean blind acceptance or unexamined conformity. Rather, it means trusting that God is
true and not a deceiver. It also means that all Christians can understand
the same things, yet explain them differently, uniquely. Different
explanations or perspectives do not necessarily mean different beliefs.
Peter was not so much calling them all to think alike as he was calling
them to maintain unity in spite of their differences.

From a trinitarian perspective like-mindedness suggests corporate
unity rather than individual sameness. It suggests that unity is complex
rather than simple. For instance, as human beings we have more in
common with other human beings than we have individual differences.
And our differences, though they seem extremely great, do not make us

other than human beings. Peter was calling people to remember their humanity, to lean on the crutch of Christian commonality and not to forget or deny that commonality by overemphasizing the ways that we differ from and disagree with one another. He was suggesting that the difference that Jesus Christ makes to humanity has as much to do with humanity as a whole as it does with particular individuals.

MISSING THE MARK

For at least forty years Westerners have been subjected to the indoctrination of shallow-minded and short-sighted multiculturalism at the expense of the deeper doctrines of God's trinitarian truth that is found with regenerate eyes exclusively in the Bible. It is an understandable error that has been made by Humanists and Secularists, who have no understanding of Christian trinitarianism. They hope that multiculturalism will solve the complex problem that occurs when ultimate claims are put upon humanity by the various religions.

Every religion claims to have the ultimate truth about humanity and reality. Every religion makes ultimate claims about reality that can best be categorized in terms of monotheism or polytheism. The various religions tend to be either monotheistic or polytheistic in character. Philosophically, monotheism and polytheism are mutually exclusive. However, the doctrine of the Trinity provides a philosophical position that includes them both without compromising the truth. The doctrine of the Trinity demonstrates the reality of both ultimate positions at the same time and without confusion with the constraints of biblical Christianity. The doctrine of the Trinity provides the actual, ultimate truth about God and His world, about our objective reality.

We can see the damage and danger posed by classic monotheistic religions from the historic and ongoing rivalries between Judaism and Islam, where both claim exclusive monotheistic religious positions. The logical conclusion of monotheism is world domination. If absolute truth is monotheistic, then that truth already rules or dominates reality. If monotheism is true, then everyone needs to believe and practice the correct monotheistic expression of truth.

But in a world where there is more than one religion that claims to be monotheistic, competition for world domination will necessarily continue until a victor arises. This is why there can be no peace between Israel and Islam, or between Islam and any other religion. From their monotheistic perspectives coexistence is not an option.

Christianity is also monotheistic, but Christianity provides a unique kind of monotheism—trinitarian monotheism. The doctrine of the Trinity is absolutely unique to Christianity among the world religions. Again, it is not that Christianity provides a philosophical compromise between mutually exclusive positions, but that Jesus Christ has demonstrated the reality of trinitarian existence. Thus, monotheism and polytheism are false or philosophically inadequate expressions of God and the reality He created.

FINDING THE MARK

There can be no like-mindedness between competing monotheistic religions, nor between monotheism and polytheism because of their ultimate and mutually exclusive philosophical beliefs. It is time to recognize this elemental truth, and abandon the compromising philosophical irrationality of multiculturalism and religious toleration. We must face the truth that multiculturalism and religious toleration are the servants of polytheism and that neither Islam, Judaism nor Christianity can ever accept them, except as a temporary truce in the long war for world domination.

Again, all monotheistic religions work for ultimate and exclusive religious and philosophical domination as the logical conclusion of their monotheism. It cannot be otherwise. However, the central and unifying characteristic of the reality that we inhabit is neither monotheistic nor polytheistic but is necessarily trinitarian. It is both one and three (many) at the same time without distortion of the central characteristic of reality's unity nor its diversity.

These same struggles or ultimate religious positions were alive and in play when Peter called Christians to like-mindedness. The monotheism of Judaism had struggled against the various polytheisms of the Pagan world since time immemorial, and those struggles were alive and well in the First Century Middle East when Peter penned this letter. It cannot be otherwise because Old Testament Judaism introduced both trinitarianism and monotheism to the world and they've been struggling against one another ever since.

The Bible teaches that God is eternal and non-changing, and the advent of Jesus Christ established that God is trinitarian in character—Father, Son and Holy Spirit. Therefore, God has always been trinitarian from His earliest biblical revelation. But the truth is that the Trinity is a complex historical doctrine and the revelation of God as trinitarian has taken time to unfold, and people need time to understand it. In the process, the historic revelation of the trinitarian God had to be revealed as both trinitarian and unitarian, and in the fullness of time to manifest as the Son of God in human flesh—yet divine.

It is not an easy truth to understand, people have seldom gotten it right. Confusion has ensued. Old Testament Israel continued to get it wrong, and God continued to send prophets for their correction. Time and again the simplicity of monotheism would irrupt in various abuses, both religious and political, and dominate and obscure the more subtle and textured complexities of trinitarianism. Most often the tendencies toward unitarianism led to social domination and abuse. And God would send another prophet to clarify and expand God's trinitarian truth for His people. Finally, God sent His Son in the flesh to manifest the truth of the Trinity for all to see.

But, as Early Church history reveals, the confusion continued, which then drove the church to clarify and establish the doctrine of the Trinity as official policy.[52] However, church creeds and policies have proven to provide too little protection against the ravages of heresy. And in the early 600s the most powerful and influential monotheistic heresy broke out in the Arabian desert in the wake of much Christian confusion. It was almost as if the confusion about Christianity, and particularly about the divinity of Christ and the Trinity, were at the root of the heresy.

Islam

Peter, didn't know this, of course, because Islam proper would not be born for another 600 years after he penned this letter. Nonetheless when it was born, Islam would meld three of the most powerful, dynamic forces in human history into its service, forces that were in existence as Peter was writing: monotheism, the Bible (though a confused and inadequate understanding of it) and the idea of evangelism. The emphasis of monotheism over polytheism was a long standing Jewish concern. The New Testament in the 600s was the newest religious scripture, and at that point little was known about it. And Christian evangelism was the newest religious movement. The Jews of the Old Testament did little evangelism, so it was a new development.

Mohammad took the idea of monotheism from the Jews and melded it with ancient Middle Eastern paganism and then fused them together with the call for aggressive evangelism that he found among Christians. But he rejected the dynamic truth of trinitarian theology and replaced it with a sense of righteous militancy and domination of others by every available means as an expression of the will of God. In his later writings, Mohammad turned to politics and military force to accomplish his goals.

This three-part mystical concoction has proven to be a powerful stimulus among sinners. It is mystical because of the irrationality of melding the idea of monotheism with the reality of various ancient pagan ideas and practices, and then calling the mixture by another name, Islam, and proclaiming it to be a unified whole. This would all

---

52 The Ecumenical Creeds (Nicene, Apotstles', Athanasian and Chalcedon) established the doctrine of the Trinity.

happen later, of course. I digress in order to put the idea of the progressive revelation of God's trinitarian character in its larger context in our own day.

Unity

In the meantime, Peter called for Christian like-mindedness that can only come from the Christian trinitarian perspective. And the need for Christian trinitarian like-mindedness which began with the birth of Christ has never been greater. Of course, every era can make this claim and it is always true.

The development of trinitarian theology went dark in the Middle Ages when it got lost in the caves of philosophical mysticism. Nonetheless, enough of the residual effects of the Trinity remained in Christendom for the development of science, technology and capitalism to develop and utterly change the world. That Christ-like, trinitarian like-mindedness has recently reemerged in the light of Christ and beckons again for the fulfillment of its destiny to provide a fuller and more complete revelation of God in Christ in our Postmodern world. All of this is to say that God's revelation continues to unfold, though not apart from the Bible.

It must be understood that Peter's call for "unity of mind," or "one mind" in the *Authorized Version*, does not mean thinking alike, though neither does it forbid thinking alike. The Greek word that Peter used (*homophrōn*) is composed of two parts: *homou*, which suggests both sameness and togetherness, and *phrēn*.

Strong's says that *phrēn* probably comes from an obsolete Greek word (φράω or *phraō*) that means to rein in or curb. It also refers to the midriff, the mid-portion of the body, that is, (figuratively and by implication of sympathy) the feelings or sensing nature, and by extension, to the mind or cognitive faculties. It suggests a common understanding.[53] The general idea behind this word involves a moral commitment to remain unified by holding to the central (midriff) aspects of Christianity, that is, not holding too fast to theological positions at the circumference or extremes, but focusing attention at the center.

However, this does not mean that Peter suggests that the central theological or biblical positions issue from any kind of compromise. They most emphatically do not. The Bible is not a document of compromise, but a document about the unique revelation of God in Christ. In part, this means that Christians must themselves rest in the central revelation of Jesus Christ.

---

53 *Strong's Hebrew and Greek Dictionaries, G3675*, www.eSword.net.

All of this suggests that Peter's call is not simply a call to the head, it is a call to the heart. It is not merely intellectual, but involves a moral commitment to all of Christ's people. Faithfulness requires both intellect and emotion, but not one in service of the other. Rather, faithfulness requires that both be in service together to God in Christ.

Peter sought to further clarify what he meant by adding the word *sumpathēs*, having sympathy and compassion for one another. To be compassionate means to understand the suffering of others and being moved to do something about it. It requires sensitivity to the pain and suffering of others and the mutual identification of that pain and suffering with one's own. And because sin is at the heart of human pain and suffering, compassion is the recognition of the reality of sin in one's own life and in the lives of others. In our sinfulness we are all prone to various mistakes and errors of judgment. And because of this Peter was calling Christians to not rush to judgment about others, but to have sympathy and understanding.

Peter also called for "brotherly love" (*philadelphos*), or the recognition of a common Father, a blood kinship that is not based in genetics, but which is based on and issues from God's grace. This is not the touchy-feely love of modern liberalism, but constitutes a mutual commitment to well-being. Families take care of their own. Families fight and squabble, but when push comes to shove they do not abandon one another.

Then, to make sure that the bond Peter was describing would be strengthened without becoming hard or coarse, he commended *pity* (*eusplagchnos*). The *English Standard Version* translated it as "a tender heart." The idea is that Christians are to be full of pity or pathos —feelings—for one another.

THE MEAN OF THE WHOLE

This is a very different idea about how Christians are to relate to one another than we find in most of our contemporary churches or contemporary literature. People today insist on emphasizing the joy of the gospel, and that is not wrong. But we must not overemphasize the joy at the expense of the pity, nor visa versa. And the thing to note about Christian joy is not the extremities of its emotional highs, but its consistency in the face of sorrow and defeat. Indeed, Christian joy sings praises to God in spite of what the world gives us. Christian joy is not dependent upon our circumstances, but is dependent upon God alone.

The final Christian characteristic that Peter commends is "a humble mind" (*philophrōn*). The *Authorized Version* translated it as "be courteous." And while humility and courtesy are most worthy

Christian characteristics, I wonder if that is really what this word means. The word is again composed of two parts: *philo* and *phrēn*. We discussed *phrēn* above.

Philo means love, and according to Strong's the bottom line for *phrēn* is understanding. For instance, Phrenology is an abandoned pseudoscience that sought the understanding of personal character traits in the shape of the human skull. And though this pseudoscience is utterly ridiculous, it does suggest the meaning of the Greek word, which is not about skull shape, but about the seat of personal character or vitality.

Similarly, schizo*phren*ia is a fracturing of the the wholeness of character or personality. The Greeks located the *phrēn* or center of thought and feeling in the midsection of the body rather than the head. So, the compound word suggests love of personal wholeness, or a fondness for what makes people whole—their center.

Surely, a genuine love of wholeness, understanding and wisdom would be both humble and courteous. But the failure to correctly identify the root meaning of the word would facilitate a great loss in terms of genuine Christian character. Christians need to know that Peter was commending the love of wholeness, understanding, knowledge and wisdom. He was not, however, commending it as a means of pride, but as a means of humility and common identification and courtesy.

The wholeness or so-called wisdom that puffs people up is not biblical wholeness or wisdom. If anything biblical wisdom humbles the plume of hot air that prideful people produce. Biblical wisdom finds wholeness in God, not self. Biblical wisdom finds wholeness through healing the breach of sin that separates self and God.

Putting all of this together, Peter commended "unity of mind, sympathy, brotherly love, a tender heart, and a humble mind" (v. 8). Peter commends the like-mindedness that is produced by participation in God's trinitarian character through healing the breach of sin. This, of course, does not mean that Christians become little gods because they eliminate sin in their lives—nothing of the sort! It simply means that Christians are changed from within by the invasion of the Holy Spirit through regeneration. Peter commends compassion, sympathy and pity for the pain and sorrow in the lives of Christians that is left in the wake of sin.

RECOVERY

Of course, Christ has taken care of the sin. We are indeed forgiven and restored to fellowship with God. But the effects of sin in our lives, our families and our institutions tend to linger. The consequences of

our broken families and marriages, the legal consequences of our mis-
deeds and misunderstandings are not healed overnight. The repentance comes in an instant, but the recovery takes a bit longer.
Repentance is the door to Christian fellowship, recovery is the ministry
we share. Fellowship is simply an introduction to recovery.

And by *share*, I mean that we help others recover from their sins
as they help us recover from ours. Forgiveness is free, but recovery
takes time and effort. Christian ministry is always mutual ministry.
Paul, the greatest Christian in history, was blinded and broken on the
Road to Damascus. He was delivered into the hands of those he had
formerly intended to kill. Those Christians then healed him and set
him free in their midst. Paul was prepared for Christian leadership by
being broken and blinded so he could have sympathy—pity—for the
brokenhearted, who became his brothers and sisters in Christ through
the unity of the Spirit.

Paul exchanged his blood inheritance as a Jew for the inheritance
of grace in Christ. Paul gave up everything—land, home, possessions,
friends, family, inheritance, everything—for Christ.

Paul wrote to the Romans:

*"Beloved, never avenge yourselves, but leave it to the wrath
of God, for it is written, 'Vengeance is mine, I will repay,
says the Lord.' To the contrary, if your enemy is hungry,
feed him; if he is thirsty, give him something to drink; for
by so doing you will heap burning coals on his head. Do not
be overcome by evil, but overcome evil with good"* (Romans
12:19-21).

Peter wrote to the "elect exiles of the dispersion" (1 Peter 1:1): "Do
not repay evil for evil or reviling for reviling, but on the contrary, bless,
for to this you were called, that you may obtain a blessing" (v. 9). This
teaching is so clear. So, why is learning it so hard?

TAKING OFFENSE

People are hardwired for vengeance. It's in the blood, and the Old
Testament stands as proof of this fact. God's plan to forgive sin and
establish His kingdom is simply a plan to overcome the human propen-
sity for vengeance because only God can accomplish such a thing (miracle), and doing so will stand as an eternal testament to God's grace
and glory.

There are two self-justifying aspects of vengeance that must be
overcome: 1) taking offense, and 2) seeking justice. Neither of these
things are bad or wrong in themselves, but they are both easily brought
into the arsenal of self-defence that God's enemies use to foster sin. Sin
and offense go hand-in-hand because sin is offensive whether we sin

against one another or against God. In addition, people are prone to usurp God's role in the world, which then further offends God. People who are offended tend to think that their indignation is righteous, that they are right and justified in their feelings of anger and being offended.

People also easily confuse being embarrassed with being offended. Embarrassment wounds our pride so we take a defensive posture in order to protect our wound from further exposure. And as soon as we come into that defensive posture we find ourselves needing to defend our defensiveness. And while we know that two wrongs don't make a right, we do it anyway, and our effort to defend our defensiveness then becomes an act of offense.

Here the word *offense* is understood in terms of sports, in the sense that the offensive team has the ball and runs with it, while the defensive team doesn't have the ball. No one will admit to taking offense for shallow and petty reasons, so we embellish our reasons to bolster our position. Thus, all personal offense taking is prohibited by God everywhere in Scripture.

Faithful Christians should simply not be offended by anything. This is what both Peter was teaching in the above verses, and what Paul teaches elsewhere. Nor should Christians take up the cudgels of defense when they think that God has been offended. God does not need our help defending His cause. Even though God often uses people in His own defense He does it His way, not ours. Indeed, people inevitably believe that their own feeling of being offended can only be assuaged by seeking the satisfaction of justice, that their cause for being offended is a cry for the execution of justice, that getting justice will alone relieve them of their offended feelings. This pattern of thinking is a self-replicating and self-perpetuating dynamo of self-justification. It issues from wounded pride in order to reinforce an embarrassed pride. Thus, pride is at its beginning and its end.

Pride

Pride was the first sin. It was the sin of Satan himself. Pride is also the root of original sin in the Garden. Pride is the greatest sin because it issues from self-love and is opposed in every way to faithfulness. Consequently, it is God's most hated sin and the one He punishes most severely. The punishment of the Angels (Hebrews 2:2), of Adam and Eve (Genesis 3:16-19), of Nebuchadnezzar (Daniel 4:27-31) and of the destruction of Jerusalem in A.D. 70 all bear witness to this.

Pride is the fountainhead of all other sins: "From pride all perdition took its beginning" (Tobit 4:14). Pride is also the most dangerous of sins, because it blinds our understanding, and unless something finally makes us realize the truth, we are liable to linger in spiritual self-delusion, imagining ourselves to be righteous and virtuous when certain of our responses are actually selfish and vicious.

There is a species of pride in every sin, whatever the particular nature of the sin itself. When we are blinded by pride we do not see our talents and abilities as God's gifts to us. Rather, we attribute our good qualities to ourselves, and grant ourselves the right to use them as we see fit. Sin has infected everyone with the virus of pride, though it manifests itself differently in different people.

Pride is a sensitive creature that is easily hurt, which is why it so often defends its self-defensiveness by taking the offensive and lashing out with a preemptive strike against a perceived threat in order to spare itself harm or embarrassment. And because pride denies the reality and extent of sin, it denies God's biblical teaching about sin by denying that God knows the truth. Pride claims to know more than God, and thus usurps God's place at the apex of human wisdom and divine authority.

So, what is the purpose of Peter's admonition? Why should people care about living in obedience to God? Peter's answer is very modern in the sense that Modernism is an expression of self-concern. The reason is so "that you may obtain a blessing" (v. 9). God intends to bless His people. He always has (Genesis 12:2, Deuteronomy 28:1-14). God's interest is in the longevity and well-being of humanity, but not merely for our own sake.

HUMANISM

God is not a servant of human well-being. No, God's concern is for His own glory. And while that may sound very self-centered in a bad way to us, for Him it is not. It would be a bad thing if God were not who He claims to be: perfectly good, righteous, omnipotent, trinitarian, etc. But because God is a kind of center without circumference, His self-concern is actually a concern for all things.

When people understand God to be in the service of human well-being, we neglect our covenantal obligations and begin to think that God's love is unconditional. It is not! God's love for us graciously produces rules and laws that are for our longevity and well-being. In return our love for God produces the desire for ardent obedience to His will in our hearts. Of course God's grace is unconditional, but God's blessings which are the fruit of His love are attached to covenantal conditions (Deuteronomy 11:13-15, 28; John 14:15, 14:23, 15:10; 1 Timothy 2:15; 1 John 2:15, 4:20).[54]

---

54 God loves humanity as a kind unconditionally, but sets conditions for individuals.
    Those conditions are at the heart of God's covenant, blessings for obedience and

And in order to help motivate us to love God and live in obedience to Him, Peter reminded his reading audience that the best thing that we can do for ourselves is to truly love God. If our pride is really all about being self-centered, then it should serve God in order to receive God's blessings for itself.

Thus, Peter turns pride back upon itself by showing that service to God's will is actually the best thing that pride can do for itself. Love of God, which requires the death of pride through service to God and His people, actually results in human health, wealth, well-being, longevity and eternal life. Indeed, there is no better prospect for human beings than to actually receive God's blessings, and to live in the service of God's glory.

---

curses for disobedience.

19. God Favors Righteousness

For "Whoever desires to love life and see good days, let him keep his tongue from evil and his lips from speaking deceit; let him turn away from evil and do good; let him seek peace and pursue it. For the eyes of the Lord are on the righteous, and his ears are open to their prayer. But the face of the Lord is against those who do evil." —1 Peter 3:10-12 (ESV)

P eter was quoting or paraphrasing Psalm 34:12-16: "What man is there who desires life and loves many days, that he may see good? Keep your tongue from evil and your lips from speaking deceit. Turn away from evil and do good; seek peace and pursue it. The eyes of the LORD are toward the righteous and his ears toward their cry. The face of the LORD is against those who do evil, to cut off the memory of them from the earth." And by doing so, He was recommending these verses from Psalms as being faithful to the intent of His own work.

But more than that, he was also recommending the Old Testament itself. He was saying that this teaching that was in the Old Testament here in the Psalms has validity in the New. Christians must not overlook the value of the Old Testament. The Old Testament provides not merely the historical foundation for Christianity, but the theological foundation, as well.

Verse 10 then suggests the key to a happy life. The goal of the verse is to live long and prosper. It is to live the good life, to live a life that is worth living. It is not merely the *pursuit* of happiness, but its *fulfillment*. However, Peter was not recommending that Christians simply party their lives away. Christians are not to be libertines who eat, drink and are merry without any concern for tomorrow. Life's goal is not self-satisfaction. But neither are Christians to be perpetual sourpusses, who think that life is to be played as a dreary dirge in a minor key. No, Peter was showing that obedience to the will of God is the very thing that maximizes human happiness, both individually and collectively. So, if you want to live a happy and fulfilling life, give your life to the service of God. Work to please God.

Actually, Peter was more specific than this. He said that we must refrain our tongues from evil, and keep our lips from speaking guile. Following Peter then, we see that happiness is not something that we receive from God or from other people, it is something that we do to or for others, or in this case, something that we should do by refraining from the opposite. Happiness is something that we give to others, and it begins by not giving them grief. If you want to be happy for the rest of your life, shut your mouth. Quit speaking evil. Quit spreading unhappiness. Quit lying. Stop stretching the truth out of shape. Quit trying to make the truth be what you want it to be, and see that it actually is what God says it is.

REFRAIN

Of course, there is more involved than keeping our lips from evil. We must also "turn away from evil" (v. 11). Paul added that we must refrain from all appearance of evil (1 Thessalonians 5:22). Even if we are not actually engaged in some sin, we must distance ourselves from both temptation and the potential suspicion by others that we might be engaged in some evil.

For instance, a man must not be in private company with a woman other than his own wife, particularly in a counseling relationship. Such a situation provides for both temptation and suspicion of hanky panky, even if nothing ever happens. The mere suggestion titillates our sinful imaginations, and is a danger because action tends to follow thought. Before a sin is engaged, it is thought about.

Peter knew, of course, that simply avoiding evil is not sufficient. Mere avoidance is insufficient to constitute a moral imperative. Remember Jesus' reference to the person who had been freed from an unclean spirit and then put his house or life in order. The implication was that he simply separated himself from the unclean spirit and was without the Holy Spirit to fill the void. And later the unclean spirit returned and found the "house empty, swept, and put in order." Then it (brought) with it seven other spirits more evil than itself, and they enter(ed) and (dwelt) there, and the last state of that person is worse than the first" (Matthew 12:44-45).

The point of the story is that it is not enough for people to simply clean up their lives. It is not enough to simply avoid evil because apart from the power and presence of the Holy Spirit through regeneration human beings are not able to keep themselves from sin and evil. To merely get your life together in such a way that you quit drinking or drugging or goofing off or gambling or sexing or whatever—even getting an education and decent job—is not enough to conquer sin.

In such a case, being devoid of the presence and power of the Holy Spirit will eventually be worse than your prior sinful condition. Why? Because being lost in gross sin pretty much guarantees personal poverty, and personal poverty tends to keep the effects of your sin to a minimum. But when a sinner cleans up his life apart from Christ, the cleaner life produces more income, and the additional income extends the reach or consequences of one's sin. Overcoming the grosser sins does not effect the more subtle and dangerous sins.

We see this in our prisons, where the inmates are encouraged to get an education so that they can get a decent job when they get out. Some inmates who embark on this path are successful. But apart from Christ, whether acknowledged or not, their success only provides them with opportunities to sin in more subtle and effective ways. Overcoming sin necessarily requires the power of Christ. But apart from regeneration in Christ, such people only become smarter sinners who because of their education are better able to sin, or better able to justify their sin, their life apart from Christ.

Education alone does not change character, it only helps people become better at what they already want to do. If they want to do the right things, then Christ's prevenient grace is already working in their lives. But if they don't, education will simply make them more effective sinners.

To educate means to develop a person's skills and abilities. Education takes what people already have and makes it better, more efficient. But what sinners need is regeneration, not mere education. Sinners need new desires, a new purpose, a new identity. Education without regeneration simply makes sinners smarter, but it does nothing to address their sin. The problem is that a smart crook can do more damage than a dumb one. And a crook who has won the respect of society is more dangerous than one who hasn't. And that was Jesus' point.

Doing Good

Similarly, Peter said that we are not to merely "turn away from evil," but that we must also "do good." We are to "seek peace and pursue it" (v. 11). While it is helpful and even necessary to stop doing the bad stuff, that's not enough. We must also actually do good. But how can sinners do good? They can't! Apart from regeneration and the active work of the Holy Spirit in one's own life it is simply not possible to do good.

Am I saying that unbelievers cannot do good works? Yes, the Bible teaches that the human condition is completely helpless and hopelessly lost in sin, and that only salvation by Jesus Christ can fix the problem. Only Christ's propitiation on the cross can atone for sin, and it has! That propitiation has already been made. Christ has already done everything that needs to be done. We are already His because all power and authority have already been given to Jesus Christ.

The Bible teaches that no good can be done apart from God in Christ.[55] So, those whom we identify as actually doing good, but who themselves do not acknowledge Jesus Christ as their Lord and Savior, are actually living a lie because they fail to recognize Christ for who He actually is. They use His light but fail to acknowledge that the house has been wired by the Lord, so to speak. If people are actually doing good, but fail to acknowledge Christ, they are at best confused about Christianity and about who they are, about their own identity, because the light of Christ illuminates everything. Unbelievers who actually do good have the appearance of godliness, but deny its origin and power (2 Timothy 3:5).

So, those who are not doing good, but who are living in blatant sin, need the regeneration that only Jesus Christ provides. And those who are doing good, but who deny or fail to recognize Christ for who He actually is in their own lives, are in need of Christian education. They will likely be ultimately saved, but don't yet know it because they have wrong ideas about Jesus and what salvation actually is, and even who they themselves are. Indeed, they undoubtedly have a host of wrong ideas about Christianity, about humanity and about human history.

We all know people who are engaged in what seems to be genuinely good—usually some sort of service to the poor—but who do not understand themselves to be Christian. Much of this sort of liberal social service today is done without the acknowledgment that concern for the poor actually issues from the love of God in Christ. Nonetheless, we must understand that failing to acknowledge Christ or Christ's involvement in one's own life does not mean that Christ is not the reigning King of the Universe, or that He is not actually involved in such an individual's life. Just because I fail to correctly understand Jesus Christ does not mean that He is not already preveniently involved in my life. Just because people fail to understand the Trinity does not mean that God does not function trinitarianly.

Of course, much of the surface motivation for doing good in our world is cut from the same works-righteous cloth as that of the Phar-

---

55 This, of course, is a highly disputed idea. It is not a simple prooftext (John 16:13) but issues from the fact of God's creation. The basic idea is that because God is the originator of everything, things are best understood from a perspective that is in harmony with God. If you don't believe it, I simply ask that you make the assumption as an act of faith and see what comes from it. For further discussion see the work of Cornelius Van Til (www.vantil.info) .

isees in Jesus' day. Indeed, all religiosity, including secular social service, apart from Christ is works-righteousness at best. Jesus was adam-
antly opposed to the works-righteousness of the Pharisees. But He was
not opposed to the good that they did—of course not! Feeding the poor
is good even when it is done out of self-centered pride. It is always better than not feeding the poor, but it never justifies the sinfulness of
pride or the consequences of sin.

Re-cognition

Jesus is always opposed to the false righteousness that such prideful people embody and employ. He was opposed to the failure of the
Jews to re-cognize Him as their long awaited Messiah, as He is always
opposed to anyone who fails to recognize who He actually is. He is
opposed to such people because, while they may do good apart from
recognizing who He is, they will always fail to recognize the trinitarianism of the Godhead because of the role and character of the Trinity in His identity.

And failing to recognize the Trinity, people will fail to give God the
glory He deserves and fail to worship Him as He commands. Failing to
recognize Jesus Christ as the trinitarian Son of God who provided propitiation for the sins of humanity means that whatever good is done
will be swallowed up in the wake of unforgiven sin that clings to unbelievers like rot to aged fruit. He was opposed to the narrowmindedness
of the ancient Pharisees and all other Christless monotheisms that
keep God's love and concern from blessing the nations, the other
people in the world.

God had saved and blessed the Jews so that they would be a blessing to the world (Genesis 12:2-3). God always intended to save the
whole world. But the Jews turned in on themselves, thinking that God's
blessings were blood related, probably because God had spoken of
inherited blessings. Sure God had been especially concerned about
raising children right, apart from exposure to sin and evil that casts
itself in a positive light. All parents understand that they are to protect
their children from evil and to teach them the necessity to honor and
respect others.

But where the ancient Jews went wrong was to think that God's
blessings issued from blood kinship with the ancient patriarchs of the
faith, and with the purity of the Jewish bloodline. They failed to
adequately understand and teach the doctrines of grace that God had
given them in the Old Testament. And failing to recognize and understand God's grace, they failed to recognize God's Son. So, God took that
failure of recognition on their part and used it to accomplish Christ's
crucifixion in history.

The historical fact of Christ's crucifixion, His bodily resurrection and the dispensation of the Holy Spirit then became the springboard for the propagation of the gospel of God's grace in Jesus Christ for the whole world. Christ's death and resurrection became the engine of Christian evangelism and outreach. And the success of the Christianization of the world has already been much more successful than people generally realize. The vine of world Christianity has yet to flower, but her roots have spread far and wide, even if unseen and unacknowledged. Indeed, the public acknowledgment of Christ's sovereignty is the capstone not merely the foundation for the glory of God in the church of Christ.

The continuing success of God's plan today has eluded many people because they have failed to adequately understand who God actually is and what salvation is actually about. They have failed to understand the meaning and the implications of God's trinitarian character having manifested perfectly in Jesus Christ, God's only begotten Son. Too many Christians have narrowly focused on God's activity in their own personal lives, and expected that God's involvement in the lives of others must match God's involvement in their own lives. So, Christians have been sidetracked with concerns about themselves, about their personal beliefs, their personal lives and their own personal expressions of Christian faith.

SHALLOW

This inward focus of contemporary spirituality has blinded people to the objective reality and work of Jesus Christ in the world. Because we have defined Christ's church too narrowly, as if it were limited to some particular administrative structure, we have failed to recognize Christ's involvement outside of our own narrowminded understanding. We have failed to understand the trinitarian character of His body, which is His church.

We ourselves have failed to adequately understand the trinitarian character of the Godhead, and the implications of the doctrine of the Trinity regarding the church of Jesus Christ, and of the actual role and function of Christ's church in human society. We have mistaken the logo for the corporation, the motto for the principle and the style for the substance. Our narrowminded vision of Jesus Christ has produced a shallow and inadequate understanding of reality.

In our day, too many Christians, like the Jews before them, have become ingrown with an inordinate concern about themselves and their churches, as if God could only work in ways that they acknowledge and understand at this moment. Rather than insisting that all Christians do things only the way that we (our particular church or denomination) do things, that all Christians understand Christianity only the way that we understand it, we must begin to acknowledge that, because God alone is good, all goodness comes only from God (Jeremiah 33:9, Mark 10:18). So, wherever any actual good is done, Jesus Christ is always necessarily involved.

This has tremendous implications for Christianity and for our world because it means that wherever good is being done, Christ is involved whether or not people yet know it or acknowledge it. Christ's involvement in our world and in our lives does not depend upon our awareness of Him. Christ can be at work in one's life without the person being aware of it. Being born again is simply the first awareness of this fact in one's own life. But the awareness of Chirst does not cause Him to be present.

Christ works the same way that gravity works, in that gravity does not depend people knowing anything about physics. When people "find" Jesus it is not that they invite Him into their lives, but that they discover that He is already there. The Holy Spirit is already involved in our world and in our lives. And what is more, we see that it was He who opened our eyes so that we can "see" God. Before He opened our eyes through regeneration, we could not see Him (John 3:3, 5). The Spirit comes in regeneration to people and one of the consequences of that regeneration is that they become aware of God's involvement in their lives. They notice that they have been regenerated, that they are not the person they used to be.

Uncommon Grace

Thus, it is not that Christians must explain how it is that unbelievers are able to do good works apart from knowing Christ, but that unbelievers must explain how they can do good works and be oblivious to the involvement of Jesus Christ in their own lives. It is not that believers and unbelievers have common ground in the secular world where certain limited aspects of God's grace are held in common.

Rather, believers and unbelievers have common ground only in the world that God created, the world that Christ has redeemed by His propitiation on the cross and that the Holy Spirit now inhabits. In reality, we all have these things in common, but unbelievers do not believe it. They refuse to believe it. And their failure to believe God's truth and to see God's active involvement in the world does not make God's truth or involvement unreal. Like gravity, it continues to operate whether anyone recognizes it or not. It just means that unbelievers don't believe it. And not believing it, they don't see it.

The burden of proof is not on believers to prove to unbelievers what is self-evident. Rather, the burden of proof is on unbelievers to explain to themselves and to the world how they are unable to see what is personally, historically and objectively self-evident in the light of Christ. Since history itself testifies that Christ has indeed come to this world, unbelievers must explain how it is that they don't see God in Christ. They must explain why they refuse to accept the gifts, grace and goodness of God in Christ Jesus.

Unbelievers assume that God does not exist and then ask believers to prove God's existence. But why is the assumption that God does not exist any more viable than the assumption that He does? Both are simply opposing assumptions that claim to be self-evident. Thus, it is at least equally viable for believers to assume that God exists and to ask unbelievers to prove that He doesn't. Indeed, the momentum of history is with believers.

The heart of this concern is not God's existence. God's existence is not something to be proven. It can only be accepted on faith, like an axiom. The issue is the character and viability of the idea of God's existence as a self-evident axiom. Where the reality of God is not self-evident, there is a failure to understand God's trinitarian character. In this case it is not that God doesn't exist, but that God has not been fully or correctly perceived and understood.

Peter said that people can prove the existence of God by keeping their own tongues from evil and their own lips from speaking deceit, by turning from evil and doing good, by seeking peace and pursuing it. So, by actively engaging God's Word in obedience our own lives will be so changed for the better that we will fall on our faces in praise of God. Only when God has changed our own lives by grace through faith in Christ, and we realize that His forgiveness has brought us growth in grace that we did not previously have and could not previously discern, will we cry out with newly discovered self-evident understanding of God in Christ, "Hallelujah! Thank you, Jesus!"

Contra Malum

How is it possible that believers and unbelievers can have such disparate ideas and experiences of God? How can believers claim God to be self-evident and unbelievers claim that the absence of God is self-evident. Peter answered this question when he said that, "the eyes of the Lord are on the righteous, and his ears are open to their prayer. But the face of the Lord is against those who do evil" (v. 12).

God is with the righteous and not with those who do evil. God is with believers and not with unbelievers. Thus, both groups accurately assess what is self-evident to them. Believers and unbelievers do not experience or understand the same things about God. They do not understand God or the world in the same ways because they do not experience God in the same ways. They each have different perspectives about their God data. Those with God consider God in their data, where those without God do not.

We could say that in a sense believers project God upon reality by presupposing His existence. And contrarily, unbelievers reject or withhold God from reality by presupposing His nonexistence. God then chooses to watch over and respond to the prayers of believers, and to turn away from unbelievers because God favors righteousness and eschews evil. Can it really be that simple? Indeed, it can and it is. Praise the Lord!

20. Christian Readiness

Now who is there to harm you if you are zealous for what is good? But even if you should suffer for righteousness' sake, you will be blessed. Have no fear of them, nor be troubled, but in your hearts honor Christ the Lord as holy, always being prepared to make a defense to anyone who asks you for a reason for the hope that is in you; yet do it with gentleness and respect, having a good conscience, so that, when you are slandered, those who revile your good behavior in Christ may be put to shame.   —1 Peter 3:13-16 (ESV)

By posing verse 13 as a question, Peter implied that no one should be against what is good. So, no one should object if you follow or do what is good. But we know that people do in fact oppose Christ, but we also know that Christ is nothing but good. So, there is more to this verse than what is in this verse. The verse must be understood in its context. Peter was suggesting that doing good to those who want to harm us will go a long way toward convincing them of the goodness of Christ's cause.

For the most part, those who oppose Christ misunderstand Him. There are precious few people who actively oppose Jesus Christ who actually understand God's actual character, mission or plan. Rather, the opposition against Christ feeds on misunderstanding, mischaracterization and misrepresentation, mostly out of ignorance but occasionally out of spite. Those who lead an upright and benevolent life should not fear anything or anyone because genuine righteousness—biblical righteousness—actually provides a widely respected social blessing. It is only when righteousness and justice interfere with people who are taking advantage of others that it is disliked.

And yet, this verse does not simply say, as it is usually translated, that Christians should be "zealous for what is good" (v. 13). It is not opposed to this idea, but the word *zealous* is not in the Greek. The *Authorized Version* reads, "be followers of that which is good." The idea of being zealous comes from the Greek word *ginomai*, which the *Authorized Version* translated as *be*. But it means more than *be*. Strong's says that it means *to cause to be*, and this causative character has led to the introduction of the word *zealous* to be added to help capture that meaning. And while there is nothing wrong with being zealous for that which is good, it misses an important nuance of meaning in the verse.

That nuance takes two forms. First, it suggests that Christians should promote the cause of all goodness, everything that is good. And that cause is God in Christ. And second, it suggests that Christians should be actively involved in causing people to do good by imitating or following Christ themselves. *Young's Literal Version* captures this sense of the verse: "and who is he who will be doing you evil, if of Him who is good ye may become imitators?"

MORAL LANDSCAPE

Note Peter's reliance on the knowledge of good and evil, first mentioned in Genesis 2:9, and forbidden in Genesis 2:17. Indeed, it was the transgression of God's instructions about this very thing that resulted in original sin or the Fall. To do what Peter here called for requires repairing the breech of original sin. And appropriate to Peter's intent is the idea that only the propitiation of Jesus Christ can—and has—repaired that breech. It is the propitiation of Jesus Christ that has repaired the breech and opens the only way that anyone can know or do what is actually good.

The truth is that we cannot know or do what is good apart from Jesus Christ because God alone provides the only objective definition of good, and has employed Jesus Christ to complete that definition. It is not that people who don't know Christ as their Lord and Savior actually do good, and that Christians must account for the good that they do apart from Christ. No, that frames the problem in the wrong way. Rather, people who don't know Christ as their Lord and Savior, but who actually do good, don't themselves know that it is Christ's presence or prevenient grace in their own lives that allows them to do any good at all.

And it is they who must account for their own failure to recognize the truth of Jesus Christ in their own lives who is actually the source of the good that they do. It is not Christians who must account for unrepentant sinners who occasionally stumble into doing something good. Rather, it is unrepentant sinners who must account for the fact that they cannot recognize their own delusion, which causes them to think that they themselves can do good and are good people.

Honor Christ

And lest we should worry too much about these things, Peter added: "But even if you should suffer for righteousness' sake, you will be blessed" (v. 14). We are to do good and encourage good in others even if it brings harm to us because the good will eventually overwhelm the evil. Peter had already addressed this idea in several previous verses. We need not fear or be troubled by anyone who works against the Lord. He will come to our aid, and will Himself work against the foolishness that opposes His goodness.

We need not concern ourselves with worrying about or working with such people because the Lord has something more important for us to do. Rather, said Peter, "in your hearts honor Christ the Lord as holy, always being prepared to make a defense to anyone who asks you for a reason for the hope that is in you" (v. 15).

How are we to honor Christ? The *Authorized Version* translated the word *honor* (*hagiazō*) as *sanctify*. We are to sanctify the Lord God. So, while it is actually God who sanctifies us, Peter tells us here to sanctify God. Sanctification is the process that God uses to bring us spiritual growth and maturity in Christ. Sanctification is a broad term that includes encouragement, chastisement, discipline, teaching, correction and satisfaction.

Of course, the root definition of *sanctify* is to separate unto God. That which is sanctified is kept or weaned from the corrupting influences of worldliness and godlessness. Paul wrote much about the process of sanctification and maturity in Christ. And in Paul's writings Christians are the subjects of sanctification. But here Peter wants Christians to sanctify the Lord. Are we to do for the Lord what He does for us? In an sense, yes.

Several Bible translations use the word *honor* here. The *English Standard Version* is representative: "in your hearts honor Christ the Lord as holy" (v. 15). The phrase "as holy" picks up the meaning of sanctify because the root of the Greek word (*hagiazō*) is often translated as *holy*. So, we are to honor and respect the holiness of Jesus Christ. We are to honor Jesus Christ as *Lord* (*kurios*).

We are to treat God as holy, and more, we are to treat Jesus Christ as holy. The idea of treating Jesus Christ as holy is necessarily a trinitarian idea because it draws on His divinity. It is about honoring both the humanity and divinity of Christ, without confusing or blending them. And that can be accomplished only through the doctrine of the Trinity.

There is a difference between God's sanctification of us and our sanctification of Him. His sanctification of us weans us from our sin and immaturity and grows us in Christ's righteousness and spiritual maturity. So, God honors us by making us more honorable over time. But our sanctification of God does not make God more holy. Or does it?

GROWTH OF PERFECTION

As Christians grow in righteousness and maturity we come to a clearer understanding and practice of God's perfect righteousness. Our understanding and practice of the propriety of Christ's righteousness, increases or deepens as we grow. And as it does, we give God in Christ more and more honor. So, while His personal righteousness does not grow because it is already perfect and does not change, ours does. And our appreciation of God also grows, which in turn adds to God's glory. So, while God Himself doesn't grow, His glory and honor grow as more and more people grow in His grace.

In addition, this sanctification of God is to take place in our hearts, in ourselves, our inner being. It is to be an inner reality, a matter of personal belief, confidence and faith. We are to assume God in Christ as the Holy Spirit that inhabits His people through regeneration. And as we assume that this is true of ourselves, we will find that it actually becomes increasingly true because the assumption itself will make it more true.

This assumption is also called faith in Christ. And it comes by grace through faith that we are saved. Faith or the realization and assumption of God in Christ in one's self is the means or mechanism of salvation. To believe it is to assume that it is true in your case. And the assumption proves itself to be self-authenticating over time as your life changes in the light of Christ.

Of course, we must be careful not to engage in the sin of presumption first mentioned in 1 Samuel 15:23, "For rebellion is as the sin of divination, and presumption is as iniquity and idolatry. Because you have rejected the word of the LORD, he has also rejected you from being king." This verse concludes the story of Saul's failure to obey God's Word. Saul thought that he had already obeyed it, but he hadn't, not fully. God had instructed Samuel to destroy *all*, and Saul had destroyed only *some* (1 Samuel 15), but assumed that he had done enough to satisfy God's command.

Divination is the error of attributing divinity falsely or wrongly. And *presumption* is thinking that something is true when it is not.

The caution here is to take care not to deny our own sinfulness or the extent of the impact of sin on humanity. Again, because of our trinitarian character, even as people grow out of their sin individually, the corporate character of our identity remains caught up in sin as long as any sin remains on earth. We will only be completely and finally cured of sin when all of humanity is cured of sin.

Nonetheless, faithful people will grow in righteousness personally and faithful communities will grow in righteousness corporately. The sin of presumption happens when people claim to be Christian, but don't act like it. They are presuming something to be true (their faithfulness) that appears to be false.

Hope

Verse 15 is huge. Christians are to always be prepared to defend their hope—their faith, their beliefs about God and Jesus Christ—with reason. Hope is the foundation of this verse because without hope we have nothing to defend and no reason to defend it. So, the hope must be real and it must actually be in us. The first thing to notice about the way that Peter phrased this concern is that he did not simply say that it was *your* hope. He only said that it needed to be *in* you. There are a variety of ways that this can be understood and the following are all true.

First, it could mean that you have hope as if it were a commodity, and that hope resides in your inner being. In this case the hope would in fact belong to you. But is it the hope that you *will be* saved, or that you *might be* saved? If it is Christian hope, it is both the assurance of your own salvation and the intention to persevere in that assurance to the end.

Could the hope belong to someone else? It could mean that the hope does not reside in you like a car resides in a garage, but involves a hoping in you like hoping that a basketball player will score a free-throw shot. Here you are the object of the hope as opposed to simply being its carrier. In this case the hope could belong to you in the same way that a basketball player owns his own hope that he can make the shot. But it could also be caught up with the hope of the other players that he will make the shot. Indeed, all those who are rooting for his team may share such a hope. Here we see that hope can and usually does contain a social element. Everyone who roots for a particular team shares a particular hope. And similarly, Christians all share a common hope for one another in the sense of this team centered hope.

But the hope could also belong to Jesus Christ. In this case, the Lord would hope for the accomplishment of His own mission. Here we must not understand the word *hope* to simply mean to pine or yearn for something that *might* happen. That is most emphatically not what Christ does! He has no doubt that His mission on earth will be fully and perfectly accomplished. His hope is an assurance or certainty.

As an aside, it is interesting to observe that, while Jesus said, "It is finished" (John 19:30), just before He died on the cross, it was *not* finished. Christianity was not finished, it was just beginning. And Jesus was not finished because He would soon be resurrected. The story wasn't finished, either. So, what was finished?

The goal of Jesus' earthly life was the propitiation of God for the sin of the world. He needed to pay the price to close the deal that would release God's grace upon humanity. And since His death as the punishment for sin was the price, the closing of that transaction finished or closed the deal. Jesus' death on the cross was like signing the final papers for a home purchase. Once the papers are signed, the sale is finished, though payment may not be complete.

BE PREPARED

The next element of Peter's charge is to be prepared. Peter did not tell us to defend our hope, but to *prepare* for its defense. The two things are related, but different. The Greek root of the word (*hetoimos*) means to be fit or to conform to some standard. Thus, our readiness can be compared to military preparedness.

Several things must be done to prepare a nation for an attack against it. Soldiers must be drafted and trained. Materials must be acquired and weapons manufactured. The actual battles that ensue in any conflict are a very small part of the process of military preparedness.

It is also significant to note that Peter was not writing to a particular individual, but to the saints as a group or whole. Of course, individual Christians need to prepare themselves to defend their hope. But when we think of the church as a whole working together to accomplish Peter's admonition the idea grows exponentially in size and complexity by a large factor. And that is what Peter was talking about. Of course, the verse means that people should know their Bibles. But that is like a soldier knowing how to clean and dress his sidearm. Of course, the weapon must be clean and function properly, but that is a very small part of what is involved in military defense.

Peter was saying that the church needed to be prepared to defend the hope that is in her—corporately. We are so used to thinking in terms of our aberrant Modern Western individualism that it is difficult for us to read and understand Scripture corporately. But if we are going to harvest the deeper meaning of this verse, we must do so corporately, together. Again, while doing so as individuals is helpful and it moves the process in the right direction, it leaves much to be desired. The church must learn to think and act like a nation that is moving toward military preparedness.

I'm not suggesting any sort of Christian militancy, not at all! Rather, I'm simply trying to envision the kind of organization and preparation that Peter had in mind. Peter was talking to the whole church when he told us to be prepared to defend the hope of the gospel. Thus, he was talking about both our hope in the gospel and God's hope for the gospel. As I said before, God's hope is not pining and whining for some preferred outcome. God's hope issues out of His foreknowledge that His will cannot be averted, His plan cannot fail. So, God confidently expects the future that He has envisioned. That's God's hope.

ORGANIC UNITY

Thus, Peter's call for gospel defense was a call to unite the churches organically. In military terminology, *organic* refers to a military unit that is a permanent part of a larger unit and usually provides some specialized capability to that parent unit. It was a call for the establishment of Christian or biblical social structure as much as anything else.

The best cultural defense will always be the establishment of appropriate social structures that work together toward the ultimate defense of its own hope. The accomplishment of any goal requires an intense and sustained focus on the goal. Goals are not accidentally accomplished. They require intentionality, effort and coordination. People misunderstand Peter's call when they interpret it in strictly individualistic terms. Of course he does mean personal preparation, but not merely that.

How is this goal of the defense of Christ's hope to be accomplished? Peter said, "with meekness and fear; having a good conscience" (vs. 15-16). This great goal of the church is to be accomplished with a spirit of meekness. If meekness is one of the instruments we are to use, then we must correctly understand it. Meekness is not mousiness, nor is it timidity or awkwardness. No, meekness is the willing submission of a racehorse to the directions of the jockey. Meekness is the willing discipline that allows a runner to win a race by pouring every ounce of strength and determination he has into the race—and more.

Christian meekness taps into more than our human strengths because it submits to the power and presence of God through regeneration. Meekness is the essence of faithfulness because meekness moves pride and the resistance of pride out of the way. Meekness is the essence of fruitfulness because meekness does not resist the power of the Vine (John 15:5). Meekness treasures its connection to the life-giving Vine. Meekness knows that its own leaf and fruit are powered by the Vine and not by its own efforts. So meekness gives itself completely to the power of the Vine. Meekness is not weakness, but strength in

Christ. Meekness is not self-centered but is other-centered by the love of Christ.

FEARFUL MEEKNESS

Meekness works with respect or *fear* (*phobos*), as the *Authorized Version* translates it. The fear of meekness is not cowardice, but courage that does not flinch at the specter of its own demise. Nor does meekness cower in insecurity, nor flee from responsibilities that are too heavy to carry. Because the meek do not depend upon themselves, they are free to accomplish more than they can themselves do. The meek do not look away when confronted, but look to the hills from whence comes their help (Psalm 121:1).

It is the fear of the meek that God turns into courage and determination. Fear alone would simply flee danger and distress. But the fear of the Lord is a fear that conquers all other fears by remembering the context of life and death—that context being God. Fear stimulates adrenalin and adrenalin provides strength, focus and responsiveness. And the greater the fear the more the adrenaline flows. So, the fear of the Lord provides great strength, focus and responsiveness for use in the defense of Christ's hope for the salvation of His people. Indeed, meekness and fear provide formidable help to the people of God for the defense of Christian hope.

There is so much power and strength that are given through meekness and fear that Peter prescribes a governor to keep them in line. That governor is "a good conscience" (v. 16). A good conscience is essential to keep believers in line with God's vision for His people. And what is this conscience? The Greek word (*suneidēsis*) literally means *co-perception*. Thus, it is first and foremost a perception, a way of seeing or thinking, even a worldview. And it is not merely the seeing, thinking, perception or worldview of the believer, but is a *co*-perception. It is a shared perception, a shared vision or way of seeing.

Shared among whom? Shared among fellow believers, to be sure. But the communal aspect of this shared perception is not what Peter means. It is not the fact that other people share your views that defines conscience. Rather, conscience is most clearly seen when it causes people to stand alone in opposition to what others think. So, the shared character of the co-perception is not its communal character, though its communal character is both real and important. Rather, the light of conscience originates in Christ. The substance of conscience does not originate from the Christian community, but issues from Christ who shares His perception with His people through the power and presence of the Holy Spirit through regeneration. The perception of conscience belongs to Christ, who shares it with His people.

People of conscience are people who see and are responsive to the moral dimensions of life. They are people who are sensitive to the needs and problems of others, and to the moral concerns of God in Christ. And yet, Christian morality is not simply a concern for the well-being of others, but it is a response to God's concern for the well-being of His people. Christian morality is biblical morality in the light of Christ. And when harnessed to the meekness and fear that Peter mentioned, it becomes Christian morality on steroids—not in the sense of being hyper-critical but in the sense of being hyper-strong.

Shame

The final purpose for the defense of hope through meekness, fear and conscience is "so that, when you are slandered, those who revile your good behavior in Christ may be put to shame" (v. 16). The Lord wants His people to be so consumed with and by social structures that are geared to the defense of Christian hope, that are so focused on the glory of God in Christ that no other motive can be conceived. In this way, when people react in disgust and slander to the righteousness of Christ, the consciences of His people will be so clear that all responsibility for the defensive behavior can be attributed to God alone. The purpose is to employ the goodness of God and the purity of an obedient conscience, in order to shame any and all who object to God.

Indeed, Peter was here recommending the use of shame as a legitimate and even preferred tool for evangelism. Yes, the purpose for defending Christian hope is evangelistic. It is a way to present the gospel as the Lord wants it to be presented, which is not simply as a verbal argument but as a way of living that is so attractive that people will engage it even though they are slandered and vilified because of it.

Gandhi, having learned from Christianity what he called nonviolence, shamed people into growing morally by suffering for the sake of what he believed was a righteous cause. Gandhi, who was not a Christian, had great success applying this biblical teaching among a people who were not Christian. Imagine the power of doing so as a Christian among Christians!

Peter wants people to be so engaged that they will not disengage even on threat of death. The goodness and beauty of God must shine in and through His people so that without saying a word those who stand against them feel the sting of humiliation and shame. The mere existence of Christ's goodness and righteousness should bring people to their knees in thankfulness for it and in embarrassment for their own lack of it. And those who are unable or unwilling to acknowledge the goodness and glory of God must be brought to the humility of shame and embarrassment as the only credible response to the opposition of

God's goodness and greatness regarding His mission in Christ Jesus. The very sight of Christ's goodness and righteousness should shame and embarrass unrepentant sinners to the point that they want to make a change in their lives for the better in Christ.

21. THE GRACE OF SUFFERING

For it is better to suffer for doing good, if that should be God's will, than for doing evil. For Christ also suffered once for sins, the righteous for the unrighteous, that he might bring us to God, being put to death in the flesh but made alive in the spirit, in which he went and proclaimed to the spirits in prison, because they formerly did not obey, when God's patience waited in the days of Noah, while the ark was being prepared, in which a few, that is, eight persons, were brought safely through water.   —1 Peter 3:17-20 (ESV)

Verse 17 joins the idea of suffering with the doing of God's will. God does not mandate human suffering, nor is such suffering a necessary part of God's will. It is not that God wants people to suffer. In fact, He doesn't want people to suffer, and He doesn't want it so much that He sent His only begotten Son to suffer and die on our behalf, to take the punishment on Himself for our transgressions.

However, He did this not simply to keep people from suffering, but to gather people up into salvation by freeing us from the consequences of our sin and the damnation that follows. God's intention is to ultimately end what He defines as sin and suffering on earth, to make earth like heaven (Matthew 6:10). And the critical issue in this regard is that God's definitions do not always match ours. In fact, they seldom do. Or perhaps a better way to say it is that our definitions don't always match His, which puts the issue in proper perspective.

Many people are frustrated with God because the world is awash in sin and suffering—and God is in charge of the world. Many people charge God with creating and promoting evil based upon His sovereignty and authority. They reason that because God created everything they think that He must have also created evil (Isaiah 45:7, Amos 3:6, Lamentations 3:38) because evil exists. But evil is not a thing, nor is it created. Rather, evil is a value attribute. We tend to objectify it and use it as a noun or a thing, but it is an adjective, a classification, a value judgment.

SAYS WHO?

It is true that God first defined evil in the Garden of Eden. So, in a sense God did create or invent evil when He spoke of the value of knowledge as being good or evil (Genesis 2:9). Things, beliefs and ideas are described as evil because they do not conform to God's values, which are provided through the whole of the biblical literature, Old Testament and New.

Because God distinguished between good and evil, he did define evil. Those things that oppose God are defined by God as evil, and apart from God's definitions of them there would be no ultimate good or evil. Only God has access to the certainty of ultimate knowledge. For the most part human beings follow God's lead and deem things that we ourselves like as being good and things that we ourselves don't like as being evil—but doing so is sinful. Nonetheless, there is a sense in which good and evil are usually seen as a reflection of our own personal preferences. We tend to think of good and evil as being related to pleasure and pain or like and dislike. We tend to think that what makes us feel good is ultimately good for us, and what makes us feel bad is ultimately and objectively evil. But God knows better.

We human beings get into trouble when we objectify our own preferences and begin believing that our own preferences yield or reflect ultimate value judgments that are objectively true. God's personal preferences are in fact objectively true because God is by definition the determiner of ultimate reality. We are not, and understanding that we human beings are not the ultimate determiners of good and evil is the central biblical lesson that God is teaching.

Because that lesson is difficult for us to learn, because it opposes our natural tendencies, because God's ways are not our ways, and because God's thoughts are not like our thoughts (Isaiah 55:8-9), He sent His Son, Jesus Christ, to mediate and mitigate God's understanding of good and evil for us. God gave us the Old Testament and all that it entails and then sent Jesus Christ to correct our accumulated errors and misunderstandings of it by giving Him the highest and most complete authority in this world.

And because Jesus Christ condescended to become one of us in human form, in our human reality, He is best able to communicate God's vision of good and evil, of God's categories of right and wrong, in a way that is understandable and useable to human beings. However, we must remember that reality is complex and understanding it all

isn't easy. It takes regeneration, time and maturity. It is Christ's trinitarian character and His ongoing presence as God's Holy Spirit through
regeneration in the lives of His people that provides the guidance and
correction that we need to see the wholeness and holiness of God's program of redemption.

Good Pain

Peter was trying to break the association between good and evil
with pleasure and pain in verse 17. Reality is not so simple as such an
association suggests. Pleasure is not always good, nor is pain always
evil. So, Peter simply noted that doing good does not always result in
pleasure, but can and often does result in pain and suffering. Why?
Because of the reality of evil. Because what is good irritates what is evil.
Because goodness threatens to destroy evil in the same way that light
destroys or dispels darkness. And yet, in spite of God's goodness and
power, evil persists.

Does the ongoing evil of sin and suffering mean that God's will is
not or cannot be accomplished? Not at all! In fact, the world is driven
by God's will. And at the same time, God's will is that sin and suffering
end and that good be done everywhere at all times. So, why do sin and
suffering persist in the world?

Sin and suffering are not willed by God, though they are used to
accomplish God's purposes. In a sense, God did create evil by defining
it, but His definition includes the fact that evil has no part or place in
Him. Thus, evil is not outside of God's ultimate purposes, but it is not
part of His desire or character. Rather, God's sovereignty is so great
that He can use evil for the accomplishment of His own good purposes.

God is good and He wills what is good. And what He determines to
be good is actually good. We human beings are in no position to criti-
cize or improve upon God's values. We must also realize that life is
complex, much more complex than previous generations ever ima-
gined.

Thus, while the elimination of sin and evil are good, the punishment of sin and evil are also good because they produce either repentance and the consequent abandonment of sin and evil, or they serve
the establishment of God's justice, which is also good. God is working
on at least two positive fronts: 1) promoting what is good, and 2) promoting justice, which is also good. And because only God's own definition of good is actually good, so God's definition of the goodness of His
justice is ultimately good, as well. Just like we human beings are tempted to define good and evil on the basis of our own experience and
value judgments, we are tempted to define justice and injustice on the
same flawed basis.

PURPOSEFUL PAIN

People are easily confused about these things because people like to think that all of what they themselves define or experience as pain, suffering and difficulties, are bad. But they are not. People sometimes suffer pain and difficulties in this world as a consequence of sin. And sometimes our suffering is simply part of our own growth and maturity or sanctification. Sometimes individuals cause their own suffering, and sometimes individuals are caught up in suffering caused by social or cultural problems. Consequently, while sin is an evil thing, pain and difficulty are not necessarily evil. We may not like them. We may not have chosen to so suffer, but that does not make it bad or evil. It is not the experience of a thing that makes it good or evil, it is the ultimate purpose that it serves.

Often the positive purpose of pain and suffering is to encourage people to avoid sin. And where sin is not avoided, pain, suffering and difficulties are the just consequences of sin. Pain and difficulties accompany sin because sin is evil and because God's justice requires punishment for transgression. Because what is good is in agreement and in harmony with God, what is evil is out of agreement and harmony with God, and dissonance results. That dissonance is then experienced as pain, discomfort and irritation.

Thus, justice and its punishment are then actually good things when they serve God's purposes. The pain and suffering are intended to provide lessons about avoiding sin and evil. So, the learning of those lessons is good, and the failure to learn from them engages God's justice and judgment, which are intended to be corrective measures. And again, God's justice is a good thing.

God's will is for people to do good. God wants what is good for all people. And if people suffer the slings and arrows of misfortune for doing what is good and right in God's eyes, then that suffering is good by definition. The reward for it is the promotion of the greater good in the world. It contributes to corporate or social goodness and provides general benefit for humanity. This kind of suffering for doing good is much to be preferred over suffering consequences for one's own sin and evil because suffering for doing good actively promotes and increases the general level of goodness in the world. There is an accumulated social benefit when a lot of people do a little good. Though you suffer, you are contributing to the greater social good.

But when people suffer the consequences of sin because of their own bad behavior, their suffering only passively promotes good when the negative example they provide links sin with suffering. In other words, it is good for God's law to punish sinners as a way to dissuade both themselves and others from sinning. It is a greater evil when unrepentant sinners do not suffer the consequences of their own sinful behavior. So, getting away with evil behavior turns out to be doubly evil because it has no redeeming value whatsoever.

The best way to deal with this concern is to use our own suffering to learn to avoid sin. And such learning is in accordance with God's will. However, God doesn't demand that people suffer in order to learn His will. But if they don't or won't learn it any other way, then the suffering is provided as a foundation for their learning.

And inasmuch as the learning fails to occur, the suffering then serves the purposes of God's justice. And God's justice is also good. So, either way God wins, and both His goodness and His justice are advanced by everything that people do. When they do good, it is His good that they increase. And when they do evil, it is His justice that they prove as He pours out His judgment upon evil. The only losers are those who fail to heed God's Word.

CHRIST OUR MODEL

In verse 18 Peter showed that Christ provided the model for our suffering. So, as Christ suffered and because Christ suffered, those who follow Him will also suffer. Whether our suffering is unjust because we are engaged in doing God's will or is just because we are thwarting God's will, that suffering serves God's purposes.

Peter began by mentioning that Christ suffered once for sins. This was a reference to His suffering and death on the cross. Peter then clarified this meaning by saying that Christ who is righteous suffered for sinners who are unrighteous, or as the *Authorized Version* translated it, "the just for the unjust" (v. 18).

Then to make sure that we understand what he intended to say, Peter added that Christ's purpose in all this was "to bring us to God" (v. 18). And because the purpose of Christ's suffering was to bring people to God, the purpose of our suffering is also to bring people to God. It is significant that people are brought to God in different ways and for different purposes. Not everyone experiences the same thing when they are brought to God.

The suffering of the righteous brings people to God for comfort by being a model of faithfulness and encouragement. And the suffering of the unrighteous brings people to God for judgment by providing a lesson about God's justice that requires punishment for sin. So, those who are so dense as to not understand or accept that Christ has already suffered their punishment for them by taking their place on the cross, must themselves suffer the consequences of their own sin in this life and the next. Those who refuse to understand and accept Christ's vicarious atonement on the cross don't get it, and they can blame no one but themselves for that failure.

DEATH/BIRTH, OLD/NEW, END/BEGINNING

The last example that Peter provided in this verse was that Christ was "put to death in the flesh but made alive in the Spirit" (v. 18). The death of the Old Man in Adam is necessary for the birth of the New Man in Christ. The death of the one is the birth of the other. Jesus spoke of the necessity of putting new wine in new wineskins (Matthew 9:17), of not sewing new cloth to an old garment (Mark 2:21). Paul spoke of being a new creation in Christ and of the old passing away (2 Corinthians 5:17), and of a New Covenant replacing the Old (Hebrews 8:13). Just as Jesus died in the flesh and rose in the Spirit, so must His people die to the flesh and rise in the Spirit.

Verse 19 has provided much confusion because of a narrow reading that is devoid of the richness and depth that is provided by the trinitarian perspective. Rather than rehash that confusion, let me suggest that this verse speaks to the same thing that Paul spoke of in Galatians 3:21-26:

"Is the law then contrary to the promises of God? Certainly not! For if a law had been given that could give life, then righteousness would indeed be by the law. But the Scripture imprisoned everything under sin, so that the promise by faith in Jesus Christ might be given to those who believe. Now before faith came, we were held captive under the law, imprisoned until the coming faith would be revealed. So then, the law was our guardian until Christ came, in order that we might be justified by faith. But now that faith has come, we are no longer under a guardian, for in Christ Jesus you are all sons of God, through faith."

Verse 19 speaks about the captivity of humanity in the chains of sin from time immemorial. Remember that Peter deals with big ideas and the general themes of human history in order to put Jesus Christ in His proper context. Humanity has been in captivity to sin, imprisoned by sin, and Christ has come to humanity's rescue. The "spirits in prison" (v. 19) simply refers to humanity's slavery to sin. The Old Man is a slave to sin.

The larger context of this verse is regeneration by the Holy Spirit. It's about having died to the old spirit in Adam and of being made alive in the Holy Spirit in Christ. Peter then illustrates this idea by associating it with the Great Flood and God's renewal of humanity by saving Noah and his family from drowning in the ancient Flood. The old humanity died in the flood, and the new humanity would be born again from the stock of Noah. Peter was simply providing an example of how God works. Noah's Flood provided a type or example of God's regeneration. Most people drowned in the Flood, but God brought a few people "through the water" (v. 20). He saved them. The flood story was but a shadow of the reality of salvation that had come in Christ Jesus.

Peter tied this example to his previous discussion of doing good by suggesting that the bulk of people in Noah's day were imprisoned by sin, which kept them out of Noah's ark and brought them to a watery death. But God spared or saved or regenerated humanity through those who joined Noah in the ark.

There's more. The people to whom the Lord proclaimed and who were described as "spirits in prison" (v. 19) are the same people who did not obey in verse 20. Thus, the "spirits in prison" (v. 19) are identified as the disobedient people of the Old Testament who drowned in Noah's Flood, and by implication they represent the people of all places and times who are disobedient to the Lord. The "spirits in prison" (v. 19) are the same people who Paul said were "dead in (their) trespasses and sins" (Ephesians 2:1).

Flood Waters

Elsewhere Paul argued that "the Scripture imprisoned everything under sin, so that the promise by faith in Jesus Christ might be given to those who believe" (Galatians 3:22). Thus, the phrase, "spirits in prison" (v. 19), refers generally to those who do not believe because it is only through belief or faith that such prisoners are set free in Christ. Since they are in prison, they have not been set free.

Calvin said that the reason that Peter used the example of Noah's Flood was to encourage believers. The argument goes something like this: the world has always been overwhelmingly dominated by unbelievers. So, believers should not lose heart because they are outnumbered. God is not interested in nor responsive to mere numbers, He is interested in faithfulness. Noah and his family were preserved and the overwhelming majority of unbelievers were drowned. Therefore, believers can take courage and hold fast to their faith without regard for their number, large or small.

The fact of this example then brought up the idea of baptism because of the example of Noah's family passing safely through the waters of the flood. Noah's Flood was thought of by Peter as a kind of baptism. Noah and his family were saved by passing through the flood waters. Perhaps he recalled that Paul had spoken of the Israelites having passed through the parting of the Red Sea as a kind of baptism (1 Corinthians 10:2), as well.

22. Saved By Baptism

Baptism, which corresponds to this, now saves you, not as a
removal of dirt from the body but as an appeal to God for a
good conscience, through the resurrection of Jesus Christ, who
has gone into heaven and is at the right hand of God, with
angels, authorities, and powers having been subjected to him.
—1 Peter 3:21-22 (ESV)

Peter here argues that baptism is salvific, that people are saved by baptism. Of course, he qualified it in two ways. First, by saying that "baptism corresponds to this" (v. 21), where the word *this* refers to that of which he has been speaking. And second, he was not talking about baptism "as a removal of dirt from the body but as an appeal to God for a good conscience, through the resurrection of Jesus Christ" (v. 21). So, while salvation through baptism is actual, and while the ceremony of baptism uses water, the reality of baptism is not about the water or the ceremony, though both are necessary for baptism to occur.[56]

Immediately we are embroiled in the old debate about the efficacy of baptism and whether baptism produces regeneration. It is important to notice that Peter doesn't use the language of production or of cause and effect. Rather, he suggests that baptism properly understood and practiced is indeed salvific. But his emphasis here is upon the proper understanding of baptism from a trinitarian perspective.

Peter was not talking about the ceremony of baptism, but about the personal and historical reality of new life in Christ. His attention was on the result not the process. However, the reality of new life in Christ necessarily issues from the trinitarian character of God and impacts the trinitarian character of the renewed person in that the Holy Spirit inter-

---

56   For more on baptism see footnote 40, page 112.

cedes and connects the renewed individual to the divinity of Jesus Christ, the second Person of the Trinity.

The historical anomaly is that the word *baptism* has been used in both Scripture and history to refer to both the end result and the process, and has done so without the specificity and clarity that we now desire. The lack of clarity in Scripture in conjunction with the desire for increased clarity on our part has fueled the historical confusion that has surrounded this debate. What the Bible refers to as baptism is actually a complex sacrament that impacts both individuals and communities in a variety of ways.

The confusion has arisen because of an unbiblical desire for simplicity in the face of complexity. Baptism is called a sacrament because by it people are ceremonially, legally and actually separated from the world and brought into Christ's church. Once people are brought into the church, once people are in Christ, they are considered to have both the necessary gifts for and obligations of obedience to His precepts— not perfect but increasing obedience. Whereas prior to baptism, people are considered to have neither the ability nor are they aware of their obligation under God's covenant. Upon baptism, then, the gifts and the obligations begin to grow.

Baptism is the historic method of church expansion through the formal membership incorporation of individuals. It is by baptism or through baptism that church membership grows. And as with all living things, growth is a complex reality that requires several inputs and produces several outputs. Correctly understanding and defining baptism is essential for correctly understanding Peter's point. What does baptism have to do with Peter's general theme?

Model Submission

Peter began this chapter with a discussion of the covenantal obligations of marriage. Wives are to live in submission to Christ through the household authority of their husbands. One of the benefits of wifely submission is that it provides a model for the children to emulate. When the wife lives in loving submission to the headship authority of her husband and actively gives glory to God in the midst of that relationship, the children of the marriage are given a front row seat from which to observe and learn about the importance of love and authority. They can learn how mom and dad deal with their responsibility under authority to operate in the harmony of mutual love and respect. And where the children do not see these things modeled, they do not learn them.

Wives are to adorn themselves with the inner beauty of a quiet and gentle spirit that is attuned and committed to the needs of her husband

and family. Husbands are to love and honor their wives, both under-standing them—which means listening to and hearing them—and giving understanding to them, which means teaching and instructing them. The husband is not just the head of the household, he is the priest of the household who represents God to his family through instruction and represents his family to God through prayer and instruction.[57]

In 1 Peter 3:8 Peter instructed all Christians to "have unity of mind, sympathy, brotherly love, a tender heart, and a humble mind." All Christians are to do what God teaches because it is good and to renounce the spirit of revenge by being willing to suffer when people misunderstand and/or oppose the good they do. This is what God wants and what Christ preached. This message and preaching of Christ awakens people as if from the dead. This message of the gospel brought new life to those who were dead in their trespasses and sins.

Thus, Peter introduced baptism as an example of how this message of the gospel changes people. Yes, God changes individuals, but God also changes people corporately. To illustrate the individual changes that are involved Peter compared baptism to a clean conscience. And to illustrate the corporate changes that are involved Peter compared baptism to Noah's Flood. Individuals are washed clean by the waters of baptism in terms of conscience. And humanity is corporately renewed through baptism as it was renewed by Noah's Flood. Baptism places people under a renewed covenant with God in Christ.

The ceremony of baptism performed by the church does not and cannot guarantee that the individual who is baptized has, will have or will continue to have a good conscience. That's between the individual and God. However, baptism does impose God's covenant in Christ upon the individual in terms of the obligation of obedience to Scripture and mutual Christian submission (Ephesians 5:21). The obligation has social elements that are to be overseen by church elders (Acts 20:28, Philippians 1:1, 1 Timothy 3). Thus, baptism is salvific regarding the church as a corporate whole in the sense that all church members are baptized, but that does not mean that every baptized individual will be faithful.

Symbol and Reality

The historic debates about baptism have proceeded along the lines of the difference between the sign and the thing signified, or the symbol and the reality, both of which issue from the difference between the classic dualistic Greek philosophical categories of abstractness and

---

57 This does not mean that fathers can or should baptize their own children or serve communion without church authority. Those are church sacraments.

concreteness. In contrast, Peter's categories are trinitarian (unity and plurality). Peter has posed the baptismal issue in terms of individual conscience and corporate renewal. However, he has not opposed them against one another, but speaks of them as being mutually supportive, as if they both belong to a greater unified reality.

To comprehend Peter's point we must not think that he had in mind the process or procedure of a baptismal ceremony, but rather Peter was writing about the purpose or end result of baptism. We confuse ourselves when we apply or perceive procedural categories in a discussion of purpose. In the case of individuals Peter spoke of a good conscience as being the result of baptism. And in the case of corporate humanity, he spoke of Noah's Flood as being a kind of corporate baptism that resulted in a new covenant. Both are about death and new life.

God flooded the whole world, but Noah and his family were prepared and saved. And the fact of their preparation, their response to God's warnings, caused a different result from Noah's Flood for them than for the rest of humanity. So, while God brought the same experience upon all humanity (Noah's Flood), those who had responded to God (Noah and his family) experienced a different result (renewal) than those who didn't (death). The same pattern can be seen with regard to God's covenant with humanity in that those who respond to God have a different result (salvation) than those who ignore God (damnation). The old saying is that the same sun that hardens the clay also melts the wax.

Different Result

When we look at Noah's Flood as a kind of baptism, we find that the Flood brought two things to humanity as a whole: death and renewal. We are used to thinking of Christian baptism as a kind of symbolic death of the individual, who then rises out of the waters of baptism into new life in Christ. And this is good symbolism, which Paul engaged in Romans 6.

However, Peter was not engaging in that kind of individual baptismal symbolism here. He was using Noah's Flood as an example of God's purpose for humanity through baptism. Noah's Flood was not a symbol, but a reality. God was not averse to wiping out populations of faithless people in order to accomplish His ultimate purpose, which is the establishment of human faithfulness and righteousness. While God's people are usually marginalized people of one sort or another, it is not God's intention to be the God of the marginalized. God's intention is to be the only trinitarian God of all humanity, that Jesus Christ be at the very center of human culture.

We know this because according to Scripture God's renewal of humanity through Noah reestablished God's covenant at the center of the post Flood human culture. Note two things about Noah's Flood: 1) 99.999 percent of the human population died, and 2) God saved Noah and his family—eight people. Now remember who Peter was writing to: Christians who were fleeing the impending destruction of Jerusalem. Peter was aware of the build up of the Roman war machine, and likely saw a similarity between the destruction of Noah's Flood and the impending destruction of Jerusalem. This similarity caused Peter to call attention, not to the destruction of the many brought about by the baptism of Noah's Flood but to God's preservation of the faithful in the midst of great upheaval. It was the fact of God's faithfulness to His covenant and to His covenant people that was the object of Peter's attention.

CONSCIENCE

Of course, the corporate body is always composed of individuals. Peter did not neglect the end, result or purpose of individual baptism—a good conscience. And exactly what was this good conscience to which Peter referred? Again, the Greek word translated as *conscience* (*suneidēsis*) refers to a kind of co-perception. Another way to understand it is to see it as a combination of two other Greek words (*sun* and *eidō*) that indicate a summary oversight, or seeing from the perspective of an overview, from a perspective that sees the wholeness of a thing, that sees a thing, idea or process start to finish, beginning to end, conception to completion.

Consequently, *conscience* refers to a perspective from which the wholeness of the world is seen and understood. The contemporary definition of *conscience* demonstrates this: "motivation deriving logically from ethical or moral principles that govern a person's thoughts and actions." Conscience sees and understands the world from ethical and moral principles. Peter found those principles in Scripture, and mostly in the Old Testament because that was Scripture for Peter. But it was the Old Testament as seen in the light of Christ. Conscience refers to a perspective about life that produces behavior that is consistent with what the Bible calls faithfulness.

Peter's reference to this conscience as being good indicates the harmonious consistency between a person's actual behavior and the behavior described in Scripture as faithful. A good conscience does not feel guilt associated with its personal behavior. And it is not that it is numb to guilt that is present, like a sociopath experiences guilt. Rather, it knows that the guilt has been taken care of by Jesus Christ. Indeed, such guilt has been washed away by the waters of baptism, and because of the forgiveness provided by Christ's propitiation on the cross.

Guilt is then continuously eliminated because of what Jesus has done and the individual's love and faithfulness to Jesus Christ. Christ's faithfulness and the sinner's response cannot be artificially separated as if they are two independent things. They are not. Rather, they are two elements of one thing—salvation. Thus, the result of this faithfulness is the maintenance of faithful behavior through conformity to biblical principles of morality by the power and presence of the Holy Spirit through regeneration.

CLUSTERING

Again, life is complex, the world is complex, people are complex, behaviors are complex. Human behaviors tend to cluster around various principles. People who deceive others are more likely to steal and to not honor agreements. People who commit adultery are more likely to lie in order to avoid revealing their adultery. And conversely, people who are honest are less likely to lie, steal or commit adultery. Behaviors tend to cluster around principles, beliefs, presuppositions and loyalties. The Bible guides human behavior by focusing on principles, beliefs, presuppositions and loyalties that God defines as good. Thus, a good conscience is a biblical conscience, a conscience that engages in personal faithfulness to Scripture through regeneration.

Peter also said that this good conscience is exercised as an "appeal to God ... through the resurrection of Jesus Christ" (v. 21). The *Authorized Version* translated this phrase as, "toward God ... by the resurrection of Jesus Christ." It must be understood that Christians do not practice conscientiousness in order to attain salvation, but practice it in the response of thankfulness for a received salvation.

Thus, they are not making an appeal to God to stay their execution, but are involved in the process of appreciating God's love and faithfulness to them, and of publicly showing the appeal of God's love and faithfulness by making God attractive to others. Believers are not motivated by trying to avoid the consequences of their sin because those consequences have already been taken care of by Jesus Christ. Believers are already on the other side of their own death.

RESURRECTION AND REGENERATION

Note also that Peter appeals to God through, not just Jesus, but through the *resurrection* of Jesus Christ. Yes, Jesus Christ is the only actual mediator between God and humanity (1 Timothy 2:5), but that is not what Peter was getting at here. He was describing the mechanism of that mediation, which is Christ's resurrection. Had Christ not been resurrected, He would not be the mediator. So, Christ's resurrection provided identification and assurance regarding His role as mediator.

And exactly what does Christ mediate? Yes, He mediates between man and God, between sinners and God. But what does He reconcile through the mechanism of His resurrection? Because God cannot tolerate sin, human sin is removed by Christ's sacrificial death which atoned for sin and allowed for God's forgiveness to manifest as grace and blessing toward humanity.

And because the mechanism from God's side regarding Christ's mediation is Christ's resurrection, the mechanism from our human side regarding Christ's mediation is our individual or personal regeneration as forgiven and repentant sinners. Thus, Christ's mediation creates a kind of bridge or conduit between His resurrection and our regeneration. Christ mediates or reconciles His own resurrection with the regeneration of believers.

In the same way that Peter was dealing with the end result or purpose of baptism and salvation, he also spoke of the end result or purpose of Christ's resurrection. That result was that Christ "has gone into heaven and is at the right hand of God, with angels, authorities, and powers having been subjected to him" (v. 22). The resurrected Christ had confirmed this purpose and result of His resurrection in Matthew 28:18 when He said that "All authority in heaven and on earth has been given to me."

Where Christ used the word *authority* (*exousia*), Peter used *angels* (*aggelos*), *authorities* (*exousia*) and *powers* (*dunamis*). Christ said *all authority*, so Peter fleshed it out. By naming angels Peter meant that all communication regarding God or heaven must proceed from the authority of Jesus Christ. No other authorities must be considered from the point of Christ's resurrection forward. This means that the only religious or spiritual communication or messages to be considered by humanity are those that concern Jesus Christ. Christ is the sole spiritual authority.

The word *authority* (*exousia*) is also translated as *power*, and must be understood to include all power of every sort, to include artistic, academic, monetary and political influence. Christ has authority over aesthetics, academics, economics and politics.

The word *powers* (*dunamis*) is also translated as *mighty works* and *miracles*, and must be understood to include medicine, healing and technology in that our contemporary practice of these things would be understood as miraculous (*dunamis)* by First Century people. People today live in the midst of scientific and technological miracles in comparison to all previous ages.

Thus, we get the sense and scope of the purpose of Christ's resurrection and our regeneration as envisioned by Peter. Where Christ has authority, Christians have responsibility. And where Christ's authority is ultimate, the responsibility of Christians is proximate. Because Christ has all authority Christians have limited, cultural authority and responsibility.

Christian Culture

To review then, Christians have the responsibility of representing Christ's authority in the following cultural areas: the arts, academics, science, economics, politics, medicine, healing and technology. Altogether the summation of these responsibilities is religious because religion is the institution of culture. And in the light of Christ's ultimate authority over all things, the culture to be institutionalized is culture that is defined, informed and illuminated by God's Word (the Bible) as seen and understood in the light of Christ. And the religious means of this institutionalization are worship, education and morality. Whereas the civil means of this institution are through various legalities—courts, police and military.

All of this is the subject of the word *this* that is referred to in verse 21. And all of *this* is the proper reference regarding baptism, in that *this* is what Christians are baptized into. The word *this* also points back to the rest of the chapter. Christians are baptized, not merely into church membership in some local church, but into personal responsibility for Christian culture, which includes the realm of the universal (not invisible) church. There is no question about being baptized into a local church. The local church that does the baptism receives the baptized person into local membership.

But Peter's point is that people are baptized into the greater universal Christian culture as well because of the personal obligations of morality involved in being a Christian and because Christians still live in the world. And the entrance fee to the universal church is a personal conscience that has been cleansed by the grace of God through the propitiation of Christ on the cross. Salvation is free, but discipleship is not free or without qualifications. Regeneration is not the end but the beginning of the process of salvation and includes discipleship and sanctification. Discipleship is costly and requires much. However, both the cost and the requirements are supplied by the grace of God. Don't for a moment think that because God is gracious that His grace somehow suspends the demands of His law. It most certainly does not! Rather, Christ provides the means for mercy, grace, regeneration and obedience.

Christ's crucifixion fulfilled the demands of God's law, it paid the debt that humanity owed. Baptism then adds the name of the individual to the class action case involving the cross of Christ. Regeneration, rising from the waters of baptism, freed from the debt of sin and with a clean conscience, is both personal (individual) and corporate (social), inasmuch as it involves new relationships with other regenerated individuals. In the same way that regeneration frees an individual from his sinful past, the corporate regeneration of the church frees it from the momentum of sinful human history and realigns the corporate body with the gravity of heaven in the light of Christ.

Thus, both regenerate individuals and the corporate body of the church are then free to follow Christ, who "has gone into heaven and is at the right hand of God, with angels, authorities, and powers having been subjected to him" (v. 22). Thus, salvation is indeed about *me* (individuals) and Jesus, but it is also about *us* (the church as the body of Christ) and society. The wholeness of salvation includes both individual and corporate salvation.

Freedom

This is important because it involves the moral behavior of the individual, who's conscience has been freed in Christ in order to follow Jesus, and it involves the social behavior of Christian society, composed of many local churches, that have been freed from the law of Adam in order to follow the law of Christ. This is the freedom from the law that Paul wrote about (Romans 7:3, 8:2; Galatians 5). This freedom is not the exemption from all law and morality, but is freedom *from* the law that results in damnation and freedom *for* the law that results in salvation (1 Corinthians 9:21, Galatians 6:2). All Scripture is always opposed to immoral behavior and lawlessness.

We see the social element of salvation in the fact that Peter points to "angels, authorities, and powers" (v. 22) being subject to Christ. And while Peter did not say *all* authority here, Jesus said *all* authority in Matthew 28:18. The point is that both earthly and heavenly societies are to honor the authority and power of Jesus Christ.

Does this therefore mean that there must be a single, worldwide, human institution that mediates the authority and power of Jesus Christ, like that conceived by the Roman Catholic Church? Or is the power and authority of Jesus Christ to be mediated by the Holy Spirit in the lives of individuals and communities in a more spiritual and institutionally diverse way? Keep this dilemma in mind as we continue to examine Peter's letters, and keep in mind that the Roman Catholic Church claims to have the power and authority of Peter.

23. SUFFERING JUDGMENT

*Since therefore Christ suffered in the flesh, arm yourselves
with the same way of thinking, for whoever has suffered in the
flesh has ceased from sin, so as to live for the rest of the time in
the flesh no longer for human passions but for the will of God.
For the time that is past suffices for doing what the Gentiles
want to do, living in sensuality, passions, drunkenness, orgies,
drinking parties, and lawless idolatry. With respect to this
they are surprised when you do not join them in the same
flood of debauchery, and they malign you; but they will give
account to him who is ready to judge the living and the dead.*
　　　　　　　　　　　　　　　　　　—1 Peter 4:1-5 (ESV)

The major theme of the previous chapter has been the suffering of
the saints for the cause of righteousness. Peter has hammered the
idea that Christians are to be fully engaged in doing good, in
doing what is right according to Scripture, regardless of the consequences. And Christians will suffer for doing good because God's
enemies are opposed to God's plan of salvation through Jesus Christ,
and will inflict ridicule, disgrace, pain, and suffering of every conceiv-
able kind in order to wreck the cause of righteousness.

The enemies of God believe God to be evil and will oppose Him with
every fiber of their being. We have seen this with current Islamic Jihad-
ist warriors who are willing to die for their cause of opposition to the
biblical, trinitarian God by turning themselves into bombs. And Peter's
point is that Christians must be more willing than the Jihadists to suffer
for the cause of Christ—but be engaged in the service of life, not death.

However, this in no way means that Christians are to engage in military warfare in the service of their cause, other than ordinary military
service of the various nations in which they live. Christians are not paci-
fists, but understand that civil governments are charged with the military protection of their populations in the light of Christ. Peter was well

aware of the extent to which God's enemies would go in the pursuit of their persecution of Christ's church. Indeed, he was himself preparing for the impending destruction of Jerusalem by the Roman army, not that he knew it would be destroyed but he was certainly aware of the increasing persecution and the build up of the Roman army. He was most certainly aware of the threat of potential war and destruction. Peter himself was purported by some to have died crucified upside down in Rome.[58]

LIFE NOT DEATH

It is significant that Peter does not call Christians to die, but to suffer. Peter refers to death only symbolically and as part of regeneration, as a means of new life in Christ. In 1 Peter 2:24 he speaks of Christ bearing "our sins in his body on the tree, that we might die to sin and live to righteousness." Nowhere does Peter speak of self-sacrifice in terms of ordinary death as being Christian. No, Christ's self-sacrifice on the cross was sufficient (2 Corinthians 3:5). Peter was calling Christians to life not death. He was preparing Christians for a life in Christ that would be difficult and painful until the fullness of Christ would one day be fully revealed, when every knee would bow to Christ and the kingdom of God in Christ would be manifest on earth as it is in heaven.

Indeed, it is much more difficult and challenging, more spiritual and more rewarding, to live for a cause than to die for one. Dying is easy. Dying is a coward's way out. Living requires courage, dedication, discipline and persistence. So, while Christians are not to emulate Christ's self-sacrifice, we are to emulate His willingness to suffer in the flesh. And this was no mere spiritual suffering of a mystical body that the Lord experienced, but was the body of flesh (*sarx*) in which the Lord of glory took human form. It was real suffering, not mystical or allegorical suffering that Christians were to prepare for and engage.

How are we to prepare? By arming ourselves "with the same way of thinking" (v. 1) or the "same (*autos*) mind (*ennoia*)" (*Authorized Version*). Same as what? Same as Christ, Peter implied. We are to engage the same kind of thinking that animated Jesus. And what kind of thinking was that?

MORAL THINKING

The Greek literally means self-reflective moral consideration. Christian self-reflection necessarily involves trinitarian self-reflection

---

58 The death of St. Peter is attested to by Tertullian at the end of the second century, and by Origen in *Eusebius, Church History II.1*. Origen says: "Peter was crucified at Rome with his head downwards, as he himself had desired to suffer." However, this view is disputed by J. Stuart Russell in *Parousia: The New Testament Doctrine of Our Lord's Second Coming*, Baker Books, 1999.

inasmuch as Christians are self-consciously trinitarian in character. Christian self-reflection, then, involves consideration or reflection on one's own individual character, and upon the corporate character of the church as defined in Scripture. To be self-reflective is to be aware of one's own identity as an individual and as a member of the body of Christ. There is both a personal element and a social element to this reflection.

In addition, Peter has called us to moral reflection, to think about how we ought to behave in the light of Christ. We are to reflect on what it means to be in our right mind, in the mind of Christ's righteousness. Such self-reflection will draw us into our trinitarian character in that it will draw us into the mind of Christ, which inhabits the body of Christ, the church—not perfectly, of course, but better over time.

Thus, while Christ does provide an example for us to follow, the mere following of Christ's example is inadequate to Peter's meaning because the mere following of an example is more akin to rote memory than serious moral consideration. Of course, we are to remember what Christ has done and how He lived and taught us to live. This kind of reflection is essential to Peter's meaning, while at the same time it is not sufficient.

Peter was not directing mindless followers about the various steps to take to reproduce a Christ-like attitude. He was insisting on the presence of the Holy Spirit through regeneration as the motivating power of both the self-reflection to which he pointed and the moral behavior that would result. The self-reflection that Peter wanted was the trinitarian self-reflection that included the Holy Spirit as part of one's own personal identity in Christ.

The last phrase of this verse, which is not the end of the sentence, reads "whoever has suffered in the flesh has ceased from sin" (v. 1). It suggests that personal suffering has an effect on sin. We can understand this in at least two ways. First, someone who is suffering for doing good is himself less involved in sin because he is doing good. Here, it is not so much that the suffering curtails sin, but that not engaging in sin brings about persecution and suffering. There is less sin because you refuse to do it. But your refusal offends other sinners, who then bring persecution and suffering on you because they are offended by your effort toward righteousness.

Secondly, enduring persecution and suffering for doing good provides a witness to the possibility of living with less sin, and inasmuch as that witness is effective, it will call others to imitate the good behavior and suffer the consequences themselves because of the nobility of the commitment to do what is right even when it is personally costly. The nobility of suffering for a righteous cause is inspiring.

Verse 2, the end of the previous sentence, explains how the will of God is to replace the passions of the flesh. Notice that Peter did not say that Christ will remove the passions of the flesh so that Christians can live in some kind of Essene state of feelinglessness or Buddhist-like nirvana, but that Christ will transform those passions to serve the will of God. The feelings and energy of those fleshly passions will remain, but their purpose and goals will change in the light of Christ.

SPIRITUAL JUJITSU

Again, Peter calls Christians to live bodily (*sarx*), not as if the body and its passions do not exist, but to engage them head on with a kind of spiritual jujitsu that flows with the power and momentum of an opponent just long enough to change it slightly in order to produce a different result. The fleshly passions do not go away, but are rechanelled into the service of God's will. Peter has called Christians to live in the flesh, in time and in the midst of the passions of the flesh, not to deny them or denounce them but to live in service of God's will in the midst of them. This is not a call to engage in sinful behavior, but to rechannel the passion for sin into passion for God. It is also a call to not neglect the body.

We don't have control of our feelings. They have a life of their own and make themselves manifest in our lives without regard for our personal will. Feelings come and feelings go, and for the most part we are not in control of them. So, how can we possibly escape from the passions of sin when they seem to control us? This is part of the problem that Peter was dealing with here. And Peter's answer was to allow the feelings of passion to arise—as if you could stop them even if you wanted to!

Nonetheless, we must allow them to arise, but refuse to engage in the sinful behavior they seem to demand for their satisfaction. Refuse to engage them because that sinful behavior will not satisfy those passions, but will actually further inflame them. Those who do engage the sinful behaviors that their sinful passions seem to demand find themselves further enmeshed in sin as the result. Sin is like the irritation of poison ivy, the more you scratch it the more it spreads and the worse it gets.

Peter knew that the itch of sin cannot be simply turned off like a water faucet, nor can it be satisfied by experience. Poison ivy itches, get used to it! The real cure is to avoid it, and if you get infected, don't scratch it. Apply the appropriate salve but don't expect the salve to eliminate the itch. Rather, use the irritation it causes to remind you of something else, in this case to remind you of God and His goodness. Use the irritation as a reminder and a prod for prayer.

When you become aware of the itch, pray for God to give you strength and to heal the irritation. God intends to put an end to sin and its enticements, its irritations—and He will. In the meantime, we must simply use the irritation of sin to fuel our commitment to serve God, and not succumb to it. Peter said to "live ... in the flesh ... for the will of God" (v. 2).

In verse 3 Peter makes an argument for breaking with the past history of the Jews, the *dispensation of Adam*. He said that in the past the Gentiles had been doing exactly what they wanted to do: "living in sensuality, passions, drunkenness, orgies, drinking parties, and lawless idolatry" (v. 3). The Jews had tried to cordon themselves off from exposure to such things and the people who do them. The Jews turned inward following God's instructions regarding holiness and godly living.

But in doing so, the Gentiles were left to themselves and the destructiveness of their own sin. And that is not what God had in mind. So, He sent Jesus Christ to atone for human sin, so that He could provide grace and mercy through Jesus Christ and reach the whole world. This is what might be called the *dispensation of Jesus Christ*, the second Adam or current covenant Head of humanity.

Thus, Peter calls Christians to put away those old behaviors: "living in sensuality, passions, drunkenness, orgies, drinking parties, and lawless idolatry" (v. 3), and step into the New Age in Christ. This is the kind of living in the flesh he was talking about, and he is making the case for not simply stopping this kind of behavior, but replacing it with faithfulness. Bad habits cannot simply be abandoned, they must be replaced with good habits.

Then He goes on to say why our suffering for Christ will ensue— because "they are surprised when you do not join them in the same flood of debauchery, and they malign you" (v. 4). Joining in such behavior amounts to a favorable vote for the morals associated with it, and not joining in amounts to your disapproval. The result of not joining in brings shame to the revelers by your good (or better) behavior, and they don't like it. So, they belittle it, malign it. And if it persists they attack the do-gooders with increasing malevolence.

Superman

People, who are like sheep, tend to flock together. *Herd mentality* is a term created by Friedrich Nietzsche to describe how people are influenced by their peers to adopt certain behaviors, to follow trends, and even to make certain purchases. Examples of herd mentality include the early adopters of high technology products such as cell phones, stock market trends, clothing fashions, cars, home decor, etc.

Sociologists study the related topics of group intelligence, crowd wisdom, and decentralized decision making.

Nietzsche divided people into two groups: one group lends itself to the religious views which direct human behaviors, the other group lends itself to influence by the media and follows media trends, social norms, etc. Nietzsche found both of these tendencies to be a human weakness that his idea of a "Superman" was to overcome. While Neitzsche's idea of a Superman was a figment of his imagination, he got these tendencies right. And the thing to notice about them is that religion and media tend to oppose one another. These two institutions tend to be hostile toward one another.

Their opposition may be more circumstantial than necessary in that the media is by definition herd thinking and contemporary Christian salvation has a decidedly individualistic flavor. The media tends to appeal to worldly people because they push worldly hype. If they pushed some other kind of hype things would likely be different. But this is the world we live in, and it has many similarities with Peter's world in that sin is dominant among human beings today as it was back then.

Nonetheless, Peter told everyone to avoid such things—worldliness and sin—because everyone "will give account to him who is ready to judge the living and the dead" (v. 5). Our lives are not actually ours. We have been bought by Jesus Christ, who paid for us with His blood. Who did Christ purchase?

All humanity. All humanity is, therefore, under the authority of Jesus Christ, and that is in fact why people go to hell. It is the judgment of Jesus Christ that consigns unrepentant sinners to hell (Matthew 28:18). If Jesus has *all* authority and some people go to hell, then they go to hell because of the authority of Jesus Christ. Christians are not free to live as they like. Rather, Christians are free to live as Christ commands. And what is more, Christ's commands provide real joy and freedom for the repentant and obedient and, at the same time, damnation for the unrepentant and disobedient.

Unrepentant sinners equate freedom with sin, and what Christians call *salvation*, the unrepentant call *hell*. "Woe to those who call evil good and good evil, who put darkness for light and light for darkness, who put bitter for sweet and sweet for bitter! Woe to those who are wise in their own eyes, and shrewd in their own sight! Woe to those who are heroes at drinking wine, and valiant men in mixing strong drink, who acquit the guilty for a bribe, and deprive the innocent of his right!" (Isaiah 5:20-23).

COVENANT

People become so committed to this reversal of values that they cannot repent of it. John of Patmos wrote, "The fifth angel poured out his bowl on the throne of the beast, and its kingdom was plunged into darkness. People gnawed their tongues in anguish and cursed the God of heaven for their pain and sores. They did not repent of their deeds" (Revelation 16:10-11). In John's vision, in spite of the fury of God's judgment, there are and will always be sinners who are utterly impervious to God's call for repentance and salvation.

So, to say that people go to hell because of the authority of Jesus Christ simply means that like Deuteronomy 28, the covenant of Jesus Christ is such that it provides for both the salvation of the repentant and the damnation of the unrepentant. However, it must be underscored that it is not Jesus' desire, nor God's "that any should perish, but that all should reach repentance" (2 Peter 3:9).

It is not that God sends anyone in particular to hell, but that because of Adam's sin humanity as a species or kind is already bound for hell. The species of Adam is condemned to extinction and hell, and that is why regeneration in Christ is essential for salvation. God sent Jesus to provide a way to avoid damnation and hell. People still have the freedom to engage sin and deny Jesus.

Only those who willingly repent and turn to Christ are saved. Thus, every human being must "give account to him who is ready to judge the living and the dead" (v. 5). This account that we must give to the Lord is not the testimony of the experience of our own salvation, but is the biblical account of Christ's salvation of humanity and our personal submission and involvement in it. The word that is translated as *account* is *logos*. It is the same word that is used in John 1:1, "In the beginning was the *Word*, and the *Word* was with God, and the *Word* was God."

It is not that we must give an account of our own personal lives, but that we—both individually and corporately—must give back to God the *Word* (*logos*) that He has given us in Christ Jesus. It was the Seventeenth Century scientist Johannes Kepler who described science as "thinking God's thoughts after Him." But more than mere science, faithfulness is a matter of thinking God's thoughts and living God's life. No, we do not become gods. We become followers in union with God in Christ.[59]

The judgment to come is about how well we can use the logic of God's Word in our own lives and in our world. Because God's Word is the source of life on earth, we can expect that Word to ultimately reveal, not the secrets of eternal life, as if God is some kind of a snake oil salesman, but the meaning and method for the development and maintenance of sustainable human culture. The Word given to us in Jesus Christ, the Word that we are to give back to God as a testimony of the efficacy of Jesus Christ in our own lives and for the world, is the

---

59   See footnote 31, page 97.

very foundation of sustainable human culture. This is the truth of God's salvation through Jesus Christ.

Interestingly, the Greek word *echō* is translated as "to him who is" (v. 5). In a sense, we are to echo God's Word back to Him, but not merely in the sense of biblical memorization, but in the sense of understanding and incorporating God's Word into our lives. Judgment is a matter of showing God that we understand what He was talking about in the Bible by using God's wisdom for the development and maintenance of sustainable human culture. And inasmuch as we can do that, we will be engaged in building the kingdom of God on earth as it is in heaven. This is the judgment or evaluation that has been ongoing in history since the time of Jesus' death. The purpose of God's judgment is not the destruction of the world, but the salvation and longevity of the world in Christ.

24. Gospel Hype

For this is why the gospel was preached even to those who are dead, that though judged in the flesh the way people are, they might live in the spirit the way God does. The end of all things is at hand; therefore be self-controlled and sober-minded for the sake of your prayers. Above all, keep loving one another earnestly, since love covers a multitude of sins. Show hospitality to one another without grumbling. As each has received a gift, use it to serve one another, as good stewards of God's varied grace.
—1 Peter 4:6-10 (ESV)

For this is why" (v. 6), said Peter summing up the reason for God's judgment. The reason that God has called humanity to account to the Judge of the living and the dead, His only begotten Son Jesus Christ, is because God's judgment serves as a foil for the gospel of Jesus Christ. God's judgment against sin is the context of the gospel. It provides the only context against which or by which the gospel makes sense, and apart from that context the gospel falls flat. Because of Adam's sin and God's impending judgment, Christ has made propitiation for those who will survive God's judgment and who will live on the other side of that judgment.

This gospel, said Peter, was also evangelically preached to the dead. There are two possible meanings of this. First, Peter was referring to the past, to history. In this case it could be that he was saying that this is the same gospel that has always been preached, and had been preached to the Old Testament saints in anticipation of judgment by God's Messiah. Our ancestors in the faith would be the dead of whom Peter spoke.

Secondly, we might benefit by translating the Greek word *judged* (*krinō*) as *distinguished* or *discerned*. The idea here is that the saints are to be seen as ordinary fleshly people, but people who live by the Spirit of God. And that living by the Spirit of God is a function of regeneration. Understood this way, Peter was saying that the dead to Christ are made alive in Christ through regeneration. Thus, the gospel is preached to the unregenerate, who are dead to Christ, that they may become regenerate in Christ.

The *English Standard Version* reverses the word order by mentioning the Spirit before God, where in the Greek *God (theos)* is mentioned before the *Spirit (pneuma)*. Suggesting that we are to live the way that God lives allows for speculation that Peter was talking about the similarities between our human being and God's being. This kind of speculation has been done in many pagan accounts regarding the *Great Chain of Being*.[60] While many people have been tempted to see it this way, this is not what Peter was actually talking about. Rather, he was simply saying that regenerate Christians live in the flesh, but by the wisdom and guidance of the Spirit of God, the Holy Spirit, who is also identified as God's Word or Scripture.

In addition, the *English Standard Version* adds the word *might*, which makes the idea of living by the wisdom and guidance of the Lord seem like a potential option, which it is not. It is not that Christians might live by the wisdom and guidance of the Lord, but that that they are called to do so. What could be more important to a Christian than this? Nothing. Yet, the *English Standard Version* word choice makes it seem to be optional.

THE END

Peter then put the church into the context of the end times. "The end of all things is at hand" (v. 7). Does Peter mean that the end of the world is near? Yes and no. The Greek word translated *end (telos)* means *purpose*, in the sense that the purpose of all things is the *end* or *cause* for which all things have been created.

Peter's point was not that the third planet from the sun called Earth is about to explode, or that humanity was about to perish from the face of the globe, but that the manifestation and revelation of Christ Himself is the end purpose for which the earth was created. And with every passing year, the world actually gets nearer to the fulfillment of its end purpose. This is not great apocalyptic prophesy, but merely common sense in the light of Christ's progressive revelation.

What is the significance or importance of the fact that the revelation of Jesus Christ as Lord and Savior is the end purpose of the world? First, notice that it is not simply the end purpose of the church, but of the entire world. Then, Peter tells us: "therefore be self-controlled and sober-minded for the sake of your prayers" (v. 7). The idea is to be *sane*

---

60 *The Great Chain of Being: A Study of the History of an Idea*, by Arthur O. Lovejoy, Harvard University Press, 1976.

(*sōphroneō*) and *sober* (*nēphō*) in prayer, to guard ourselves against wild speculation about or intoxication regarding God's purpose in Christ. And particularly to guard ourselves against such things in prayer and worship.

Why the focus on prayer and worship? Because prayer and worship serve to both establish and reveal our innermost beliefs and values. God does not want His people to have their own speculative or intoxicating beliefs and values regarding Jesus Christ, nor does the Lord want us to hope for such things or to communicate such hopes to others through public prayer or worship (John 4:24).

Understanding Peter here requires knowing what he means by sanity and sobriety. Christians are not to indulge in theological insanity or intoxication, and those who already do will not and cannot understand Peter's message correctly until they repent of their errant theological speculations and apocalyptic intoxication.

END OF HYPE

Of course, he meant that Christians are to be free of blood chemistry disorders, whether self-initiated like depression and drunkenness or socially imposed like orgiastic cult behaviors or ungodly governmental policies. To be theologically sane and sober precludes all hyper theological positions and beliefs, be they hyper-Preterist, hyper-Calvinist, hyper-Arminian, hyper-Charismatic or hyper-whatever. Clearly Peter was concerned that Christians would be tempted to hype or sensationalize Christianity with regard to what he was saying in his letters.

He was concerned about this because he was putting Christ in the context of world history, and because that context is of central importance for the entire world. Peter was talking about big ideas. It is tempting to turn Christian life and living into a speculative drama of supernatural proportions, as was being done in the extra biblical literature[61] of Peter's own day and has also been done in contemporary literature in ours.[62] Such literature and thinking fails to treat Scripture with sanity and sobriety, yet it has always been wildly popular.

---

61 *The Old Testament Pseudepigrapha, Vol. 1: Apocalyptic Literature and Testaments*, Doubleday & Company; 1983; *The Old Testament Pseudepigrapha, Vol. 2: Expansions of the Old Testament and Legends, Wisdom and Philosophical Literature, Prayers, Psalms, and Odes, Fragments of Lost Judeo-Hellenistic works*, by James H. Charlesworth, Anchor Bible, 1985.

62 For instance, the *Left Behind* is a series of 16 best-selling novels by Tim LaHaye and Jerry B. Jenkins, dealing with Christian dispensationalist End Times: pretribulation, premillennial, Christian eschatological viewpoint of the end of the world. The primary conflict of the series is the members of the Tribulation Force against the Global Community and its leader Nicolae Carpathia—the Antichrist. *Left Behind* is also the title of the first book in the series, published by Tyndale House.

Peter's concern about *prayer* (*proseuchē*) included both informal supplication and formal worship. Christians were not to engage in the speculations of insanity and insobriety in either their own private thoughts or their behavior, and they were also to disdain public worship that engaged or promoted such things.

Human beings are naturally inclined to make the error of taking an ordinary truth too far, of absolutizing a general principle, of turning a general rule into an absolute truth. To guard against this tendency in this case Peter cautioned, "Above all, keep loving one another earnestly, since love covers a multitude of sins" (v. 8).

Peter knew that the general rule regarding sanity and sobriety would be abused in precisely this way because he saw it happening in his day. Yet, Peter did not intend his directions here to be understood as the hyper-sobriety of teetotalism or the hyper-sanity of a joyless, cloistered life. Peter knew that people would be so tempted because he was trying to explain how the revelation of Jesus Christ effected world history. He knew how the absolute centrality of Christ in all things can easily lead people into various hyper theological positions that damage the cause of Christ with various versions of Christian hype and speculation. No doubt, Peter hoped to put an end to speculative Christian hype. Lord knows the damage it has done to genuine Christian faithfulness in our day.

FERVENT LOVE

Therefore, said Peter, if Christians are to be fervent about anything, we must be fervent in our love and charity toward one another. If we are to err in our natural tendency toward exaggeration and hype, we should err by being hyper-loving and hyper-gracious. And it is not simply that love covers sin, but that *charity* (*agapē*) covers sin. The difference is that charity is love with legs. It is love in action, and it opposes love without action. Charity insists on the activity and actions of love to accompany the proclamations and words of love.

HOSPITALITY

In verse 9 Peter added *hospitality* (*philoxenos*) to this list of things to exaggerate. Hospitality is related to the love of foreigners or strangers, those who are not related by family or geographical nearness. We must also note the linguistic root of the words *hospitality* and *hospital* because the care of hospitality is not different than hospital care when such is needed.

There is an element of healing that is involved in hospitality that can be discerned by thinking of the health problems that could result when travelers are not accorded the common benefits of food, fellowship and shelter. Sleeping in the rain can bring on pneumonia. Starvation and poor nutrition are the cause of much illness. And the failure of fellowship can lead to crime and even war. Thus, hospitality toward strangers is essential to human health and welfare.

At this point we must also note that Peter wanted Christians to be hospitable to "one another" (v. 9). While hospitality to all is an ideal to strive for, hospitality among Christians is essential for fellowship. The one is a goal while the other is a minimum expectation. Christian hospitality should serve as a means of evangelism, not in the sense of simply hosting people who are not Christian and sharing the gospel with them, but in the sense of showing the world how Christians love and care for one another and doing it so well that non-Christians are envious of such deep and precious relationships.

Peter knew his audience so he added that they were to engage in hospitality without *grumbling* (*goggusmos*). He knew that Christians would be tempted in this way. He understood that people cannot be genuinely hospitable unless they actually want to and enjoy the process. Those who do it out of duty rather than love do so begrudgingly, and that was precisely what Peter forbade here.

Begrudging compliance is forbidden because it comes out of a spirit of duty, envy or revenge. Christians must actually want to be hospitable. We must actually enjoy interaction with people who are foreign or different than we are. And we must be particularly hospitable to those Christians who engage in foreign (or different) ways of conceptualizing and practicing Christianity. We should want to get to know these people and their various beliefs and practices as a way knowing Christ more fully. The discussion of Christian doctrine and practice should be joyful, interesting, exciting (but not hyper-exciting, or intoxicating) and motivating.

Of course, we must not deny the limits of orthodoxy that have been wrought into existence by the various historic Christian creeds. We must honor both the creeds and the diversity of expression. We must understand that Christianity is not universalism. But neither must we be unwilling to engage other people's thoughts while holding to orthodox Christianity. We must always be willing to grow personally and corporately by ceding to better positions and explanations of the faith without abandoning biblical orthodoxy. Indeed, this is a high calling and will require much study, patience and understanding. And this is exactly what Peter was calling for.

ENGAGING THE CONVERSATION

Christianity is intended to be an eternal conversation about the glory of God in Christ that eventually fills and dominates every thought of every person (2 Corinthians 10:5, 2 Peter 3:9) as it grows into maturity. It is not just that we come to maturity in Christ as individuals, but that Christianity as a social movement and an institution also grows and matures over time.

Yet, most Christians grumble about other Christians for one reason or another. People also grumbled about Jesus. So, what is the nature of this grumbling? John reported that there was much *muttering* (same Greek word) about Jesus among the people. "While some said, 'He is a good man,' others said, 'No, he is leading the people astray'" (John 7:12). At the heart of this concern lies the theological discussion about Jesus' character and mission. Those who thought that Jesus was good could not possibly be those who grumbled against Him, so the grumbling must have been a reference to those who did not believe or support Jesus or His mission.

Thus, at the root of grumbling lies unbelief. Unbelief grumbles and complains. This does not mean that all grumblers are unbelievers, but it does mean that all grumbling issues from doubt and unbelief. We can also say it this way: faithfulness does not grumble. Thus, the negative command to not grumble is also the positive command to be faithful. Belief tends to be spotty and inconsistent.

The purpose for all of Jesus' instructions here is the establishment of Christian culture, or the kingdom of God. People are not simply saved so that they can go to heaven. It is *not* true that it doesn't really matter what we do here on earth—not at all. It matters very much! Peter was very concerned that Christians work together in mutually supportive and beneficial ways in order to improve life in the here and now. God intends that things be "on earth as (they are) in heaven" (Matthew 6:10).

Gifts & Stewards

In verse 10 Peter then shows us how this is to work. "As each has received a gift, use it to serve one another, as good stewards of God's varied grace" (v. 10). These are the same gifts that Paul spoke of in 1 Corinthians 12, and they are to be used for the same purpose. But while Paul spoke of the various gifts being used in the church, Peter expanded that vision to include the exercise of gifts as a kind of division of labor within the Christian community.

For instance, carpentry skills (a gift) can be used around the church, but they can also be used in the community as a method of financial support. And the same thing is true regarding other kinds of gifts. We can think of them as being spiritual gifts in that they come from God. But we can also think of them as ordinary talents and skills that are God given. But however we think of them, Peter's point was that we are to use our gifts and talents in the context of the Christian community.

An economy is developed by working and spending money in the local community. Local work and support begets local economic development. Peter was telling the Christians fleeing Jerusalem, to band together in local, mutually supportive economic relationships. We know that social, economic and technological development flourishes when built upon a Christian foundation of honesty, integrity and industry. There is no reason to think that this is not what Peter wanted them to do. For them to do so would establish Christianity in the new areas and would further the cause of Christ and the planting of His church(es), and would benefit both the Christians and the foreign societies in which they were being planted. And this is exactly what happened.

The Greek word translated as *serve* (*diakoneō*) is the same word used in 1 Timothy 3:13 to describe the office of Deacon. However, here Peter was not referring to a church office, but to the common Christian activity of service through the use of one's gift. And because of this, we can differentiate between the formal office of Deacon and the ordinary activity of Christian service. We note that they are the same kinds of things discussed in different settings.

Thus, every instance or use of the word does not necessarily suggest that the person involved in service is a formal, elected, official Church Deacon. Christian service is to be common to all Christians. All Christians are to *deac* (serve), if I may turn the word in to a verb. This is what John meant when he said that God made us kings and priests (Revelation 1:4, 5:10). This does not mean that every Christian is an actual king with a castle or a priest with a church, but that all Christians are to serve God with their gifts, and that such service is both kingly and priestly in character. It also means that actual kings and priests are to be faithfully engaged in Christian service.

All Christians are called to service, to the small *d* diaconate. But this calling does not mean that all Christians are to be church leaders. The ordinary dictates of organization require a few leaders and a lot of workers engaged in service. Service through the use of our God-given gifts is to be in the DNA of all Christians. It is toward the establishment of this mindset that Peter was driving. And it is the establishment of this mindset that all Christians must peruse as an expression of their love for Christ.

25. God's Charisma

As each has received a gift, use it to serve one another, as good stewards of God's varied grace: whoever speaks, as one who speaks oracles of God; whoever serves, as one who serves by the strength that God supplies—in order that in everything God may be glorified through Jesus Christ. To him belong glory and dominion forever and ever. Amen.
                                        —1 Peter 4:10-11 (ESV)

Verse 10 provides a translation difficulty that is seldom seen or acknowledged. The English translations have added an article to the verse. The article *a* or *the* has been added to the word *gift* (*charisma*). In grammar an article is a determiner that indicates the specificity of reference of a noun or phrase. The *English Standard Version* reads "As each has received a gift." The *American Standard Version* reads, "according as each hath received a gift." The *Authorized Version* reads, " As every man hath received the gift." There is no article in the Greek. It has been added in the hope of improving clarity.

Add to this situation the definition of the Greek word *charisma*, translated as *gift*, and the issue looms large. *Charisma* can indicate a gift or an endowment, or it can indicate a qualification or faculty. An alternative translation is *deliverance*—each has received *deliverance*. And because the Greek word is difficult to translate into English we have the English transliteration *charisma*, a personal attractiveness or positive contagiousness that enables one person to influence another. Of course, *charisma* is a gift, but it is not something that can be wrapped up and given to another because it is a characteristic.

However, the *Authorized Version* translators understood that the added clarity was the fact that the gift that God has given was not unique to each believer, but was the common gift of grace. Each received *the* gift, the same gift. Each believer was endowed with the same gift of *charisma*, originally understood as the gift of belief. The gift that each received was the same gift. We can also call it faith. The modern translators, who were more in tune with the individualism of Modernity, understood the gift to be unique to each believer, and reflecting Paul's thought in 1 Corinthians 12.

At issue is understanding exactly what it is that has been given by God and received by the saints. Was Peter talking about individual giftedness or about the gift or grace of salvation? To whom was Peter writing? To individual Christians or to the church as a body of believers? Here, the *English Standard* Version reads, "As each has received," and is closer to the Greek because the word *man* is not in the Greek. The idea is that each individual received something.

However, Peter was not addressing individuals, he was addressing the church, the body of believers. He was saying that each individual in the corporate body had received something special, but not something different or unique. Sure we each receive Christ in a unique way with unique consequences, and we do have unique talents and gifts, but the context suggests that Peter was talking about the same Christ who has been received by each believer.

The Gift

And exactly what has been received by the saints? To be sure, the general grace of God given through salvation is more than just the particular giftedness given by the Spirit spoken of by Paul in 1 Corinthians 12. It is that, but the particularity of the gift is secondary to its commonality. The difference has to do with the particular fruit(s), or the growth and development of God's general gift of deliverance or salvation. And yet, we must understand that *grace* (*charis*) and the *gifts* (*charisma*) are near synonyms, and that this wordplay is heavily exploited throughout the New Testament. The fact of the repeated wordplay suggests that the difference is important because it is being highlighted.

Does Peter engage in this wordplay here? Yes. "As each has received a gift (*charisma*), use it to serve one another, as good stewards of God's varied *grace*" (*charis*, v. 10).

From a trinitarian perspective we understand that God has given a corporate gift of grace to humanity through Jesus Christ, and that gift has been described as salvation, redemption or regeneration. The gift is new life in Christ that issues from God's forgiveness, which has been given in response to Christ's sacrifice and propitiation on the cross. And there are two sides to the gift: the giving and the receiving. Every gift involves an exchange, not that the receiver has to give something in return, but that the ownership of the gift changes hands. One who was not an owner becomes the owner of the gift. That's what it means to give something to another.

Two Sides

These two sides or aspects of God's grace provide the difference that is the subject of the biblical wordplay between *charis* and *charisma*. It is as if God gives wholeness to humanity and God's wholeness is then received and incorporated individually. Like in the feeding of the five thousand (Matthew 14:13-21), where God gave the wholeness of the bread and that wholeness was received and incorporated individually as each individual ate it. God's wholeness is sufficient for all humanity, but only those who actually receive it are incorporated.

The wholeness is the miracle, which is not available to individuals in their solitude or in their individuality. The reception of the miracle produces the corporality or unity of those who received it. It incorporates individuals into a social or spiritual unit(y), and the wholeness of the unit(y) is miraculous in that it is super natural. The wholeness of human corporality is not a part of human biology, but is apart from or superimposed upon individuals who compose the group. The unity of the group is of a different order than the membership of the members.[63]

Indeed, God's wholeness, God's unity in Christ is always central to both the giving and the receiving of God's miraculous grace. It is by grace that we are saved through faith. It is by God's gift of wholeness that people are saved and that wholeness is received, assimilated and manifested individually—particularly. Thus, the wholeness of God and His gracious gift of salvation (deliverance) is the basis or foundation for the individuality of each Christian.

Christians are more unique than non-Christians because they have received the incorporation of wholeness into God by grace through faith in Christ. And that gift of wholeness manifests individually, particularly and uniquely. God is always wholeness, unity, corporality and oneness. But in Christ God's corporality changes human individuality as it manifests in Jesus Christ, and through the dispensation of the Holy Spirit in the particular lives of His people.

Thus, we might translate verse 10: *because you, all and each, have received regeneration in Christ, which is the central characteristic of God's corporate gift to humanity, you are to serve one another automatically, that is, without requiring specific instructions, as if mutual*

---

63 In the mathematics of set theory, an ordinal number is the order type of a well-ordered set. Two ordered sets X and Y have the same order type when they are order isomorphic. When two sets are order isomorphic, they are "essentially the same" in the sense that one of the orders can be obtained from the other by the substitution of one for the other.

service and genuine consideration to one another is the very desire and delight of your souls because that is how the gift of God's goodness manifests as unity in the midst of the diversity of the community of God's people.

SERVICE

Here we find that every Christian is called to *diakoneō*, to loving, careful and responsible service in the body of Christ. However, this service is not the work of supervision that is required by those who are called and elected to the office of Deacon, but is composed of the various services engaged by individual Christians that the Deacons are to supervise and coordinate. All Christians are to serve in this capacity, and the Deacons elected to office are to supervise this work, coordinate and/or direct this service in order that specific needs within the church are not overlooked or neglected. *Diakoneō* sometimes refers to the particular service that is rendered by every Christian, and sometimes to the task of overseeing that service in order to insure that no one is left out in either its giving or its receiving. The overseeing belongs to the office holders, but the work belongs to everyone.

In verse 11 Peter provides two examples of what he was talking about: "whoever speaks, as one who speaks oracles of God; whoever serves, as one who serves by the strength that God supplies." Here Peter divided church work into two types: speaking and serving. Obviously, he does not mean to suggest that speakers don't serve or that servers don't speak. Rather, he was characterizing the two kinds of service. Those who speak are to speak as if God is speaking through them, and whoever serves is to serve as if God is directing and doing the work.

Immediately, we must be cautious regarding speakers to keep from thinking that God actually speaks through particular individuals. When speakers are thought to be mouthpieces for God, their words are elevated to the status of Scripture. However, individual human words are not words of Scripture. We are not to think of ourselves as oracles of God in the sense that our words and ideas come with the entirety of God's wisdom and authority. We are not God, and are not in the process of becoming God. Rather, Peter means that all of our speaking, in church and out, is to be built on, based on and in reference to God's Word, to Scripture. We are here called to speak God's Word after Him, to structure our thoughts and words on the model of Scripture.

We are to follow and restrict ourselves to the categories of thought and analysis that are given in the Bible. Doing so, however, involves neither the curtailment or suppression of human freedom, but rather protects people from the dangers of believing that our own foolish speculations can be trusted to reveal truth about the nature or character of reality. God shows us the actual nature and character of reality in the Bible, and it is both miraculous and dangerous. The greatest danger is believing that we as human beings are able to discern and discriminate between the miraculous and the dangerous. The problem is that the stupendousness of the miraculous blinds us to the reality of the dangerous. The Bible provides a guide or standard for discernment between them.

Clearly, Peter does not mean that we can never say anything without explicitly referring to the Bible. Rather, Peter was talking about preaching and teaching in the church, and about establishing our intellectual categories and structures of discourse upon biblical categories and logic. He was simply saying that the Bible is the model for human thinking and doing, for conversation and organization. We are to engage what the Bible teaches, and eschew what the Bible forbids. Again, God is not curtailing our human freedom, but is providing for human sustainability. We must not do everything we are able to do, just as we must not speak everything we think. Rather, we must discern what is actually truthful and useful.

Nonetheless, we must speak as if God is directing our thoughts because He is. But neither must we forget or ignore our sin or the way that sin deludes and tricks us. In order to not be fooled by sin we must acknowledge the reality of the possibility that we can be fooled by sin, that sin provides a real and present danger in our lives. And in order to not be unnecessarily limited or bound by sin we must acknowledge that Christ's forgiveness of sin is real, and we must actually receive it. Thus, our categories of analysis are bounded on one side by the reality of our own sin and on the other by the reality of Christ's forgiveness.

GLORY OF WORSHIP

And why must we do all this? Peter concludes, "in order that in everything God may be glorified through Jesus Christ" (v.11). The objective is to glorify God through Jesus Christ, and the method is to live within the bounds of the Bible in regard to human imagination and the intellectual categories of analysis and understanding. Doing so is the manifestation of wisdom by honoring God in Christ. At the heart of Peter's understanding of the purpose of life is to give glory and honor to Jesus Christ, or in a word—worship.

Note first that the proper context for worship is everything. Worship applies to *everything* (*pas*). There are two focal points regarding worship that are captured by two New Testament Greek words: 1) *doxa* points to God, who is the object of Christian worship and veneration, and 2) *proskuneō*, which points to the proper attitude of the worshiper.

Peter used the word *doxa* here in order to magnify the object of Christian worship—Jesus Christ.

When the supernatural object of Christian worship is correctly received and perceived, the attitude of the worshiper follows in its wake. However, the object of Christian worship—God in Christ—is only perceived by those who are born again (John 3:3, 5), those who have eyes to see and ears to hear (Matthew 11:15; Mark 4:9, 23; 7:16; Luke 8:8; 14:35). The perception requires the reception.

Christian worship can only be engaged by regenerate believers because genuine belief only issues out of personal regeneration, the gift of grace. Apart from having eyes to see, the real object of worship cannot be properly seen or understood. But when the object of worship is seen and properly understood as God in Christ, the worshipers add glory and honor to God through their worship. Each worshiper adds his honor of God to the collected historical honor of God that has accumulated throughout the ages.

And it is not that the honor of God by the worshiper happens only during the hour of worship. Rather, when the worshiper is properly aligned to God in Christ through regeneration by the Holy Spirit, the attitude of the worshiper honors God in everything that he does and says, twenty-four/seven. Worship in spirit and truth (John 4:24) is a function of the worshiper's attitude toward life, which means that everything is engaged in the attitude of worship. But again, this attitude of worship is not some mystical, hush-hush, head-bowed, eyes-closed posture, but is a matter of speaking as if God is listening and serving as if God is actively involved.

Dominion

At this point Peter could not contain himself or his love of God, and he broke out in praise: "To him belong glory and dominion forever and ever. Amen" (v. 11). We have discussed *glory* (*doxa*), to which Peter here added *dominion* (*kratos*). Strong (G2904) suggests that the root meaning of the word is vigor. Nonetheless, the translators have used the word *dominion*, which is a kind of dominance or power through spiritual and legal authority. And while the acknowledgment of legal authority is correct, and while it does in fact provide for domination through legal and lawful imposition, Peter does not mean that God dominates by imposing His will upon others against their will.

Rather, God's greatness and goodness inspires people to willingly and gladly follow His lead because God has planted His Holy Spirit in them lead and guide them. God is like a great athlete who dominates other competing athletes with his abilities, but does not dominate his fans. Rather, He inspires His fans to appreciate Him. Fans honor their heroes. Heroes don't dominate or impose themselves upon their fans. Of course, God is not an athlete, and Christians are not fans, so this analogy breaks down if it is pressed to far.

As if Peter suspected that there might come a time in the future when people might think that they have outgrown their need for God's care and direction, Peter also proclaimed the duration of God's sovereignty: forever and ever. There will never be a time when God is not sovereign or unworthy of glory and honor.

26. THE LORD OF HOSTS

Beloved, do not be surprised at the fiery trial when it comes upon you to test you, as though something strange were happening to you. But rejoice insofar as you share Christ's sufferings, that you may also rejoice and be glad when his glory is revealed.
—*1 Peter 4:12-13 (ESV)*

The fiery trial that Peter mentions is one word in the Greek: *purōsis*, which is a kind of fire that is heated up as hot as possible for smelting. Ore is smelted in order to extract and purify the metals that it contains. The process makes the ore much more valuable because the various metals are put in a form that makes them better available for their specific uses. Thus the fiery trials are part of the Christian soul mining process, whereby rough Christians are purified and made more valuable. It provides an analogy for spiritual growth, maturity and sanctification.

As odd as it might at first seem, success, wealth and ease of life do not produce Christian growth and maturity. Rather, success tends to stimulate pride and self-centeredness. In contrast, difficulty, failure, poverty build character and maturity. This is not an appeal for Christians to seek poverty or to make everything difficult. Poverty itself is not a blessing, nor is the inflated self-esteem of the prideful. Wallowing in poverty is not a Christian virtue. Nor is the pride that usually accompanies success and wealth.

Rather, Christians are to engage their spiritual gifts in order to escape poverty through the creation of wealth. As this is done, however, a caution applies because success in this area can lead to pride and self-concern. The Christian ideal is to work hard to create wealth, to understand that all wealth belongs to God, and to use the wealth for God's purposes, not our own.

The Christian path or way is the way of spiritual growth and maturity. It is the more difficult path, not the easy path. The Christian path leads to success, but does not start there. Christianity is most successful when it is difficult. But it is not that struggle and difficulty are virtuous, but that struggle builds strength and discernment. A healthy society is one that strives toward biblical goals, both personal and social, and makes progress along the way. But the danger is that the progress that makes life easier and more manageable, also reduces the struggle, which undermines the strength and discernment that come from overcoming difficulties.

I suspect that this is why God insists that Christians continuously strive for perfection. Perfection, being unattainable, keeps the goal of the struggle forever ahead of us. To strive for perfection is to strive forever because the goal is beyond our abilities to attain. The greatest danger for Christians is to think that we have attained an acceptable degree of maturity and discernment that we can rest on our laurels.

Necessary Struggle

Thus, struggle and strife are necessary for Christian growth, maturity and sanctification. This means that Christian peace is not the end of personal or social struggle and strife, but rather, Christian peace is a matter of living in a social environment wherein this struggle for righteousness and orthodoxy can be rigorously engaged without appealing to war or violence. War and violence are to be avoided because they impede and undermine the progress of maturity and sanctification.

The struggle is spiritual, emotional and intellectual. The struggle is a matter of clashing worldviews. And the means of winning the struggle of worldviews is education and persuasion, not force. The most righteous, orthodox and compelling worldview must win adherents through honest persuasion, not manipulation, trickery or force. Thus, all parties must have sufficient freedom to research, present and honestly discuss their arguments to the best of their ability, without engaging in exaggeration, manipulation, trickery or bullying.

The best, the most righteous, most orthodox, most biblical and most compelling worldview must be allowed to grow and mature in perpetuity toward perfection. It must grow out of personal engagement and struggle. Because persuasion issues out of argument or discussion, argument and discussion are essential to the process. And discussion must be done honestly, openly and in good faith by all participants.

Acceptable forms of argumentation employ both logic and affection. Repetition can also be used as a method of argumentation where people are simply acclimated to an idea by repeated exposure to it. Over time whatever is repeated tends to become more accepted. Unacceptable methods of argumentation include deceit, denigration, extortion and intimidation.

Inasmuch as religion and faith are related to one's worldview, they are essential to the process of argumentation and discussion. To remove religion and faith from discussion related to worldview in the name of objectivity is an attempt to win the argument by disallowing the very thing under consideration—the character of objectivity itself.

It is not that religion and faith are biased and scientific objectivity is not. Rather, there is no such thing as human objectivity, every perspective is biased in one way or another. Human beings cannot be unbiased. The very idea that being unbiased is superior to being biased is itself a bias. A bias is simply a preference, and everyone has all kinds of personal preferences about all sorts of things. The ideal should not be *being unbiased*, it should be *having the right bias*, or being biased in favor of what is good and right.

Good and right for whom, and according to what? Asking these questions again puts us into a deep and divisive argument that has been going on forever. In a nutshell, people have competing ideas about good and evil. All discussion about such topics is fatally biased by our upbringing, education, social position, personal preferences, religion, politics, etc. Thus, God has provided His Word to discern and adjudicate between good and evil because we cannot. That is both the subject and function of the Bible.

Peter was saying that this path of Christian perfection that issues out of difficulty and struggle must not be perceived to be odd or unusual. It is neither. It is quite ordinary. And it is to be the central activity of our personal lives and pursuits as Christians. We must also remember that God is drawing us into the fulfillment of His vision of perfection. Note two things: 1) it is God's vision of perfection, not our own, and 2) we are being drawn into it, not pushed into it. While God issued His decrees in the past, the subject of those decrees is in the future. God is not bound by time, like we are.

Pulling History Forward

God is pulling us forward through history. The past is not pushing us forward, Jesus Christ is pulling us into the future that He has already secured for us (John 14:2-3). We are not dependent upon the past, upon human history, nor upon our own personal histories. We are not dependent upon some version of broad Christian history, nor upon our narrow denominational or theological histories.

Rather, our pasts and our histories are simply the record of our growth, our mistakes and errors. History is not something that we need to get back to. There never has been a Golden Age that can or should be the target of our return. History does not flow backwards. As we learn better (more of God's truth) we must be willing and able to let our historical errors go, and not get caught up in a spirit of revenge against those who oppose us or who support others.

God's grace and Christ's forgiveness cover all that. That is why Christ came—so we can escape the gravity of our past, our history. We must trust that God's forgiveness is both real and sufficient for all humanity. Accepting God's forgiveness means letting our past go. Accepting God's forgiveness means that we are not driven nor constrained by our past, not by our old errors and mistakes, not by our own views, not by our Old Man. The Old Man is dead and the New man is alive in Christ.

Accepting God's grace means not perpetuating old mistaken ideas and worldviews, nor engaging in revenge against others because of their mistakes and errors or because of their history. Entering the Kingdom of God requires the abandonment of our own claims, our own histories, and accepting the claims of God in Christ. That's what forgiveness is all about.

But this is not a matter of simple agreement or some kind of personal pledge. Our agreements and pledges are too cheap and easy to both make and break. They are what Bonhoeffer called *cheap grace*.[64] Rather, accepting God's grace must include the heartfelt conviction and intellectual embrace of the truth and goodness of God, and of His Word, personally arrived at by the difficulties and struggles of study, argument and conflict with those who disagree. Indeed, the truth will set us free (John 8:32).

We cannot take our worldly baggage into God's Kingdom, be it emotional, personal or historical. We must leave it all behind and step into God's future in faith. We are presently on the doorstep of this struggle, and this is where we are called to be. We must embrace God's future by relinquishing our past in a way that we don't simply ignore the past, but that we learn from history the lessons of our mistakes and errors. Thus, history has a positive function in God's future. We do not abandon history, but learn from it by abandoning its false ideas and misconceptions.

Rejoice!

Peter's transition in verse 13 is extremely important, but it is often missed. At least I have only recently come to see its importance. "But rejoice" (v. 13), said Peter. We are called to rejoice, not merely in spite of the difficulties and struggles we experience, but we are to rejoice

---

64 *The Cost of Discipleship, by* Dietrich Bonhoeffer, New York: Macmillan, 1966.

because of them. God chastens those he loves (Hebrews 12:6). So, when we feel God's chastening, it is a sign of His love.

God does not chasten those whom He does not love. He gives them up to their desires. He allows them to do what they want, knowing that it will destroy them (Romans 1:26). God doesn't need to soil His hands with the destruction of unbelievers; they will destroy themselves by their refusal to see the wisdom and truth of God's Word.

Contrary to this response of disbelief regarding God's grace and mercy by unbelievers, Christians rejoice. In the face of our own struggles and difficulties, in the face of the opposition that comes against us in our stand for Christ, in the face of the world's rejection of God and His Word, we are called to rejoice, to raise our voices in praise and worship. The Christian response to everything is the joy of praise and worship. "Rejoice in the Lord always. Again I say, Rejoice!" (Philippians 4:4). Always, in all things.

When King David was distraught, downtrodden and persecuted he did not give up or get depressed. What did he do? Consider Psalm 7. David complained that the enemies of God were in ascendance, that they were attacking him and his godly beliefs. He was so frustrated that he prayed for their destruction because they were not merely his enemies but were the enemies of God Himself. At the end of this diatribe against the success of God's enemies David provided God's solution to this problem: "I will give to the LORD the thanks due to his righteousness, and I will sing praise to the name of the LORD, the Most High" (Psalm 7:17). There are many psalms and biblical stories like this.

In the face of the apparent success and fire power of God's enemies, God's people are to rejoice in the Lord and sing praises to His name. God's primary weapon against the forces of unrighteousness is the corporate worship of God's righteousness. We are to lift up God's righteousness in praise and honor because His righteousness alone is the only weapon that can win this kind of battle. God's righteousness in Jesus Christ is the light that shines in the darkness. The beauty and truth of God's righteousness in and through Jesus Christ provide the light that scatters the darkness.

We cannot argue darkness or willful ignorance out of existence. We cannot defeat it at the polls. We cannot defeat it on the battlefield. We are helpless against it, but God isn't. It requires a change of mind or opinion that is equivalent to a new birth because it involves a new beginning based on loving, trusting and honoring the God of the Bible in the man called Jesus Christ. The light of God's truth and beauty, lifted up and honored in public worship cannot be overcome by darkness. It cannot be defeated by the forces of darkness and ignorance because it dispels them. It is the light of God in Christ alone that dispatches the Holy Spirit unto souls for their regeneration, and the only way to increase that light is to celebrate it in worship.

Peter calls the saints to rejoice to the same degree that they know or experience hardship, affliction and suffering, and then some. Christians are called to identify with Christ and with His persecution and suffering. We are to bear it to the same extent that Christ bore it, but more than merely bearing it we are to use it as a springboard for praise and worship. Doing so will help us bear with it, but that is not its purpose. Its purpose is to forge an identification with Christ so that as His glory is increasingly and progressively revealed we will contribute to Christ's glory with our praise and worship. Our honoring of Christ in all things will increase the light of His glory and the joy of His people.

We are to put on the whole armor of God as preparation for engagement with the enemy. However, putting on the armor is not the battle. The armor is not the strategy, nor the war. The armor of God provides us with the tools of engagement—the belt of truth, the breastplate of righteousness, the shoes of the gospel of peace, the shield of faith, the helmet of salvation, and the sword of the Spirit which is the Word of God (Ephesians 6:11-20).

And while every soldier must prepare for engagement and must actually be engaged, no one is engaged alone. Warfare is a team sport. Platoons, battalions and armies are engaged on the battlefield, not individuals. We are not each fighting our own war against Satan. Rather, we are soldiers in God's army as He fights His war against Satan. The difference is that on our own we can engage other individuals in discussion and maybe persuade a few to believe in God.

But when we gather as God's army in public worship and lift up Jesus Christ in praise and honor the Lord of hosts takes prominence. When Christians worship and work together in harmony, first with Jesus Christ and then with one another, a sense of wholeness and unity issues from amidst the participants that is both at one with the participants and other than the participants. It is analogous to the unity of the Trinity that stands apart from the diversity of the Trinity, and yet holds the diversity together in unity. The Lord of hosts is the Spirit of oneness and unity that holds the diversity of the Trinity together.

The Lord of hosts is the God of the aggregate. He is the oneness and unity of His people, who are in harmony with God and with God's purposes. The aggregate is the wholeness or unity of a group. That unity and wholeness are essential to the revelation of God in Christ through regeneration by the power and presence of the Holy Spirit.

Only the regenerate can know this unity and wholeness, and as the regenerate gather in worship to praise and honor Christ, the manifestation of the Lord of hosts in their midst provides a confirmation and assurance of faith that is undeniable. It is undeniable precisely because it has changed you, the believer.

That assurance then brings joy and gladness to believers. And the more that God is revealed in and through Jesus Christ, the greater the assurance, which increases the joy, which increases the gladness. The *Authorized Version* translates it as "exceeding joy" (v. 13, *agalliaō*). We might even call it extreme joy.

27. HUMAN DECONSTRUCTION

*If you are insulted for the name of Christ, you are blessed,
because the Spirit of glory and of God rests upon you. But let
none of you suffer as a murderer or a thief or an evildoer or as
a meddler. Yet if anyone suffers as a Christian, let him not be
ashamed, but let him glorify God in that name. For it is time
for judgment to begin at the household of God; and if it begins
with us, what will be the outcome for those who do not obey
the gospel of God?* —1 Peter 4:14-17 (ESV)

Verse 14 provides a specific example of the persecution, struggle
and difficulty that comes to Christians, and an explanation of
what it means. When a person is insulted for being a Christian, it
is a blessing because it is a badge of honor, a confirmation of faith by an
unbeliever. At first glance this might seem odd, even ridiculous, but it is
not. Why not? Because the only kind of people who will insult Christians
for being Christians are enemies of God. They have no incentive to make
such an accusation. There is no benefit in it for them, which means that
they are simply reporting their honest perception that you belong to
Jesus Christ. And they can perceive it because they see in you something
that is not in themselves.

This report is a blessing because it provides a witness to your faithfulness who is hostile to Christ. It is not a blessing because it is hostile to
Christ, but because it is a testimony about your faith from someone hostile to Christ. If I tell you that I am a Christian, you might believe me
and you might not because my own testimony about myself will always
be biased in my favor. But when an enemy of the gospel goes out of his
way to denigrate you for your faithfulness, his testimony of your being a
Christian is much more trustworthy because he has no incentive to say
so. He is not doing himself any favors with his acrimony.

The *Authorized Version* goes on to say that the accuser is committing blasphemy, that his failure to recognize the Holy Spirit in or through you constitutes blasphemy on his part (Matthew 12:31-32), but at the same time it is a glorious testimony to the reality of the Spirit in you. The enemies of God only attack the people of God. Satan does not waste his time with people who pose no threat to him. So, if you are attacked by them, that attack provides a confirmation of your faithfulness.

To insure that God's people don't abuse this insight Peter reminded them that not all suffering and accusation works like this. Some kinds of accusations and difficulties do not reveal faithfulness. Discernment is necessary. For instance, God's people should not suffer or be accused of being a murderer or a thief or an evildoer. Christians must not be accused of these kinds of things, nor are they to do them. Peter is speaking only of being accused or suffering as the result of one's faithfulness.

This idea is reiterated in verse 16: "Yet if anyone suffers as a Christian, let him not be ashamed, but let him glorify God in that name." Originally, the word *Christian* was intended to denigrate the followers of Jesus because Jesus had been crucified as a common criminal. It was intended to be a slur. But here Peter reclaimed the term by using it in a positive way.

QUEER THEORY

In our day, homosexuals have done the same thing with the word *queer*. They have taken a term of denigration and turned it into something that is now viewed as a positive thing by many people, and they have done so in the same way. They have also done a similar thing with the word *gay*, except in the reverse. It was originally a word that had a good positive meaning, but now provides an offense to God. The difference between what Peter did with the word *Christian* and what homosexuals have done with the words *queer* and *gay* pertains to the different character and definition of the words. The word *Christian* points to the biblical character of the righteousness of Jesus Christ, whereas the words *queer* and *gay* point to the very heart of what the Bible calls unrighteousness.

The root understanding of the word *queer* is defined as "beyond or deviating from the usual or expected." It refers to a deviation from a norm, a turning aside and being at variance with what is commonly understood to be normal or right. The definition, while pertaining to sex, is much more broad-based than that. It constitutes an attack on the social construction of human society as historically and biblically understood.

As a verb it means to disrupt the norm or to understand a thing from a non-normative perspective. Where God is working to establish biblical righteousness as the human norm, homosexuals are working to establish a different, unrighteous human norm.[65] The objectives of Queer Theory (now a department of study on many university campuses) are not limited to human sexuality, but they do focus on sexuality because of the role that sexuality plays in human identity.

This line of intellectual endeavor is trying to dislodge human identity and experience from its biblical foundations by suggesting that human sexuality is socially constructed rather than biologically and biblically defined by the God who created us. Their arguments are complex and heady, but fatally flawed because they fail to honor the role of context and history regarding human identity and experience. Queer theorists rightly understand that something is very wrong with our historic human identity, that there is a flaw or problem that must be addressed by all people—and there is! But they deny and refuse the biblical framing, understanding and solution of the problem. The Bible identifies the problem as sin and the solution as forgiveness in Christ.

But the Queer Theorists deny the reality of sin and attempt to establish that the problem is God's imposition of human identity and norms, particularly sexual norms, upon humanity. Their solution is the celebration of the radical freedom to sin, even casting it as the obligation to sin as an expression of personal freedom, a freedom which they define as being fundamental to the essential character of all human beings. They identify this radical freedom, this obligation to oppose common norms of every sort, as the very essence of our humanity. Thus, their goal is the eradication of God's moral standards because they understand that those standards are not natural.

And indeed, they are not! They are supernatural norms. Where God applies a supernatural identity and norms (behaviors) upon people by creating people in His own image, and renewing them in Christ, Queer Theorists work to undo that supernatural (and biblically understood) identity and return to their original created (and fallen) identity in Adam. They want to return to a kind of pre-Fall condition, before Adam sinned. They do this by denying sin or redefining sin or redefining humanity by attacking human sexual definitions and practices. They correctly understand the defining role that sexuality plays in the development of human character and identity. But they refuse to accept God's authority over human sexuality, and assert their own. They deny God's gift of sexuality through redefinition and abuse of bib-

---

65 *Plastic People—How Queer Theory is Changing Us*, by Peter Sanlon, The Latimer Trust, London, 2010; *The History of Sexuality*, by Michel Foucault, Vintage Books, 1990 (Random House, 1978).

lical sexual norms, and work to desecrate its foundational role in marriage and reproduction.

Thus, while homosexuality is a forgivable sin like most others, Queer Theory is entirely blasphemous and therefore unforgivable. It is, however, not unforgivable simply because it justifies immoral sexuality, but because it denies both the need for forgiveness and God's ability to provide it. It constitutes blasphemy against God, but is also blasphemous against all established human norms. It is unforgivable because it refuses to accept the need for forgiveness.

And what is more—because all sustainable human life requires and depends upon the establishment of various limits and norms regarding human behaviors, it ultimately goes against the longevity and sustainability of humanity itself. While homosexual sex cannot reproduce life, Queer Theory actively undermines various norms that are required to sustain humanity, according to the Bible. It courts the social policies of death and destruction. Homosexuality does not provide a viable model for human behavior because widespread adaptation to it will lead toward death by depopulation.

Human beings are creatures of habit and to undermine or destroy fundamental human sexual habits (biblical patterns of marriage and sexuality) in the name of freedom will ultimately undermine honesty, integrity, truth, justice, science and technology, all of which are built upon the habits of honesty and discipline. Indeed, discipline itself is a habit and an essential Christian norm that is undermined by Queer Theory. Of course, it is not consistent in this regard, nor can it be.

In contrast, God's mission has been to create and enforce good habits, to define, support and encourage honesty, integrity, truth, justice, science and technology as the fruit of faithfulness to God's established habits of human identity in Christ. In Christ the old habits are left behind and new habits of righteousness are born and flourish. Thus Queer Theory undermines God's central purpose of reforming humanity in the image of Jesus Christ—God's central purpose in history. Again, it is not that homosexual practice or experience itself is an unforgivable sin, but the kind of intelligent, creative, willful, systematic denial of God and His purposes that are endemic to Queer Theory provide a powerful and deadly attack against the God of the Bible, and the sustainability of humanity.

God can tolerate a lot of accidental or unconscious sin. Forgiven sinners continue to lie, cheat and steal to some degree as they grow out of their addictions to sin. And God's mercy provides grace and forgiveness as long as people are improving in their faithfulness to God's righteousness. But God cannot tolerate any intelligent, creative, willful, systematic denial of the righteousness of His character. Thus, Queer

Theory is completely intolerable of and incompatible with biblical faithfulness.

Of course, forgiven sinners may continue to struggle with renouncing their homosexuality, but people cannot entertain or embrace Queer Theory in the least, for to do so is to utterly abandon trust in and fidelity to God. It must be completely denounced and abandoned because it is an intellectual path that leads to death, not merely the death of individuals but the death of human kind (Proverbs 8:36). So, the failure to abandon it will bring the full force of God's wrath as an act of God's mercy, as He excises a social cancer that threatens His favorite species. Queer Theory is, as the poet says, the very seed of death and destruction.[66]

God's Purpose

Peter has put forth God's plan and shown that Jesus Christ will continue to be revealed throughout history as people grow in grace, sanctification and maturity. Thus, the revelation of Jesus Christ as the Son of the trinitarian God is not simply a book of the Bible, but is the long process of the unfolding of God's purposes in a world that is growing in God's grace—eternally.

As the disciplines of theology, philosophy, history, science and art mature through history, they will each and all provide new and valuable perspectives and insights about God's Word and purposes that will provide for the continuing revelation of God in Christ throughout history. This ongoing historic revelation of Jesus Christ is itself an element of Christian worship. The engagement of theology, philosophy, history, science and art in the light of Christ is an act of worship. The process of engagement with Jesus Christ is itself a function of worship, and the many fruits of such engagement are themselves fruits of Christian worship.

Having established all of this, Peter turned his attention to the judgment of God as the engine of Christian development and maturity. God's purpose is not to destroy the world, but to save it. And He will save it through the manifestation of His judgment. Of course, we know that God has given all power and authority for judgment to Jesus Christ. And Christ's judgment, His faculties of assessment and evaluation, provide the only hope for humanity and the only way of salvation

---

66 Note that *destruction* can also be rendered *deconstruction*, which is the stated purpose of Queer Theory. *Deconstruction* is an approach, introduced by French philosopher Jacques Derrida, which rigorously pursues the meaning of a literary text to the point of exposing the presuppositional contradictions and internal oppositions upon which it is founded in order to show that those foundations are irreducibly complex, unstable, or impossible. It is an approach that may be deployed in philosophy, theology, literary analysis, or other fields. –http://en.wikipedia.org/wiki/Deconstruction.

because of the superiority of Christ's righteousness in the history of the world. He alone is able to judge rightly because He alone is the righteous judge.

Thus, Peter said in verse 17: "For it is time for judgment to begin at the household of God." The time that had come to a head in Christ was a *kairos* time, a special time. This special time is not the kind of time that can be measured with a clock or by a calendar. Though *kairos* moments happen in time, they are not a function of time. So, such times cannot be known by the calendar or the clock, and the attempt to predict the fulfillment of *kairos* time through the judgment of God by the calendar is futile.

Jesus Himself made no such prediction, and neither did Peter. Thinking of God's judgment in terms of time and prediction is simply an indication of one's own ignorance. Those who predict do not know what they are talking about. Religious predictions are superstitious leftovers from a time that did not know the fulfillment of Christ, a pre-Christian time, and those who try to work out the dates are simply facing in the wrong direction and working toward the wrong purpose. They are reaching for what cannot be grasped, grasping for what cannot be reached.[67]

The *kairos* moment of God's judgment began with the pregnancy of time itself, with the decree of God inseminated into the history of the world at the very birth of time itself. Peter's point was that the birth of this *kairos* moment had come with the fulfillment of time through the delivery of the Messiah to an anxious world. Christ's birth constituted the birth of this *kairos* moment. And Christ's death on the cross constituted its manifestation in history.

Peter, as we know, was writing after the birth, death and resurrection of Jesus Christ. He was not anticipating the coming of the Messiah, nor a return of Christ's birth, but the fulfillment of the fullness of God's promises through the maturation of Christ in His people. Peter was writing about the reemergence of the Lord of hosts as promised by Malachi, the last book of the Old Testament. Peter was proclaiming the fulfillment of the final biblical prophecy of the Old Testament through the revelation of Jesus Christ in history as the Lord of hosts.

The *judgment* (*krima*) that begins among God's people (v. 17) and in Christ's church is often translated as *condemnation* and *damnation* elsewhere in the New Testament. The Greek word signifies a decision or discernment that is made. Peter did not necessarily mean that God was going to damn the people of God before He damned the rest of

---

67   It is an effort to return to a kind of superstitious Oracle of Delphi prediction of the future. For more on this see: *Arsy Varsy—Reclaiming the Gospel in First Corinthians*, Phillip A. Ross, Pilgrim Platform, Marietta, Ohio, p. 233-ff.

humanity. Such a view is simply contrary to God's stated purpose of saving the world, contrary to God's promises and is contrary to the overall tenor of Peter's letter.

The translation of the Greek word *krima* as *judgment* in verse 17 is unfortunate, even if it is technically correct. Its grammatical correctness does not help us understand Peter's intended meaning. Peter did not intend to say that the church would be the first institution to fall apart during periods of God's judgment, though that is also true. The church acts as the canary in the mine, to serve as an indication of the health and well-being of society generally.

Rather, Peter had been teaching the scattered church about finding and discerning God in Christ in their own midst as they fled the destruction of Jerusalem and set up new communities, mostly to the West. What those fleeing saints needed most at that time was discernment and discretion—biblical wisdom—to be at the center and foundation of their new communities. Thus, Peter was saying that the time had come for this kind of biblical discernment and discretion to manifest as the wisdom of Christ in their various churches.

This kind of wisdom can only begin in the house or household of God. Because God is at its center, it cannot begin where God is not at the center. Peter was telling them to put God in Christ at the center of their lives, in their families and in their churches, in their waking and in their sleeping, in their hearts and in their children.

CHRIST'S PURPOSE

Peter was then overwhelmed with another thought: "and if it begins with us, what will be the outcome for those who do not obey the gospel of God" (v. 17)? Peter was not speculating about the future here, but was clarifying the purpose of God. The outcome or end of which Peter spoke is the *telos* or purpose of God. Peter was not talking about the end of a series of events or the final calendar day of the Lord. Peter was talking about the purpose of God's *kairos* moment that had its birth in Christ Jesus.

Christ's purpose in the world is to provide righteous judgment for an unrighteous people. It is to provide correct discernment for an undiscerning people. It is to provide direction for a directionless people. We unrighteous sinners must learn to judge righteously in the light of Christ. We must learn to judge lightly in the righteousness of Christ.

How can unrighteous people ever make righteous judgments? First, we must give up our unrighteousness. We must abandon those thoughts, values and actions that are unrighteous. And receive instruction in righteousness from someone who is righteous—Jesus Christ.

However, righteousness is a complex subject, not because it is hard to understand but because it is so easy for sinners to pervert it. Thus, God chose to manifest Himself trinitarianally over a long period of time in order to demonstrate the consistency of His righteousness across various cultures and epochs, and to provide a transnational and transhistoric stability for human longevity that can be found nowhere else.

If the purpose of God in Christ was the self-revelation of God through history for the purpose of growing and saving humanity through the development of honesty, integrity, truth, justice, science, technology and art, then what is the purpose of those who just don't understand it, those who refuse to stand under Christ, who is the foundation of all of this?

Peter asked the question, but didn't answer it. He left it for us to answer in order to demonstrate the reality of the unfolding revelation of God in Christ in us. It is an important question and it deserves an honest answer. Peter wants us to answer it teleologically, where teleology is the supposition that there is purpose and principle in the works and processes of the world. To think teleologically is to assume or presume purpose in the world. And if there is a purpose, there must be a higher intelligence that infused the world with purpose.

PURPOSE OF UNBELIEVERS

Peter asked about the purpose of those who don't believe the gospel. If salvation is so difficult for those who do believe, what about those who don't? He has been showing the purpose of those who believe, how God is directing the unfolding revelation of Jesus Christ in history, and how obedience to the gospel will bring persecution, and that the purpose of the persecution is to further reveal the glory of God in Christ in us. Peter has been arguing the positive case for faith in Christ as the foundation for human longevity through science, technology and art, and asks us—his readers—to try to argue the negative case. He wants everyone to engage the process of argument because he knows that God wins all arguments.

It is time, said Peter, for discernment and discretion to begin to be practiced in the house or household of God. It was time then, and it's even later later now. So, begin we must! Ask the hard questions, and dare to suggest some biblical answers. And be sure to listen to your brothers and sisters in Christ.

28. LORD OF THE AGGREGATE

For the time has come for the judgment to begin from the house of God. And if it first begins from us, what will be the end of those disobeying the gospel of God? And if the righteous one is scarcely saved, where shall the ungodly and the sinner appear? Therefore let those who suffer according to the will of God commit their souls in well-doing, as to a faithful Creator.
—1 Peter 4:17-19 (ESV)

The first word of verse 17 (*hoti*) literally means *because*. So, Peter is setting up a logical proof in verses 17-19. Because of this (v. 17) and that (v. 18), therefore v. 19. Because the world is in the midst of a *kairos* moment with regard to the revelation of Jesus Christ, the people of God are called to exercise judgment—discretion.

The idea of verse 17 is that the people of God are those who are faithful and obedient to Christ because faithfulness and obedience are the foundations upon which Godly judgment rests. And because Godly judgment cannot rest upon any other foundation, Peter asks about the end or purpose of those who do not believe the gospel of Jesus Christ. Peter said that our only hope is the exercise of Godly judgment understood as biblical discernment in the light of Christ. Therefore, those who do not, cannot or will not exercise biblical discernment in the light of Christ are without hope, without the hope of ultimate salvation or longevity.

The idea of verse 18 provides a similar contrast. Because the righteous find salvation difficult, or because difficulties are a necessary part of salvation, what will become of those who do not, cannot or will not exercise the biblical discipline that is required for biblical discernment? It is not so much that Peter was asking the question in order to find the answer, but that he was asking the question in order to point out the consequences of faithlessness.

Remember that Peter has been arguing that the revelation of Jesus
Christ in history is progressive (not liberal, but developmental) because he understood that the passage of time in the light of Christ
would necessarily bring humanity to greater maturity. We know now
that part of that social maturity involved the development of science
and technology out of the philosophical foundations and implications
of God's trinitarian character.

The Future

Peter had a vision that as humanity would grow more mature in
the light of Christ (over time and in history), more and more people
would come to the realization—because of the dispensation of the Holy
Spirit—that God actually exists and that Jesus Christ is His only Son.
Peter did not know anything about science and technology *per se*, of
course.

Rather, he was filled with the hope that the progressive revelation
of Jesus Christ was the foundation for great things, miraculous things,
things that were formerly unknown to history. He also knew that
growth and maturity are always hard won, that growth and maturity
develop as a consequence of struggle, difficulty and hard work. They
are not the result of laxity, leisure or laziness.

So, in order to encourage the saints to persevere in faithfulness
and Godliness, he pointed out that while salvation is a free gift of God's
grace, it does not mature without struggle and difficulty—and therefore
requires discipline.

The translation of the Greek word *molis* as *scarcely* is unfortunate
because it makes the verse sound as if salvation is a scarce commodity.
But that is not what Peter was saying. Rather, he was saying that the
maturity of salvation in Christ comes out of struggle and difficulty, that
Christian discipleship would require more effort than people were used
to making. And that it would generate struggle and difficulty (conflict)
in the process because the natural tendencies of people are to be sinful
and lazy. Unpacking the implications of the Trinity would bring in a
new way of thinking about God and His world. It would upset established religious and political ideas.

When Peter asked what would happen to the "ungodly and the sinner" (v. 17), he was suggesting that they would simply be left behind,
that they would not be caught up in God's salvation in Jesus Christ,
that they would self-select themselves out of God's kingdom because of
laziness or commitment to a false church or a pagan state or whatever.
Because the Jewish people were unwilling to concede that the fulfillment of the Old Testament's promised Messiah had come in the Person

of Jesus Christ, they cut themselves off from the Messiah for whom they hoped.

And because Rome, the dominant civil government of the time, had embraced every form of Paganism, it cut itself off from the only form of civil government that is compatible with the Bible—representative government that issues from the application of trinitarianism to gifts and the division of labor.

GOVERNMENT

Biblical civil government can take several forms, depending upon the faith and maturity of those involved. But whatever form it takes, it must provide for genuine representation between the governors and the governed, whether a kingship, a republic or a democracy. The capacity of civil government to actually govern breaks down as the degree and quality of representation between leaders and people fails to actually be representative.

There is an additional element that is also involved. There must be genuine representation between the ultimate leader, Jesus Christ, and humanity as well. This is what it means for Jesus Christ to be the only mediator (Hebrews 9:12, 12:24) between God and man. However, the jurisdictional elements of that relationship (between God and His people, individually and collectively) are not to be held by civil government.

That jurisdiction belongs to personal conscience and God's church.[68] Where civil government is involved with civil law, church government is involved with church or moral law. And while the church is to provide a beacon of biblical morality for society generally, it only has jurisdiction with regard to church members, and even then some things are left to conscience. The regenerate have the grace and advocacy of Jesus Christ to mediate between themselves and God's law.

Non-members are not under the jurisdiction of the church, which means that they continue to be under the jurisdiction of civil government. The jurisdiction of the church is to provide a kind of buffer between civil law and God's law. So, the unbeliever enjoys no such buffer. The unregenerate have no advocate or mediator between themselves and God's law. Thus, they are completely liable to Old Testament law apart from Christ. Lord, have mercy.

In addition, not everything that is legal is moral, nor is everything that is sinful actually illegal. Some things that are legal with regard to the civil law are immoral in the eyes of the church (or the Bible, in that

---

68   *Westminster Confession*, Chapter 20 and *Savoy Declaration*, Chapter 21, *Of Christian Liberty, and Liberty of Conscience.*

the church is charged with representing the Bible to humanity). And conversely, some things are sinful but are not against civil laws.

The flexibility and tensions between these things provides for the jurisdiction of conscience. It facilitates the personal discrimination between good and evil (or conscience) that is directed by the Holy Spirit, regarding biblical understanding and application in consultation with God through prayer and among other regenerate Christians. This is the area in which personality is developed, expressed and matured. It is the area in which God's law meets particular contexts, the area in which will and choice are exercised, the area in which principles and practice intersect. Moral conscience is the area—spiritual, intellectual and moral—in which personal relationship with Jesus Christ is exercised, or not.

It is upon this basis that Peter asked about what would become of the ungodly and the sinner. His intent was to bring his readers to consider their own lives apart from the guidance of God through the presence of the Holy Spirit through regeneration. Apart from this personal relationship with Jesus Christ, which operates through the individual interaction with God's covenant or Word (the Bible) in the light of Christ (under the influence of the Holy Spirit through regeneration). However, it must not be thought that this interaction is limited to God interacting with you (the individual) alone. No. God interacts with all of His people through prayer, conscience, worship, etc.

Corporate Relationship

Thus, believers are called into relationship and discussion with other believers as a way to further develop their relationship with Jesus Christ, in that He is also manifest in others through regeneration. It is through this relationship and discussion that Christian unity is manifest, or not. This unity, however, does not begin with doctrinal or theological agreement. In fact, quite the opposite!

When believers begin to interact with one another, they find a lot of disagreement. This initial disagreement provides much struggle and difficulty. However, the difficulties are to be engaged and endured because they (the struggles and difficulties) are the engine of Christian maturity in Christ. The struggles, the interactions with others, the discussions and difficulties bring all parties in Christ to greater maturity and sanctification. They provide a kind of proving ground for Christian maturity and discernment.

However, the idea here is not to simply prove one's self theologically competent, but to learn about the depth and breadth of God's Word, the sufficiency and perfection of Jesus Christ, the diversity of God's people, and the wideness of God's mercy. The purpose is to meet other Christians, to broaden one's horizons, to develop patience and understanding, to refine one's beliefs, to experience the benefits found in many counselors, to develop the ability to work with others and to improve the development of social conscience.

People often think that conscience is a personal matter, but it is not. Conscience is a community matter because it has to do with how we treat one another and/or the social consequences of our beliefs and behaviors on others. But neither is conscience a public or civil matter. It is not a function of civil jurisdiction or influence. Rather, it is a matter of one's relationship with Jesus Christ and one's relationship with other people.

Again, it is often assumed that one's personal relationship with Jesus Christ is a private matter. But it is not. It is a community matter because it is has to do with how we treat one another in the light of Christ. There is no such thing as a completely independent individual or isolated Christian. Christians are always necessarily associated with or connected with other Christians, with Christ's church in one way or another. To be a Christian is not simply to be in personal relationship with Jesus Christ, but it is to be in personal relationship with God's people, as well. To be saved is to be brought into personal relationship with Jesus Christ, who also gathers with His people. Christianity is necessarily social.

AGGREGATE

Jesus Christ is the Lord of hosts, the Lord of a vast multitude that exists as One in Christ, in unity with Christ. He is Lord of the human aggregate. He is the whole that is greater than the sum of its parts. He is the human archetype in Jesus Christ, and salvation in Christ provides an archetypal upgrade from the old Adamic archetype. He is the poetic bloom on the proverbial rose, and when the bloom is off the rose, it means, figuratively, that whatever you are talking about has lost its first freshness, it's former beauty and allure.

Thus, Christ provides a human archetype that is eternally fresh and beautiful. And the engagement of that archetype provides an allurement that is both attractive and charming. How can I say that? Because "we know that for those who love God all things work together for good, for those who are called according to his purpose" (Romans 8:28), and because what is good is also beautiful.

On account of all of this, said Peter, "let those who suffer according to God's will entrust their souls to a faithful Creator while doing good" (v. 19). Notice that Peter was not talking about all suffering, but only suffering according to God's will. Peter was not talking about whether God causes suffering in the world, and we will do well not to steer biblical terms and ideas in directions that the Bible doesn't take them. Peter was not suggesting the abstract idea that God is the author of human suffering. Nor was he saying that it is God's will for His people to suffer. Rather, Peter was highlighting those Christian people who are persecuted in any way because of their beliefs or practices—those who suffer because of their faithfulness to Jesus Christ.

Those who are making an effort to be faithful need to entrust their souls to God. The *Authorized Version* translated the word (*paratith-ēmi*) as "commit the keeping of." The word indicates, not merely a decision, but the transfer of possession or ownership. Christian faithfulness is both active and passive because it involves the active surrender of one's will to God. Once that surrender has been made, life does not become passive, as some versions of spirituality seem to suggest. Rather, surrendering one's will to God means actively engaging God's will for your life.

It does, however, mean that once that initial surrender is made, one's own will becomes passive in the sense that one becomes passive toward one's own will, where previously one's own will was the driving force of life. Faithfulness is not passive in the sense that the driving force of life becomes passive. But rather, in the sense that our response to our own will, our own desires, becomes passive in order that God's will may become active. And the first activity to be engaged is the discovery of God's will for your life. John The Baptist said it this way, "He must increase, but I must decrease" (John 3:30).

The discovery of God's will for your life is made through interaction with God's Holy Spirit through regeneration in the context of the reading and understanding of God's Word. God's will is found in God's Word because God's will for His people is always the same—faithfulness or loyalty to God in Christ (Messiah, the human archetype). History brings God's people to various contexts regarding the application of faithfulness, and different people find themselves in different situations, which require different ways to manifest faithfulness to God.

But the essential principle of faithfulness (the archetype) is always the same in every circumstance. The Lord of the aggregate intends to bring the principles of the aggregate to bear upon all individuals in all situations. The archetype of Jesus Christ is able to serve as a model of both belief and behavior in all human situations. There is no situation for which the archetype of Jesus Christ does not apply.

Old Becomes New

People might wonder how the archetype of Jesus Christ applies to Old Testament saints, whose archetype was Adam. This can only be understood from an historical perspective because the human context is always historical. Adam (humanity) was created in the image of God, and the first instance of humanity was named Adam, who then served as the archetype of humanity. Adam's role as archetype continued until Christ came and replaced him as the Federal Head of humanity. All of the essential elements of humanity were contained in the archetype of Adam, and his helpmeet, Eve. Nonetheless, their Fall resulted from a moral breach introduced by the Serpent. That breach was then healed by Jesus Christ. And because the Fall had been historic, the repair also needed to be historic.

Not only did Adam provide the human archetype, but Adam's relationship with Eve was also covenantally archetypal. In order to understand this, we must understand that the biblical archetypes are not individualistic. There is no such thing as an individual who exists independently of others. Obviously, individuals exist but complete human individual independence is an illusion. Individuals cannot reproduce. Individuals exists, but are not whole, not complete, and not independently sustainable.

Human identity requires both an individual pole and a social or corporate pole. The point is simply that people are necessarily socially dependent. As Eve is to Adam regarding the old archetype, the church is to Christ regarding the new. Man (humanity) is a social being. Humanity is the aggregate of human individuals. The whole is composed of the parts, but is more than the sum of the parts because the aggregate (the body) is itself an entity or being. We experience this aggregation as various national and regional characteristics that are manifested by individuals, yet belong to the various national or regional groups, such as accents and mannerisms.

Christ's archetype provided an adjustment to Adam's archetype. The archetype of Christ did not replace the archetype of Adam. It corrected it. Christ corrected Adam by providing forgiveness and the crowning element of humanity—God's Holy Spirit. Those who are regenerated in Christ are renewed by the forgiving and renewing power of God's Holy Spirit. And to be renewed by the Holy Spirit is to be renewed by God Himself, because God is trinitarian. God the Father, God the Son and God the Holy Spirit are each uniquely personal in themselves and at the same time they are one Person.

Individual renewal or regeneration brings individuals into conscious participation with God's trinitarian character, which brings the redeemed into contact with one another, as well. Thus, regeneration is always social as well as personal. People cannot be Christian apart from participating in Christ's church(es) because being Christian means consciously participating in God's trinitarian character, which is necessarily social as well as individual.

What does it mean to entrust our souls to God? What is a soul (*psuchē*)? The Greek word literally means breath or breathing, and suggests a constituent element of life. The soul of a person is like oxygen to fire. And fire is not a thing but a process or chemical interaction. We often speak of souls as if they were like marbles that can be collected, as if the soul is an eternal thing that exists inside of our bodies, and will someday transcend this body and this earth to dwell in eternity in heaven with God. But this is a Greek, Gnostic idea, not a biblically Christian idea.

Soul Confusion

We must realize that our minds, our thought patterns or ways of thinking, have been shaped by Greek philosophy more than by biblical Christianity. For millennia Western society has imposed Greek categories upon the Bible and Christianity. So, all too often our patterns of thinking are more Greek, more Pagan and secular, than they are biblical.

The theological and biblical confusion that has manifested in the modern world is a function of the imposition of unbiblical (or extrabiblical) ideas and definitions upon biblical terms and concepts. And the problem is not simply an East/West philosophical and theological difference because the Eastern/Western philosophical dichotomy is itself a false dichotomy.

Indeed, the central problem that we face manifests itself as the forcing of various ideas, definitions and interpretations into false dichotomies of various kinds. In politics it manifests as the political Right against the political Left. In physics it manifests as our understanding of light as particles against light as waves. In philosophy it manifests as essence versus process, or constancy versus change, or ultimacy versus particularity.

Plato identified the problem as the one and the many. The problem of the one and the many issues out of a dualistic interpretation and understanding of reality. Thus, the problem cannot be solved from within a dualistic perspective because that perspective can do nothing other than oscillate between the dichotomous poles. Greek philosophy and thinking is essentially dualistic, and thus, it has been unable solve the problem.

Societies built on dualism lack social stability because they oscillate between various kinds of false dichotomies that produce growth on the one hand and decline on the other, a boom and bust progression. Every dualistic society experiences cycles of expansion and decline as they oscillate between the poles of their dualistic understanding.

Jesus Christ and biblical Christianity provide the only possible solution to the problem of philosophical dualism. Theologically dualism manifests itself as monotheism versus polytheism. Historically, Paganism has always been polytheistic. Then along came the proposition of monotheism as seen, for instance, in the creation of humanity (Genesis 1:26-27) or First Commandment (Exodus 20:3). God separated Israel from the other nations so that Israel (God's people) could wrestle with being faithful.

Unimany

Note the pattern: God, who is One, created the world and then created Adam (humanity). Adam required Eve for propagation, and Eve was created from the rib of Adam, from a part. Thus, humanity was divided into two parts—"male and female he created them" (Genesis 1:27). Then there were two, but God called the two "one" (Genesis 2:24), *e pluribis unum.*

God created this problem of the one and the many. Why? So that He could provide the solution to the problem. And what is God's solution to this problem? Himself, the Trinity, and specifically the Holy Spirit. How does the Holy Spirit solve this problem? By being Himself, in the fullness of His trinitarianism, by bridging the one and the many.

The Holy Spirit has been widely dispatched to this world following Christ's birth, death and resurrection in order to renew God's people, the people of God's covenant, in Christ. So, the Holy Spirit fills the lives, the hearts and minds of God's covenant people through regeneration.

This means that God Himself abides in His people, which means that human identity in Christ is caught up or incorporated into God's identity. We don't become God, but we find our true identity in God through Christ. As Jesus described it: "I in them and you in me, that they may become perfectly one" (John 17:23). Note that in Christ the identity of Christians, the many individuals who have been regenerated in Christ, becomes one.

In Christ the many become one. In Christ the false dualism of monotheism versus polytheism becomes trinitarianism, which solves the philosophical problem, not by establishing a compromise half way between monotheism and polytheism, but by integrating the dichotomy into an entirely different dimension. This new dimension in Christ is a supernatural dimension. However, we must guard ourselves from interpreting or understanding the word *supernatural* from a dualistic perspective as has been done historically by various occult teachings (books, writings, movements, etc.). This supernatural dimension is not magical, mystical or other worldly.

Rather, the *supernatural* involves the superimposition of God—
God's story, God's Word, God's history—upon this world, as if God is
an alien being who has infected this world with Himself. *Infected* is not
the right word, of course, because God does not bring disease to an
otherwise healthy world, but brings healing to an otherwise sinfully
diseased world.

Nonetheless, the point is that the conscious involvement of God's
Holy Spirit in this world and in the lives of God's people changes and
restores the character of humanity—both the character of the individuals who compose humanity and the character of the human aggregate.

New Dimension

What is this new dimension in which the Holy Spirit lives and
moves and has our being (Acts 17:38)? For that matter, what is a
dimension? A dimension is a realm of measurement. For instance,
height, width, depth and time are all dimensions, realms, ideas or areas
of measurement. The supernatural dimension of the Holy Spirit is also
a dimension, realm, idea or area of measurement.

There are two questions that must be answered for us to understand this supernatural dimension. First, what is being measured? And
second, what is the standard by which it is measured? We can answer
these questions by asking another, *Where does the Holy Spirit dwell?*

He dwells in human hearts and minds. Thus, His abode is within
humanity, both in individuals and in the human aggregate. He dwells
in both of these areas because He is trinitarian in character, so He is
both one and many, ultimate and proximate, etc. His character overlaps or touches upon our character, both individually and corporately.
Therefore, the Holy Spirit dwells in what we call morality. His being is
in what we call the moral dimension, and again we must include both
the morality of individuals and the morality of cultures.

In fact, He ties the individual to the social, the particular to the
principle, the proximate to the ultimate, etc. And because of this, He
also provides the standard by which to measure—Himself, His Word,
the Bible. But because His own being is so difficult for us to perceive
and/or understand, He manifests Himself as the Person of Jesus Christ
on our behalf and for our good. He became one of us so that we can
better understand Him and His mission in this world.

It is critical to our understanding of Him to realize that He became
only one Person, a fully human and divine Person. He did not, nor does
He intend to, manifest as any others. Rather, in order to highlight His
role in the Trinity, He must always maintain the integrity of being only
one Person in order that He alone may bridge the gap between the one

and the many, the individual and the principle, the proximate and the ultimate.

Do Good, Be Well

Peter said that we are to be engaged in a particular activity while at the same time entrusting our souls to God. That activity is *doing good* (*agathopoiia*, v. 19). Other versions translate it as *well-doing*. The Greek word is composed of two words that literally mean *good* and *make*. To make is to be engaged in an activity. And to determine that a thing is good (or bad) requires a moral judgment—a discernment.

Therefore, we are to be engaged in the activity of making good moral judgments. This is the dimension in which the Holy Spirit dwells. It is the dimension in which he measures our souls with His judgment, His discernment. We ourselves, the new temple of the living God, are to be measured by the standard provided by God's Holy Spirit —Jesus Christ.

However, we are not to measure one another until we have first measured ourselves against the Prototype of Christ. The Christian's first and highest calling is to magnify the Lord in his or her own thinking and living, in our own hearts and minds. By magnifying Christ in our own lives we grow in sanctification (moral maturity in the light of Christ and according to the Bible), and we grow in unity as we each and all "attain to the unity of the faith and of the knowledge of the Son of God, to mature manhood, to the measure of the stature of the fullness of Christ, so that we may no longer be children, tossed to and fro by the waves and carried about by every wind of doctrine, by human cunning, by craftiness in deceitful schemes" (Ephesians 4:13-14).

May this day arrive soon. Come, Lord Jesus!

29. Who, Me?

So I exhort the elders among you, as a fellow elder and a wit-
ness of the sufferings of Christ, as well as a partaker in the
glory that is going to be revealed: shepherd the flock of God
that is among you, exercising oversight, not under compul-
sion, but willingly, as God would have you; not for shameful
gain, but eagerly; not domineering over those in your charge,
but being examples to the flock. —1 Peter 5:1-3 (ESV)

Whether Peter wrote exclusively to the elders mentioned in chapter one ("elect exiles of the dispersion," 1 Peter 1:1) or to the whole church is debatable. But here he explicitly turned his attention to church leaders by exhorting them. He didn't simply call their attention to what he had to say next, but he demanded that they pay more attention generally. His plea was passionate and intense as he insisted that they lead their churches in a particular way.

By what authority did he exhort them? He identified himself as a fellow elder, but more than being a fellow elder he was an older elder. He cited his knowledge and experience of Jesus, having personally witnessed the sufferings of Christ. Unlike them, he had known Jesus personally and had witnessed the suffering of the Lord in His earthly life and His death on the cross. Peter played his apostle card. Peter was an apostle and those to whom he wrote were not apostles. He had known Jesus personally, and they had not. Reaching into the past he appealed to his greater knowledge and experience of Jesus as the foundation of his authority.

But he also reached into the future to establish his credentials and authority to provide direction for church leaders. He identified himself as a partaker of the glory of Christ's ongoing and future revelation, the "glory that is going to be revealed" (v. 1)—future oriented glory. Peter seems to have been aware that his ministry would contribute in a foundational way to the unfolding of God's revelation in and through Jesus Christ.

It is not sufficient that Christian authority issues from the past, from history, as if gospel authority can be handed down like a trident from one person to another. While that kind of authority was traditional among earthly kings, and while Christian authority will always honor the saints who have preceded the ongoing present era, the authority of the past is not sufficient for the present. An authority that is anchored only in the past is too narrowly conceived. It is anchored in death, not life, in what has been, not in what already is or what will be in the ever increasing fullness of Christ's revelation.

As the Chinese proverb says, "Water down stream cannot be used to turn the mill." While we must always learn from the past, we must not insist that memories of yesterday's manna provide sustenance for tomorrow's journey. Knowledge of the past is incredibly useful, even essential, but wisdom grows and adapts to meet today's needs. Much of Peter's overall message was that God has provided for the ongoing guidance of the Christian community by providing for the ongoing revelation of God in Christ now and in the future.

DRAWN FORWARD

The revelation of Jesus Christ in history would continue to provide wisdom and guidance over time because God's direction and leadership for the present moment was not being pushed into the present by the past, but was being pulled into the present by the future, like a plant being drawn toward the light of the sun. God's decree is pulling history forward into a future that had been then (and is now still being) prepared in advance of history. What was being revealed about Christ in the present had already been established in the future. If I am going to reveal to you tomorrow what I hold hidden in my hand today, what you will see tomorrow already exists today.

From a practical standpoint, Peter was calling church leaders to look forward to the fullness of the establishment of Christianity rather than to look backward to the history of the Old Testament. Clearly, Peter was not calling for the abandonment of the Old Testament. Rather, he simply acknowledged that Christ had fulfilled the law and the prophecy, and a new chapter of God's story was unfolding among those who were called Christians, even as they were relocating all over the known world. They were to face toward the future, not the past. They were to look to the glory that was going to be revealed in the future, and was then and still is now in the process of being revealed in the present. And in fact, Peter's letter(s) would provide—and have in fact provided—a foundation for that revelation.

So, because those Christian leaders to whom Peter was writing would be called to lead their people in the midst of new and unfolding circumstances Peter wrote them to warn them about three vices that would tempt them to veer off course, three characteristics that are too often found among Christian leaders: laziness, ambition and greed.

Laziness

To guard against laziness he clarified their obligation as Christian leaders—shepherds—to feed God's people. And while bodily nutrition is necessary and important, his primary intention was to feed them spiritually and intellectually. In order to be the people that God wants Christians to be, they would need to be faithful, educated and intelligent. There is no place for laziness or sloth in Christian life. Christians must be attentive and Christian leaders must model this virtue.

It is possible to be faithful, but neither educated nor intelligent. It is also possible to be educated, but neither faithful nor intelligent. And it is also possible to be intelligent, but neither faithful nor educated. To be the people that Christ has called us to be means engaging all of these things to the best of our abilities. In Christ there is the fullness of Christian character toward which we are to strive (1 Corinthians 14:12). The wholeness of salvation in Christ is also the manifest fullness of our human potential. In Christ we will be all that God has created us to be as His people, to fully represent Him on earth, to be Christ's representatives on earth.

Ambition

To cure the second temptation of ambition Peter insisted on moderation and meekness. Peter did not mean to suggest that all of these character flaws always infect Christian leaders. Clearly, laziness and ambition don't always go together. Nonetheless, for those who would be driven by ambition and success in ministry Peter called for temperance and humility.

Because the call to Christian leadership is a high calling, it is often an object of covetousness. Because Christian leadership provides a social position of power and authority, it is sought after by those who would abuse it for their own benefit. The temptations to abuse power and authority increase as one's power and authority increase.

Thus, success in Christian leadership requires an increasing ability to resist the increasing subtleties of abuse. In other words, the more power and authority that one has, the easier it is to abuse. For an analogy think of the operation of a large machine. The larger the machine the more delicate and careful the operator must be because of the sheer weight and momentum of the machine.

GREED

In opposition to the third vice of greed Peter set the positive character qualities of liberality, generosity and charity. Church leaders are not to work for *filthy lucre* (*Authorized Version*) or *shameful gain* (*aischrokerdōs*, v. 2). This does not mean that gospel workers should not be compensated for their work. The threshing ox should not be muzzled (1 Corinthians 9:9). Church leaders have families to feed and care for just like other people. Peter's point, however, was that Christian leaders should not labor for the purpose of receiving wages.

Ministry is not a job, it is a calling. Actually, all work from a Christian perspective is to be engaged as a calling, which means that the primary purpose for work should not be money. Rather, the primary work in one's calling is to promote and extend the kingdom of God. It's not that making money is bad, it's not. But it should not the central focus of one's calling.

Money was/is not to a priority for ministry. Ministry is not a job in the sense that its purpose is to put bread on the table. When ministry becomes a job, when the purpose of laboring for Christ becomes the receiving of a paycheck, when church leadership becomes an employment in the sense of a profession, it no longer serves Christ as Christ is to be served—sacrificially. When church leaders are focused on feeding their families or laboring for a wage, they are focused on themselves and their own families rather than on Christ's people and on His concern for them.

This admonition must be heard by Christian laity as well as Christian leaders because both groups can be tempted to make this error. Personal gain must not be the motivation for Christian leadership. And leaders can fall into this sin all by themselves, or they can be funneled into it by churches and their pastoral committees who make this error in judgment by insisting that the pastorate is a job like any other. And they begin treating it as such by generating job related expectations for their leaders. At that point, they are directing the leader rather than being directed by the leader. At that point the roles of leader and follower have been reversed to a degree. This is not to say that church leaders should be exempt from supervision. They most certainly should not be. It is, rather, a comment on the character of the supervision that is appropriate for ministry.

PETER'S LOVE

Peter's exhortation in verse 1 was very dear to him because of the special instruction that he had received from the resurrected Christ. John recounted the story:

"He said to him a second time, 'Simon, son of John, do you love me?' He said to him, 'Yes, Lord; you know that I love you.' He said to him, 'Tend my sheep.' He said to him the third time, 'Simon, son of John, do you love me?' Peter was grieved because he said to him the third time, 'Do you love me?' and he said to him, 'Lord, you know everything; you know that I love you.' Jesus said to him, 'Feed my sheep'"(John 21:16-17).

No doubt Peter had been thinking about this for years by the time he wrote this letter. There is no question that he remembered it because, as John reported, Peter had been disturbed by the resurrected Christ's instructions that had been given specifically to him. Over the years, Peter came to see that he himself had needed to be cured of his own delusions about Messiah Jesus. That was what Jesus was doing as He asked Peter about his love and directed Peter to care for His people in John 21.

Over the ensuing years Peter had come to understand that Christian sanctification and maturity involved a process of disillusionment. For the most part people need to be freed from various Pagan superstitions and religious falsities that have wormed their way into the human heart. He knew this because Christ had purged him of his own hardheadedness, hard-heartedness, superstitions and foolish religiosity.

Peter had been the perfect representative or example of the Jews of his time. He was a lowly fisherman, and as such was a common man. He was uneducated but hard working, opinionated but uninformed, yet boldly honest. He was honest enough to plainly say what he thought, but not smart enough to see his own internal inconsistencies.

For instance, consider the fact that Peter had boldly identified Jesus as the Messiah of God (Matthew 16:16). It was upon Peter's bold and plain identification of Jesus as Messiah that Christ founded His church. Indeed, what other foundation could Christ's church be built on than the simple, plain and honest confession that Jesus is Christ and Lord.

Yet, two verses later Peter criticized Jesus' teaching regarding His impending crucifixion and resurrection. Peter had correctly identified Jesus as the Christ, and in the next breath he tried to correct the theology and/or the end times scenario laid down by Jesus! Peter had such bold honesty, yet such unmitigated audacity. The Lord rebuked Peter, the very man upon whom rested the foundation of the Lord's church. Yes, Christ's church was founded on the bold confession of Jesus as the Christ, in spite of the fact that at that point Peter didn't understand his own words.

Christ's church was founded, not on the full-blown realization of Jesus as the Christ of God, but on the honest but seriously flawed confession that Jesus is the Christ by Peter. Peter provided a model of God's grace and mercy—and of God's power to work in His people even when they don't fully understand Him. Where Paul's model was that of a scholar and academician who had a complete and almost instantaneous conversion, Peter's model was that of an ordinary yokel who continued to bumble along, two steps forward and one step back. Peter still had a lot to learn, and his learning curve was uneven. Peter's model balanced Paul's by demonstrating that there was more to the gospel than scholarship and academics. Peter would demonstrate learning of a different kind. In Peter we see God's ability to keep His people growing rightly in spite of their (our) resistance and stupidity.

For Paul, the appearance of Christ answered questions that Paul had struggled with and studied all of his life—theological questions. But Peter had yet to even think of the deeper questions of life and eternity. Peter was smart enough to see that Jesus was the Christ, but dumb enough to think that he could correct the theology of the Messiah of God. Only now as Peter was writing these letters did he begin to see the greater questions and issues, and their implications and applications regarding humanity.

And, based on his own growth and maturity in Christ, Peter understood that those who would follow Christ in the future would, like him, continue to grow and mature in perpetuity. That ongoing growth, that continual development of Christians as both individuals and as the incorporation of Christ's church was the heart of Peter's vision. Christ first showed Peter the contents of his own mind and heart that were filled with sin, error, superstition and confusions of every sort. Only after Peter saw his own sin and confusion and recognized them for what they were could he know enough to renounce himself and his own ideas and receive the grace and wisdom of Jesus Christ through regeneration. This is the foundation upon which Christ founded His church.

This foundation was nothing new. Jeremiah had said, "The heart is deceitful above all things, and desperately sick; who can understand it?" (Jeremiah 17:9). But Peter, having been a Jew, prior to meeting Jesus undoubtedly thought that he had overcome this particular malady. What Jew wouldn't have thought so? The Jews who had read and studied the Old Testament for centuries were not celebrating the wickedness of their human hearts as the they practiced their Temple rites, but were working to overcome that wickedness with their faithfulness, their sacrifices and various religious and cultural practices.

And if those Old Testament sacrifices and practices did not or could not overcome this malady of the human heart, those who maintained those sacrifices and practices in the presence of what actually could overcome it—Jesus Christ—would have been deluded beyond all hope (1 Corinthians 15:19). Their delusion would be beyond hope because they would have falsely believed that their religious observances were efficacious. Thus, they would falsely believe that their sinful hearts were cured by their various Old Testament beliefs and practices. And falsely believing that they were already cured, they would not see their need for Jesus. And this is what happened.

Love Revisited

This would likely have been Peter's mindset prior to his own regeneration and sanctification. To some extent this would have been Peter's mindset when Jesus instructed him in John 21:16-17. Here in 1 Peter 5:2 Peter was passing along the wisdom that he had gained in the light of Christ since his regeneration (Acts 2). So, what had Peter learned?

In John 21 Jesus asked Peter if he loved Him. 1) Do you love (*agapaō*) me? Peter answered, yes, Lord, I love (*phileō*) you. 2) Jesus asked again, do you love (*agapaō*) me? Yes, Lord, I love (*phileō*) you. 3) And again, do you love (*phileō*) me? Disturbed by the repeated question, Peter answered, Yes, Lord, you know that I love (*phileō*) you.

Note that Jesus asked about one kind of love and Peter answered with another. At this point in Peter's life he does not seem to have understood the kind of love that Jesus called for. Peter consistently spoke of *phileō*, when the Lord asked about other kinds of love. Eventually, Jesus appears to have accepted Peter's lack of understanding and accepted whatever kind of love that Peter could muster up. The third time, Jesus asked about the only kind of love that Peter seemed to understand. Perhaps, Jesus was using Peter's faulty understanding of Christian love as an example of the necessity for regeneration and growth in grace, which awaited Peter at this time.

In addition, Jesus' instructions were different each time as well, as if Jesus was calling attention to a kind of progression. Jesus answered: 1) Feed (*boskō*) my lambs (*arnion*). 2) Feed (*poimainō*) my sheep (*probaton*). 3) Feed (*boskō*) my sheep (*probaton*).

The first time Jesus answered with *boskō arnion*. The literal meaning of these words is something like: *send my baby lambs out to pasture to feed in the open fields*. The second time He said *poimainō probaton*. This means to tend as in supervise or rule over those sheep who advance or move forward in maturity. But there is also a sense here that Jesus was speaking of the sheep as a group or flock rather than individually.

The third time Jesus used the same word for sheep as the second time. So, by repeating it He may have meant to underscore it as a priority, as if to suggest that those sheep who continue to advance in maturity will need further special attention, and that this special attention will be a kind of group attention rather than an individual oriented attention. It may have been as if Christ was suggesting that growth in Christian maturity involved the growth from individuality into a more corporate centered identity. We might think of it as originally a concern for their own personal salvation, and as they grew in sanctification, that concern gave way to concern for God's people.

And this fits the model of Christian maturity where at first baby Christians (lambs) are sent into God's pasture (Scripture) to feed on whatever interests them. But as they grow and mature, they require more specialized instruction and direction to keep from chasing down rabbit holes or false leads. And at the highest levels of growth and maturity, they themselves become instructors and caretakers of the community known as the church. It suggests growth from self-concern to concern for others.

Passing Forward

In 1 Peter 5:2-3, Peter used slightly different words himself as he passed on what he had learned from all of this. Peter said, in essence, feed or shepherd (*episkopeō*) the flock of God of which you are a member, those who are already in your personal orbit by imposing direction or *purpose* upon them. But don't force yourself upon them, rather inspire them to follow your direction willingly, as Christ has so inspired you. Don't operate out of shame or greed, and don't try to manipulate people with shame or greed. Rather, be a model of attentive intelligence (*prothumos*) that will inspire others to want to be like you.

Christian leaders, those who grow in genuine maturity, must continuously and eagerly seek additional maturity, more sanctification. It is out of this spirit of eager striving for Christ that Christian leaders are to be motivated and drawn. Christian leaders must be willing and eager for service, and not motivated by sloth, power or greed.

Rather than focusing on the literal translation of Peter's words, I am trying to capture Peter's intention. How can I know what Peter's intention was? Because Peter was serving the God of the Bible, who does not change, but who has changed both Peter and me in the same ways. This does not mean that I am on a par with Peter—not at all. It only means that both Peter and I have been regenerated with the mind of Christ, as was Paul (1 Corinthians 2:16) and as are all Christians. Of course, having the mind of Christ does not mean that we all have the same level of understanding, only the same kind of understanding.

This sense of Peter's message in these verses is summed up as Peter insisted that Christian leaders be "not domineering over those in your charge, but being examples to the flock" (v. 3). All Christians are to willingly and eagerly work to be the best examples of the spirit of Jesus Christ that they can be. Christians are to work to outdo each other in their own personal efforts to accurately model biblically informed Christian thinking and living. And those who do the best job of this are to serve as elders and leaders of the churches. Such people are to lead by example. That is the model for Christian leadership that Peter was planting, and to which we today are to aspire to.

Lord, make it so.

30. MORALITY & SCIENCE

And when the chief Shepherd appears, you will receive the unfading crown of glory. Likewise, you who are younger, be subject to the elders. Clothe yourselves, all of you, with humility toward one another, for "God opposes the proud but gives grace to the humble." Humble yourselves, therefore, under the mighty hand of God so that at the proper time he may exalt you, casting all your anxieties on him, because he cares for you. —1 Peter 5:4-7 (ESV)

T he central difficulty with church leadership is that the world and the flesh are opposed to Jesus Christ. The world hates Jesus, and that hate is aimed at all who represent Him, and the better a person is at representing Him the more opposition he will receive from the world and the flesh. Ministry is difficult because it is largely unappreciated by worldly people. And contemporary churches tend to be worldly. It is difficult to persist in a job that produces deprecation and opposition.

This situation persists even in the most faithful of congregations because the focus on both evangelism and sanctification (or spiritual growth) means that congregations always contain a spectrum of faithfulness on the part of its members.[69] Every church has worldly and faithless people among its members, and during times of church weakness, like today, many worldly people find their way into church leadership as deacons, elders and even pastors. Consequently, the weakness or faithlessness of churches as a whole contributes to a kind of momentum of increasing spiritual weakness and faithlessness.

Peter, being acutely aware of this situation, calls elect members and leaders generally to not look to other Christians for guidance and support, but to look only to the Great Shepherd who is none other than

---

69 *Westminster Confession of Faith*, Chapter XXV, Of the Church, IV, V, 1646.

Jesus Christ. The Great Shepherd (*archipoimēn*) is not a reference to someone who holds an office like the Pope, but refers specifically to the archetypal Christian—Jesus Christ.

We are to emulate church leaders when they are worthy of emulation, and we are to call them out when they are not. And we are to have the spiritual discernment to know the difference.

Peter spoke of Christ's appearing or manifesting (*phaneroō*), which is another way of (or word for) referencing the unfolding revelation of Jesus Christ. Christ will appear or manifest with increasing clarity and intensity as He is revealed in history. Thus church leaders, and all Christians really, are to look to the author and finisher of their faith (Hebrews 12:2). The Lord will complete the revelation that began in Christ through His church and in this world (Philippians 1:6). Nothing will stop the ongoing unfolding of the revelation of Jesus Christ in history.

Thus, the leadership, guidance and example of the Great Shepherd will always be available through the reality of the Holy Spirit for all church leaders in all times. And what is even more encouraging and exciting is that over time and history the revelation of Jesus Christ will continue to accumulate, which means that the quality and availability of Christ's leadership, guidance and example will continue to become clearer and fuller until the trinitarian reality of Jesus Christ simply cannot be denied by anyone alive. That day will be the day of the appearance of the Great Shepherd.

GLORY

Peter went on to say that on that day Christ will bring a "never fading crown of glory" (v. 4). The various translations use the word *you*, which the Authorized Version translates as *"ye shall receive a crown of glory,"* which uses the plural form of *you*. However, the Greek does not contain the word *you*. So, the question about exactly who would be the recipient of this crown of glory is not as clear as we want it to be.

The question arises because we know that all glory belongs to God alone (Revelation 16:9, 19:1), that we human beings are not worthy of glory, and furthermore, that glory is the essence of worship. In worship we ascribe and give glory to God in Christ, but that glory does not accrue to the repentant sinners who are saved by the grace of God. Thus, the suggestion that believers or even elect church leaders will themselves receive a crown of glory is suspect of being potentially infected with a bit of human pride.

It is likely that Peter was referencing the "crown of glory" mentioned in Isaiah 28:5. There, however, Isaiah suggested that the Lord Himself would *be* a crown of glory upon His remnant people. Here the idea was that God would not simply bring or give a crown of glory, but that He would Himself be a crown of glory. This is undoubtedly what Peter was talking about because Isaiah was the central Old Testament writer to use that phrase.[70]

As Christ became increasingly manifest through His progressive revelation in history, He would manifest as the trinitarian God in or through history, uniting the particular with the universal and the proximate with the ultimate in the minds of believers. That manifestation would then serve as a kind of crown in the sense of being the sign and symbol of God's kingship regarding the assimilation of that kingship in the minds (or heads) of men.

The crown of glory would then not be given in honor of the believers it would be given to, but would be given in honor of the completion of the progressive revelation of Jesus Christ, and would symbolically rest on or in the minds of believers. Thus, the honor of the crown would not accrue to repentant sinners, but would accrue to Christ alone.

GLORY'S FLOWER

Peter also mentioned that this crown would be *unfading* (*amarantinos*). The word refers to a blood-red flower (amaranth) that does not wither when picked as long as it is kept in water or moistened. It was an ancient symbol of perpetuity and immortality. And perhaps more importantly, it is edible. The fact that it is edible is significant because of the character of the plant itself. Amaranth seeds, like buckwheat and quinoa, contain protein that is unusually complete for plant sources.[71]

Most fruits and vegetables do not contain a complete set of amino acids, and thus different sources of protein must be consumed for a balanced diet. As a food, amaranth is particularly wholesome, complete and nutritious. Thus, the fact that Peter said that the crown of glory to be received by God's people was unfading or amaranth-like suggests, not merely that Christ provides wholesome nutrition for the soul, but that the wholeness of body and soul are essential for a full understanding of this analogy.

GLORY'S AUTHORITY

Verse 5 establishes biblical authority, which is always a matter of submission. Biblical authority is not the permission to dominate others, but is the responsibility of obedience to those over us, and ultimately obedience to Christ Himself as revealed in Scripture. Clearly, the youngers are to be in submission to the elders. This, however, sug-

---

70   It is also mentioned in Proverbs 4:9 and 16:31.
71   http://en.wikipedia.org/wiki/Amaranth.

gests a principle not a hard and fast rule, as if authority were completely and merely a function of age. It's not. It's primarily a function of
Christian maturity and sanctification, which includes knowledge, wisdom and experience. As a general rule people should honor their elders
by submitting to their wisdom. But where wisdom is lacking among the
elderly, submission to their folly is not advisable.

The context of Peter's comments suggest an existing or assumed
structure of authority in the churches and in society in general. Peter
did not have to define all of his terms because he knew that people
would understand what he meant by them. Inasmuch as those historical structures have deteriorated, we today know and understand them
less than our forefathers knew them because of their deterioration. But
Christians still have a general idea of what it means to live in an biblically authoritative social structure, even though we have no recent
experience of it.

The subtext of Peter's message here was to honor existing social
and legal structures by conforming to them. Remember that Peter was
writing to the "elect exiles of the dispersion" (1 Peter 1:1), to those who
were fleeing the destruction of Jerusalem and establishing communities in the Roman Empire. Part of Peter's concern was that the new
communities reflect the teachings and values of Jesus Christ, that they
honor civil government and reflect the authority of Christ. Thus, Peter
was establishing that Christian communities are to be orderly and
respectful of traditional laws and values. He meant essentially Old
Testament values that are seen and interpreted in the light of Christ,
but also Roman values and laws that do not conflict with Christianity.
Remember that Jesus Himself obeyed Roman law unto His own death.

Respect for authority was to be the foundation of Christian communities. The idea of being in submission one to another could easily
lead to chaos and anarchy if all hierarchical leadership were to be
abandoned in some kind of radical mutual submission. Sure, husbands
and wives were to be mutually submitted, and yet the so-called bottom
line was and still is that the husband has the greater authority in marriage. So, in marriage mutual submission works as long as both parties
are mutually submitted to Christ and His representatives. The husband
is not to lord it over the wife, but to serve her in the light of Christ.

Mutual submission in a larger society is more difficult. Thus, it is
likely that Peter's comment to "be subject one to another" (v. 5, *Authorized Version*) suggested that each person should be obedient to the corporate will of the body, as long as that corporate will genuinely reflected
the will of God in Christ. Clearly, Christians are to agree about morality
and values, laws and behaviors, because we are to have unity in the
mind of Christ (1 Peter 3:8). Clearly, there must be some social mechan-

ism for such determination regarding disputed values. Even if the bulk of the body was to defer to the leadership of the elders, the elders themselves would need some way to come to agreement or consensus.

Humility

A foundational element of that mechanism was to wear humility toward one another like a cloak. In the same way that clothing hides most of our body from view, wearing humility would mean practicing it in such a way that it would dominate in our interactions with others. Humility should always be the first and most comprehensive thing that others should notice about us.

God's opposition to the prideful and his favor toward the humble is well-established in Scripture. The original reference is probably Proverbs 3:43: "Toward the scorners he is scornful, but to the humble he gives favor." However, James 4:6 employs the same quotation.

Does God's grace *come to* those who are humble? Or does God's grace *make* people humble? I think that both are true, but that God first makes people humble by dispensing His grace upon them. In grace God's people then grow in humility by relying upon God's grace. So, God takes the initiative in humbling people by saving them. Saved people then continue to rely upon God's grace and grow in it.

Verse 6 reverses this order by demanding that people humble themselves (*tapeinoō*), though a literal translation would be more like the command: *Be humble!* Again, Peter was writing to saints on the run, so he wasn't writing evangelistically. He wasn't calling the nations to convert to Christ. He was calling Christians to act like Christians. He was bolstering the faith of hatchling Christians and their new communities.

Peter provided several contrasts in this verse to drive his point home. The most obvious contrast was to humble themselves so that God could exalt them later. Another contrast was that it was better to humble one's self than to be humbled by God. This may sound as if it contradicts what I said previously about whether grace comes to the humble or makes people humble. But it doesn't. People are to be meek to the humbling influences of God's grace, which means that people should be sensitive to it.

People should respond when God brings a little humbling pressure upon them so that God doesn't have to bring greater pressure upon them. It is far better to humbly respond to God than to defy Him, which is the contrast here. Peter was suggesting that they should respond to the hand of God in the destruction of Jerusalem, lest God think that He needs to bring additional difficulties upon them in order to humble them.

What sort of exultation did Peter have in mind for those who humbled themselves before God? The Greek word translated as *exalt* (*hupsoō*) means to raise to the very summit of opulence and prosperity. Peter, speaking for God here, promised that through humble obedience to Jesus Christ great prosperity would come to the people of God, not simply to individual Christians but to God's people as a whole. Christian values and practices produce prosperity, financial prosperity in that markets thrive in social situations of honesty, integrity and consistency, which are the result of Christian faithfulness. And thriving markets provide for the leisure and cultural pursuits that contribute toward the development of science and technology, which in turn drive social prosperity.

REAR VIEW

Yes, I am reading the history of Western Civilization back into the Bible here. Because the history of Western Civilization provides the proof of Peter's words. By saying that such blessings would come in "due time" (v. 6, *kairos*) Peter acknowledged that such exaltation would take a long time to develop. In the same way that Christ was born in due time, *kairos* time. In a similar way, God would exalt His humble people in due time with the opulence and prosperity of science and technology through the engine of capitalism. And this has already occurred, though I suspect that it is still in its infancy historically.

Answering how all of this can happen, Peter said, "casting all your anxieties on him, because he cares for you" (v. 7). He was reminding them of Psalm 55:22: "Cast your burden on the Lord, and he will sustain you; he will never permit the righteous to be moved." The idea is to abandon our temptation to worry about the future and our own well-being by simply trusting that God will provide for our needs. And why would this simple abandonment of worry lead to the development of capitalism, science and technology?

In itself, it wouldn't. But when coupled with faith in Jesus Christ, the Christian values and practices of socially shared honesty, integrity and consistency contribute to the foundations of social and economic development, which in turn then bring what can only be described as opulence and prosperity. That's where Western civilization with its Christian foundation has already brought us.

What does it mean to cast our cares or burdens on the Lord? It is similar to Jesus sermon on the mount in Matthew 6:25-30. There Jesus advised His people to not be anxious about anything but to consider the birds of the air and lilies of the field. They provide an example because they do not worry, yet God cares for them by providing for all their needs. The central concern in this admonition is God's provision or God's providence, as it was known in former generations. Clearly the topic under consideration is what we call the economy, the system of production, distribution and consumption, and/or the efficient use of resources.

The idea is that we don't need to worry because God will provide what we need—food and clothing. How are these things actually provided? There are more productive ways to use our time than to wile the day away in worry. Jesus was not suggesting that God would miraculously beam food and clothing to us from heaven. The Bible is not a book of superstitious or fantastic ideas that defy common sense. Not at all!

Rather, the Bible is the most common and ordinary of books in that part of its historic purpose has been to put an end to the ideas and beliefs of magic and ancient spiritual superstition. The Bible does not deny the miraculous or mysterious. Rather, it establishes what ancient societies attributed to magic and superstition to the powers of human organization and cooperation guided by the righteousness of Jesus Christ.

It is not simply a matter of human organization and cooperation in themselves, but the fact that they are guided by Christ's righteousness that makes them both good and productive regarding human beneficence. Christ's righteousness is central to beneficial human organization and cooperation because that righteousness provides for truth, wisdom, honor and integrity as constituent elements of human character where that character has been regenerated in the likeness of Christ.

Why are these things not available apart from Christ? Because of the reality and extent of human sin, and because of the clarity and articulation of righteous moral character provided by the Bible when understood in the light of Christ through regeneration.

There is no greater teacher of moral righteousness than reading the Bible in the light of Christ through the presence and power of God's Holy Spirit through regeneration. And moral righteousness provides the only sufficient foundation for the development and maintenance of science and technology. But this is not to say anything particularly odd or unusual about science and technology, other than specifically associating them with Jesus Christ. The connection between righteousness and Jesus Christ has not been seriously considered for several generations. So, it is about time to reconsider what we have been doing.

Rudiment

The long arc of the biblical story is about the determination of good and evil or right and wrong. This story arc begins in the Garden of Eden with the tree of the knowledge of good and evil (Genesis 2:9), and is only resolved with the advent and administration of Jesus Christ (Hebrews 5:14). The central lesson is that right and wrong cannot be determined by humanity apart from the trinitarian presence of Jesus Christ. Human morality provides the foundational character of those who develop and work with science and technology in that morality is not merely about good and evil, but about correct and incorrect discernment of truth, which is the source of intelligence and good scholarship.

By casting our cares or burdens on the Lord, our hearts and minds are then free from the habits and compulsions of selfishness or self-centeredness because our general well-being is not at risk. The lessening of old habits and compulsions then frees the mind for greater consideration of more objective concerns, like science and technology.

But why am I so concerned about relating science and technology with Jesus Christ? Because the arc of human history has demonstrated that modern science, technology and capitalism grew out of the soil of Western Christendom, and that the providence of the modern world intimately involves these three things.[72] In every sense imaginable God has given humanity science, technology and capitalism as instruments of His providence and care. As we cast our cares and burdens—worries —upon God, He frees us from superstitious habits and compulsions by schooling us in Christ's righteousness, thereby growing us into Christ's likeness and demonstrating the value of moral character with regard to the development of moral intelligence—discernment, which is the ground for the development of science and technology.

Conversely, moral corruption undermines science and technology because corruption destroys our ability to function objectively or righteously, honestly and with integrity and consistency. And that loss of character in turn affects the integrity of data collection, evaluation and maintenance regarding science and technology. This also contributes to the fact that, for instance, dishonest and/or inconsistent people cannot collect reliable scientific data. Good science requires the ability to do honest observation and analysis, and not skew the results for the highest bidder or because of some ax to grind or some other reason. Good science requires moral integrity, both personally and socially.

---

72 This assertion is based on 1) the preeminence of God's trinitarian character and the veracity of the biblical account of Creation, 2) the trinitarian character of reality discussed in several of my books and 3) the necessity for honesty, integrity and wisdom in the development and practice of science and technology. Christian faith is both a requirement for and a product of this perspective. And as such it is self-authenticating through study in the light of Christ. Much of my writing works to establish this understanding of the Bible and history.

31. The Plan

Be sober-minded; be watchful. Your adversary the devil
prowls around like a roaring lion, seeking someone to devour.
Resist him, firm in your faith, knowing that the same kinds of
suffering are being experienced by your brotherhood through-
out the world. And after you have suffered a little while, the
God of all grace, who has called you to his eternal glory in
Christ, will himself restore, confirm, strengthen, and establish
you. To him be the dominion forever and ever. Amen.
—*1 Peter 5:8-11 (ESV)*

To suggest being sober-minded sounds like Baptist teetotaling prudery. The Greek word (*nēphō*) suggests being circumspect, cautious, prudent and watchful by examining carefully all the circumstances that may affect a decision or determination. It suggests that some consistent measure be adopted as a guide, and then paying close attention to it. Christ Himself is that measure.

The idea of sobriety applies because the opposite of sobriety is drunkenness or the impairment of one's judgment. Excessive alcohol causes a narrowing of the focus of one's attention in the sense that things are blurred and discernment becomes difficult. The blurring refers to logic and the ability to think complex thoughts. Inebriation interferes with the ability to think clearly, contrary to the idea the world promotes that suggests that drinking helps whenever a serious thought is under contemplation. It doesn't.

It is commonly understood that alcohol and drugs break down moral barriers. People behave more immorally under the influence of alcohol and drugs than they normally would. So, Peter's admonition to be sober means to hold fast to one's morality. Other versions translate it as *sensible*. It is a call to maintain common sense, where common sense is a function of social morality. It is indeed a call to prudence and circumspection. Webster says that "prudence differs from wisdom in this, that prudence implies more caution and reserve than wisdom, or is exercised more in foreseeing and avoiding evil, than in devising and executing that which is good."[73]

Webster's definition helps us to see that Scripture calls people to both the doing of good and the avoidance of evil. Both are necessary, and they are very different things. The avoidance of evil requires great personal awareness and attention to detail. In particular, the detail to be attended to is the chain of cause and effect, such that a leads to b and b leads to c, so c is to be avoided. Therefore, a and b are also to be avoided lest c follow in the train. Indeed, this is the kind of watchfulness or vigilance that Peter intended.

In a word, the avoidance of evil involves the increase of awareness, and in particular, moral awareness. Because morality issues from the comparison and evaluation of human behavior according to some standard, it involves both an elevated sensitivity to the implications of various behaviors and an increasing familiarity with the standard upon which good judgment depends. Thus, genuine morality is always a function of both heightened sensitivity and keen intelligence. Moral behavior requires both intelligence and discretion. It is a function of refinement, taste and tact because genuine morality issues out of personal discipline, care (love) and consistency. Here we can see the connection between Christian morality and the arts of science and technology discussed previously.

SEX

Too many people think that Christian morality is simply a prudish attitude about sex. And it does include that, but is actually much more than that. Unfortunately, modern people have been so desensitized by the godlessness of worldly culture that they are unable to think through the complex set of relationships about sex that are beyond the self-interest of basic sexual expression.

In fact, the worldly culture that dominates today has so reversed the ideas of good and evil (Isaiah 5:20) that society now believes and teaches that free sexual expression is the very apex of human relationships, that love is either equated with sex or that the two things have nothing in common. At least, that's the modern and postmodern Romantic version of things.

For instance, the pornographic version of sex decouples it from love and understands it to be a simple bodily function like eating. The deceit of worldly sin holds these opposite ideas together in conflict and in ignorance of the actual moral connection between love and sex. On

---

73 *Webster's 1828 Dictionary*, "prudence," public domain.

the one hand the worldly view of love and sex is all about romance and emotional sensuality, but on the other hand it decouples love from sex by rejecting any necessary connection between them. Both positions are worldly and sinful. Believing this perversion requires the denial of logic that blinds worldly people and keeps them from seeing the logical disconnect between these two contradicting ideas about love and sex. It condemns them to the consequences of their blindness.

In contrast, it is God alone who opens the moral eyes of the soul so that they can see the delicate textures of reality that tie together the nearly infinite complexities of human behavior and ground humanity both individually and corporately in the interrelated aspects of being fully human in the context of the world in which we actually live. Sex and marriage play central rolls in that world, and are tied together by God and history.

Therefore, those who deny God find themselves denied by God of the full range of sensitivity and intelligence that bring untold and uncommon joy in the fullness of life in the light of Christ. That fullness, that joy, comes only in the wake of Christ through regeneration with confession and repentance that alone restore the holiness, the wholesomeness and the wholeness of human life in Christ.

Why should God's people be sober and vigilant? Why not imbibe in the turpitude of moral laxity? Why struggle to maintain Christian morality, clarity, precision and logical fidelity in all of one's dealings? Because, said Peter, "your adversary the devil" (v. 8) lurks in the darkness and fuzziness of faithlessness. The devil (*diabolos*) is prowling in the darkness and intends to devour whoever he can. He is like a lion in the sense that no one can defend himself against a lion.

DELIVERY

However, King David defeated a lion when he was a young boy (1 Samuel 17:34-35). Clearly, Peter has this story about David in mind when he calls Satan a lion because the manner of David's defeat of the lion is the recommended implication of this verse. Satan prowls like a lion looking for people to devour. So, people must defend themselves against this threat. So exactly how, then, did David defeat the lion? "The Lord ... delivered me from the paw of the lion" (1 Samuel 17:37), David reported.

David's delivery was not magical nor mysterious, but was quite practical. David used his sling to defeat the lion. So, how is it that David attributed this defeat to the Lord? Actually, God's involvement in the defeat was active at every level. God created the circumstances for David's role as a shepherd, which brought him into the situation that required him to defend his flock. God had also given David an interest in the sling, the opportunity to practice, and the skill to excel at it. Then God gave him the courage to face the lion, the wisdom to depend upon his skill and the ammunition for his sling. But the over-arching point was that David didn't defeat the lion on his own, but with the guidance and protection of God.

Thus, in the same way that God protected David from the lion by orchestrating the lion's death at David's hand, so God will provide for His people by giving them the desire, the training, the trust and the cir-cumstances to prevail over Satan. These things are to be engaged by God's people in this specific order. They must desire God, engage in the discipline and discipleship that God provides in Christ, trust the Lord to see them through it and then be attentive to their own circumstan-ces.

ADVERSARY

So, exactly who is this adversary? He is the personification of evil. Being an adversary (*antidikos*), he opposes the beliefs of believers and everything that supports God's truth. And what determines the adver-sary's character is not merely his opposition, but the character of that which he opposes. He opposes God. He stands against everything that God stands for. He is the principle, not merely of opposition, but of the opposition of everything godly and good, everything true and trust-worthy.

His logic is the logic of opposition that exists in philosophical dual-ism. There is a consistency to dualistic logic, but not an adequacy or sufficiency. It fails to consider the fullness of both the ultimacy and the particularity, the unity and the diversity, of reality. Satan operates from a dualistic worldview and tends to see the world in dualistic terms, in black and white opposites.

The devil is dark and black because he opposes God's light. The radical divisive worldview of the devil, or dualism, falls short of the subtleties and delicate textures of God's trinitarian reality. His view is insufficient to the complexities of reality, and that is why it is evil. It falls short of God's mark. Satan is not merely an accuser, but a false accuser. He accuses falsely because he understands falsely.

Remember that God also accuses sinners of sin, but His accusa-tions are not false. God's accusations are full and complete because they do not issue from dualism, but from the trinitarianism of His own character and reality. God's accusation includes the full-orbed trinit-arian cure provided in Jesus Christ, His Son through His Holy Spirit. Thus, God's accusations are intended for our good, where Satan's false accusations are intended for our destruction. Satan stops short of God's trinitarian cure by calling guilty sinners to death through death.

But God's cure calls guilty sinners through death to new life in Christ through regeneration.

THE WAY

Peter then provides the way for this to happen. "Resist him, firm in your faith" (v. 9). We are to resist Satan's accusations with firm resolve and stand our ground in Christ. Note that we do not fight Satan with Satan's weapons. We do not respond to Satan's accusations with our own counter accusations against Satan or with self-defense. We are not to give him what he gives us. Rather, we are to resist the temptation to buy into the dualism of the devil by not responding to it. We must deny the premise of dualism. False accusations do not warrant a response. They deserve no defense nor any response because they are themselves nothing. To respond to nothing is to create an unnecessary offense. We must not rise to the bait of false accusations.

Rather, we are to keep our eye on the Prize, on the caduceus of Christ who alone is our protection and our stay. We are to hold fast to the trinitarian reality of Christ Jesus by engaging in the biblical disciplines of Christian discipleship. We are to resist the devil and his various temptations, and resist responding to his false accusations.

This is very much related to Jesus' teaching about turning the other cheek (Matthew 5:39) and loving our enemies (Luke 6:27). When vitriol is added to vitriol the only outcome possible is vitriolic. When false accusations are met with counter accusations the original accuser is encouraged to amplify his accusations, usually by turning up the volume. When force meets force the results are explosive.

But when an empty, offensive threat is ignored, it dissipates. It has no substance or reality beyond invoking a fearful response. So, when that response of fear is withheld, the accusation is seen for what it is—an empty threat.

Peter said that we should do this "knowing that the same kinds of suffering are being experienced by your brotherhood throughout the world" (v. 9). Here he ties this resistance of the devil to his larger subject—Christian suffering. This idea of suffering for the sake of promoting Christ's righteousness is not simply the idea of feeling pain or discomfort. Rather, the emphasis is not on the pain or discomfort at all, but on the endurance, on the strength that Christ gives for such endurance. The image to have in mind is not a wounded and defeated soldier lying helplessly on a battlefield writhing in pain. Rather, the image is that of a wounded soldier on a battlefield who fights on triumphantly in spite of his wounds, and without regard to the pain.

In addition, Peter explains that those who suffer for Christ are not alone because Christians all over the world are experiencing the same kinds of suffering and the need for endurance. Again, this is not a call to wallow in corporate pity for the people of Christ. But rather it is a call to encouragement because Christ's cause is being advanced in every corner of the globe. *Though you may feel alone and defeated in your pain and suffering, you are neither*, said Peter.

COMMON-UNITY

The *Authorized Version* translates this phrase: "knowing that the same afflictions are accomplished in your brethren that are in the world" (v. 9). The use of the word *accomplished* reveals the essential character of the Greek word (*epiteleō*), but falls short of Peter's intention. In what sense is suffering an accomplishment? None. It is not the suffering that gets accomplished, but the endurance. Suffering just happens, but endurance is a discipline. And to do it well requires practice and mastery. Endurance must be mastered and such mastery is an accomplishment of personal discipline.

This is, of course, not to suggest that all Christian discipline results in personal pain and suffering. It doesn't. Quite the opposite, the major element of Christian experience is joy, not suffering. But it doesn't take much suffering to overwhelm the joy. That's just the way that people are wired. We are weak reeds. And perhaps this is why Peter was trying to convert Christian suffering into a badge of honor and glory for Christ. In the long run the suffering will end, but the joy will continue eternally. So, the eternal and dependable nature of the joy is to be our focus.

Nonetheless, suffering will take a toll. So, Peter addressed the cost of discipleship. Sure, it will be difficult and demanding, but "after you have suffered a little while, the God of all grace, who has called you to his eternal glory in Christ, will himself restore, confirm, strengthen, and establish you" (v. 10). Peter calls us to the hope that pulls the past into the present, the hope that shapes the present in the likeness of God's decree regarding the end purpose of the world. After the pain, after the endurance, when it's all over at the end of the world God will restore, confirm, strengthen and establish.

Notice that Peter did not say that the world would end in pain, suffering and destruction, but in restoration, confirmation, strength and the establishment of God's kingdom. Pain and suffering would be part of the process, of course, but not the purpose. The end of the world is not destruction. The end of the world is the purpose for which the world was created—God's glory and the establishment of His kingdom.

This is the central message of Peter's letters. He was countering the popular ideas of the Zealots and Gnostics in his own day, counterfeit prophets predicting the end of the world as they knew it. And though these prophets were counterfeit because they opposed God and the cause and purpose of His Son, they did suspect the end of the known world. That world ended with the destruction of Jerusalem and the Temple and the end of the ancient Jewish Temple administration in A.D. 70. At least that was the beginning of the end. As it has turned out, the end of that world, as the beginning of the New World in Chirst, has turned out to be a longer process than people first thought.

Our Time

We currently live in between these two great dispensations or eras: the Old Testament era and the fulfillment of the kingdom of God on earth—the promised kingdom of God. The end of the old world was at the same time the beginning of the reign of Jesus Christ and the long march of the gospel to all the nations of the world. The end of the old world was a real end because it involved the transfer of covenant authority from Adam to Christ. While the spirit of Christ defeated the spirit of Adam by conquering the cross and even death itself, the destruction of Jerusalem and the Temple in A.D. 70 by the armies of Rome established that defeat in the history of the world.

Moreover, the fall of Jerusalem and the Temple in A.D. 70 generally coincided with the Acts 2 coming of the Holy Spirit, the birth of the Christian church and the subsequent scattering of the saints into the Gentile nations across the face of the globe. God didn't wait for the saints to decide to get all evangelistically enthused, raise the necessary funding and then go off into the world for Christ. He scattered them by destroying Jerusalem and the Temple. They went, running for their lives, and Peter and the apostles sent letters to them as they went to give them both encouragement and understanding about what was happening to them. With that encouragement and understanding, they were able to frame their situation in the light of Christ, and began telling others about their situation because it made so much sense to them. And we called them *evangelists*.

Dominion

Thus, God's actions were the actions of the sovereign God of history who was in the process of establishing dominion through His people. Peter, acknowledging this, proclaimed doxologically, "To him be the dominion forever and ever. Amen" (v. 11). The *Authorized Version*, using a different Greek manuscript, reads, "To him be glory and dominion for ever and ever. Amen."

The idea of Christian dominion is troublesome for a lot of people. The Greek word translated as *dominion* (*kratos*) means power and might—strength. Webster defines *dominion* as sovereign or supreme authority, the power of governing and controlling.

Dropping the word *glory* (*doxa*), or adding it, whichever view of the Greek manuscript issue you prefer, is significant. By affixing glory to dominion, the idea that dominion must be in the service of God's glory is secured. It is essential that we understand that God's interest in dominion is not the dominion of one group over all of the others, but is to be the dominion over all by God Himself through the expression of His glory through worship and fueled by discipleship. God's dominion is not that of a minority over a majority, nor a majority over a minority, but is the agreement of people with God that God is right in His assessments and judgments, and their willing compliance with God's Word, without concern for majorities or minorities. The concern is to be truth and faithfulness, not popularity.

Sinners who worship worldly political power mistakenly think that Christians want the same kind of social and political structures that they do, except with Christians in control. This is a huge error that cannot be corrected until those who commit it are able to see and understand the real Christian position. Indeed, seeing and understanding the Christian position is the solution. Christian dominion is not a matter of replacing those who are in control but dominated by sinful, worldly values and worldly political practices with so-called "Christians" who are dominated by sinful, worldly values and those same worldly practices. Rather, Christian dominion is a matter of replacing the sinful values and worldly political practices themselves—in everyone. Those worldly practices are dominated by the values and practices of malice, deceit, hypocrisy, envy, slander, etc.

God's plan is to change the values of both the governors and the governed from things like "sexual immorality, impurity, sensuality, idolatry, sorcery, enmity, strife, jealousy, fits of anger, rivalries, dissensions, divisions, envy, drunkenness, orgies" (Galatians 5:19-21) to things like "love, joy, peace, patience, kindness, goodness, faithfulness, gentleness, self-control" (Galatians 5:22-23). Doing so will utterly change the world and the way that it operates apart from God.

God's government is always representative government. We see this in the way that Christ represented His people on the cross as He received punishment for their sin. In this world, political leaders always actually do represent the people they govern. Corrupt leaders are the evidence of a corrupt people. The power of human politics ultimately flows from the people to the leaders, regardless of the kind of government.

So, the best and most effective way to change the quality of political leadership is to change the quality of the people governed. That is part of the goal of Christian dominion. It starts at the local level in the hearts and minds of ordinary people, and over time it spreads to neighboring local areas until all of the local people and their politicians reflect the values and mores of Jesus Christ—truth, goodness and beauty according to God's definitions.

SUBTERFUGE

Unfortunately, unrepentant people have taken advantage of Christian trustfulness and done various unchristian things and practiced unchristian values in the name of Christianity, while not themselves manifesting Christian character traits, and given genuine Christianity a bad reputation. And the unregenerate and unrepentant do not have the necessary discernment, care or discipline to see through the ruse. So they tend to think poorly of Christianity because of such people. They don't realize that the people who do such things are not actually Christians, regardless of what they say about themselves. Power hungry sinners have often seized the mantel of Christianity, whether by popes or princes, in order to accomplish dastardly deeds—and the undiscerning can only see it as the failure of Christianity, rather than it being unchristian at worst and unfaithful at best.

Thus, such undiscerning people continue to think that Christians want only what everyone else wants, and will do whatever it takes to get their own way. They tend to think that Christians intend to force their worldview on everyone else just as they tend to force theirs. So, for them Christian dominion means top-down, shove-it-down-your-throat domination by Christians rather than people's willing agreement with biblical truth in the light of Christ.

Christian dominion does not include forcing people to conform to Christian values, other than conformity to a civil law that generally conforms to the Ten Commandments, which is already in place almost everywhere in the world. Christians are law abiding people and will support reasonable laws and other social mores that encourage biblical virtue. The only sense in which Christians support any kind of political domination is that Christians are committed to the rule of law, where the same laws equally apply to all people.

Christian dominion will not be imposed from the top down, but will grow organically and willingly from the bottom up.

32. The End

By Silvanus, a faithful brother as I regard him, I have written briefly to you, exhorting and declaring that this is the true grace of God. Stand firm in it. She who is at Babylon, who is likewise chosen, sends you greetings, and so does Mark, my son. Greet one another with the kiss of love. Peace to all of you who are in Christ.   *—1 Peter 5:12-14 (ESV)*

It is not clear whether Sylvanus helped write this letter or simply delivered it. But it doesn't really matter because it is certain that both Peter and Sylvanus, being faithful to Jesus Christ, would agree to its content. It is also probable that in either case Sylvanus was available to Peter for conversation and consultation about it. It is difficult to imagine that two faithful brothers in Christ would not have discussed the contents of the letter and much more. Thus, Peter's mention of Sylvanus was not merely an authenticating detail of the reality of their relationship and theological proximity, but would also encourage the acceptance of the letter because it had the virtual signature of both men to attest to its truth.

Peter's mention that this letter is brief suggests that there is much more that can be said about his central topic—the progressive revelation of Jesus Christ as the Son of God in history. Note also that the fact that Christ's divinity establishes the reality of the Trinity. Thus, wherever Christ's divinity is received, the Trinity of God is established in or through the body of Christ. The brevity of Peter's letter stands as a prelude to that unfolding revelation in history.

It is also instructive to note Peter's tools for this revelation—*exhortation* (*parakaleō*) and *declaration* (*epimartureō*). *Parakaleō* literally means to call near and is translated as *comfort, beseech* and *pray.* Peter was both calling them together, calling them to live in close Christian unity, and calling them to spiritual unity in Christ. They were not simply to be close to one another, but they were to be close to Christ, as well. In fact, their unity with Christ was the more important aspect of their being together because it provides the foundation for their unity.

Unity

Christian unity cannot be attained or retained by the effort of Christians to be close to one another. Inasmuch as we attempt to achieve a unity that is based upon ourselves or our various traditions (Mark 7:8), doctrinal positions or administrative structures we will fail in our efforts. The problem with trying to establish Christian unity on the basis of our own histories (traditions), beliefs, doctrines and structures is that our own spiritual growth and sanctification continue to lead us out of this or that particular doctrinal position or way of understanding or organizing something to a better, more refined and more biblical understanding, a more faithful way in the light of Christ's progressive revelation.

Thus, our own practices, beliefs and doctrines are to be in continual improvement and development. For the most part Christians are not all at the same place in their growth, which means that there is little basis for any broad-based doctrinal or administrative Christian unity that is based on some historic position. The history of Christianity clearly evinces the futility of the effort to forge doctrinal agreement or administrative conformity as the central basis of Christian unity.

This observation, however, does not mean that doctrine or administration are unimportant. They are important, in fact, extremely important. Our very maturity and sanctification in faithfulness depend upon our continuing growth and development in right, orthodox doctrine and submission to the right faithful authorities. So, while our unity cannot be based upon our various traditional practices, doctrinal understandings and assessments or our administrative structures at any particular stage in our development, it is essential that our growth and development bring us all into closer agreement with true, biblical praxis, doctrine and administration.

This is, in part, undoubtedly why Peter called attention to the fact that history is not an outgrowth of the past as much as it is a coalescing into the future hope and glory of God's decree. Because the present is being pulled into the future rather than pushed by the past, Christians and their churches can shed the outgrown husks of historic shortsightedness while simultaneously and faithfully clinging to the core truths of the unchanging gospel as the progressive revelation of Christ in history gains additional clarity, depth and articulation.

And yet, for all intents and purposes, it is likely that the quintessential truth of ultimate biblical doctrine, practice and administration will continue to be both within our reach and beyond our grasp for the foreseeable future. Indeed, it is the hope of gospel truth, provided by God's decree from time immemorial, that serves as the beacon that draws us forward in history, deeper in sanctification and closer in unity. We must therefore steadfastly cling to our vision and pursuit of God's truth with honesty and integrity, passionately forging doctrinal clarity and administrative harmony on the anvil of Scripture with the hammer of history and the grace and mercy of God in Christ.

We must each and all grapple tooth and claw for the most rigorous and generous expressions of God's truth that the greatest faithfulness tempered with godly scholarship and colored with genuine humility can muster. At the same time we must not flippantly, rashly or prematurely brand others with the hot iron of heresy. Rather, we must encourage disagreement in the effort to arrive at harmony if not a consensus that is neither broader nor narrower than the wholeness of God's revealed truth. Why encourage disagreement? Because disagreement fuels diligence, patience, tolerance and mercy, and because serious disagreement will keep us from lazy self-contentment. Better theories and greater understanding come out of disagreements.

The context of this grappling is fervent discussion (*dialogizomai*) within the bonds and bounds of covenant faithfulness. We must be willing to discuss our views and values with passion, alacrity and clarity, holding our views with the firmness of commitment, the graciousness of forgiveness and the eager willingness to admit our own errors and shortcomings, trusting that the power and presence of the Holy Spirit through personal regeneration in Christ will lead and guide all of Christ's church into God's kingdom.

This is the essential character of Peter's exhortation. Christ will continue to be revealed in increasing depth and clarity as people wrestle with the deep biblical issues. So, rather than avoiding doctrinal discussions, we must engage such discussion willingly and gladly, and with enough humility to admit our own errors and shortcomings.

At the same time we must understand that doctrinal clarity is not a denominational or sectarian contest. All genuine believers are on the same team, though they have different skills, positions, resources and perspectives.

DECLARATION OF MUTUALITY

Note also that Peter didn't just exhort. He also declared or testified to the truth of God's Word and his own faithfulness. By using this word (*epimartureō*, v. 12) Peter indicated that God's truth is not found by argument or compromise. In fact, God's truth is not found at all. God gives it. God's truth is not something that we human beings produce, conclude or establish. We cannot go on an archeological journey and dig it up or recover it from antiquity. God's truth is not in the past, nor is it a product of the past.

It does not come to us from the past, but comes from the future. It resides in the future as the husband of hope. God's truth is a declaration, a proclamation, a resolve. God declares it and we receive it—or not. It is not the conclusion of a logical argument, nor the summation of constituent parts, but the very foundation of all logic and deliberation.

God's truth is not based on anything, nor does it issue out of anything. It simply is. But it is what it is dynamically and creatively. Truth is alive, which means that it assimilates and replicates, but does so without changing its central character (Hebrews 13:8). It stands as the declaration of the living God—"I am" (Exodus 3:14, John 8:28, 13:9).

So, Peter exhorted and declared, but what did he exhort and declare? What was the content of his message? He exhorted and declared "that this is the true grace of God" (v. 12). The *this* to which he referred was the central message of his entire letter—the progressive revelation of Jesus Christ through history. This was and remains the guiding truth of Christ's church(es) in the sense that Christ lives in and through His church by the power and presence of the regeneration of His people in His own likeness. God's people, both individually and collectively, continue to grow and mature to the fullness of the stature of the fullness of Christ (Ephesians 4:13). The church, the body of Christ, grows broader and deeper, ever bringing new glory to God.

ANALOGY OF ADOLESCENCE

Similarly, people reach adulthood, not as a consequence of adolescence, but in spite of it. Adolescence is not the foundation for adulthood, but is a lingering vestige of childhood. The hope for maturity in adulthood draws people out of their adolescence. Adolescence does not grow and mature into adulthood. Adolescent experience does not develop and accumulate into adulthood. A thousand adolescent experiences do not add up to or produce an adult experience. The two things are of completely different characters.

Rather, adulthood arises out of the rejection and abandonment of adolescence. Adolescent foolishness is not the foundation of adult wisdom. Adolescence is the conclusion of childhood, where childish thoughts and ideas are irrationally clung to in immature fears and intellectual insufficiencies. Adult wisdom is the repudiation of adolescent immaturity in the hope of greater wholeness and fullness in Christ. Adolescence does not push maturity forward. Adolescence holds maturity back. Maturity is something altogether different than adolescence, just as wisdom is not constructed from foolishness. Adolescence should be short, not long because it delays the onset of genuine growth and maturity.

STANDING

The *English Standard Version* turns the last phrase of verse 12 into a new sentence: "Stand firm in it." The *Authorized Version* makes it part of the existing sentence: "this is the true grace of God wherein ye stand." There is little difference between the call to stand firm and the call to remain standing firm. But because the latter testifies to the existing reality of the Spirit in the lives of the faithful, it provides more than a hopeful admonition. It provides the additional impetus of the existing reality of Immanuel, God with us. It adds power to the gravity of God by acknowledging His nearness, His involvement, His direction. And the nearer to the gravitational center, the greater the centripetal force. So the *Authorized Version* provides a better, more effective reading.

The Greek word *histēmi* simply means *stand*. And the many definitions of stand are instructive. Here it means to be upright, not simply to be on one's feet, but to stand for something righteous. A stand is also a support or foundation like the base of a lamp—a lamp stand. It can also mean to be in some specified state or condition. For instance, someone could say, "I stand corrected." It can indicate a position where something is, or the idea of occupying a place or location, whether actual or metaphorical. For instance, people can stand on common ground. It can indicate a growth of similar plants (usually trees) in a particular area, like a stand of trees. It can be the action of holding one's ground or maintaining a position. Or it can suggest a point of view or a perspective from which things are viewed or understood. It can also mean that something remains in force. I think that Peter intended all of these various meanings.

IN COMMON

At verse 13 Peter said, "She who is at Babylon, who is likewise chosen, sends you greetings." Three things need to be clarified here: 1) Who was Peter referring to? 2) What is the significance of Babylon? And 3) the fact of the election of the church.

The word *church* is not in the Greek but is an implied reference to the church at Babylon. By referring to the church Peter implied that his letter was authorized or supported by the church at Babylon, or that the church agreed with what Peter had written. It gave the letter additional authority because it came not merely from Peter, nor merely with Sylvanus' blessing, but with the authority of the church at

Babylon. Because of the close fellowship that these early Christians enjoyed, we can imagine that Peter discussed the contents of the letter with others in the church. Indeed, he probably preached and taught in Babylon what he was teaching and preaching in this letter to the beleaguered saints in exile.

Peter mentioned the church at Babylon because he was there at the time he wrote the letter. Peter was known as the apostle to the circumcision or Jews, and Babylon would have been a capital city of Jewish exiles. There is no good reason to think that Babylon was a code word for Rome here. It is a much better hermeneutic to avoid the appeal to code words whenever possible. We should accept the plain meaning of words unless there is a compelling reason not to.

Lastly then, Peter referred to their common election. The fact that Peter began this letter by addressing the "elect exiles of the dispersion" (1 Peter 1:1) and ending with a salutation to those who were "likewise chosen" (v. 13) is of interest. Clarifying the process, Peter wrote in 1 Peter 1:2, that he was writing to the "elect according to the foreknowledge of God the Father, through sanctification of the Spirit, unto obedience and sprinkling of the blood of Jesus Christ." Note that the process of election involved the Father, the Son (Jesus Christ) and the Holy Spirit. It was and is a trinitarian election. This is important because it provides for the fact that God's election involves a process that unfolds over time and takes place in history.

God, standing outside of time, foreknew it. The Spirit, standing in the hearts and minds of believers, was growing them through the process of sanctification. And the Son, Jesus Christ, had manifested God's election in history by shedding His blood on the cross. But more than this, these elect exiles were themselves like droplets of Christ's blood that were being sprinkled upon the nations as they fled the destruction of Jerusalem. Peter, writing from Babylon, was aligning himself and the church at Babylon with them, with these Christians in exile. They had all been cut from the same cloth, so to speak. He was identifying with them and their scattered plight in Christ.

He was letting them know that, even if they had not themselves consciously chosen to be part of the Christian church before the destruction of Jerusalem, God had chosen them by the fact of their exile. And that the various churches that had been scattered by God's Roman hammer stood ready and willing to consider them and their needs to now be the common concern of Christ's people everywhere. Even in this salutation Peter was pressing the evangelism envelope. He didn't want them to think that because God was opening up the gospel to the Gentiles that God was turning His back on the Jews. He was not!

Sure, Christ ended the Jewish Temple administration, but that did not mean that Jewish people would themselves be excluded from God's grace. Heaven forbid such a thought! The whole purpose of the Jewish election and administration in the first place was that the Jews themselves would be a blessing to the nations (Genesis 12:2). The fact that the Pharisaic Jews had made a mess of God's purpose did not divert or curtail that purpose. In fact, it served God's purpose by demonstrating historically that people cannot accomplish God's will apart from the power and presence of the Holy Spirit through regeneration. That is the central message of the failure of Judaism and the destruction of the Temple. And that was the central message that Peter was communicating to the new Jewish exiles produced by God's Roman hammer.

Tribute

Peter said that his church at Babylon did not merely send greetings but *saluted* (*aspazomai*) them. The greeting or salute was a symbol of camaraderie, of brotherhood and fellowship. Peter wasn't simply exerting authority and control over the other churches by dictating theology and policy to them, but was more sharing with them what he had been teaching at Babylon.

Peter included a greeting from Mark, probably the writer of the gospel, but Mark's identity is not certain. Scholars think that Peter was the spiritual father to Mark, as Paul was to Timothy. Regardless, the letter was strengthened by adding Mark's name to it. It was as if Peter suggested that Mark would also be in enthusiastic agreement with the letter.

Concluding this letter, Peter recommended that the saints "greet one another with the kiss of love" (v. 14). The kiss of love or peace has become a common cultural expression of fidelity and shared brotherhood in the Middle East. It still is today. Because we in the Modern West do not practice this custom I am tempted to dismiss it as being a mere cultural practice. But it is also important not to simply dismiss various biblical details as being unimportant because they appear to be culturally specific to a particular time and place.

In the same way that we should not dismiss Paul's injunctions about head coverings, we must not discount such things without a compelling reason. As Paul's concern about head coverings dealt with important symbolic issues regarding gospel authority,[74] it is possible that the practice of the holy kiss may also include some important symbolism. Clearly, the holy kiss symbolizes Christian unity, and the fact that Western Christians have both abandoned the practice and experi-

---

74 See: Phillip A. Ross, *Arsy Varsy—Reclaiming the Gospel in First Corinthians*, Pilgrim Platform, 2009, pgs. 190-197.

enced fractured unity is noteworthy. Yet, in no way does this suggest that unity can be achieved or restored by simply practicing the holy kiss, nor that the abandonment of the holy kiss caused or contributed to the loss of unity. Nonetheless, it is interesting that the two things coincide.

There is no good reason not to continue the practice of the holy greeting, and indeed, it might help to call attention to our casual treatment of Scripture and the need to exercise various cultural practices that can contribute toward an environment more hospitable to Christian unity. And curiously, the holy kiss establishes a kind of biblical formality to social relationships that is likely to be healthy in that it may mitigate against the sorts of informalities that that tend to undermine social and personal morality. Immorality often (usually) begins when and where traditional (biblical) social formalities are discarded and various informalities are engaged as various kinds of flirtations that work to undermine various social norms.

It is also noteworthy that the kiss of love is actually a kiss of *agapē*, where agape is defined in our contemporary world as the selfless love of one person for another without sexual implications, and especially love that is spiritual in nature. How such a kiss is choreographed is less important than its simple practice, though again there is no compelling reason to alter the traditional choreography.

PEACE

Just as the holy kiss is an expression of agape love, Peter also spoke a blessing of peace: "Peace to all of you who are in Christ" (v. 14). And just as the holy kiss is an expression of common affection and brotherly care, Peter's blessing targeted those in common fellowship, those who are in Christ. The idea of being in Christ points to regeneration, which provides the only significant division of humanity. The whole of Scripture deals with the change of covenantal administration from Adam to Christ brought about by regeneration. The Old Testament set up the coming of Christ to a lost world. And the New Testament paved the way for the birth of a new humanity in Christ, regenerated in Christ.

The process of that regeneration began in earnest in Acts 2 with the dispensation of the Holy Spirit to the Gentiles, and will continue until the fulfillment of the kingdom of God with the return of Christ in the flesh. We currently live between these two historical markers, during a time of gospel advancement. To date, not all humanity has been born again in Christ, but the number of Christians continues to grow. The kingdom is advancing.

Yet, the wheat and tares also to grow together. The great harvest is yet to come. As such, there is still a division in humanity between the followers of Adam and the followers of Christ, between those who are in Christ and those who are not, between the regenerate and the degenerate. Peter's blessing calls attention to this division with the words "in Christ" (v. 14). Both the blessing of peace and the holy kiss are for those who are in Christ. There is great value in establishing and maintaining the cultural expressions of Christian unity.

However, we would be remiss not to also take notice that Peter blessed "all of you who are in Christ" (v. 14), not *some* who are in Christ, but *all*. Thus, while Peter's blessing facilitates the division between covenant keepers and covenant breakers, it also facilitates the unity of the church(es) by insisting that both the holy kiss and the blessing are for all Christians because there is unity among all Christians, all those who are in Christ. There is nothing in Scripture that calls Christians to separate from one another—separate from unbelievers, yes of course. But we are not to separate from fellow Christians.

The focus on Christian denominations has made a wreck of Christian unity with an unbiblical emphasis upon doctrine apart from brotherhood, scholarship apart from faithfulness, and sectarianism in the face of commonality.[75] Without a doubt, every denomination has been undermined from within its own ranks and by its own denominational emphases because of the faithless disregard for the seriousness and the application of Peter's admonition to strengthen Christian unity by both maintaining the central division between believers and unbelievers, and by intentionally engaging the cultural practices of symbolic unity among all believers.

Given the state of things today—monetary crises, moral collapse, cultural clash with Socialism, Islam, etc.—it is well past time to seriously begin to rethink and reform the meaning and practice of Christian unity. However, given the state of the churches—rabid factionalism, theological ignorance, spiritual apathy, and covenantal disregard —it is very unlikely that the denominations will be able to hold any kind of reforming synod in order to address these concerns. Therefore, if there is to be any progress made in these areas, it will come from local churches and individual Christians.

And because Christian unity is not a matter of funding or forwarding some kind of global super denomination, the emphasis on local and diverse expressions of Christian unity that cut through the false divisions that separate us, while strengthening the protective walls that nurture us, could not be more timely or appropriate. Much of the prob-

---

75   This is the central thesis of *The True Mystery of The Mysterious Presence*, see footnote 31, page 97.

lem with the ecumenical efforts of the past toward Christian unity comes from the failure to understand the Christian Trinity and its implications regarding Christian character and church unity.

The Father, Son and Holy Spirit are in corporate unity without sacrificing the uniqueness of the individual identities, their hierarchical structure of authority or their essential equality in union in the Godhead. And because church unity is a reflection of the spiritual unity of the Trinity (not identical to it, but a reflection of it), trinitarian church unity will reflect both the characteristics of the unity and diversity of the Trinity.

TRINITARIAN UNITY

Consequently, Peter's injunction to seek peace, given to all who are in Christ, is an appeal to trinitarian unity as the only way to manifest genuine peace in this sinful world. That peace comes through the prior peace with God that issues only from the forgiveness of sin by those who are actually in Christ. And the most effective progenitor of world peace is then the incorporation in Christ of all of His people, not as a kind of super-denominational, top-down corporate structure or the imposition of some super-doctrine, but as a kind of non-denominational, bottom-up individual Christian and local church initiative that forgoes the failed national and international denominational structures, and institutes the mindset or worldview of trinitarian unity among believers that is taught in Scripture.

Church unity is not a function of denominational agreements, but of Christian neighborliness and the neighborliness of local congregations one to another. Forget the press releases and denominational announcements of Christian unity that issue out of worldly structures and media outlets. Forget the international confabs that are working in old wineskins. The media outlets will be the last to know and acknowledge the reality that Christ's love makes on sinners and the instruments of sin. Christian unity is not an individual or social achievement that is forged and maintained by the best or that is driven by a survival-of-the-fittest mindset.

Rather, Christian unity is a gift that has already been given, first to repentant sinners, and then through repentant sinners, one to another in Christ. Don't look for it in the headline news, but rather preveniently give it to your neighbor across the street who attends a different church or no church because s/he has given up on failed models of Christian faithfulness. Receive it, acknowledge the unity of the Godhead through the love of Jesus Christ. Then, give it, extend the grace and forgiveness to others that Christ has given to you.

Don't expect your church or denominational leaders to do it for you. But do it for yourself, for your family, for your local church and most of all for Jesus Christ. Give it as a personal or church-wide act of sanctification (1 Peter 1:20-25). Give it as an act of evangelism (John 13:35, 2 Corinthians 8:8). Don't wait for someone else to lead the way, take the lead yourself and step out in faith today for Christ's sake!

Scripture Index

OLD TESTAMENT

Genesis 1:12.................33
Genesis 1:11, 12, 21, 25..61
Genesis 1:26...............127
Genesis 1:26-27.........259
Genesis 1:27.........60, 259
Genesis 1:31.................60
Genesis 12:2........177, 294
Genesis 12:2-3............183
Genesis 2:17....61, 65, 121, 189
Genesis 2:18.................60
Genesis 2:19.................61
Genesis 2:24...............259
Genesis 2:7..................96
Genesis 2:9..189, 199, 277
Genesis 3:15...............127
Genesis 3:16-19...........176
Genesis 3:22...............127

Exodus 3:14................291
Exodus 20:3...............259
Exodus 29.....................21

Deuteronomy 1:17........25
Deuteronomy 10:17 25, 59
Deuteronomy 11:13-15 177
Deuteronomy 11:28....177
Deuteronomy 16:19 25, 59
Deuteronomy 28. 20, 220
Deuteronomy 28:1-14. 177
Deuteronomy 28:1-15. 133

Leviticus 11:14.............55
Leviticus 19:15.............63
Leviticus 19:2..............55
Leviticus 20:7..............55
Leviticus 8:30...............7

Job 34:19......................59

Psalm 7:17..................240
Psalm 34:12-16...........179
Psalm 34:14.................62
Psalm 37:27.................62
Psalm 55:22.................276
Psalm 63:11.................122
Psalm 89:6-7...............131
Psalm 111:10........63, 131
Psalm 118:22................97
Psalm 119:142..............44
Psalm 121:1.................195
Psalm 139:24...............44

Proverbs 3:43.............275
Proverbs 8:36.............247
Proverbs 23:23.............74
Proverbs 24:23.............25
Proverbs 24:23-24.......59
Proverbs 28:21.............25

1 Samuel 15.................191
1 Samuel 15:23............191
1 Samuel 17:34-35......281
1 Samuel 17:37............281

2 Samuel 23:5..............44

2 Chronicles 19:7....25, 59

Ecclesiastes 3:1.............79
Ecclesiastes 4:12.........128

Jeremiah 13:23...........145
Jeremiah 17:9.............267
Jeremiah 33:9............185

Lamentations 3:38.....198
Lamentations 4:16.......25

Isaiah 5:17....................44

Isaiah 5:20...........62, 280
Isaiah 5:20-23............219
Isaiah 6:3.....................58
Isaiah 28:5.................272
Isaiah 40:3-5...............19
Isaiah 40:6-8...............80
Isaiah 40:8...................44
Isaiah 45:7.................198
Isaiah 51:6...................44
Isaiah 51:8...................44
Isaiah 52:15...............122
Isaiah 53:6.................148
Isaiah 55:8-9.............199

Ezekiel 34:11-12..........150

Daniel 4:27-31...........176

Amos 3:6....................198
Amos 5:14-15.............62

NEW TESTAMENT

Matthew 3:1-3..............19
Matthew 5:14................77
Matthew 5:39.............283
Matthew 5:48.............164
Matthew 6:3................77
Matthew 6:10 33, 94, 198, 227
Matthew 6:25-30.......276
Matthew 6:33................8
Matthew 7:14...............45
Matthew 7:17-19..........62
Matthew 7:21-ff..........20
Matthew 9:17.............203
Matthew 11:15.............234
Matthew 12:31-32......244
Matthew 12:44-45......180
Matthew 12:48-50........76
Matthew 14:13-21.......231

Matthew 16:16...........266
Matthew 19:28............95
Matthew 20:16.............46
Matthew 21:21-22......166
Matthew 21:22...........167
Matthew 22:14............46
Matthew 24...................2
Matthew 24:3.............95
Matthew 25:14-30......141
Matthew 28:18. .160, 211,
                213, 219
Matthew 28:18-20.....121

Mark 2:21.................203
Mark 4:23.................234
Mark 4:9...................234
Mark 7:8...................289
Mark 7:16.................234
Mark 10:18................185

Luke 1:35....................15
Luke 2:10..................139
Luke 2:11....................62
Luke 6:27.................283
Luke 8:8...................234
Luke 9:14..................161
Luke 12:40..................43
Luke 14:35.................234
Luke 20:21...................59
Luke 22:42................166

John 1:1.....................220
John 1:9.....................110
John 3:3.......58, 185, 234
John 3:5.............185, 234
John 3:30.................256
John 3:35..................139
John 4:24..........224, 234
John 6:37...................139
John 6:39...................139
John 6:56....................75
John 6:66....................72
John 7:12...................227
John 8:28...................291
John 8:32...................239
John 8:44....................76
John 10:16.........148, 150
John 11:27...................62
John 12:32..................139
John 13:3....................139
John 13:9....................291
John 13:34....................77
John 13:35.................298
John 14:2-3.........64, 238
John 14:13..........177, 166
John 14:23.................177

John 15:5...................194
John 15:10..................177
John 16:13..................182
John 17:20-23.............56
John 17:21..................139
John 17:23...........75, 259
John 19:30.................193
John 20:31.................109
John 21.......................268
John 21:16-17....268, 266

Acts 2..................285, 295
Acts 5:29...................120
Acts 10:34...........25, 59
Acts 10:36...................62
Acts 17:26....................96
Acts 17:38..................260
Acts 20:28.................207
Acts 25:3........................4

Romans 1.......................49
Romans 1:17................92
Romans 1:26.............240
Romans 3:11..................11
Romans 3:23......141, 162
Romans 5:1-5...............98
Romans 6.......................208
Romans 6:5...................13
Romans 6:17-18.........140
Romans 7.....................88
Romans 7:3.................213
Romans 8:15-17...........15
Romans 8:2.................213
Romans 8:28.............255
Romans 8:29.............143
Romans 9...................100
Romans 9:33................98
Romans 12:19-21........175
Romans 13:4..............153
Romans 14:11..............43

1 Corinthians 1:26........71
1 Corinthians 2:16.....269
1 Corinthians 3:11-16....44
1 Corinthians 9:9.......265
1 Corinthians 9:21......213
1 Corinthians 10:2.....204
1 Corinthians 10:6.......34
1 Corinthians 11:1.....47
1 Corinthians 12 227, 230
1 Corinthians 12:12....108
1 Corinthians 13:11.....49
1 Corinthians 13:12....129
1 Corinthians 14:12....264
1 Corinthians 15:19....268
1 Corinthians 15:52......15

1 Corinthians 15:54.....68

2 Corinthians 2:9........42
2 Corinthians 3:5.......215
2 Corinthians 3:15-16..20
2 Corinthians 3:16.......64
2 Corinthians 5:4........68
2 Corinthians 5:17......86,
                        203
2 Corinthians 8:8........298
2 Corinthians 10:5.....227

Galatians 2:6..............59
Galatians 2:20............92
Galatians 3:11-12.......92
Galatians 3:21-26......203
Galatians 3:22...........204
Galatians 3:28....98, 102,
                        165
Galatians 5.................213
Galatians 5:1..............135
Galatians 5:19-21......286
Galatians 5:22-23.....159,
                        286
Galatians 6:2.............213
Galatians 6:7-8...........59

Ephesians 2:1...........204
Ephesians 3:9-11.........44
Ephesians 4:13...........291
Ephesians 4:13-14......261
Ephesians 5:21..........207
Ephesians 6:4............93
Ephesians 6:9........25, 59
Ephesians 6:11-20.....241

Philippians 1:1...........207
Philippians 4:4..........240

Colossians 3:11..........102
Colossians 3:25...........59
Colossians 3:25...........25

1 Thessalonians 4:17....43
1 Thessalonians 5:15-22
...................................144
1 Thessalonians 5:22. 180

2 Thessalonians 2:16...44

1 Timothy 2:15............177
1 Timothy 2:5.....128, 210
1 Timothy 3...............207
1 Timothy 3:13..........228
1 Timothy 3:6...............91

2 Timothy 3:5............182

Titus 1:1-3..................44
Titus 3:5......................44

Hebrews 2:2.............176
Hebrews 4:16..............91
Hebrews 5:14............278
Hebrews 8:13............203
Hebrews 9:12.......44, 253
Hebrews 10:10............85
Hebrews 10:19-22.........7
Hebrews 10:38............92
Hebrews 11:1..............32
Hebrews 11:3..............19
Hebrews 11:9..............92
Hebrews 11:11.............19
Hebrews 11:28..........7, 19
Hebrews 11:33.............19
Hebrews 11:39............19
Hebrews 12:2............272
Hebrews 12:6............240
Hebrews 12:24..........253
Hebrews 13:8............291
Hebrews 13:20.....44, 148

James 1:21-27.............93
James 2:9....................25
James 4:6..................275

1 Peter 1:1 24, 35, 45, 148,
      175, 262, 274, 293
1 Peter 1:1-2...................1
1 Peter 1:2..4. 5, 6, 7, 104,
      293
1 Peter 1:3...10, 14, 18, 78
1 Peter 1:4..............15, 28
1 Peter 1:5......28, 56, 108
1 Peter 1:5..............18, 19
1 Peter 1:6..................23
1 Peter 1:7 24, 56, 66, 108
1 Peter 1:9..................32
1 Peter 1:10............34, 43
1 Peter 1:12.................35
1 Peter 1:13 39, 41, 42, 45,
      55, 108
1 Peter 1:14................157
1 Peter 1:15..................49
1 Peter 1:16............55, 56
1 Peter 1:17 25, 55, 57, 63,
1 Peter 1:18-19............63
1 Peter 1:19............65, 66
1 Peter 1:20-21............66
1 Peter 1:20-25..........298

1 Peter 1:21.................67
1 Peter 1:22.................76
1 Peter 1:22-25...........158
1 Peter 1:23......78, 79, 81
1 Peter 1:25.................81
1 Peter 2:1...........83, 92
1 Peter 2:2.................87
1 Peter 2:2-3..............86
1 Peter 2:4..................89
1 Peter 2:5....90, 92, 97
1 Peter 2:6......96, 97, 98
1 Peter 2:7................100
1 Peter 2:8..........99, 100
1 Peter 2:9. 104, 106, 107,
      108, 109
1 Peter 2:10................111
1 Peter 2:11. .114, 116, 117,
      118
1 Peter 2:12................119
1 Peter 2:13...............120
1 Peter 2:13-14...........152
1 Peter 2:14...............120
1 Peter 2:15...............122
1 Peter 2:16........126, 132
1 Peter 2:17..130, 131, 132
1 Peter 2:18...............132
1 Peter 2:19...............133
1 Peter 2:20...............133
1 Peter 2:21........139, 143
1 Peter 2:23...............145
1 Peter 2:24.......146, 215
1 Peter 2:25...............148
1 Peter 3:1.........153, 154
1 Peter 3:1-2.............155
1 Peter 3:3-4..............156
1 Peter 3:4.................157
1 Peter 3:5.................162
1 Peter 3:7. .163, 164, 165,
      166
1 Peter 3:8. .174, 207, 274
1 Peter 3:9...........175, 177
1 Peter 3:11.........180, 181
1 Peter 3:12...............186
1 Peter 3:13...............188
1 Peter 3:14...............190
1 Peter 3:15........190, 192
1 Peter 3:15-16...........194
1 Peter 3:16........195, 196
1 Peter 3:17.......143, 200
1 Peter 3:18.......202, 203
1 Peter 3:19.......203, 204
1 Peter 3:20...............204
1 Peter 3:21.205, 210, 212
1 Peter 3:22.........211, 213

1 Peter 4:1..........215, 216
1 Peter 4:2..........217, 218
1 Peter 4:3.................218
1 Peter 4:4.................218
1 Peter 4:5. .219, 220, 221
1 Peter 4:7................223
1 Peter 4:8................225
1 Peter 4:9........225, 226
1 Peter 4:10 227, 230, 231
1 Peter 4:11 232, 233, 234
1 Peter 4:13........239, 242
1 Peter 4:16...............244
1 Peter 4:17 248, 249, 252
1 Peter 4:18...............251
1 Peter 4:19........255, 261
1 Peter 5:1..........262, 265
1 Peter 5:2.........265, 268
1 Peter 5:2-3..............269
1 Peter 5:3.................269
1 Peter 5:4.................272
1 Peter 5:5.........273, 274
1 Peter 5:6.........275, 276
1 Peter 5:7.................276
1 Peter 5:8.................281
1 Peter 5:9.........283, 284
1 Peter 5:10...............284
1 Peter 5:11...............285
1 Peter 5:12........291, 292
1 Peter 5:13........292, 293
1 Peter 5:14 294, 295, 296

2 Peter 1:10......46, 68, 78
2 Peter 1:19-21..........121
2 Peter 3:9...42, 43, 220,
      227

1 John 1:5..................110
1 John 2:15.................177
1 John 4:20.................177

Revelation 1:4..........228
Revelation 3:16...........73
Revelation 3:18...........73
Revelation 4:8.............58
Revelation 5................162
Revelation 5:10.........228
Revelation 11:15..........44
Revelation 16:10-11...220
Revelation 16:9.........272
Revelation 19:1.........272
Revelation 21:2...........95

Tobit 4:14..................176

INDEX

1960s...........................120
a.d. 708, 37, 150, 176, 285
a.d.1004......................106
Aaron...........................21
abandoned...................142
abandonment..............48
abode of God..........16, 25
Abraham.............162, 163
abstinence...................114
abuse..................165, 264
academics...................267
accepting Christ...........20
accomplish.................284
actions speak louder than
    words......................155
Adam....11, 60, 61, 62, 64,
    65, 76, 80, 85, 89, 92,
    102, 105, 108, 115, 116,
    121, 127, 128, 176, 203,
    213, 220, 222, 245,
    256, 259, 285, 295,
    296
Adam, dispensation of
   218
Adam, new.............86, 113
Adam, scientist.............61
Adam, Second.............147
Adam's death...............65
Adamic archetype......255
administrative harmony
   290
adolescence........291, 292
adoption...........15, 96, 165
adornment............81, 156
adrenalin....................195
adultery..............114, 210
aesthetics.....................40
aesthetics, academics,
    economics and politics
   211
affinity groups.....136, 137

affliction.......................24
against the grain.........134
agape....................77, 295
Age of Enlightenment...51
agency of salvation.......18
aggregate....241, 257, 260
agnosticism..........48, 122
agreement...................254
agriculture....................67
alcohol........................279
alien...........................260
all at once....................15
amaranth....................273
amazement.................134
ambition.....................264
amino acids.................273
analysis........................62
anarchy...............160, 274
ancient pagan mythology
   128
angel.....36, 108, 139, 213,
    176
anger..........................134
Anno Domini...............22
anxiety disorder..........131
apathy.........................296
apocalyptic prophesy. 223
apostasy.........................1
apostle card................262
apostles........................31
appointed or elected......2
archeology..................291
archetype......11, 255, 256,
    272
argument....................237
Arminian....................224
art156, 211, 212, 247, 250,
    280
asleep.................100, 101
assume God................102
assumptions. 136, 137, 191

assumptions, opposing
   186
assurance 7, 100, 192, 211,
    242
astonishment..............134
atheism.......................122
athlete........................234
attitude.......................233
attraction.....................62
audacity.....................266
Augustine.....................51
authenticity................154
authoritarian..............154
authority. 4, 16, 17, 25, 57,
    72, 91, 108, 120, 121,
    131, 142, 153, 154, 160,
    161, 162, 164, 177, 182,
    198, 199, 206, 211,
    212, 213, 219, 220,
    232, 245, 247, 263,
    264, 273, 274, 285,
    286, 292
authority, abuse of......165
authority, all 211, 213, 219
authority, anchored in
    death.....................263
authority, begins with
    wives.....................154
authority, hierarchical
   297
authority, legal...........234
authority, ultimate......121
authorized....................21
avoidance of evil........280
awake..........100, 101, 103
axiom..........................186
babes in Christ.............84
Babylon......292, 293, 294
backslide.......................88
bait...............................83
Baptism....204, 205, 207,

208, 212, 213
baptism, result of......208
baptism, salvific 205, 207
baptized infants.........165
Barnes, Albert.............46
beauty. 156, 157, 158, 159,
    162, 196, 206, 240,
    255
beginning and end points
   13
beginning to end.......209
behavior.......................65
being is headwaters of
    doing.......................41
belief.............................20
belief without obedience
   100
believe hard enough...167
benediction....................7
better and worse........139
biased...........................238
biblical logic................92
biblical principles........50
big picture....................23
biology................117, 231
Bishop..........................148
black and white..........282
blasphemy.........244, 246
blessing.......177, 183, 211,
    236, 243, 294, 295,
    296
blessing, inherited.....183
blindness42, 58, 109, 281
blood chemistry........224
blood kinship.............173
blood of Christ. .7, 22, 65,
    91
blood-red flower........273
body of Christ. 15, 42, 66,
    68, 111, 112, 143, 216,
    232
bond servant...............65
bondage.......................20
bondage to Christ........40
Bonhoeffer, Deitrich. 239
boom and bust............80
born again. .10, 11, 12, 14,
    15, 16, 18, 21, 42, 63,
    67, 78, 81, 82, 87, 92,
    105, 111, 129, 157, 203,
    234, 295
born again, definition of
   185
bottomless pit.............83
boundaries...................72
brain damage.............149

Brethren.......................53
bribery..........................15
brotherhood......130, 132,
    294
brotherly love..............76
Buddhist.....................217
bullying.......................237
burden of proof..........185
bygone era....................30
cable broadcasting.....137
caduceus....................283
call for action..............70
calling 109, 138, 140, 159,
    162, 164, 226, 232,
    261, 263, 264, 275,
    284, 288
Calvin, John....18, 46, 51,
    52, 70, 82, 105, 204
canary in the mine....249
capitalism...172, 276, 278
captivity......................203
categories of analysis 233
cataloging the world....61
catastrophe..................32
cause and effect........280
ceaselessness..............15
ceding to better positions
   226
center without
    circumference........177
central act of evangelism
   91
central biblical lesson 199
central message. 291, 294
central teaching of
    Scripture.................96
Charismatic..................26
chain of command....153,
    154, 160
change the world.......286
character......67, 157, 158,
    174, 186, 188, 192,
    245, 277, 278
character and education
   181
character qualities. 75, 78
Charismatic................224
charity....76, 77, 225, 265
chastisement.....190, 240
childhood...................291
children......................206
choreography............295
chosen as a group........25
Christ corrected Adam
   257
Christ in the OT...........34

Christ is Lord..............62
Christ, law of..............213
Christ's mission...........65
Christendom...............278
Christian age...............23
Christian colleges........30
Christian commonality
   169
Christian culture........212
Christian discipline.....57
Christian dispersion......2
Christian factions........25
Christian intellectuals. 53
Christian militancy....194
Christian stories begin
    with redemption.....86
Christian unity......27, 28
Christianity as a social
    movement.............227
Christianity is textured
   128
Christianity, bad
    reputation.............287
Christianization of the
    world.....................184
Christians are more
    unique...................231
Christianity, failure of
   287
Christlike....................146
church..........................21
church and state........106
church apathy..............73
church contamination. 72
church foundation.....266
church government...105
church in exile...............4
church leaders 46, 48, 57,
    72, 108, 121, 160, 161,
    175, 228, 262, 263,
    265, 269, 271, 272,
    275
church leadership.....264
church membership. .108
church, birth of.........285
circumspection..........279
citizenship.................161
city of God..............14, 35
civil disobedience......120
civil government...40, 77,
    105, 106, 120, 131,
    152, 160, 214, 253,
    274, 286
Civil Rights Movement
   120
civility........................132

civilization..4, 7, 120, 152
clarity, limits of..........136
classification...............62
climate change............34
closed eyes..................61
clothing......157, 158, 218, 275
co-perception....195, 209
code word...................293
Codex Sinaiticus..........46
cohesion....................138
coin............................16
community..................14
come forward..............88
comeuppance............134
coming of age..............84
common access............91
Common Era...............23
common gift of grace 229
common ground........185
common language.......52
common sense...135, 137, 223, 277, 279
common story............137
communication. 128, 129, 136, 137, 138, 211
community............10, 54
compassion........173, 174
competition for world domination...........169
complex corporate structure.................89
complexities of faithlessness...........83
compromise......259, 290
compulsion................149
conscience.................160
consensus..................290
condemnation...........248
conduit between resurrection and regeneration..........211
confirmation of faith. 243
conflict.....................252
conformity....50, 53, 168, 210
confusion.............30, 139
conscience....7, 207, 208, 209, 212, 213, 253, 254
conscience, definition 209
conscience, good 194, 195
conscience, not personal 255
consciousness 33, 62, 210

consecration..........50, 56
consequences.............154
consequences of faithlessness..........251
consequences of sin...201
conservative................50
Constantine...............106
constituent element of life..........................258
construction not destruc-tion.........................32
consultative unity......129
consumption..............277
contemporary churches 271
context. 28, 137, 172, 203, 224, 228
context of the gospel. 222
continuum.................121
contract....................153
conversation.............226
cookie-cutter similitude 168
corporate....................63
cornerstone.....97, 98, 99
cornerstone laid in Zion 94
corporate. 14, 33, 42, 129, 192
corporate body..............6
corporate centered identity.................269
corporate character of humanity................85
corporate church.........16
corporate holiness.......56
corporate identity.......111
corporate regeneration 213
corporate renewal....207, 208
corporate resurrection 64
corporate will of the body......................274
correct and incorrect dis-cernment..............278
correction..................190
corrective measures...201
corrosion.....................15
corruption. 15, 34, 56, 57, 67, 92, 142, 154, 278, 286
cost of discipleship....284
counseling relationship 180
counterfeit prophets. 284

courage......................195
courtesy.............131, 173
courts........................212
covenant....21, 22, 23, 37, 60, 74, 91, 115, 117, 139, 153, 156, 157, 163, 206, 207, 209, 218, 220, 254, 259, 285, 290, 296
covenant keepers and covenant breakers 101, 153
covenant, character of 139
covenant, justice........139
covenant, universal....139
covenantal change.......23
covenantal conditions 177
covenantal disregard. 296
covetousness.............264
cradle of civilization...154
created in God's trinitarian image.....14
creation....................259
creativity..............50, 149
creeds, confessions, commentaries. 31, 226
Crouch, Andre.............43
crown of glory....272, 273
crucifixion..........213, 266
cultural fragmentation 136
cultural improvement..71
cultural longevity........78
culture. 57, 60, 63, 65, 71, 91, 94, 114, 117, 118, 137, 138, 139, 156, 208, 212, 227, 260
culture of Christ..........65
culture of doubt.........143
culture of maturity and responsibility.........115
cycles of expansion and decline.................258
damnation....45, 99, 103, 119, 139, 198, 208, 213, 219, 248
darkness.....................83
darkness has no choice 109
darkness of humanity. 68
dastardly deeds.........287
data collection...........278
David......19, 66, 240, 281
Day of the Lord...........43
Deacon......160, 228, 232

death....14, 18, 63, 65, 67, 102, 208, 247
death of human kind. 247
death on the cross.....202
debt and credit..........142
debt of life....................65
deception 76, 83, 92, 145, 186, 238, 280, 286
decision......................256
declaration........288, 291
deconstruction..........247
decoy...........................83
decree of God.........12, 19
defensiveness..............176
deliverance 229, 230, 231
delusion.....................268
delusions about Messiah 266
democracy..................253
demographics............157
denial of God.............281
Dennis the Short.........22
denomination, super global....................296
denominational histories 238
denominations. .296, 297
deny the premise.......283
deposit of faith..........102
depravity....................125
description matches reality......................81
desire God..................282
destruction.....22, 32, 62, 65, 73, 95, 102, 114, 118, 154, 240, 247, 284, 294
destruction of Jerusalem 3, 5, 23, 30, 37, 44, 148, 150, 176, 209, 215, 249, 274, 275, 285, 293
destruction of the world 23, 54, 221
destruction of unbelievers...........240
development................42
developmentally progressive............129
deviation....................244
devil...................281, 283
diagnosis......................5
diaspora........................3
dichotomy, false........258
dictating theology and policy....................294

dictionaries.................131
dimension. .128, 146, 259
dimension and measurement.......260
dimension of the Holy Spirit....................260
dimension, no other....95
Diocletian....................22
Dionysius Exiguus.......22
directing the leader...265
disagreement..............254
discernment......148, 237, 244, 248, 251, 261, 272, 278, 279, 287
discipline....................283
discipleship................286
discipleship is not free 212
discipline.......72, 91, 194, 246, 251, 252, 280, 282, 284, 287
discourage evil 120
discreet........................39
discretion31, 39, 40, 249, 250, 251, 280
discrimination. 2, 39, 233
discussion. 226, 237, 238, 241, 290
dishonesty....................15
disillusionment..........266
disobedience........99, 139
dispensation of the Holy Spirit................21, 231
Dispensational end times speculation.............22
dissonance..................201
distribution................277
diversity.......21, 118, 170, 226, 232, 241, 254
divination...................191
divinity......................288
divinity of Christ 150, 190
division........................54
division of humanity. 295
division of labor. 227, 253
doctrinal clarity.........290
doctrinal clarity is not a denominational or sectarian contest. .290
doctrine.............289, 296
doctrine, improvement of...........................289
doctrines of grace. 55, 183
doing good. 181, 182, 185, 186, 188, 189, 200, 201, 204, 214, 216,

232, 261, 280
dominion..234, 285, 286, 287
dominion as domination 287
doubt...100, 122, 141, 166
doubt begets doubt....142
drawn not driven.........65
drink the milk.......88, 93
droplets of Christ's blood 293
dualism....258, 259, 282, 283
dwelling....................164
dye............................112
dying is easy...............215
e pluribis unum.........259
early adopters............218
Early Church..............34
Early Church Fathers...51
ears to hear....21, 35, 234
Easter.........................22
Eastern/Western philosophical dichotomy.............258
economy......................77
economic crisis............78
economic depression. 150
economic development 78, 79, 115, 117, 133, 276
economic viability......142
economy...78, 79, 89, 97, 150, 228, 277
Ecumenical Creeds.....171
ecumenical efforts.....297
education...160, 163, 164, 181, 212, 237
education, Christian..182
elders 160, 207, 262, 273, 275
elected to office............46
election...46, 48, 82, 100, 104, 148, 292
election, Jewish.........294
Elliot, T.S...................43
embarrassment...74, 110, 176, 177, 196
embellishment..............3
emergent/emerging church....................71
emotion......................173
emotional frenzy........161
emotionalism.............122
emperor.......131, 152, 153
empty threat.............283

encourage disagreement 290
encourage good....120
encouragement.190, 202, 284, 285
end of the world...23, 35, 284
end time....22, 23, 44, 54, 223, 249, 266, 284
end to war....130
endpoint of history....12
endurance....283
enemies of God believe God to be evil....214
engine of salvation....141
engineering....67
engines of God's glory. 67
envy....83, 92, 286
equality....165, 297
equality of being....153
equality of men and women....153
Erasmus....70
eternal life....95, 178
eternal promise....32
eternal security....118
ethereal realm....95
European kings....106
evangelists....36
evangelism..3, 68, 72, 76, 133, 134, 155, 171, 271, 285, 293, 298
evangelism and hospitality....226
evangelism and shame 196
evangelism, engine of 184
evangelism, Jewish....171
evangelism, not an answer....134
evangelists....36
Eve....60, 61, 76, 116, 121, 176, 257, 259
everything....234
evil 74, 119, 120, 126, 180, 282
evil persists....200
evil, God's fault....198
evil, not a thing....198
exaggeration....237
exaltation....276
excellence....109
exhortation....288, 290
exile....2
existentialism....129
exodus....151

expansion of Christianity 8
extend Christ's ministry 147
extortion....238
extreme....172
eye salve....74
eyes to see....21, 35, 107, 234
Ezekiel....150
Ezekiel's prophecy....150
face the future, not the past....263
factionalism....296
failure of Christianity 142
faith....18, 19, 20, 24, 25, 32, 36, 102, 167, 186
faith is an assertion....92
faith, as assumption...191
faith, correct....167
faithful, educated and intelligent....264
faithfulness....100
faithfulness does not grumble....227
faithlessness....165
faithlessness, natural. 165
Fall....87
Fall of Jerusalem....1
false divisions....296
false start....86
falsehood, ugliness and evil....67
family...78, 152, 154, 155, 163, 164, 165, 166, 173, 298
family corporation....155
family government....153
family rights....15
farming....79
fasting....10
father/son relationship 111, 113, 116
fear of the Lord....63, 195
fear, withheld....283
feeding of the five thousand....231
feelings....122, 176, 217
fellowship. .225, 293, 295
fellowship, with God..174
feminine....116
fiery trial....236
filioque....106
financial management.78
finding Jesus....185
fire and brimstone....81

First Commandment. 259
flatten out the complexities....26
flirtations....295
flock....268
followership....81
foolish religiosity....266
foolishness. 122, 190, 292
foot in both eras....23
forgiveness....28
forefathers....63
foreign folds....150
foreknowledge. .5, 25, 66, 104, 143, 194, 293
forever finding Christ..88
forgiveness....41, 90, 134, 145, 186, 210, 211, 230, 233, 239, 246, 257, 290, 297
fornication....114
founding of America...34
free will....20, 149
freedom....21, 39, 40, 48, 50, 62, 84, 124, 126, 129, 135, 149, 152, 160, 213, 219, 232, 233, 237
freedom and selfishness 125
freedom and sin....219
freedom and slavery. .125
freedom from godless assumptions....135
freedom is slavery to God 126
freedom not subjugation 65
freedom requires limits 40
freedom to live above the law....40
freedom to sin....245
freedom, responsible. 130
freely choose....20
freewill....254
freewill, passive....256
frustration....24
fulfillment of the revelation....54
fullness of time....15, 38
fundamentalism....54
future. .3, 11, 12, 290, 291
future oriented glory. 262
gambling....181
Gandhi....196
Garden of Eden...35, 115,

277
gender..................98, 159
genetic sequence. .95, 116
genetics.....................173
genocide.....................65
Gentiles.....4, 5, 7, 21, 64,
116, 119, 218, 295
Germany........................3
ghetto...........................91
gift of the Word.........128
gifts of the Spirit........102
giving and receiving..230
glory..24, 44, 63, 90, 177,
183, 191, 206, 226,
233, 234, 241, 250,
262, 272, 284, 286,
289
glory, new..................291
Gnostic........25, 258, 284
goal............................194
goal of Christianity......66
God alone is good......185
God as Father................5
God called the two "one"
...............................259
God causes suffering. 255
God does not honor
persons...................59
God does not respect
individuals..............60
God doesn't love us for
our uniqueness.......60
God favors righteousness
...............................187
God judges...................55
God literally holds the
world together........63
God loves Himself.....140
God of the aggregate..241
God of the marginalized
...............................208
God of the Old
Testament...............55
God phobia.................131
God possesses us...........11
God provides the only
objectivity...............63
God wins all arguments
...............................250
God's decree..............238
God's active involvement
...............................185
God's authority..........154
God's blessings.............7
God's central purpose
...............................246

God's chastening.......240
God's condemnation....21
God's curses...............102
God's decree. 32, 99, 263,
284, 289, 290
God's earthly mission..94
God's end or purpose for
creation...................35
God's enemies....154, 215
God's eternal hope......32
God's expectations.....101
God's freedom....125, 126
God's future...............239
God's garments...........74
God's glory.................67
God's goodness.........232
God's government.....286
God's gravitas..............66
God's greatness..........125
God's hope............41, 194
God's image..56, 107, 129
God's imposition of
human identity.....245
God's intention..........198
God's judgment. .63, 139,
220, 222, 248
God's justice..............200
God's kingdom..284, 290
God's law...................201
God's love............36, 126
God's mission..............55
God's plan. .5, 8, 127, 175,
184, 286
God's power................28
God's primary weapon
...............................240
God's provision.........276
God's purpose. .7, 8, 208,
249, 294
God's reflexivity.........129
God's Roman hammer
...............................293
God's salvation......33, 34
God's salvation promise
...............................32
God's selection was
group oriented........25
God's solution...........259
God's story................260
God's timeless being...58
God's timelessness......66
God's trinitarian will...28
God's truth..........14, 290
God's truth is not found
...............................290
God's two fronts........200

God's ultimate intention
...............................139
God's ultimate truth....64
God's vision................81
God's warnings.........208
God's will. 26, 76, 93, 121,
123, 141, 147, 178, 198,
200, 202, 217, 255,
256
God's will is to silence
ignorance..............122
God's Word.................80
God's wrath...............247
Godhead......21, 107, 108,
111, 125, 127, 150, 183,
184, 297
Golden Age.................238
good and evil...61, 62, 63,
115, 121, 189, 199,
200, 238, 254, 277
good and evil confused62
good and evil, reversed
.......................117, 280
good intentions...........72
good irritates evil......200
good news....................36
good people...............190
good, definition of.....189
goodness............189, 196
governors and the
governed................286
grace8, 10, 12, 20, 34, 45,
63, 133, 141, 163, 165,
173, 186, 193, 212,
234, 239, 246, 267,
294, 297
grace alone...................93
grace and humility.....275
grace and humility, cause
or effect.................275
grace and identity........95
grace not race.....104, 165
grace through faith19, 21,
25, 186, 191, 231
grace under fire.........134
grace vs. justice..........133
grace, cheap...............239
grace, gift of...............140
grace, inheritance of. .175
grace, true..........291, 292
grace, unlocked...........20
grace/gifts wordplay. 230
graciousness under fire
...............................133
grapple tooth and claw
...............................290

gravity.........................185
gravity of God.............292
gravity of our past.....239
Great Chain of Being. 223
Great Flood...............203
Great Shepherd.........272
greater good...............201
greed. .142, 264, 265, 269
Greek philosophical
    categories.............207
Greek philosophy......258
Greek rationalism........51
ground of performance
   101
grumbling..........226, 227
guarded from loss........16
guarding......................24
guilt. 36, 64, 83, 110, 122,
    209
habits...84, 218, 246, 278
halfway commitment to
    the errors of both
    extremes.................54
happiness, giving.......180
hardheaded..........42, 44
harmony and
    cooperation...........107
harvest......................296
hate32, 49, 100, 132, 134,
    271
head coverings..........294
head of household....164,
    166, 207
headship....132, 147, 156,
    206
healing......................212
heart...173, 174, 191, 204,
    267
heart of Peter's vision 267
heaven. 16, 18, 22, 25, 33,
    61, 117, 227
hell.........99, 117, 139, 219
helping......................163
herd mentality...........218
heresy.................171, 290
hermeneutic..............293
hidden.........................20
hieroglyph...................90
history. 99, 246, 285, 289
historic shortsightedness
   289
history..12, 14, 19, 22, 24,
    34, 46, 64, 66, 80, 86,
    87, 89, 111, 112, 127,
    128, 129, 138, 147,
    182, 183, 186, 203,

222, 224, 225, 238,
    239, 247, 248, 250,
    260, 272, 273, 276,
    278, 285, 288, 289,
    291, 293
history, distortion of..133
history, early church. .171
history, pulled.............64
history, pulling forward
   238
history, unparalleled
    changes...................37
history, watershed.....139
Hitler............................3
holding to the center..172
holiness.....50, 53, 54, 55,
    56, 90, 91, 190, 218,
    281
Holiness movement....53
holy...........................190
holy kiss....294, 295, 296
holy nation................108
Holy Spirit. .10, 11, 15, 19,
    26, 31, 34, 36, 41, 50,
    55, 62, 65, 68, 79, 91,
    113, 121, 127, 130, 140,
    160, 170, 180, 184,
    185, 191, 203, 205,
    213, 216, 223, 241,
    244, 254, 256, 257,
    259, 261, 272, 277,
    290, 294
Holy Spirit dwells in
    morality................260
Holy Spirit, coming of
   285
Holy Spirit, dispensation
    of..........................295
Holy Spirit, invasion of
   174
homosexual......244, 245,
    246, 247
honesty 115, 117, 119, 160,
    162, 246, 250, 276,
    290
honesty, integrity and in-
    dustry...................228
honor....60, 115, 119, 130,
    132, 154, 156, 160,
    162, 165, 190, 213,
    234, 240, 273, 277
honor, unforced.........162
hope.....12, 18, 27, 28, 32,
    34, 41, 67, 68, 192,
    193, 194, 195, 196,
    251, 268, 284, 289,

290, 291, 292
hope fuels the church..68
hope, future fulfillment
   42
hope, husband of.......291
hope, shared...............41
hospitality.................225
hot Christianity...........73
household of God......249
household stability......78
how God works.........204
human potential........264
human race.................61
human weakness.........74
humanism..........169, 177
humanity...64, 65, 75, 79,
    80, 89, 96, 98, 105,
    129, 138, 140, 142,
    146, 169, 177, 191, 193,
    201, 208, 218, 220,
    230, 231, 239, 246,
    250, 253, 254, 257,
    259, 260, 267, 278,
    295
humanity, new..........295
humanity, old...........203
humanity, purchase of
   219
humanity, redeemed...85
humanity, redefining.245
humanity, salvation of
   139
humanity's rescue.....203
humiliation................196
humility.....132, 162, 173,
    196, 264, 275, 290
Hus, John....................52
husband............153, 164
husband, wayward.....155
husbandry...................79
hype...................219, 225
hypocrisy. 77, 83, 92, 132,
    286
I am............................291
identity.11, 14, 33, 56, 60,
    62, 98, 99, 100, 107,
    108, 111, 112, 113, 127,
    130, 163, 181, 216,
    245, 259
identity drives behavior
   41
identity is based upon
    our belongings and
    associations............40
identity, confusion.....182
identity, false...............96

identity, not by blood. .95
identity, two poles of. 257
ideology....................50
idolatry..............128, 218
ignorance.....48, 122, 157,
    188, 296
ignorance, willful......240
image of God.....116, 126,
    257
imagination....32, 64, 99,
    219, 233
imitate Jesus..............145
imitation....................102
immaturity....................49
immortality...33, 68, 273
impairment of judgment
   279
imperishable....15, 17, 65,
    80, 157, 162
impose meaning and
    purpose..................92
impose trinitarian
    categories...............58
imposition.231, 234, 258,
    269, 297
improvement...............42
inaccurate
    understanding of
    reality.....................26
incarnation.................138
individualism...............51
individual and corporate
   66
individual interpretation
   121
individualism....130, 193,
    194, 219, 230
individuality................25
individuality and unity
   116
indoctrination............169
indoctrination in our
    schools...................131
infallible......................13
infants.........................21
infinitude of God.........44
information...............137
inheritance. 15, 16, 18, 19,
    38, 96, 165, 175
inhibitions...................39
inspiration...................28
inspire........................269
instrumentality of faith
   21
instrumentality of
    heaven...................16

instrumentality of the
    Holy Spirit...........6, 16
integrity......115, 117, 142,
    154, 160, 246, 250,
    276, 277, 278, 290
intellectual............51, 173
intelligence.......164, 269,
    278, 280, 281
Internet......................137
intimacy....................161
intimidation..............238
introspective..............83
invested......................68
irrational fear............131
irrationality...............171
irritation............201, 217
Isaiah..........................19
Islam...116, 169, 170, 171,
    214, 296
isolated Christian......255
Israel.......66, 85, 94, 169,
    204, 259
jealousy.......................83
Jeremiah....................267
Jerusalem............94, 150
Jerusalem, new...........95
Jesus isn't lost.............89
Jesus' birth...............139
Jesus' name..............166
Jethro........................161
Jewish age...................23
Jewish bloodline........183
Jewish establishment. .35
Jewish people not
    excluded...............294
Jihad..........................214
John The Baptist. 19, 256
Jordan, James.......43, 76
Josephus........................1
joy...18, 30, 32, 126, 226,
    242, 281, 284
joy of the gospel.........173
joyless........................225
Judaism........37, 116, 170
Judaism, failure of....294
Judeo-Christian heritage
   126
judge lightly..............249
judgment.......62, 63, 173,
    201, 202, 247, 248,
    249, 265, 286
judgment according to
    works.....................55
judgment as discernment
   55
judgment defined......221

judgment serves
    goodness...............202
judgment to come......220
judgment, as faculties of
    assessment and
    evaluation.............247
judgment, exercise of as
    discretion..............251
judgment, good.........280
judgment, on basis of
    wholeness not parts98
judgment, other side of
   222
judgmental.................135
Julian calendar...........23
jurisdiction......16, 17, 25,
    105, 139, 161, 253
jurisdiction, ultimate. 121
justice..119, 133, 154, 175,
    176, 188, 200, 201,
    202, 246, 250
justification...............103
kairos..........................22
Kepler, Johannes......220
key to the Scriptures....19
kind.............................33
kindness....................134
Kingdom of God. 4, 8, 25,
    239
Kingdom of God on earth
   66
kingdom of heaven....139
kingdom of heaven on
    earth.......................25
kingdom work.............36
kingship....................253
kiss of love................294
knowledge.................274
knowledge of good and
    evil..................63, 277
knowledge, secondhand
   31
knowledge, ultimate. .199
labeled......................157
language....................128
Laodicea................73, 81
last time....22, 23, 54, 56,
    58
Latin..........................52
laws of nature.......51, 125
laziness.............252, 264
lead by example........270
leadership.............4, 272
legal sanctions.............40
legalism......................50
liberal.........................50

liberal social service. .182
liberalism..52, 54, 71, 173
libertines....................179
life in Christ is difficult
.................................89
life is complex...........200
life not death........65, 215
light dispels darkness
.................................200
light of Christ..64, 68, 77,
    83, 87, 92, 97, 110,
    121, 163, 172, 182, 186,
    196, 213, 214, 216,
    217, 241, 247, 251,
    252, 254, 255, 261,
    274, 277, 281, 285,
    287
like begets like...........142
like-minded.......168, 170,
    172, 174, 215
limited atonement.......43
lion....................281, 282
literalism....................161
literature.............30, 173
live by faith, not by sight
.................................92
live long and prosper. 179
living a lie...................182
living stones................97
local church...............298
local level...................287
logic............118, 279, 291
logic of God's Word...220
logic, of opposition....282
logical disconnect......281
logo............................184
long march of the gospel
.................................285
long-suffering..............43
longevity......79, 102, 177,
    178, 221, 246
Lord of hosts.....241, 248,
    255
Lord of the aggregate 256
Lord of time.................12
love.......77, 140, 154, 157,
    206, 240, 268, 280,
    295, 297
love and sex.......280, 281
love our enemies......120,
    283
love with legs.............225
love, everyone...........130
love, kiss of................294
love, reciprocal............76
love, truth and beauty. 65

love, unconditional....177
loyalty.........................256
lukewarm....71, 73, 74, 81
lust..............................49
Luther, Martin.......51, 52
Lutheran......................53
machine.......................264
magnify the Lord.......261
magic..166, 259, 277, 281
magnet........................100
magnetic attraction.....12
magnetic forces...........62
making good moral
    judgments.............261
Malachi........................248
male and female.........116
malice...........................83
man/humanity social 257
manners......................152
manipulation.....237. 269
manliness...................109
manna.........................263
manners.......................132
many become one.....259
marriage.....153, 246, 274
Mark...........................294
markets........................276
marriage. 60, 74, 115, 116,
    154, 156, 163, 206,
    246
marriage is a threesome
.................................60
marriage, not between
    one man one woman
.................................75
Mary.............................15
masculine....................116
math............................147
maturity....30, 53, 57, 66,
    72, 73, 75, 80, 84, 87,
    88, 91, 93, 115, 129,
    133, 157, 164, 165,
    190, 191, 200, 201,
    227, 236, 237, 247,
    252, 254, 266, 267,
    268, 269, 274, 289,
    291
maturity, moral.........261
maturity. engine of....254
me-and-Jesus mentality
.................................45
mechanism of salvation
.................................191
mechanical Christianity
.................................51
mechanism of mediation

.................................210
mechanism of salvation
.................................146
media outlets.............297
media trends..............219
mediator...........210, 253
medicine.....................211
medicine is bitter.........73
meekness...132, 194, 196,
    264
membership...72, 82, 111,
    112, 206, 212
memorization............221
mercy.....10, 12, 212, 246,
    247
mercy, wideness of....254
Messiah......................248
messenger..................108
Messiah....19, 32, 38, 111,
    183, 222, 252, 266
metaphor........61, 80, 292
Methodism....................53
Middle Ages..........71, 172
Middle East...............294
migration.......................4
military..............212, 214
military force...............171
mind of Christ...269, 274
ministry is not a job. .265
miracles 51, 125, 211, 231,
    233, 277
misdirection................61
mission 7, 92, 95, 96, 156,
    163, 188, 192, 227,
    260
misunderstanding......27,
    188
mob mentality............161
moderation................264
Modernism...................52
Modernity..................230
modest.........................39
Mohammad................171
monetary crises.........296
money......65, 78, 81, 142,
    150, 228, 265
money, income...........181
monotheism. 35, 112, 115,
    118, 127, 128, 130,
    140, 169, 170, 171, 259
monotheism, Christless
.................................183
monotheistic......126, 127
moral commitment....173
moral compass............63
moral dimension.......260

moral fence-sitters......49
moral government.......33
moral imperative.50, 180
moral judgment...55, 261
moral law..................253
moral laxity.................74
moral principles..........50
moral standards........245
morality....40, 50, 52, 92,
   115, 120, 152, 164, 196,
   210, 212, 213, 260,
   274, 278, 279
morality, undermine. 295
morally blameless.......49
Moravians...................53
more Greek than biblical
  16
more substance than
   style.........................87
Moses........19, 21, 66, 161
Moses, new.................151
motivation.................265
multiplication of grace
   and peace..................8
multiculturalism.......135,
   138, 169, 170
multiplication function
  95
mutual exclusion........118
mutual ministry.........175
myopia........................58
mystery.....................281
mystical...........129, 215
mysticism...171, 172, 234,
   259
narrow gate.................45
narrowminded.....45, 50,
   130, 148, 183, 184
natural born.................15
natural spiritual urge...10
natural tendencies.....199
navel gazing.................36
Nebuchadnezzar........176
negative command......48
New Age...22, 23, 95, 218
new dimension..........260
new heaven and a new
   earth.......................44
new human model.....102
New Israel..................151
New Jerusalem...........35
new light on the ancient
   texts........................39
new starting point.......87
new story of redemption
  90

new wineskins...........203
Nietzsche, Freidrich. .218
nirvana......................217
Noah..........................203
Noah's Flood....204, 207,
   208
nobility.......................216
non-denominational. 297
nonviolence...............196
norm.........244, 245, 246
not finished...............193
nutrition....................226
obedience....7, 21, 48, 49,
   76, 99, 101, 126, 133,
   140, 147, 153, 157, 158,
   177, 186, 206, 212,
   250, 276
obedience, to parents.155
object of faith..............19
object of worship.........67
objectivity...........61, 238
obligation..................206
obligation of obedience
  207
ocean of being............68
offense..............175, 283
office vs. service........228
Old Testament.19, 20, 31,
   34, 36, 37, 38, 55, 58,
   65, 85, 86, 96, 104,
   112, 127, 150, 162, 163,
   170, 175, 179, 199,
   204, 209, 222, 248,
   256, 263, 268, 295
Old Testament
   administration........37
Old Testament era.....285
Old Testament Temple
   administration........22
omnipotent.............13, 16
omnipresent...............16
once burned twice shy141
one and the many.....107,
   116, 118, 258, 259,
   260
opposition..120, 271, 275,
   282
optimism...............13, 42
oracles of God...........232
ordinary......36, 108, 238,
   267, 277, 287
ordination service........21
organic......................194
organism...................161
orgiastic cult..............224
original authority.......154

original sin 61, 62, 63, 76,
   176, 189
orthodox.....50, 226, 237,
   289
other world.................25
overemphasis on the
   intellect...................53
overemphasized the
   heart.......................53
overpopulation......27, 34
overseer.............148, 149
oversight...................209
ownership..................256
oxygen..............149, 258
pacifist.......................214
Paganism......16, 115, 123,
   171, 253, 259
Pantheism..................118
parable of the fig tree.166
parable of the talents. 141
participation.......112, 147
particular and universal
  66
particular redemption. 43
particular universal...107
passing forward.140, 269
passion....48, 49, 115, 217
passionate relativity....49
passover.......................19
pastor........................160
pastoral committee...265
patience....................255
Patmos.......................219
patriotic propaganda. 122
Paul.........................4, 98
peace......8, 112, 181, 186,
   237, 241, 295, 297
peculiar people. .107, 108
Pentecostalism......26, 53
people are adaptable....71
people are not the same
  153
people are untrustworthy
  141
personal preference. .238
perception requires
   reception...............234
perfection. .146, 164, 237,
   238
perfectly one..............259
perishable versus
   imperishable...........79
perpetual motion
   machine.................126
perpetuity...................15
persecution 2, 4, 8, 11, 22,

23, 24, 114, 150, 215, 216, 241, 243, 250
perseverance.............133
personal discrimination 254
personal orderliness...131
personal preference...199
personal relationship 160, 254
personal relationship, not private............255
personality.........174, 254
persuasion.................237
pessimism....................42
Peter's love........265, 268
Peter's intention........269
Pharisees...........182, 294
philosophical opposition 118
philosophical relativity 49, 127
philosophy....61, 63, 108, 147, 247, 258
phobia.......................131
phrenology.................174
physics...............185, 258
pietistic curriculum and new music.................53
piety.................51, 53, 54
pilgrim status.............114
pity.............173, 174, 284
Plato.................118, 258
pleasure and pain.....200
pledge........................239
plethora.........................7
plurality....................208
poetic bloom on the proverbial rose......255
poetry...........................80
poison ivy...................217
police.........................212
Political Correctness Movement..............39
political leaders.........286
politics......238, 258, 286
pollution..............34, 142
polytheism. 127, 169, 170, 259
Pope...........................272
pornography.............280
positive and negative pole.....................100
Postmodern.................49
poverty........115, 181, 236
power hungry sinners 287

power of God.............134
practice and mastery.284
praise....24, 92, 109, 120, 126, 133, 173, 240, 241
prayer....10, 92, 133, 166, 207, 224, 225, 254
pre-Fall condition.....245
preaching...............36, 81
preached to the dead.222
preaching....................233
precious.....................159
predestination...100, 102
predestination, complicated..........101
prediction.................248
preeminence of God. .109
preemptive strike.......177
preferences..........63, 135
preparation...38, 64, 194, 208, 241
prepared in advance of history..................263
preparedness.............193
presumption...............191
presupposing, or not..187
presupposition..........102
presuppositional foundation............130
pretending.................149
Preterist....................224
prevenient grace........189
pride...154, 162, 174, 176, 183, 194, 236, 272, 275
pride and self-interest 178
priest...........90, 207, 228
principles...........143, 209
principle of animation 149
printing press.............52
Probus Junior.............23
produce, distribute and consume.................97
procedure vs. purpose 208
proclamation............291
procreation.................74
prodigal son................88
production...........97, 277
profession.................265
prognosis.................5, 21
program for humanity 50
progress.....8, 32, 42, 237
progressive............56, 57
progressive glory.........44

Progressive Movement 29
progressive revelation 29, 34, 42, 45, 54, 58, 127, 170, 172, 223, 241, 247, 252, 262, 263, 272, 273, 288, 289, 290, 291
proof of regeneration. .78
proper places.............159
prophecy....................263
prophets.......................36
prosperity..................276
protective walls.........296
protein.......................273
Protestant Christianity 55
protoevangelium.......127
prototype.....24, 101, 103, 109, 110, 116, 138, 141, 143, 147
prototype, integrity of 102
prove the existence of God......................186
providence.........277, 278
proving the saints........24
prudence..............39, 279
psyche...................75, 117
pulled into the future 289
pulled into the present 263
pulling history forward 64, 238
punishment.......120, 146, 201, 202, 286
puppets........................20
purchase of godliness. .73
purification 7, 24, 70, 115, 117
Puritans.......................30
purpose....23, 24, 28, 32, 56, 80, 92, 109, 141, 168, 202, 223, 241, 249, 250, 251, 284, 294
purpose of all things..223
purpose of God...........111
purpose of life.............27
purpose of salvation....89
purpose, ultimate......201
purpose, wrong.........248
purse............................16
pursuit of happiness. .179
qualifications............212
Queer Theory...244, 245, 246
question God plants...134

race..............................105
race and nationality are
    insignificant............96
race, chosen................104
rational element of
    human thinking.....117
re-cognition...............183
re-experience Adam's sin
   87
reached into the future
   262
reality..103, 112, 118, 147,
    169, 233, 258, 282
reality, objective........184
reason..............33, 75, 115
recovery....................175
Red Sea....................204
redeemed community
   140
redemption...64, 90, 230
redemption as new
    starting point..........86
redemption not punish-
    ment.......................65
redemption, renewal,
    revival, reformation,
    reconfiguration,
    reconstruction,
    renovation,
    restitution,
    reclamation,
    revitalization..........44
refinement.................163
refinement...40, 157, 280
Reformation....30, 34, 51,
    52, 53
reforming synod........296
regeneration.....10, 11, 13,
    14, 19, 21, 28, 41, 50,
    62, 63, 79, 82, 84, 88,
    91, 95, 105, 109, 111,
    113, 127, 129, 130,
    140, 158, 160, 174,
    180, 181, 182, 185,
    191, 194, 200, 203,
    210, 212, 215, 216,
    220, 222, 230, 231,
    241, 253, 254, 256,
    257, 259, 267, 268,
    277, 281, 283, 290,
    291, 294, 295
regeneration, baptismal
   205
regeneration, ongoing
   105
regeneration, social...257

reign of God................16
rejected by Christ........20
rejection of forgiveness
   99
rejoice.......................239
relationship.................50
relativity....................127
relevant.......................80
religion is the institution
    of culture..............212
religiosity..................183
religious behavior........10
religious struggle.......127
religious toleration....170
renewal.....................208
repentance....28, 43, 175,
    200, 220
representative
    government..........253
representation and
    priestcraft..............90
Representation Theory
   147
representation, genuine
   253
representative............154
representative authority
   150
representative
    covenantal hierarchy
   91
representative
    government. .160, 161,
    286
reproduction.............246
republic.....................253
repulsion.....................62
resolve......................291
respect authority.......120
respecter of persons...25,
    98, 101, 102, 140, 162
responsibility......30, 115,
    152, 164, 165, 206, 212
restoration................284
resurrection 11, 13, 14, 18,
    19, 28, 184, 210, 211,
    248, 266
resurrection of humanity
   146
return good for evil....119
return of Christ.........295
revelation..45, 56, 58, 62,
    66, 86, 110, 140, 163,
    223, 225, 248
revelers.....................218
revenge..............119, 134

reversal of values.......219
rhetoric.......................81
rhetoric serves logic.....81
right thinking..............38
righteousness............277
righteous indignation 176
righteous judgment...249
righteous militancy and
    domination............171
righteousness..40, 67, 73,
    81, 101, 102, 140, 159,
    188, 192, 208, 214,
    216, 237, 240, 241,
    244, 246, 248, 249,
    278, 283
righteousness, as norm
   245
rivalries between
    Judaism and Islam
   169
Road to Damascus.....175
role of the church in
    society..................106
Roman Catholic Church
    ....52, 106, 213
Roman Empire...4, 7, 22,
    150, 274
Roman military buildup
   150
Romania......................22
Rome.................253, 285
rot................................15
royal priesthood 105, 106,
    108
rule of law..................287
ruse............................287
Sabbath, eternal..........23
sacrament, baptism. .206
sacrifice....................154
sacrifice of Christ.........21
saints........................222
salute........................294
salvation.....32, 103, 204,
    208, 210, 213, 219,
    221, 230, 247, 251,
    264
salvation is a process. .89
salvation of human
    culture....................33
salvation, whole world
   183
sanctification.6, 7, 21, 24,
    53, 54, 56, 57, 70, 72,
    90, 93, 133, 190, 191,
    201, 236, 237, 247,
    266, 268, 269, 271,

274, 289, 290, 293, 298
sanctify the Lord.......190
sanity....................28, 224
Sarah............19, 162, 163
Satan. .61, 74, 76, 83, 115, 117, 176, 241, 244, 282
Satan, as lion.............281
Saul, King...................191
saved by baptism.......205
Savoy Declaration.....253
Scarlet Letter.............165
schizophrenia............174
scholarship. 52, 267, 278, 290, 296
science 61, 62, 63, 67, 117, 142, 147, 157, 172, 246, 247, 250, 252, 276, 277, 278, 280
science and technology depend upon righteousness..........67
secondary resources....31
sectarianism..............296
Secularism...........52, 169
seeking..........................11
segregation...................56
self-assessment..........157
self-authenticating....191, 278
self-centered.......45, 178, 236, 278
self-claimed...............154
self-concern........129, 177
self-control..................40
self-defensiveness......177
self-delusion...............177
self-esteem.................236
self-evident........185, 186
self-governed...............39
self-governed cooperative freedom 129
self-identity.................99
self-improvement........36
self-inhibited...............39
self-interest.................36
self-justification. .115, 176
self-love......................176
self-perpetuating cycle of anger and revenge. 119
self-reflective moral consideration........215
self-restraining...........39
self-sacrifice...............215
self-satisfaction....36, 179

self-select..................252
self-service.................125
self-serving.................77
selfishness.................130
Semper reformanda...30
sensationalism..........224
sensitivity..........280, 281
sentimental fiction.....122
separation.53, 70, 76, 90, 91, 296
serpent..........................61
servant leadership.....164
service..36, 126, 154, 182, 228, 232, 269
service to others.........125
service, two kinds......232
sex.....74, 75, 84, 114, 115, 116, 118, 120, 164, 181, 244, 245, 280, 286, 295
sex and love..............280
sexual permissiveness. 52
shame..64, 196, 218, 265, 269
short attention span. .148
shortsighted....72, 58,148
sign and seal of the covenant.................21
sign and signification 207
sign and symbol........273
simplicity in the face of complexity.............206
simple but not easy.....83
sin..21, 27, 28, 34, 36, 39, 53, 56, 57, 62, 72, 83, 84, 87, 90, 92, 99, 113, 115, 125, 126, 128, 130, 134, 135, 145, 146, 147, 148, 149, 157, 165, 173, 174, 175, 176, 182, 183, 191, 193, 198, 211, 217, 220, 222, 233, 245, 252, 267, 277, 280, 297
sin imposes itself.......135
sin in drag..................149
sin of presumption.....191
sin, abandonment of.200
sin, denial of...............99
sin, end of..................218
sin, exposure to.........183
sin, infectiousness of....71
sin, pride of...............176
sin, remove..................95
sin, smarter...............181
sin, unforgivable.......246

single, worldwide, human institution. 213
singularity....................80
sinnerhood to sainthood 84
sinners are not free.....39
slander..................84, 92
slavery. 125, 130, 132, 140
slavery to self.............126
slavery to sin.......20, 203
slavery-to-sin to slavery-to-Christ................140
small group................161
smart, powerful and influential................71
smelting....................236
sober-minded............279
social bonding............161
social conscience.......255
social construction....244
social formalities.......295
social isolation.............57
social limitations to human freedom....124
social order. .117, 161, 162
social position.....59, 264
social progress............133
social structure...194, 196
social values..............135
Socialism...................296
sociopath...................209
sojourners.....................3
soldier........................283
soldiers in God's army 241
Solomon.......................66
Son of Man..................43
sophistication..............71
soul...33, 75, 83, 117, 149, 157, 258, 273, 281
soul confusion...........258
soul is the prize.........117
soul mining...............236
sourpuss....................179
sovereignty....16, 66, 139, 150, 184, 198, 235, 285
speaking in tongues.....79
species.........................33
speculation 224, 225, 233
sphere sovereignty....106
spheres of influence...163
spiritual growth.........190
spiritual misers..........141
spirits in prison.........204
spiritual disciplines.....10

spiritual gifts.....159, 162, 227, 228, 229, 230, 236
spiritual growth.....36, 58
spiritual jujitsu..........217
spiritual milk...............93
spiritual sacrifices.......92
spiritual weakness.....271
spirituality....................11
spite.............................188
sports...........................176
sprinkled....................293
sprinkling..............5, 7, 21
stand for something righteous..............292
standard....260, 261, 280
steward.........................79
stone of stumbling......98
story............................137
story, biblical arc.......277
story, universal..........138
struggle..............252, 254
stumbling stone...32, 100
sub-mission.......153, 155, 162, 163
subconscious...............26
subject to government 119
subjectivity.................63
submission....7, 142, 152, 194, 206, 273, 274, 289
submission, mutual...274
submission, to husbands 153
substitutionary atonement.....146, 147
subtext.......................137
success.....71, 74, 81, 236, 237, 240, 264
suffer for doing good. 146
suffering.....141, 173, 196, 198, 200, 201, 214, 215, 216, 218, 241, 244, 255, 262, 283, 284
suffering for Christ....147
suffering is not the point 143
suffering to learn.......202
suffering, righteous vs. unrighteous..........202
super-denomination..297
super-doctrine..........297
superimposition of God 260

Superman..................219
supernatural.....224, 231, 234, 245, 259, 260
superstition. 63, 141, 248, 266, 267, 277, 278
superstitions...............28
supervise....................268
surrender....................256
surrogacy....................146
survival-of-the-fittest 297
sustainability.............233
sustainability of human culture....................117
sustainability of humanity..............246
sustainable culture.....34, 79, 95
sustainable economic development.........133
sustainable human culture...................220
sustainable human freedom.................149
Sylvanus............288, 292
symbolism.........294, 296
sympathy.....173, 174, 175
syncretism....................80
syntax............................28
taste and tact............280
tax deductions.............77
tax incentives..............78
taxonomy............62, 157
team sport..........162, 241
technology.....62, 67, 117, 136, 137, 142, 157, 172, 211, 218, 228, 246, 250, 252, 276, 277, 278, 280
teetotalism.................225
teleology....................250
television....................137
temperance...............264
Temple........66, 285, 294
Temple rites..............267
temptation. 57, 61, 72, 85, 87, 88, 180, 264, 276, 283
temptation, fall and redemption 85, 87, 88, 89
Ten Commandments.287
tested by fire................24
testimonies.................88
testimony of Christ's salvation...............220
Textus Receptus..........46

thanksgiving...18, 92, 126
theology. 27, 51, 127, 140, 247, 266, 267
thinking.......................62
threefold office...105, 106
threshing ox..............265
time 12, 13, 15, 66, 75, 111, 112, 113, 129, 146, 200, 238, 290
time mirror...................12
time to grow up...........89
time, fullness of.........139
time, kairos......248, 249, 251, 276
timidity......................194
Timothy.....................294
tongue................179, 180
tools of engagement...241
totalitarianism...127, 160
transcendent..............156
translate......................80
transnational and transhistoric stability 250
tree of knowledge........61
tree of life....................62
tree of the knowledge of good and evil....61, 65, 121
trials.......................23, 24
trickery......................237
tried............................24
Trinity................106, 183
trinitarian church unity 297
trinitarian election....293
trinitarian monotheism 169
trinitarian perspective...5
trinitarian relationships 26
trinitarian unity..........27
trinitarianism.....112, 259
Trinity...5, 6, 9, 11, 14, 15, 26, 33, 34, 35, 40, 50, 54, 56, 58, 62, 63, 68, 80, 89, 94, 96, 97, 98, 102, 103, 107, 112, 116, 117, 118, 121, 126, 127, 130, 138, 140, 146, 150, 160, 169, 170, 171, 182, 184, 190, 206, 241, 252, 257, 259, 260, 272, 282, 283, 288, 297
Trinity provides actual,

ultimate truth.......169
Trinity, application of..27
Trinity, common........127
Trinity, commonly
  assumed................108
Trinity, complexity of. .21
Trinity, cornerstone of
  mission...................95
Trinity, defining
  characteristic of God's
  actuality..................97
Trinity, Judaism and
  Islam......................116
Trinity, not understood
 26
Trinity, power of.........28
trust...................141, 143
trust, source of...........141
truth...120, 142, 154, 221,
  233, 239, 240, 246,
  250, 277
truth is alive...............291
truth, absolute...169, 287
truth, beauty and good-
  ness........................67
truth, distortion of.....142
Turkey...........................4
twinkling of an eye.......15
tyranny...............125, 126
ultimate truth..............48
unafraid to sin.............84
unbelievers.........131, 204
unbelief grumbles......227
unbelievers..99, 100, 119,
  130, 134, 181, 185,
  186, 240, 296
unbelievers must explain
  obliviousness........185
unbelievers, purpose of
 250
unbelievers, treated
  differently.............139
unclean spirit............180
undeniable................242
under the influence.....39
undermined from within
 296
understanding.45, 61, 81,
  100, 132, 135, 137,
  160, 163, 164, 174,
  184, 186, 191, 199,
  207, 221, 226, 233,
  250, 255, 256, 259,
  260, 268, 269, 273,
  285, 286, 289
understanding,

differently.............186
understanding, shallow
 184
unifying force.............67
union...........................91
uniqueness of
  Christianity.............27
Unitarianism.......127, 171
unity. 21, 54, 56, 118, 132,
  138, 151, 168, 170, 174,
  208, 231, 232, 241,
  254, 255, 274, 288,
  290, 294, 296, 297
unity in diversity.........25
unity of mind.............172
unity of the church......27
unity, organic............194
unity, rethink and reform
 296
universal church........212
universalism......139, 226
university educated
  Christian intellectuals
  and the uneducated 52
unjust suffering.........134
unmitigated
  trustworthiness.....142
unrepentant sinners...68,
  202
unveiled........................44
valor...........................109
value neutral................61
Van Til, Cornelius......182
veiled.........20, 26, 64, 96
veneration..................233
vengeance..................175
vicarious atonement. 203
vices...........................264
vigilance....................280
vigor..........................234
Vine...........................194
violence......................237
violent revolution......133
virtue...115, 156, 236, 287
vision.........................195
vulnerability..............141
wages.........................265
wallow in the past.......88
war.............142, 150, 237
war of words and ideas
 118
Washington D.C..........78
watershed..................139
weaker vessel.............164
wealth........................236
welfare........................77

well-being....42, 125, 173,
  177, 178, 196, 249,
  276, 278
Wesley, John...............53
Wesleyanism...............53
Western Civilization.....4,
  142, 276
Western philosophy...118
Westminster Confession
  ....253, 271
wet blanket................149
wheat and tares. 123, 139,
  296
wholeness.....60, 96, 105,
  107, 111, 112, 174, 209,
  213, 231, 241, 264,
  273, 281, 290, 291
wholeness of humanity
 65
wickedness of
  worldliness.............84
wideness of God's grace
 45
wifely resistance........166
will power....................84
wisdom...............274, 291
wisdom.....30, 31, 63, 84,
  131, 132, 146, 163, 174,
  177, 223, 232, 233,
  240, 249, 263, 267,
  277, 280, 292
wisdom, lacking.........274
witness.......................155
wives...152, 153, 154, 158,
  162, 163, 165, 168,
  206, 274
women132, 153, 156, 158,
  159, 162, 164, 165, 167
Women's Movement..164
wonder.......................110
work to outdo each other
 270
works...........................20
works-righteousness....11
works-righteousness...41,
  45, 101, 182
world domination......170
worldliness.....70, 72, 190
worldly baggage........239
worldview......48, 63, 118,
  143, 160, 237, 238,
  239, 282, 287, 297
worry.........................276
worship......10, 16, 26, 67,
  161, 164, 183, 212,
  224, 225, 233, 240,

241, 247, 254, 272,   writing.......................128   296
286   Wycliffe, John.............52   Zealots.......................284
worship, context of....233   Year of Our Lord.........23   zealous.....................189
wrath...........................64   you all....16, 24, 105, 272,   Zion.............................94

9606441R0019

Made in the USA
Charleston, SC
26 September 2011